Nonverbal Communication in the Clinical Context

CONTRIBUTORS

Larry I. Benowitz
Department of Psychiatry and
  Program in Neuroscience
Harvard Medical School
Mailman Research Center
McLean Hospital

Peter David Blanck
Stanford Law School
Stanford University

Joan C. Borod
Department of Psychology
Queens College, CUNY
Department of Neurology
Mount Sinai School of Medicine
Department of Psychiatry
New York University School of
  Medicine

Ross Buck
Departments of Communication
  Science and Psychology
University of Connecticut

Bella M. DePaulo
Department of Psychology
University of Virginia

M. Robin DiMatteo
Department of Psychology
University of California, Riverside

Howard S. Friedman
Department of Psychology
University of California, Riverside

Judith A. Hall
Department of Social Medicine and
  Health Policy
Harvard Medical School

Jinni A. Harrigan
Research Director, Department of
  Family Medicine
University of Cincinnati College of
  Medicine

Monica J. Harris
Department of Psychology and Social
  Relations
Harvard University

Ron Hays
Behavioral Science Department
RAND Corporation

Elissa Koff
Department of Psychology
Wellesley College

Louise M. Prince
Department of Psychology
University of California, Riverside

Robert Rosenthal
Department of Psychology and Social
  Relations
Harvard University

Esther Strauss
Department of Psychology
University of Victoria

Don M. Tucker
Department of Psychology
University of Oregon

Marsha Vannicelli
Director, Outpatient Service
Appleton Treatment Center
McLean Hospital

Miron Zuckerman
Department of Psychology
University of Rochester

NONVERBAL COMMUNICATION IN THE CLINICAL CONTEXT

Edited by
Peter David Blanck,
Ross Buck,
and Robert Rosenthal

THE PENNSYLVANIA STATE UNIVERSITY PRESS
UNIVERSITY PARK AND LONDON

For Wendy Jo, Marianne, and Marylu

Library of Congress Cataloging-in-Publication Data

Main entry under title:

Nonverbal communication in the clinical context.

Includes bibliographies and index.
1. Psychotherapist and patient. 2. Physician
and patient. 3. Nonverbal communication (Psychology)
I. Blanck, Peter David, 1957-. II. Buck, Ross, 1941-.
III. Rosenthal, Robert, 1933- . [DNLM: 1. Nonverbal Communication.
2. Physician-Patient Relations. W 62 N814]
RC 480.8.N66   1986   610.69'6   84-43059
ISBN 0-27-00394-4

Contents

Preface

The past twenty-five years have witnessed a revolution in our understanding of human nature. This revolution has been based upon a series of interrelated and interdisciplinary developments in the areas of brain functioning, stress-related disease, and emotional expression and communication. The developments can be grouped in at least three categories: new appreciation of the role of cerebral lateralization, with the discovery of important functions of the right hemisphere, previously viewed as "silent" and subservient to the verbal "major hemisphere"; analyses of psychosocial influences on disease, with new evidence linking stress, immune system responding, and susceptibility to a wide variety of illnesses; and study of emotional expression and nonverbal communication. These developments have been mutually reinforcing, in that findings in one area are relevant to the others. There is evidence, for example, that nonverbal expressiveness involves right versus left hemisphere brain functioning, and is a factor with implications for susceptibility to stress-related disease.

Revolutions are usually supposed to be noisy affairs, but this one has proceeded quietly and has often been unnoticed, for it has been fragmented: it has been based upon the work of many individuals in different and apparently unrelated areas of research. However, when one considers what has taken place in these widely diverse fields of study, the reality of the revolution is beyond question. This volume brings together the results of a number of investigations which, on the surface, appear to be little related. In doing so, we hope to demonstrate not only that these programs are relevant to one another, but that they reveal something of the character of the ongoing revolution. In addition, we hope to point out the relationships between this revolution and the clinical context. The clinical context provides data which when evaluated carefully are found to be indispensable and unavailable from any other source. On the other hand, the clinical context is where our knowledge of human nature is applied to real human problems of health and disease.

In our introductory chapter we discuss the emerging view of human nature in general terms, suggesting something of the nature and scope of the underlying revolution. We argue that many important aspects of this revolution involve directly or indirectly the phenomenon of nonverbal communication: the capacity of one person to influence another without the use of words. We argue also that, in order to relate the different aspects of this revolution to one another in a coherent way, a hierarchical view of human nature is demanded. The different programs of research presented in this book can be considered to be at different levels of the hierarchy. We then discuss each of the chapters, relating the content of each to the others in terms of how they illuminate the nonverbal communication process, even though they approach it at different levels of the hierarchy. Finally, we discuss the relationship of the chapter content to the clinical context, in terms both of how data from the clinic are used in the analysis and of what the analysis implies for clinical practice.

This book is intended for graduate, professional, and advanced undergraduate students, faculty members, and researchers in the psychological, psychiatric, medical, and health sciences; it is also intended for practitioners who draw on these fundamental fields for the scholarly bases of their practices. Courses for which this book may be most relevant include those in abnormal, clinical, counseling, developmental, health, medical, personality, and social psychology; nonverbal communication; psycho- and sociolinguistics; communication; speech; behavioral medicine; psychiatry; and neurology.

Preparation of this book was supported in part by the National Science Foundation's sponsorship of much of the research described in it and by Harvard University, Stanford University School of Law, and the University of Connecticut. Research underlying some of the chapters was supported by other agencies and institutions—including the National Institute of Mental Health, the American Heart Association, the National Institutes of Health, the University of California at Riverside, the National Academy of Education, the Andrew W. Mellon Foundation, the Canadian Medical Research Council, the Natural Sciences and Engineering Research Council of Canada, the United States Public Health Service—and full acknowledgment of their support is given in the chapters.

1 General Introduction: Nonverbal Communication in the Clinical Context

Developments in the social and behavioral sciences often tend to be faddish, exciting much activity and interest for awhile and then disappearing from the scene. Some might argue that the current high level of interest in nonverbal communication is just a new fad, which will soon run its course. We think that this will not be the case, however, and instead that studies of nonverbal communication have contributed, and will continue to contribute, to a fundamentally new view of human nature. There are two major reasons for our confidence. First, the study of nonverbal communication has excited common interests in widely different kinds of researchers whose approaches have heretofore been separated due to differences in methodology and focus of interest. These researchers include anthropologists, aphasiologists, ethologists, linguists, neurologists, psychiatrists, and psychologists ranging from clinicians and social/personality researchers to physiological psychologists. Second, nonverbal communication allows a new level of objective measurement of emotional phenomena. The study of emotion is making a major comeback in the social sciences after a long period of domination by cognition, partly as a result of the increased ability to measure emotional phenomena via nonverbal behavior.

Integrating Diverse Views of Human Behavior

There is a parable about ten blind men gathered around an elephant, each trying to describe the nature of the beast from his own restricted experience—feeling a leg, a trunk, a tail—arguing violently. In many ways this parable is analogous to the ways that investigators in different disciplines are attempting to describe the nature of the human beast.

Investigators accustomed to a given research tradition and specific methodological techniques become used to a view of the beast afforded by their particular point of view, and tend to ignore or even disparage descriptions based on other points of view. Each feels that his or her view is in some way superior to others, if only because it is more familiar. In science, as in politics, such territoriality can be destructive. Investigators avoid topics of study that are unfamiliar, or potentially relevant to another discipline, perhaps in part for fear of attack from an unfamiliar quarter. As a result, a topic which should be an area of common ground becomes a no-man's land (Geschwind, 1975). A welcome exception to this rule of scholarly specialization appears in the current resurgence of interest in nonverbal communication.

A comprehensive understanding of human behavior demands that investigators using different approaches take the time and trouble to learn about and appreciate other points of view and other techniques of approach (Buck, 1976). This book reflects the conviction that research in the areas of nonverbal communication in social behavior, cerebral lateralization, and psychosocial factors in stress-related illness have much to contribute to one another. There is a potential area of common ground that must not be overlooked.

Spontaneous Communication and Emotion

The basis for this common ground lies in the distinction between spontaneous emotional communication as opposed to intentional or linguistically structured behavior (Buck, 1982; 1984).

The spontaneous communication process involves motivational and emotional states based in subcortical and paleocortical structures of the brain: what MacLean (1970, 1978) has termed "reptilian" and "old mammalian" structures in his theory of the triune brain. The reptilian structures underlie basic instincts and drive states, including sex and dominative aggression; while the old mammalian structures are associated with "primary affects" such as happiness, sadness, fear, anger, surprise, and disgust (cf. Buck, 1984). The modulation and control of all these states involves neocortical, or "new mammalian," structures. Thus, brain functioning can be seen as a hierarchy which has evolved in stages, each evolutionary stage being associated with particular modes. Spontaneous nonverbal expression arises from "lower" structures; "higher" structures mediate learned "display rules" which control this expression.

There is evidence that the right and left cerebral hemispheres play markedly different roles in this control process. There is clear evidence of hemispheric differences in the ability both to send (encode) and to receive (decode) spontaneous nonverbal behavior. In addition, there is evidence that the anterior and posterior parts of the brain play different roles in emotion, cognition, and communication. Thus, there are at least three dimensions of brain activity relevant to communication: a "higher/ lower" neocortical-subcortical dimension, a right/left cerebral hemisphere dimension, and an anterior/posterior dimension (see Tucker, this book).

Nonverbal communication therefore brings us into contact with the biological bases of social behavior. This idea is not new, having been put forward brilliantly and convincingly by Charles Darwin in 1872 in *Expression of the Emotions in Man and Animals* (cf. Ekman, 1973). Darwin's thesis is simple and compelling: that any kind of coordination of behavior between organisms—for example, for the purpose of sexual reproduction—requires communication between those organisms, and that innate mechanisms for sending and receiving relevant information have therefore evolved in each species.

A Hierarchical View of Behavior

One might ask why evolutionary processes are of interest in understanding human communication, given our great power of cognition and language. This question makes the common but mistaken assumption that old systems are replaced by new systems during the course of biological evolution, much as old buildings are torn down before new ones are erected in the evolution of a city. In fact, the evolving brain may be compared to a city with a long history of new buildings being built, new transportation and communication systems being conceived and constructed, new centers of learning emerging from new conceptions of the world, and new commercial enterprises developing.

In the brain, however, things are rarely "torn down." It is as if the old buildings remain, the old transportation systems continue to function, the old learning centers based upon old conceptions continue to operate, the old commercial enterprises survive: all side-by-side with the new structures. The new structures may tend to hide the functioning of the old, but they rarely replace them completely. The old structures continue to function much as they always have, hidden yet continuously present. However, their effects are now interacting with, and at times conflicting with, the functioning of the new structures (cf. Sagan, 1980, pp. 276–79). The phenomenon of cerebral lateralization is intimately involved in this interaction, in ways just beginning to be understood.

Thus, human behavior involves the simultaneous and interactive influence of both ancient and more recently evolved systems of behavior control, which in turn involves the interaction of the two cerebral hemispheres. In the evolution of a city, changes allow a new system of organization to replace the old, resulting in the replacement of old systems by faster and more efficient ones. The consolidated school replaces the one-room school, the superhighway replaces the two-lane road. In effect, a new system of organization replaces the old, and few vestiges remain. In much the same way, the evolving brain has led to more efficient ways of dealing with, or adapting to, the environment. However, as new behavioral systems evolve, they do not usually replace the old, but merely add to them. The old systems continue to function, much as they always had, often but not always hidden by the powerful new systems. It is as if the modern city is simultaneously a temporary campsite, an ancient village, a medieval castle, a renaissance town.

This evolutionary fact is basic to the understanding of human behavior and communication: we can see old systems of organization and control existing side-by-side with more recent, and often apparently more important, systems of organization and control. The importance of the old systems, ancient and apparently obsolete as they may seem to be, should not be underestimated. We are just beginning to appreciate the extent to which human nature and social behavior are influenced by systems of behavioral organization and control with roots deep in our evolutionary heritage.

These systems of organization, and the accompanying types of communication, can be seen and studied in both animals and humans. In humans, however, communication is dominated by language. Language constitutes a special kind of communication, whose content (if not form) is independent of biology. Language supports uniquely human patterns of logic and reasoning that make human behavior and communication qualitatively different from animal behavior and communication. There are kinds of behavioral organization that occur in humans but that do not occur in animals. However, the converse is not the case. Patterns of behavioral organization that can be seen clearly in animals also occur in humans, but often are hidden by our powers of language.

The study of nonverbal communication demonstrates how human communication, and by extension the human social order, is based upon and influenced by the same motivational and emotional systems, the same fundamental learning experiences, as is animal communication. In effect, the study of nonverbal communication has drawn back the "curtain of language" to reveal the emotional forces underlying communication and social behavior.

Communication, Bodily Responding, and Illness

This view of human nature as reflecting two interacting streams of influence—an innate, emotionally-based, and spontaneous stream versus a learned, cognitively-based, and intentional stream—has important implications for the analysis of the relationships between psychosocial factors and disease. Our conscious and rational linguistically structured behavior is constantly accompanied by bodily responses over which we have little or no knowledge or control. When we go in to ask the boss for a raise, the same autonomic and endocrine responses accompany us that were once useful in fighting or fleeing from tigers. However, in our linguistically structured society, the person who *actually* fights or flees generally winds up either in jail or in a mental hospital. Thus, even though its role in the control of behavior has been replaced by social rules, the fight-or-flight response continues to affect the body.

New techniques for the study of the biological bases of behavior have allowed a fundamentally new view of the systems that underlie human communication, health, and disease. These developments have spawned entire new disciplines, with names like psychoneuroendocrinology, psychoneuroimmunology, and social psychophysiology indicating their diverse origins. These disciplines allow new ways of conceptualizing the interaction between social and psychological factors and biological systems. They provide a basis for the rigorous study of phenomena that have long resisted scientific explanation. Thus, endogenous substances have been identified which appear to mediate pleasure and pain, elation and depression, memory and forgetting, resistance to stress, and even psychosis. Psychoactive drugs operate upon these behavioral systems, and there is evidence that social and psychological factors affect them as well. There is reason to believe that some of the strongest effects involve nonverbal communication. A touch, a glance, or the tone of one's voice can have biological influences that are objectively similar to those of drugs.

REFERENCES

Buck, R. (1976). *Human motivation and emotion.* New York: Wiley.

Buck, R. (1982). Spontaneous and symbolic nonverbal behavior and the ontogeny of communication. In R. Feldman (Ed.), *The development of nonverbal behavior in children.* New York: Springer Verlag.

Buck, R. (1984). *The communication of emotion.* New York: Guilford Press.

Ekman, P. (Ed.). (1973). *Darwin and facial expression: A century of research in review.* New York: Academic Press.

Geschwind, N. (1975). The borderland of neurology and psychiatry: Some common misconceptions. In D. F. Benson & D. Blumer (Eds.), *Psychiatric aspects of neurologic disease.* New York: Grune & Stratton.

MacLean, P. D. (1970). The limbic brain in relation to the psychoses. In P. H. Black (Ed.), *Physiological correlates of emotion.* New York: Academic Press.

MacLean, P. D. (1978). Effects of lesions of globus pallidus on species-typical display behavior of squirrel monkeys. *Brain Research, 149,* 175–96.

Sagan, C. (1980). *Cosmos.* New York: Random House.

PART I
Social Functions and Nonverbal Communication in the Clinical Context

Part I brings together the results of several new programs of research, each examining the role of nonverbal communication and related social processes in the clinical context. The challenge to the editors was to assemble in a meaningful way fresh and exciting research paradigms, each bearing on the book's general themes. In order to make it easier to identify the themes of Part I, we step outside the realm of social science for a moment and enter a novelist's world. Many of the themes present in this part of the book have been conveyed brilliantly in Ken Kesey's classic novel of the 1960s, *One Flew Over the Cuckoo's Nest.*

Kesey's "cuckoo's nest" is life in a mental hospital as described by a half-Indian patient called Chief Bromden. The Chief acts as our naturalistic observer of the social relations between patients and staff. He has deceived the staff into thinking he is deaf and dumb, and his acute observations often reveal the intricacies of the nonverbal world that he sees and we often take for granted. The head of the ward is Miss Ratched, known by the patients as "Big Nurse." Ratched is autocratic and cold. Her goal is to control the men of the ward. The patient most controlled by Nurse Ratched is Billy Bibbit. He has been controlled all his life by an autocratic and cold mother, who incidentally is a good friend of Miss Ratched. Billy is constantly trying to please his mother during her visits, but she never allows him to become close. She coldly controls Billy by playing on his fears. Billy stutters for fear of emotional contact. The hero, and newcomer to the cuckoo's nest, is Randle P. McMurphy. McMurphy is full of life and passion. He is horrified by the controlling and rule-oriented Nurse Ratched and the hospital staff.

The story portrays the clash between the rule-oriented staff and the brawling, life-loving McMurphy. McMurphy brings a refreshing view of life to the patients of the ward. Although McMurphy's free spirit is ultimately destroyed by a frontal lobotomy, the other patients in the ward realize they must eventually leave the security of the cuckoo's nest and return to life in the real world. But, before the Chief escapes, he smothers his friend, the now broken McMurphy. Kesey's view of life in a mental hospital provides a shocking view of nonverbal communication in the clinical context. Nonverbal cues are used to control, threaten, and deceive the patients. For years the patients have been lied to by the staff. But, when McMurphy arrives, he shows the other patients how to begin to judge the honesty of deceptive messages and how to uncover the specific information, or true meaning, that the deceiving staff is trying to hide.

Deception and Lie Detection

The first chapter in Part I is concerned with how people lie and how they detect lies. Miron Zuckerman, Bella DePaulo, and Robert Rosenthal's quantitative summary, or meta-analysis, of all the relevant studies of humans as deceivers and lie detectors complements many of Kesey's intuitive observations. The Zuckerman group demonstrates that certain nonverbal channels are more "leaky" than others, or more likely to reveal emotional information involuntarily. Their meta-analysis supports Ekman and Friesen's (1969, 1974) proposition that all communicative channels, verbal and nonverbal, can be placed on a continuum of controllability. Leaky channels, such as tone of voice, are more likely to give away deception than more controllable channels, such as the face.

Zuckerman and his colleagues show that the more leaky the channel, the more likely it is to convey a sender's true emotional message. Subtle nonverbal cues may give away attempts at deception or sarcasm, or inconsistencies in social messages. Bateson and his colleagues' (1956) classic work on "double-bind" messages discusses the influences of inconsistent and leaky nonverbal messages on the nature and outcome of social interaction. They hypothesize that some mothers control their children by sending contradictory social messages, and prolonged exposure to these messages may be related to the onset of schizophrenia in their children.

Nurse Ratched and Billy Bibbit's mother use double-bind messages to control Billy and other patients of the ward. Kesey describes how Nurse Ratched "has the ability to turn her smile into whatever expression she wants to use on somebody, but the look she turns it into is no different, just a calculated and mechanical expression to serve her purpose" (p. 45). Billy Bibbit's stuttering fits and eventual suicide are similarly linked to his mother's double-bind messages. In one meeting, Billy's mother sits stiff and cold while sensually asking Billy if she looks "like the mother of a middle-aged man" (p. 281). Nurse Ratched's pathological use of social messages shows the manipulative quality of tone of voice in leaking her underlying message:

> "What worries me Billy," she said—I could hear the change in her voice—"is how your poor mother is going to take this." She got the response she was after. Billy flinched and put his hand to his cheek like he'd been burned with acid. [p. 301]

Her tone of voice conveys disappointment in the context of a socially approved and relatively innocuous verbal statement. Stricken with guilt, Billy then commits suicide. While leaky and inconsistent messages may not always be this damaging, more research is needed to assess how such social messages endanger the mental health of children and adults.

Zuckerman and his colleagues next discuss the behavioral correlates of deception. They describe how deceivers' attempts to control their expressions may result in well-organized and less spontaneous behavior, like the "precise and automatic gestures" of Nurse Ratched (p. 5): "her face is smiling, pitying, patient, and disgusted all at once—a trained expression" (p. 167).

The ability to detect lies is also summarized by examining how people interpret and weigh multi-channel nonverbal messages. Perceived deception, for example, is shown to influence nonverbal decoding skills and styles. As a start toward specifying the accuracy of receiving or decoding inconsistent messages in social interaction, Blanck, Rosenthal, and Vanicelli (chapter 5) briefly discuss a new instrument designed to assess sensitivity to discrepant and consistent social messages.

After Zuckerman and his colleagues provide a quantitative examination of the subtle feelings expressed and detected in social interaction, two chapters apply these substantive conclusions to nonverbal communication in the ongoing clinical context. Jinni Harrigan and Robert Rosenthal (chapter 3) and Robin DiMatteo, Louise Prince, and Ron Hays (chapter 4) describe the nonverbal components of the physician-patient interaction.

Nonverbal Interaction

Harrigan and Rosenthal's discussion of the nonverbal aspects of empathy and rapport in the physician-patient interaction provides a rare example of a field experiment in the clinical context. They describe how empathy and rapport serve as major components of effective doctor-patient interactions. They are specifically concerned with how cues from nonverbal channels serve as significant factors in the expression of empathy. The studies summarized by Harrigan and Rosenthal provide evidence that several types of nonverbal behavior are important in the expression of empathy and warmth in the effective therapeutic relationship. Kesey's descriptions of Nurse Ratched show us just how cold and non-empathic a "therapeutic relationship" can become: he says she "walks around with that same dull smile aimed between her chin and nose and that same calm whir coming from her eyes, but down inside of her she's tense as steel. I know. I can feel it" (p. 26).

In their naturalistic investigation, Harrigan and Rosenthal discuss the important relationship between body movement and physicians' rapport with their patients. Chief Bromden understands this relationship as he describes the doctor's body movements in the therapeutic session:

> At two o'clock (toward the end of the session) the doctor begins to squirm around in his chair. The meetings are uncomfortable for the doctor. . . . He squirms around and finally clears his throat . . . [till] the nurse looks at her watch and tells us . . . we'll resume the discussion again tomorrow. [p. 53]

Harrigan and Rosenthal suggest that physician-patient rapport is most enhanced when physicians nod their heads in interest and lean toward the patient. Kesey's disinterested doctor, squirming in his chair, may lack this essential ingredient for developing interpersonal intimacy and patient rapport.

The next chapter in Part I reports Robin DiMatteo, Louise Prince, and Ron Hays's ground-breaking work on the effect of physicians' nonverbal skill on behavioral measures such as patient commitment and compliance. DiMatteo, Prince, and Hays demonstrate the importance of physicians' nonverbal communication skills, both sending and receiving skills, in influencing medical treatment. As if he had studied the findings of DiMatteo et al., Chief Bromden describes the reasons for his lack of commitment to the hospital's therapeutic program: "The Big Nurse recognized [our] fear and knows how to put it to use; she'll point out to an Acute [patient], whenever he goes into a sulk, that you boys be good boys and cooperate with staff policy which is engineered for your 'cure,' or you'll end up on that side [the Chronic side] of the ward" (p. 17). Physicians' "use" of nonverbal cues certainly have important implications for both patient satisfaction and commitment to the physician. Taken together, these two chapters demonstrate the importance of nonverbal communication in the therapeutic relationship. Each chapter contributes to a broader definition of the role of the clinician's socioemotional skill, and applies much of the experimental work summarized earlier by Zuckerman and his coworkers.

Emotional Dimensions

A key question remains: how do we learn to assess clinicians' nonverbal sensitivity? Effective training requires full knowledge of the dimensions of nonverbal communication in the clinical context. As a start toward this goal, Blanck, Rosenthal, and Vannicelli (chapter 5) describe their systematic investigation of the therapist's tone of voice. Blanck and his coworkers document a systematic approach and research strategy. Their chapter describes, for example, how content-filtered speech samples can be employed by clinical researchers, and what nonverbal dimensions may tap the expression and communication of emotion in tone of voice. Chief Bromden's description of Nurse Ratched's tone of voice and her inconsistent social messages capture the complexity of the emotions that can be expressed via tone: "She continued to glare at us as she spoke. It was strange to hear that voice, soft and soothing and warm as a pillow, coming out of a face as hard as porcelain" (p. 302).

Blanck and his colleagues describe a series of studies aimed at delineating many of the emotional dimensions in tone of voice. They show how the stylistic variables associated with the therapist's clinical interactions can be reliably assessed from very brief segments at different points in the therapeutic interview. Next, they examine the therapist's tone of voice as a predictor of the therapeutic process, for example, to identify whether the therapist is talking to an in-patient or an out-patient. Finally, the Blanck group shows that therapists' tone of voice in talking *about* patients can be used to make significantly accurate predictions about therapists' tone of voice in talking *to* patients. Brief clips of content-filtered speech are shown as promising tools not only for future research on clinical interaction processes but also for the selection and supervision of clinicians.

Part I closes with an exciting new area of research with important implications for our understanding of the physiological behaviors leading to heart disease. Judith Hall, Howard Friedman, and Monica Harris describe the diagnostic value of nonverbal communication in assessing the Type A behavior pattern and ultimately heart disease and related physiological states. Hall and her colleagues summarize a body of research suggesting that the Type A personality is manifested in a constellation of nonverbal expressive tendencies such as a general tendency for loud and fast speech. They draw on rigorous methods of nonverbal cue analysis and theoretical concepts from social-personality psychology. Although

Kesey gives us no indication of Nurse Ratched's blood pressure, Hall and her colleagues' research suggest that the nurse's controlled and automatic gestures are symptomatic of the Type A's physiological constellation: "down inside [Nurse Ratched] is tense as steel" (p. 26).

The chapters in Part I are hoped to be of practical value to researchers and health care practitioners interested in 1) understanding nonverbal communication in ongoing clinical interactions; 2) aiding in the development of training programs in interpersonal skills for health care professionals and their patients; 3) assisting selection procedures for the optimal pairing of health care professionals and their patients; 4) developing systematic programs of research on nonverbal communication styles and skills; and 5) understanding the diagnostic potential of nonverbal communication in the clinical context. If these chapters aid in the long-term goal of understanding the therapeutic importance of nonverbal communication, we should be better able to help the Billy Bibbits, Chief Bromdens, and Randle P. McMurphys of our society, and also better able to train or select-out the Nurse Ratched's of the helping professions. More generally, we should be in a better position to investigate new approaches to nonverbal communication in the clinical context and in the cuckoo's nest.

REFERENCES

Bateson, G., Jackson, D., Haley, J., & Weakland, J. (1956). Toward a theory of schizophrenia. *Behavioral Sciences, 1,* 251–64.

Ekman, P., & Friesen, W. V. (1969). Nonverbal leakage and cues to deception. *Psychiatry, 32,* 88–106.

Ekman, P., & Friesen, W. V. (1974). Detecting deception from the face or body. *Journal of Personality and Social Psychology, 29,* 288–98.

Kesey, Ken. (1962). *One flew over the cuckoo's nest.* New York: Viking (Penguin edition cited in text).

2 Humans as Deceivers and Lie Detectors

Miron Zuckerman, Bella M. DePaulo, and Robert Rosenthal

What a patient says to a doctor or therapist can often be very different from how the patient really feels. It is therefore important for the clinician to be sensitive to the patient's subtle nonverbal cues, which very often convey or "leak" the patient's true underlying feelings. This chapter summarizes a body of research that has examined how deception is communicated by deceivers and how it is detected by those who receive it. Included in this summary is also a description of the types of nonverbal cues that are more or less likely to be associated with attempts at deception. In chapter 4 of this book Robin DiMatteo and her colleagues address the issue of how abilities to deceive and detect deception seem to affect the doctor-patient relationship.

Lying and lie detection are common aspects of interpersonal interaction. Lying involves an act intended to foster in another person a belief the deceiver considers false (Krauss, Geller, & Olson, 1976). Lie detection involves two tasks: (a) judging whether a message is true or false and (b) uncovering specific information that the deceiver is trying to hide. Ekman and Friesen (1969) differentiated these two tasks when they described the behaviors that give away the fact of deception (without revealing the hidden information) as *deception cues,* and the behaviors that betray the concealed information as *leakage cues.* We start with a consideration of the concept of "leakage hierarchy" and the accuracy of lie detection.

THE LEAKAGE HIERARCHY

Folk wisdom holds that while people can lie with their words, their nonverbal behavior will give them away. Freud (1905) expressed this idea best in a well-known comment: "if his lips are silent, he chatters with his fingertips; betrayal oozes out of him at every pore" (p. 94). However, not all nonverbal channels are alike and some seem less likely than others to reveal information involuntarily. Specifically, Ekman and Friesen (1969, 1974) suggested that relative to the body, the face is a more controllable channel because (a) it can send a larger number of messages at a faster rate; (b) it is more likely to elicit feedback from others; and (c) people are more aware of their facial expressions than of their body movements. Because the face is more controllable than the body, it serves as a primary means of communication when senders wish to express their true feelings. However, when senders try to conceal information and/or deceive their audience, the less controllable body serves as a better source of both deception and leakage cues.

More recently, investigators have pointed out that tone of voice is also a relatively uncontrollable channel (DePaulo & Rosenthal, 1979a; De-Paulo, Stone, & Lassiter, 1984; Rosenthal & DePaulo, 1979a,b). Because of the altered "bone– to air-conduction ratio," people are relatively unaware of their voices; what they hear is actually quite different from how their voices sound to others (Holzman & Rousey, 1966). Consistent with this finding, Zuckerman, Larrance, Spiegel, and Klorman (1981) have found that senders are more aware of their ability to send information via facial expressions than via tone of voice. In addition, studies by Weitz (1972) and Bugental and her colleagues (Bugental, Caporael, & Shennum, 1980; Bugental, Henker, & Whalen, 1976; Bugental & Love, 1975) have shown that tone of voice leaks information that is not revealed by the verbal content of the message. For example, Bugental et al. (1976) found that, in a free-interaction situation, subjects who felt powerless to affect events relevant to them showed less assertiveness in tone of voice than in verbal content. In contrast, subjects who believed in their ability to affect events in the environment showed the opposite pattern.

The foregoing evidence suggests that the dichotomy between the spoken controllable word and the less voluntary nonverbal display may be generalized to a concept of leakage hierarchy: the proposition that all channels, verbal and nonverbal, can be arranged on a continuum indicating different degrees of controllability. For example, verbal content and face may be located at the controllable end of the continuum, whereas the body and tone of voice may be classified as less controllable and leakier channels.

The concept of the leakage hierarchy entails the hypothesis that leaky channels are more likely to give away deception than are controllable ones. Evidence relevant to this hypothesis was examined in studies on the ability of human judges to detect lies from verbal and nonverbal cues. In the typical study of this kind (cf. DePaulo, Zuckerman, & Rosenthal, 1980), a group of senders is asked to lie and tell the truth in response to various questions; a group of judges is then asked to identify when senders are lying and when they are telling the truth. When investigators employed an equal number of truthful and deceptive messages, as most did, judges obviously should have made correct identifications 50% of the time through chance alone.

To examine accuracy of lie detection for different channels we conducted a quantitative summary or meta-analysis of all relevant studies. (An outline of the statistical procedures used can be found in Rosenthal, 1978, 1980, 1983, and Rosenthal and Rubin, 1978.) For each study, differences between obtained and chance accuracies were transformed into standard deviation units (Cohen's d, 1977), defined conceptually as $(M_1 - 1 M_2)/\sigma$ and computed as $2r/\sqrt{1-r^2}$ or, equivalently, as $2\sqrt{F}/\sqrt{df}$. Essentially, Cohen's d is an estimate of the size of the effect in question—Cohen suggests that ds of .2, .5, and .8 should be viewed as small, medium, and large effects, respectively. In the present analysis, positive ds indicated that detection accuracy was above chance, whereas negative ds indicated that accuracy was below chance. Separate ds were computed for each channel so that a single study provided as many ds as the number of channels examined.

Overall, we analyzed 35 separate studies yielding 72 d estimates of detection accuracy. Five separate channels were identified—face, body, speech, tone of voice, and transcript. The facial channel included studies of facial cues above the neck, whereas the body channel included studies of body cues from the neck down. The speech channel included all studies of unaltered speech, either live or tape-recorded. Studies of tone of voice employed either standard content speech (e.g., senders saying "yes" in response to all questions) or content filtering (a process that eliminates the high frequencies of the voice, thus rendering the speech unintelligible while leaving most other vocal characteristics intact). Finally, the transcript channel included studies of the transcripts, i.e., the verbal content of the messages. The 72 ds were classified into 10 categories; eight of the categories were created by all possible combinations of face, body, and speech; the remaining two categories were tone of voice and transcripts. Mean ds for each category and the number of studies upon which they are based are presented in Table 2.1.

The following procedure was then used to compute the overall com-

Table 2.1   Accuracy of Detecting Deception (in Standard Deviation Units)

	Visual Cues				
	Face		No Face		
Auditory cues	Body	No body	Body	No body	Means
Speech	1.00(21)[a]	.99(9)	1.49(3)	1.09(12)	1.14
No speech	.35(6)	.05(7)	.43(4)	.00[b]	.21
Means	.68	.52	.96	.54	.68

Transcript only: .70(6)
Tone only: .20(4)

[a]Number of studies upon which d is based is enclosed in parentheses.
[b]Theoretical accuracy.

SOURCE: Zuckerman et al., 1981.

bined p or significance of each of the mean ds presented in Table 2.1. We first computed the 72 one-tail ps, and the corresponding standard normal deviates (zs), of the differences between obtained and chance accuracies. The zs were assigned positive values if detection accuracy was higher than chance and negative values if accuracy was lower than chance. For each of the categories presented in Table 2.1, the relevant zs were added and the resulting sum was then divided by the square root of the number of studies being combined. The product is a combined z, which indicates the significance level of the associated mean d.

Which cues produced greater detection accuracy? In accordance with the suggestion that the face does not leak involuntary information, detection accuracy of the facial channel alone ($d = .05$) was low and, in fact, not significantly greater than chance (combined $z = .66$); accuracy of all the remaining channels was greater than chance at $p < .05$ (one-tailed) or better. In addition, availability of facial cues actually decreased detection accuracy from .75 (which is the mean d of the two columns in Table 2.1 with no facial cues) to .60 (which is the mean d of the two columns with facial cues). It is as if the addition of facial cues misled the judges.

In contrast to the face, body and tone of voice yielded detection accuracies (mean ds = .43 and .20, respectively) significantly above chance. Furthermore, the availability of body cues increased detection accuracy from .53 (the mean d of the two columns with no body cues) to .82 (the mean d for the two columns with body cues); similarly, the availability of tone of voice increased detection accuracy from .70 (the mean d for transcript) to 1.09 (the mean d for speech, i.e., transcript plus tone of voice). Thus, it appears that human judges can detect deception from the two least controllable channels in the leakage hierarchy.

Unexpectedly, the results showed that the most controllable channel in the leakage hierarchy—verbal content or transcript—is the best single channel source of deception cues: detection accuracy based on transcript alone (mean $d = .70$) was higher than detection accuracy associated with any other single channel. Furthermore, availability of verbal content increased detection accuracy from .20 (the mean d for tone of voice) to 1.09 (the mean d of speech, i.e., tone of voice plus transcript). This evidence is in direct contradiction to the proposition that verbal content is highly controllable and thus not likely to disclose deception. Accordingly, transcript evidently should be divided into two channels: the content or theme and its semantic structure. Senders are able to control the general content of the message but seem less able to control other aspects of what they say. Thus, the well-known distinction between what people say and how they say it probably should be reinterpreted. How something is said is usually understood as a reference to paralinguistic aspects of speech, e.g., tone of voice, speech errors, etc. Perhaps how something is said should also refer to the semantic structure of the message, which can be independent of its content. Most important, semantic structure possibly is more leaky than body or tone of voice.

If leaky channels are more likely to give away deception, then directing judges' attention to these channels should increase accuracy of lie detection. Consistent with this prediction, a study by DePaulo, Lassiter, and Stone (1982) showed that judges instructed to pay attention to the tone of voice or words of messages were more accurate at detecting deception than judges instructed to pay attention to the visual cues (facial expressions) or judges who did not receive any specific instructions.

Finally, it is important to comment on the overall mean accuracy for detecting deception. Although all ds in Table 2.1 are positive and some are substantial, in reality even a big effect may correspond to only a few percentage points above chance accuracy. In fact, the examination of actual accuracy indicated that most of the results fall in the .45–.60 range with a chance level of .5 (see also Kraut, 1980; Knapp & Comadena, 1979).

Since accuracy of detecting deception is generally above chance level, there must be some behavioral cues or combinations of cues that distinguish between lie- and truth-telling. Furthermore, since deception can be detected from transcripts as well as from bodily and auditory cues, the behaviors associated with deception must be verbal as well as nonverbal. We now turn to the question of what these behaviors might be.

BEHAVIORAL CORRELATES OF DECEPTION: A FOUR-FACTOR MODEL

Deception hypothetically involves various processes or factors that can influence behavior. Four such factors are discussed below: attempted control, arousal, felt emotion, and cognitive processing.

Attempted Control. Since deceivers try not to disclose what they really think, they may try to exercise greater control over their behavior than do truth-tellers. The attempted control may induce at least three behavioral cues to deception. First, deceptive behavior may appear too planned, rehearsed, or lacking in spontaneity. Second, the deceivers may try to be too persuasive, presenting a too slick and/or exaggerated performance. Third, since people cannot monitor all aspects of their behavior and since some channels are leakier than others, deceptive communications may be characterized by discrepancy between the more controllable and the less controllable components of the message.

Arousal. Research on psychophysiological detection of lying has shown clearly that truth and lie-telling are associated with different autonomic responses (for reviews, see Lykken, 1974; Orne, Thackray, & Paskewitz, 1972; Waid & Orne, 1982). Interestingly, there is no agreement on the precise interpretation of this phenomenon. For example, Davis (1961) suggested three possibilities: (a) the conditioned response theory—questions related to the concealed information, which must be of some importance to the deceiver, act as conditioned stimuli and thus enhance autonomic responsivity; (b) the conflict theory—conflicting tendencies to tell the truth and to lie enhance physiological responsivity; and (c) the punishment theory—anticipation of punishment in case of discovery enhances physiological responsivity. Two other interpretations attribute the autonomic activity associated with deception to the concealed information (termed "guilty knowledge") which is made salient by the crucial question in the interrogation procedure (Lykken, 1959, 1960); and to deceivers' motivation to succeed on the deception task (Gustafson & Orne, 1963, 1965).

Whatever produces physiological arousal in response to deception may also produce several other behavioral reactions. For example, Hemsley (1977) suggested that arousal causes an increase in the intensity and frequency of various nonverbal behaviors. Such an effect is almost the opposite of the planned and rehearsed impression predicted by the control which deceivers must exercise over their behavior. This contradiction conceivably may be resolved if controllability of the channels is taken into account. Behavior in controllable channels may appear as more planned and organized, whereas behavior in less controllable channels may appear more intense and less organized.

The arousal associated with deception can also affect specific behaviors, including pupil dilation, eyeblinks, fundamental frequency (voice pitch), speech errors, and speech hesitations. Several studies have shown that arousal-producing stimuli, such as the signal for the firing of a gun, trigger an increase in pupil dilation (Nunnally, Knott, Duchnowski, & Parker, 1967; Scott, Wells, Wood, & Morgan, 1969; Simpson & Hale, 1969). An increase in the rate of eyeblinks was viewed by Meyer (1953) as a correlate of general arousal. Two related reviews by Scherer (1980a,b) indicated that arousal induces higher voice pitch. Specifically, fundamental frequency seems to increase with stress (Scherer, 1980a) as shown, for example, by the finding of higher fundamental frequency in pilots' voices during flight difficulties as opposed to before these difficulties occurred (Williams & Stevens, 1969). In addition, emotions classified as higher in arousal were characterized by vocal expressions of higher fundamental frequency (Scherer, 1980b). Finally, Kasl and Mahl (1965) reported that manipulation of the level of anxiety in an interview produced concomitant changes in speech errors and hesitations, which were also related to palmar sweat. The above evidence suggests that, to the extent that deception is an arousal-producing stimulus, it can also produce increases in pupil dilation, eyeblink rate, fundamental frequency, speech errors, and speech hesitations.

Felt Emotion. In general, deception is believed to be associated with negative affects such as guilt and anxiety—guilt about engaging in deception and anxiety about being caught. Ekman (1980) added to this list the "duping delight," that is, the joy associated with meeting the challenge of a successful deception. Clearly, such affects may also account for the arousal associated with deception. In fact, anxiety about being caught is at the core of Davis's (1961) punishment theory, and the duping delight is related to Gustafson and Orne's (1963, 1965) motivation to succeed on the deception task. Nevertheless, predictions based on the arousal and the felt emotion approach are somewhat different. Proponents of the latter approach see behavioral responses to deception as a direct reflection of specific affects rather than as a consequence of a more general arousal.

The experience of guilt and anxiety under deception hypothetically may result in direct expressions of negative affects, e.g., facial expressions may become less pleasant and verbal content may become more negative. According to Ekman and Friesen (1972), anxiety can also increase the frequency of adaptors—self-manipulating behaviors that satisfy some self-needs or body-needs (e.g., grooming, scratching, etc.) Deceivers may also try to disassociate themselves from the deceptive messages so as to minimize the negative experience. Consequently, they may employ fewer self-references in the message and more nonimmediate expressions (cf. Wiener & Mehrabian, 1968). Nonimmediacy implies a less direct relationship between the communicator and the object of the message (e.g., "I like John's company" is a less immediate statement than "I like John"). Finally, such withdrawal can also cause a decrease in the frequency of illustrators—hand movements that accompany and change (emphasize, augment, etc.) what is being said verbally (Ekman, 1980).

Cognitive Processing in Deception. Lying can be considered a more difficult task than truth-telling. The deceiver must construct a message from scratch, and the content of the message must be both internally consistent and compatible with what the listeners already know. Consequently, lying could give rise to speech characteristics, pupillary responses, and gestures indicative of complex cognitive activities.

Goldman-Eisler (1968) showed that when subjects are required to make verbal statements of greater than usual cognitive complexity, they start the response later and pause more frequently. Numerous investigations, particularly those conducted by Kahneman (1973), have shown that higher levels of mental effort or processing load lead to an increase in pupil dilation (for a recent review of this literature, see Beatty, 1982). Finally, Ekman and Friesen (1972) suggested that a high level of concentration and absorption in a speech would lead to a decrease in the frequency of illustrators.

Thus, it can be hypothesized that the more complex nature of lie-telling results in longer latencies, more frequent hesitations, increased pupil dilation, and fewer illustrators. Note that changes in some of these behaviors have been predicted previously on the basis of other factors. Specifically, the increase in pupil dilation and frequency of speech hesitations was previously hypothesized from the arousal associated with deception; and the decrease in frequency of illustrators was previously derived from the lower involvement of the speaker in the deceptive message. Even if the empirical data support these predictions, we have no way of isolating their exact causal antecedents. It is possible, of course, that some behavioral correlates of deception have more than one cause.

CORRELATES OF DECEPTION: EMPIRICAL FINDINGS

To examine which behaviors distinguish between truth and deception, we conducted a meta-analysis of all relevant studies. The typical investigation of this kind employed either judges or some mechanical device (e.g., a pupillometer) to measure some aspects of the senders' behavior as they were lying or telling the truth. To be included in the present analysis, a behavioral cue must have been examined in at least two studies. The list of cues to be presented, plus a brief description of the measurement technique, is shown in Table 2.2. It is important to note here that most investigators reported rates of occurrence for each behavior rather than absolute values, thus controlling for response length. In addition, investigators have occasionally used different techniques to measure the same or what appeared to be the same behavior. Consequently, somewhat arbitrary decisions had to be made regarding the inclusion or exclusion of particular behaviors from the analysis.

The statistical procedures were identical to those used in the meta-analysis of detection accuracy. For each of the behaviors listed in Table 2.2, we computed the average effect size (Cohen's d, 1977) and significance (based on a combined z) of the difference in the occurrence of this behavior between deceptive and truthful messages. Positive ds and zs indicated that the behavior in question occurred more frequently under deception. The left-hand part of Table 2.3 presents the results of the analysis. It can be seen that 14 of 24 behaviors (58%) distinguished reliably between truth- and lie-telling, a proportion that exceeds substantially the 5% that would be expected if there were no relationships between deception and the occurrence of these behaviors.

To what extent are the results consistent with the four-factor model? It was suggested that the first factor—deceivers' attempts to control their expressions—may result in well-organized and less spontaneous behavior, exaggerated performance, and discrepancies between more controllable and less controllable channels. Well-organized behavior may be more homogeneous and therefore less segmented; and indeed, Table 2.3 does show that deception was related to a smaller number of perceived segments of behavior in a controllable channel such as the face. Single studies of behaviors not included in the meta-analysis also provide evidence consistent with this aspect of the control factor. Thus, Zuckerman, DeFrank, Hall, Larrance, and Rosenthal (1979) found that deceptive answers gave rise to impressions of less personal involvement; and De-Paulo, Rosenthal, Green, and Rosenkrantz (1982) and DePaulo, Lanier,

Table 2.2   Behaviors Potentially Related to Deception

Visual Behaviors

(1)   Pupil Dilation: Measured by a pupillometer, which assesses variations in the pupil's diameter.

(2)   Gaze: Measured by duration or frequency of attempts to establish eye-contact with the listener.

(3)   Blinking: Measured by frequency of blinks.

(4)   Smiling: Measured by duration or frequency of smiles; sometimes also measured by judges' ratings of overall facial pleasantness.

(5)   Facial Segmentation: Segmentation is performed by judges instructed to break the sequence of facial behavior into units that appear meaningful to them (Newtson, 1976); the number of units identified in a message serves as the measure of segmentation.

(6)   Head movements: Measured by the frequency of either head nods or any head movement.

(7)   Gestures or Illustrators: Measured by frequency or duration of hand movements designed to modify and/or supplement what is being said verbally.

(8)   Shrugs: Measured by frequency of hand- and shoulder-shrugs.

(9)   Adaptors: Measured by duration or frequency of self—manipulations (e.g., scratching); unlike gestures, adaptors are not directly related to what is being said verbally.

(10)   Foot and Leg Movements: Measured by frequency count of movements.

(11)   Postural Shifts: Measured by frequency count of shifts.

(12)   Bodily Segmentation: Measured in the same manner as facial segmentation except that judges are requested to segment bodily movement rather than facial expressions.

Paralanguage

(13)   Latency: Measured by the amount of time between the end of a question and the beginning of the answer.

(14)   Response Length: Measured by the duration or number of words associated with the response.

(15)   Speech Rate: Measured by the number of words divided by the duration of the message.

(16)   Speech Errors: Measured by frequency of nonfluencies, grammatical errors, word and/or sentence repetition, sentence change, sentence incompletion, tongue slips, and the like.

(17)   Speech Hesitations: Measured by frequency of pauses, including those filled with "ahs," "ers," and "uhms."

(18)   Pitch: Fundamental frequency of the voice is extracted and analyzed by electronic devices.

Verbal Behaviors

(19)   Negative Statements: Measured by frequency of negative and disparaging statements or by judges' overall ratings of the negativity of the message.

(20)   Irrelevant Information: Measured by frequency of statements judged as irrelevant to the theme of the message or by judges' overall ratings of the relevance of the message.

(21)   Self-References: Measured by frequency of references to the self (e.g., *I, me, mine*).

Table 2.2   continued
(22)   Nonimmediacy: Measured by frequency of indirect forms of expression (e.g., "he is considered to be a bore" is nonimmediate whereas "he bores me" is immediate).
(23)   Leveling: Measured by frequency of overgeneralized statements, which are characterized by leveling terms such as *every, all, none, nobody*.

General Variables
(24)   Discrepancy: Measured by judges' ratings of the overall perceived discrepancy between channels associated with the same message or of the extent to which the message appears to communicate simultaneously several different emotions.

SOURCE: Zuckerman and Driver, in press.

and Davis (1983) found that deceptive messages were viewed as more indifferent and less spontaneous than truthful messages. One behavioral cue presented in Table 2.3, leveling, is relevant to the second aspect of control, that of exaggerated performance. The fact that deceivers are more likely to express their opinions in absolute leveling terms, barring any exceptions to the position presented, can be viewed as a form of exaggerated and extreme performance. Finally, in accordance with the third predicted aspect of the control factor, deceptive messages were judged as more discrepant than were truthful communications.

We hypothesized that arousal increases the intensity and frequency of behaviors in uncontrollable channels. An increase in the frequency of behavior might be expected to be associated with an increase in the number of identifiable units, and indeed, Table 2.3 does show that deception was related to a higher number of perceived segments of behavior in the body. We also hypothesized that arousal increases pupil dilation, frequency of blinking, voice pitch level, and frequency of speech errors and of hesitations. As can be seen in Table 2.3, all 5 behaviors were reliably associated with deception. Finally, in the study by DePaulo et al. (1982) deceptive messages were perceived by judges as more tense, indicating perhaps a higher level of arousal.

Turning to the factor of felt emotion, we hypothesized that the negative affect associated with deception gives rise to direct expressions of negativity, to behaviors that signal anxiety and discomfort, and to various forms of withdrawal from the content of the message. As can be seen in Table 2.3, deception was associated with a close to significant decrease in smiling ($z = 1.67$, $p < .10$), and with a significant increase in verbal negative statements; deception was also associated with an increase in the frequency of adaptors, a behavior that can serve as an indicator of discomfort. Finally, deceptive statements were more nonimmediate than truthful ones, perhaps

Table 2.3 Behaviors Associated with Deception

Behavior	All Studies			Low Motivation		High Motivation		
	N of studies	Mean d	Combined z	N of studies	Mean d	N	Mean d	z of difference
Visual								
Pupil dilation	5	1.37	6.82***	2	1.65***	1	1.52**	1.31
Gaze	18	-.03	.13	12	.13	6	-.33	2.33*
Blinking	8	.50	1.96*	6	.85***	2	-.57**	4.60***
Smiling	19	-.09	-1.67	10	-.14*	9	-.02	1.65
Facial segmentation	5	-.27	-2.00**	5	-.27*	—	—	—
Head movements	10	-.18	-1.20	5	.16	5	-.52**	3.01**
Gestures	12	-.12	-.19	6	.09	6	-.32	1.03
Shrugs	4	.38	1.81	3	.14	1	1.10*	.71
Adaptors	14	.34	3.50***	7	.49***	7	.19	1.55
Foot and leg movements	9	-.03	-.22	4	.01	5	-.06	.10
Postural shifts	11	-.03	-.88	5	.22	6	-.24*	2.51*
Bodily segmentation	3	.83	2.84**	3	.83**	—	—	—
Paralanguage								
Latency	15	-.02	.28	8	-.05	7	-.00	.20
Response Length	17	-.19	-1.98*	7	.07	10	-.36***	2.92**
Speech rate	12	-.07	-1.36	5	.35	7	-.38***	3.03**
Speech errors	12	.23	2.14*	4	.40	8	.15	.24
Speech hesitations	11	.54	4.06***	6	.55*	5	.52***	.63
Pitch	4	.68	2.26*	2	.08	2	1.27**	1.99*

Table 2.3 continued

Behavior	All Studies			Low Motivation		High Motivation		
	N of studies	Mean d	Combined z	N of studies	Mean d	N	Mean d	z of difference
Verbal								
Negative statements	5	.95	5.34***	3	.34	2	1.88***	3.50***
Irrelevant information	6	.40	2.17*	5	.42	1	.28	.60
Self-references	4	.05	-.38	3	.22	1	-.44	1.13
Immediacy	2	-.77	-3.37***	2	-.77**	—	—	—
Leveling	4	.44	2.16*	2	.29	2	.60*	1.28
General								
Discrepancy	4	.64	4.31***	4	.64***	—	—	—

*$p < .05$
**$p < .01$
***$p < .001$

NOTE: Positive values indicate that an increase in the behavior was associated with deception.

SOURCE: Zuckerman and Driver, in press.

signalling withdrawal from the content of the message. However, two other indices of withdrawal, self-references and illustrators, were not associated with deception, raising some doubts about the extent to which deceivers tend to disassociate themselves from their deception.

The conceptualization of deception as a more complex cognitive activity than truth-telling led to predictions of increase in latency of response, speech hesitations, and pupil dilation, as well as a decrease in the frequency of illustrators. Of these four behaviors, only speech hesitations and pupil dilation were related to deception, and these relationships can be accounted for by the arousal factor. On the other hand, the two remaining correlates of deception in Table 2.3—a decrease in response length and an increase in irrelevant information—do suggest that deception involves more complex cognitive processing. Since deceptive messages are constructed without a factual basis, the deceiver has fewer things to say (shorter response length) and may use irrelevant information as a stopgap mechanism. It can be concluded, then, that the description of deception as a complex activity remains a viable hypothesis.

Although the empirical findings of the meta-analysis provide some support for the four-factor model of deception, they also raise a number of questions. Clearly, the meta-analysis of cues to deception is constrained by the empirical data available. Thus, a large number of behaviors are left out and the measurement of others is imperfect. For example, the five verbal variables included in the analysis cannot possibly account for the semantic structure of the messages. Thus, the means by which transcript leaks deception cues remain unknown. In addition, some variables such as gestures, adaptors, and head movements are global categories of behavior. Perhaps lie-telling is more strongly associated with specific subcategories of these movements. Finally, a model of cues to deception should benefit from a factor-analytic approach. That is, the suggestion that behavioral cues are organized around particular factors should be tested by a factor analysis of these cues. The emerging factors would show how these variables may be grouped and thus indicate how deception is structured.

DIFFERENT TYPES OF LIES

While the previous analysis suggests that there may be some common cues to deception, it also indicates that deception is far from being a homogeneous phenomenon. Fully 42% of the behaviors presented in

Table 2.3 were not related to deception, and the median d of the significant relationships was .52, only slightly above what Cohen (1977) considered a medium effect. The suggestion that lies are not all the same is consistent with the results of a study by DePaulo, Rosenthal, Rosenkrantz, and Green (1984). They found that speech cues that indicate a person is dissimulating liking were not the same cues that indicate a person is dissimulating disliking; furthermore, speech correlates of deception for male senders were different from the corresponding correlates for females.

In an exploratory attempt to identify behavioral cues related to different types of lies, the studies summarized in Table 2.3 were classified according to senders' motivation to succeed on the deception task. Motivation was considered high if subjects were provided some monetary rewards for doing well on the deception task or if deception was described as a test of some skill or ability. The righthand part of Table 2.3 shows the ds representing the differences between deceptive and truthful communications in separate columns for low- and high-motivation studies, as well as the zs of difference between the significance levels associated with each d (Rosenthal & Rubin, 1979). It can be seen that 9 of 24 behaviors (38%) listed in the low-motivation group were significantly associated with deception compared with 10 of 20 behaviors (50%) in the high-motivation group. Furthermore, there were 8 significant differences between the low- and high-motivation levels, where only one would be expected by chance.

With the exception of shrugs, visual behaviors associated with highly motivated deception show a decrease in frequency and/or intensity. Specifically, compared with the low–motivation condition, deception under high motivation was associated with less gazing, less blinking, more neutral facial expressions (less smiling, $p = .10$), fewer head movements, fewer adaptors ($p = .12$), and fewer postural shifts. In the area of paralinguistic behaviors, the analysis showed an association between highly motivated deception and slower pacing, specifically shorter response length and slower rate of speech. Finally, under verbal behaviors, Table 2.3 shows only one significant difference between the two motivation levels—negativity of deceptive messages was greater in the high-motivation condition.

In general, results of the meta-analysis suggest that the highly motivated deceivers tried harder to control their behavior and consequently moved less and displayed more behavioral rigidity. It should be noted that this explanation appears somewhat inconsistent with the association found between highly motivated deception and greater increases in shrugs, level of pitch, and frequency of negative statements. Since pitch is relatively uncontrollable, one can hypothesize that it should increase under high motivation. However, the increases in shrugs and negative statements under high motivation remain without clear interpretation.

THE LIE DETECTOR'S PERSPECTIVE

Models of lie detection must address two issues facing the lie detector: which cues or channels should be attended to and how should these cues be interpreted? The attention given to a channel should depend on the location of this channel in the leakage hierarchy. Under ordinary circumstances, receivers of a multichannel message could be expected to weigh more heavily the less leaky and more controllable components of the message. Since controllable channels yield more information, this strategy would allow the receivers to obtain the maximum amount of information from the message. Consistent with this proposition are studies indicating that less leaky channels exert more influence on receivers' judgments (DePaulo, Rosenthal, Eisenstat, Rogers, & Finkelstein, 1978; Mehrabian & Ferris, 1967; Zuckerman, Blanck, Driver, Koestner, & Rosenthal, 1982b)—a phenomenon termed primacy effect by DePaulo et al. (1978). Additionally, it has been shown that channels roughly similar in leakiness (e.g., speech versus face) exert a similar degree of influence (Ekman, Friesen, O'Sullivan, & Scherer, 1980; Krauss, Apple, Morency, Wenzel, & Winton, 1981) on receivers' judgments. Finally, Zuckerman et al. (1982b) found that the primacy effect was even more pronounced when there was a greater difference in degree of leakiness between the two channels combined in the message. That is, when one channel was particularly controllable and the other particularly leaky, receivers gave even more weight to the controllable channel than they did when the difference in degree of leakiness was smaller. This effect was termed primacy strategy.

The primacy effect may change, however, as a function of actual deception or anticipation of deception. Thus, Ekman et al. (1980) showed that receivers' judgments of deceptive messages were more influenced by the speech than by the face or body cues associated with the messages; receivers' ratings of truthful messages were equally influenced by all three channels. In a related study, Zuckerman, Amidon, Bishop, and Pomerantz (1982a) found that receivers' ratings of deceptive messages were more influenced by tone of voice relative to facial cues, whereas receivers' ratings of truthful messages were more influenced by the facial cues. Perhaps changes in pitch or other voice qualities associated with deception drew attention to the vocal channel when the senders were lying.

Suspicion of deception may also affect the weights assigned to the various channels. Thus, Zuckerman, Spiegel, DePaulo, and Rosenthal (1982) found that subjects suspecting deception were less influenced by facial cues relative to vocal cues, compared to subjects who did not suspect deception. However, this effect was not replicated in a more recent study by Zuckerman et al. (1982b) and therefore should be treated with caution. What Zuckerman et al. (1982b) did find was that male subjects suspecting deception decreased their use of the primacy strategy, i.e., they decreased the tendency to rely more on particularly controllable channels when such channels were combined with particularly leaky channels. This effect is consistent with a behavioral pattern of trying to uncover the truth. Females suspecting deception did the opposite, actually increasing their use of the primacy strategy. This effect may counter their success in lie detection and is therefore consistent with a large body of evidence supporting the concept of "females' accommodatingness" (Rosenthal & DePaulo, 1979a, b)—the tendency of women to avoid decoding unintended, leaked, or discrepant messages.

Overall it appears that either actual or suspected deception may change the weight assigned to various channels so that controllable channels lose and leaky channels gain some influence on the judges' impressions. In the case of the primacy strategy, the change has been observed for males alone.

As previously noted, the receivers must not only attend to certain cues but also interpret them. Thus, the investigator must determine not only which cues are related to judgment of deception (regardless of the accuracy of this judgment) but also the extent of correspondence between these cues and cues that are related to actual deception.

Studies on cues related to perception of deception were examined in a meta-analysis using the same procedure employed in the analysis of cues related to actual deception. As before, we included speakers' behaviors that were examined in two or more studies. The question of interest concerned the relationship between these behaviors and judges' perceptions of deception—regardless of (a) the relationships between these behaviors and actual deception and (b) the accuracy of judges' perceptions. For each behavior we computed the average d estimate and the corresponding combined z. The results are presented in Table 2.4. Positive ds and zs indicate that an increase in the frequency of the behavior was associated with judgments of deceptiveness (rather than truthfulness).

It can be seen that of 10 behaviors, 8 (80%) were significantly associated with perceived deception, a proportion that is higher than the proportion (58%) of behaviors associated with actual deception. This difference is consistent with Kraut's (1980) assertion that behavioral cues are more strongly associated with judgments of deception than with actual deception. Cues to actual deception apparently vary with the type of lie, deceiver, and deceptive context; cues to perceived deception seem to be more consistent and less likely to vary with different lie detectors and lie detection context. Additional experimental support for this conclusion was provided by Kraut and Poe (1982) and DePaulo et al. (1984). Kraut and Poe (1982) found that customs officials and laypersons did not differ

Table 2.4   Behaviors Associated with Judgment of Deception

Behavior	Judgment of Deception		
	N of studies	Mean d^a	Combined z
Visual channel			
Gaze	4	−.45	−3.25**
Smiling	5	−.32	−2.97**
Adaptors	3	.30	.51
Postural shifts	2	.50	3.00**
Auditory channel			
Response latency	5	.36	3.61***
Response length	4	−.11	−.61
Speech rate	2	−.67	−2.84**
Speech errors	4	.27	2.00*
Speech hesitations	2	.58	3.17**
Pitch	2	.68	2.82**

^{a}Positive values indicate that an increase in behavior was associated with the judgment of deception.
*$p < .05$
**$p < .01$
***$p < .001$
SOURCE: Zuckerman et al., 1981.

in their perception of which cues indicate deception. DePaulo et al. (1984) reported substantial agreement between male and female perceivers and between different types of lies (dissimulation of liking versus dissimulation of disliking) in the cues perceived as indicators of deception (see also DePaulo & Rosenthal, 1979b). As previously noted, there were substantial differences between male and female senders and between different types of lies in the cues related to *actual* deception.

It should be noted that most of the vocal correlates of perceived deception appearing in Table 2.4 were also examined in a related but separate research domain, that of speakers' credibility and trustworthiness (e.g., Apple, Streeter, & Krauss, 1979; Miller, Maruyama, Beaber, & Valone, 1976). In general, it appears that variables that give rise to suspicion of deception—speech errors and hesitations, higher pitch and lower speech rate—also decrease perceived credibility and trustworthiness of speakers.

What is the correspondence between cues to perceived and actual deception? A quantitative answer to this question was first provided in a study by DePaulo et al. (1982). These investigators first computed correlations of each of 20 verbal and paralinguistic cues with both actual deception and perceived deception. They then computed correlations between the 20 correlations associated with actual deception and the 20 correlations associated with perceived deception separately for every combination of sender sex, perceiver sex, and type of affect (positive versus negative). The resulting 8 correlations ranged from .33 to .86 with a median r of .52, $p < .002$. The analogous correlation in the present data between the 10 d estimates of cues to perceived deception (Table 2.4) and the corresponding 10 d estimates of cues to actual deception (Table 2.3) was .70, indicating that the behavioral cues to actual deception serve, to some extent, as cues to perceived deception as well.

The identification of cues to perceived deception suggests that a message will be judged deceptive when the relevant cues are displayed by the deceiver and perceived by the lie detector. A quite different approach to the inference of deception is suggested in a study by Kraut (1978, Experiment 2). He showed that observers suspicious of a self-serving answer became even less trusting when the answer was preceded by a long pause; in contrast, judges trusting a self-damaging answer became even more trusting if it was preceded by the same period of hesitation. Kraut suggested that the pause preceding the self-serving answer was interpreted as time needed to create the lie, whereas the pause preceding a self-damaging answer was interpreted as the time needed to decide on the answer and phrase it in the least damaging way. Thus, the previously offered view that perceived deception is related to specific cues (which are also cues to actual deception) is now challenged by the view that behavioral cues are nonspecific activators that are interpreted as deceptive or not according to the context in which they are perceived.

The resolution of this apparent contradiction gives rise to a model of the interpretation process. Specifically it is proposed that receivers interpret behavioral cues differently when they have to decide whether a message is deceptive or not, as opposed to when they have already arrived at a preliminary decision. Receivers seeking to judge whether a message is deceptive or not may be able to use the appropriate behavioral cues; that is, their judgment may be based on cues that actually distinguish between truth and deception. On the other hand, receivers who have already formed an opinion may use any cue to support their judgment. Thus, a cue to actual deception may convince the judges that a message is either deceptive or truthful depending on their already existing opinion. Of course the model needs empirical testing.

CONCLUSION

The significance of this kind of research lies in its potential for increasing understanding of nonverbal decoding processes generally and specifically in relation to the clinical process. Many times during the therapeutic process, for example, a clinician encounters a patient who is unwilling, or perhaps afraid, to acknowledge a physical or emotional problem. Some of the research described in this chapter eventually may help clinicians and clinical supervisors to develop measures for use in the training of decoding skills in the clinical context. Additionally, the research described here has implications for forensic medicine and clinical practice. In the legal context, for instance, a clinician's decoding abilities can be central to the accurate application of the insanity plea (Blanck, Rosenthal, & Cordell, in press).

In sum, clinicians have a clear need to detect lies and attempts at deception systematically and reliably. The description and development of measures for such detection may help clinicians toward a more effective understanding of patients' underlying needs and feelings. This understanding should contribute to more accurate diagnosis and treatment of both physical and emotional disorders.

ACKNOWLEDGMENTS

Preparation of this chapter was supported in part by grants from the National Academy of Education and NIMH to Bella DePaulo and from the National Science Foundation to Robert Rosenthal.

REFERENCES

Apple, W., Streeter, L. A., & Krauss, R. M. (1979). Effects of pitch and speech rate on personal attributions. *Journal of Personality and Social Psychology, 37,* 715–27.

Beatty, J. (1982). Task-evoked pupillary responses, processing load, and the structure of processing resources. *Psychological Bulletin, 91,* 276–92.

Blanck, P. D., Rosenthal, R., & Cordell, L. H. (in press). The appearance of justice: A study of judicial influence and expectancy effects. *Stanford Law Review, 38.*

Bugental, D. B., Caporael, L., & Shennum, W. A. (1980). Experimentally-produced child uncontrollability: Effects on the potency of adult communication patterns. *Child Development, 51,* 520–28.

Bugental, D. B., Henker, B., & Whalen, C. K. (1976). Attributional antecedents of verbal and vocal assertiveness. *Journal of Personality and Social Psychology, 34,* 405–11.

Bugental, D. B., & Love, L. (1975). Nonassertive expression of parental approval and disapproval and its relationship to child disturbance. *Child Development, 46,* 747–52.

Cohen, J. (1977). *Statistical power analysis for the behavioral sciences,* Rev. ed. New York: Academic Press.

Davis, R. C. (1961). Physiological responses as a means of evaluating information. In A. D. Biderman & H. Zimmer (Eds.) *The manipulation of human behavior.* New York: Wiley.

DePaulo, B. M., Lanier, K., & Davis, T. (1983). Detecting the deceit of the motivated liar. *Journal of Personality and Social Psychology, 45,* 1096–1103.

DePaulo, B. M., Lassiter, G. D., & Stone, J. I. (1982). Attentional determinants of success at detecting deception and truth. *Personality and Social Psychology Bulletin, 8,* 273–79.

DePaulo, B. M., & Rosenthal, R. (1979a). Ambivalence, discrepancy and deception in nonverbal communication. In R. Rosenthal (Ed.), *Skill in nonverbal communication.* Cambridge, MA: Oelgschlager, Grunn, & Hains.

DePaulo, B. M., & Rosenthal, R. (1979b). Telling lies. *Journal of Personality and Social Psychology, 37,* 1713–22(b).

DePaulo, B. M., Rosenthal, R., Eisenstat, R. A., Rogers, P. L., & Finkelstein, S. (1978). Decoding discrepant nonverbal cues. *Journal of Personality and Social Psychology, 36,* 313–23.

DePaulo, B. M., Rosenthal, R., Green, C. R., & Rosenkrantz, J. (1982). Diagnosing deceptive and mixed messages from verbal and nonverbal cues. *Journal of Experimental Social Psychology, 18,* 433–46.

DePaulo, B. M., Rosenthal, R., Rosenkrantz, J., & Green, C. R. (1984). Actual and perceived cues to deception: A closer look at speech. *Basic and Applied Social Psychology, 3,* 291–312.

DePaulo, B. M., Stone, J. I., & Lassiter, G. D. (1985). Deceiving and detecting deceit. In B. R. Schlenker (Ed.), *The self and social life.* New York: McGraw-Hill.

DePaulo, B. M., Zuckerman, M., & Rosenthal, R. (1980). Detecting deception: Modality effects. In L. Wheeler (Ed.), *The Review of Personality and Social Psychology,* Vol. 1. Beverly Hills, CA: Sage.

Ekman, P. Mistakes when deceiving. (1980). Paper presented at the conference on the Clever Hans Phenomenon, New York Academy of Sciences.

Ekman, P., & Friesen, W. V. (1969). Nonverbal leakage and clues to deception. *Psychiatry, 32,* 88–106.

Ekman, P., & Friesen, W. V. (1972). Hand movements. *Journal of Communication, 22,* 353–74.

Ekman, P., & Friesen, W. V. (1974). Detecting deception from the body or face. *Journal of Personality and Social Psychology, 29,* 288–98.

Ekman, P., Friesen, W. V., O'Sullivan, M., & Scherer, K. (1980). Relative importance of face, body, and speech in judgments of personality and affect. *Journal of Personality and Social Psychology, 38,* 270–77.

Freud, S. (1959). Fragments of an analysis of a case of hysteria (1905). *Collected Papers,* Vol. 3. New York: Basic Books.

Goldman-Eisler, F. (1968). *Psycholinguistics: Experiments in spontaneous speech.* New York: Academic Press.

Gustafson, L. A., & Orne, M. T. (1963). Effects of heightened motivation on the detection of deception. *Journal of Applied Psychology, 47,* 408–11.

Gustafson, L. A., & Orne, M. T. (1965). Effects of perceived role and role success on the detection of deception. *Journal of Applied Psychology, 49,* 412–17.

Hemsley, G. D. (1977). *Experimental studies in the behavioral indicants of deception.* Unpublished Ph.D. dissertation, University of Toronto.

Holzman, P. S., & Rousey, C. (1966). The voice as a percept. *Journal of Personality and Social Psychology, 4,* 79–86.

Kahneman, D. (1973). *Attention and effort*. Englewood Cliffs, New Jersey: Prentice-Hall.

Kasl, S. V., & Mahl, G. F. (1965). The relationship of disturbances and hesitations in spontaneous speech to anxiety. *Journal of Personality and Social Psychology, 1,* 425–33.

Knapp, M. L., & Comadena, M. E. (1979). Telling it like it isn't: A review of theory and research on deceptive communications. *Human Communication Research, 5,* 270–85.

Krauss, R. M., Apple, W., Morency, N., Wenzel, C., & Winton, W. (1981). Verbal, vocal and visible factors in judgments of another's affects. *Journal of Personality and Social Psychology, 40,* 312–19.

Krauss, R. M., Geller, V., & Olson, C. (1976). Modalities and cues in the detection of deception. Paper presented at the meeting of the American Psychological Association, Washington, D.C.

Kraut, R. E. (1978). Verbal and nonverbal cues in the perception of lying. *Journal of Personality and Social Psychology, 36,* 380–91.

Kraut, R. E. (1980). Humans as lie detectors: Some second thoughts. *Journal of Communication, 30,* 309–16.

Kraut, R. E., & Poe, D. (1980). On the line: The deception judgments of customs inspectors and laymen. *Journal of Personality and Social Psychology. 39,* 784–98.

Lykken, D. T. (1959). The GSR in the detection of guilt. *Journal of Applied Psychology, 43,* 385–88.

Lykken, D. T. (1960). The validity of the guilty knowledge technique: The effects of faking. *Journal of Applied Psychology, 44,* 258–62.

Lykken, D. T. (1974). Psychology and the lie detector industry. *American Psychologist, 29,* 725–39.

Mehrabian, A. (1967). Attitudes inferred from non-immediacy of verbal communication. *Journal of Verbal Learning and Verbal Behavior, 6,* 294–95.

Mehrabian, A., & Ferris, S. R. (1976). Inference of attitudes from nonverbal communication in two channels. *Journal of Consulting Psychology, 31,* 248–52.

Meyer, D. R. On the interaction of simultaneous responses. (1953). *Psychological Bulletin, 50,* 204–20.

Miller, M., Maruyama, G., Beaber, R. J., & Valone, K. (1976). Speed of speech and persuasion. *Journal of Personality and Social Psychology, 34,* 615–24.

Newtson, D. (1976). Foundations of attribution: The perception of ongoing behavior. In J. H. Harvey, W. J. Ickes, & R. F. Kidd (Eds.), *New directions in attribution research,* Vol. 1. New York: Wiley.

Nunnally, J. C., Knott, P. D., Duchnowski, A., & Parker, R. (1967). Pupillary response as a general measure of activation. *Perception and Psychophysics, 2,* 149–55.

Orne, M. T., Thackray, R. I., & Paskewitz, D. A. (1972). On the detection of deception: A model for the study of the physiological effects of psychological stimuli. In N. S. Greenfield & R. A. Sternbach (Eds.), *Handbook of psychophysiology,* New York: Holt.

Rosenthal, R. (1978). Combining results of independent studies. *Psychological Bulletin, 85,* 185–93.

Rosenthal, R. (1980). Summarizing significance levels. In R. Rosenthal (Ed.), *Quantitative assessment of research domains.* San Francisco, CA: Jossey-Bass.

Rosenthal, R. (1983). Assessing the statistical and social importance of the effects of psychotherapy. *Journal of Consulting and Clinical Psychology, 51,* 4–13.

Rosenthal, R., & DePaulo, B. M. (1979a). Sex differences in eavesdropping on nonverbal cues. *Journal of Personality and Social Psychology. 37,* 273–85.

Rosenthal, R., & DePaulo, B. M. (1979b). Sex differences in accommodation in nonverbal communication. In R. Rosenthal (Ed.), *Skill in nonverbal communication: Individual differences.* Cambridge, MA: Oelgeschlager.

Rosenthal, R., & Rubin, D. B. (1978). Interpersonal expectancy effects: The first 345 studies. *The Behavioral and Brain Sciences, 3,* 377–86.

Rosenthal, R., & Rubin, D. B. (1979). Comparing significance levels of independent studies. *Psychological Bulletin, 86,* 1165–68.

Scherer, K. R. (1980a). Vocal indicators of stress. In J. Darby (Ed.), *The evaluation of speech in psychiatry and medicine.* New York: Grune & Stratton.

Scherer, K. R. (1980b). Speech and emotional states. In J. Darby (Ed.), *The evaluation of speech in psychiatry and medicine.* New York: Grune & Stratton.

Scott, T. R., Wells, W. H., Wood, D. Z., & Morgan, D. I. (1967). Pupillary response and sexual interest reexamined. *Journal of Clinical Psychology, 23,* 433–38.

Simpson, H. M., & Hale, S. M. (1969). Pupillary changes during a decision making task. *Perceptual and Motor Skills, 29,* 495–98.

Waid, W. M., & Orne, M. T. (1982). The physiological detection of deception. *American Scientist, 70,* 402–8.

Weitz, S. (1972). Attitude, voice, and behavior: A repressed affect model of interracial interaction. *Journal of Personality and Social Psychology, 24,* 14–21.

Wiener, M., & Mehrabian, A. (1968). *Language within language.* New York: Appleton.

Williams, C. E., & Stevens, K. N. (1969). On determining the emotional state of pilots during flight: An exploratory study. *Aerospace Medicine, 40,* 1369–72.

Zuckerman, M., Amidon, M. D., Bishop, S. E., & Pomerantz, S. D. (1982a). Face and tone of voice in the communication of deception. *Journal of Personality and Social Psychology, 43,* 347–57.

Zuckerman, M., Blanck, P. D., Driver, E., Koestner, R., & Rosenthal, R. (1982b). *The leakage hierarchy in verbal and nonverbal communication: Sex differences in response to threatened deception.* Unpublished manuscript, University of Rochester.

Zuckerman, M., DeFrank, R. S., Hall, J. A., Larrance, D. T., & Rosenthal, R. (1979). Facial and vocal cues of deception and honesty. *Journal of Experimental Social Psychology, 15,* 378–96.

Zuckerman, M., & Driver, E. (in press). Telling lies: Verbal and nonverbal correlates of deception. In A. W. Siegman & S. Feldstein (Eds.), *Nonverbal communication: An integrated perspective.* New York: Erlbaum.

Zuckerman, M., Larrance, D. T., Spiegel, N. H., & Klorman, R. (1981). Controlling nonverbal cues: Facial expressions and tone of voice. *Journal of Experimental Social Psychology, 17,* 506–24.

Zuckerman, M., Spiegel, N. H., DePaulo, B. M., & Rosenthal, R. (1982). Nonverbal strategies for decoding deception, *Journal of Nonverbal Behavior, 6,* 171–86.

3 Nonverbal Aspects of Empathy and Rapport in Physician-Patient Interaction

Jinni A. Harrigan and Robert Rosenthal

Sometimes miscommunication merely results in confusion, annoyance, and mistaken impressions. But in situations where needs are critical and expectations high, miscommunication can result in serious consequences. One such situation is the doctor-patient relationship, where the patient's needs are cogent and anxiety-producing, provoking feelings of vulnerability and fearfulness. Miscommunication in the medical setting can lead to errors in diagnosis, treatment decisions, and medication use, as well as noncompliance, poor rapport, and frustration (Blackwell, 1973; Ley, 1977; Schmidt, 1977).

The problem of patient noncompliance has been the most researched concern. Reports of noncompliance range from 4% to 92% (Charney, Bynum, Eldredge, Frank, MacWhinney, McNabb, Scheiner, Sumpter, and Iker, 1967; Marston, 1970; Stimson, 1974). Even the most commonly accepted estimate, one-third to one-half (Blackwell, 1973) of all patients as being noncompliant, is remarkably high. The reasons for noncompliance are complex, but the single most consistent factor is the relationship between doctor and patient (Becker and Maiman, 1975; Davis, 1971; Hall, 1979; Korsch and Negrete, 1974). A thorough review of issues involved in patient compliance and satisfaction may be found elsewhere (DiMatteo and DiNicola, 1982; Haynes, Taylor, and Sackett, 1979; Stone, 1979; Wilson, 1973).

Patient satisfaction with health care has been studied less directly, usually in relation to compliance or recall of health information. While no criteria currently exist to characterize the degree of patient satisfaction, several studies have shown that the most important element in patient satisfaction with health care involves the interaction between doctor and patient (Ben-Sira, 1980; Vuori, Aaku, Aine, Erkko, and Johansson, 1972; Ware, Davies-Avery, and Stewart, 1980; Woolley, Kane, Hughes, and Wright, 1978). Bertakis (1977) and others (Comstock, Hooper,

Goodwin and Goodwin, 1982; Glassman and Glassman, 1981; Hulka, Kupper, Cassel, and Mayo, 1975) have shown that providing more information to patients increases patient satisfaction and retention of diagnostic and treatment facts. Wolinsky and Steiber (1982) found that patients often chose physicians on the basis of the physicians' affective behavior. Patients' descriptions of the "ideal" doctor revealed that supportive behaviors involving interpersonal relations and expressive qualities were the most salient (Congalton, 1969). Patient satisfaction is also influenced by the degree to which physicians conform to patients' expectations of the physicians' role performance (Larsen and Rootman, 1976). Bernarde and Mayerson (1978) and Hayes-Bautista (1976) discuss issues involving negotiation between doctor and patient to bring about patient compliance and satisfaction. Haug and Lavin (1979) described attitudes of rejection of and challenge to physicians by various patient populations. Finally, physician characteristics such as gender have been found to influence patient satisfaction (Adams, 1977; Engleman, 1974). These and other studies emphasize that improved therapeutic results are obtained when greater attention is given to the establishment of a positive doctor-patient relationship (Fisher, 1971; Gillum and Barsky, 1974; Kasteler, Kane, Olsen, and Thetford, 1976; Vaccarino, 1977).

The importance of effective communication in the process of health care delivery has not been lost on those within medicine (Carroll and Monroe, 1979; Engel, 1973; Gorlin and Zucker, 1983; Jensen, 1981). Balint (1964; Balint and Balint, 1962) and others (Clyne, 1973; Schüffel, 1977) analyzed the characteristics of medical interviews and concluded that one of the most important aspects of the therapeutic process is listening intently to the patient so as to understand the patient's complaints and illnesses. By the process of selective attention and selective neglect (Balint, 1973; Platt and McMath, 1979) the physician is able to know the focal area requiring attention, and is thus able to help the patient become well.

The interpersonal relationship between physicians and patients is the subject of much discussion and recent investigation within medicine and behavioral science (DiMatteo, 1979a; Friedman, 1979; Pendleton and Hasler, 1983; Waitkin, 1984). Since the mid-1970s medical educators have recognized the need to focus on teaching interpersonal communication skills, at both undergraduate and graduate levels, and have developed curriculum material and training programs in response to this need (Hornsby and Payne, 1979; Kahn, Cohen, and Jason, 1979). Significant improvements from pre- to post-test training have been demonstrated in teaching interpersonal communication skills (Engler, Saltzman, Walker, and Wolf, 1981; Quirk and Babineau, 1982; Werner and Schneider, 1974) and in training students to become more empathic (Robbins, Kauss, Heinrich, Abrass, Dreyer, and Clyman, 1979; Sanson-Fisher and Poole, 1978).

While interpersonal skills may be enhanced by training, recent research indicates that these skills can fade or diminish over time (Barbee and Feldman, 1970; Kauss, Robbins, Abrass, Bakaitis, and Anderson, 1980). There are several possible explanations for the inability of training programs to demonstrate long-lasting results. Interpersonal skills training programs have been carried out most frequently in the preclinical years, when students are concerned with learning the basic sciences and have not yet begun providing patient care. Later, when students become involved with learning about diagnosis and medical management of illness, reinforcement of communication skills is not provided. It has been suggested that if interpersonal skills training were to be given to those actively involved in day-to-day patient care, the newly acquired skills would be more likely to be retained over a longer period of time (Hornsby and Payne, 1979; Engler, Saltzman, Walker, and Wolf, 1981). Kauss et al. (1980) emphasized that it is essential to the success of interpersonal skills training programs for faculty preceptors to act as role models, reinforcing the students' and residents' newly acquired skills. Interestingly, many medical faculty have themselves not received specific training in interpersonal skills. Enhancing the qualities of interpersonal communication skills is critical because communication is an essential feature in establishing rapport and is required in interviewing, the physical examination, prescribing medications and therapy, patient education, and counseling and psychotherapy.

THE CONCEPT OF EMPATHY

A major component of effective doctor-patient interactions seems to be the expression of empathy and development of rapport. Empathy is a core process of social interaction and an essential ingredient in developing interpersonal intimacy. The concept of empathy has a long history of study (Smith, 1759, in Schneider, 1948). It has been examined from several perspectives within psychology and psychiatry: those of psychotherapists, cognitive-developmental psychologists, and social psychologists. Concepts relevant to empathy include role-taking or perspective-taking (Chandler and Greenspan, 1972; Flavell, Botkin, Fry, Wright, and Jarvis, 1968; Johnson and Matross, 1975), social comprehension (Feshbach and Roe, 1968), and altruism (Aronfreed, 1970; Moore, Underwood, and Rosenhan, 1973). A thorough review of the concept of empathy is not the focus of this paper; reviews can be found in Buchheimer (1963), Hoffman (1978), Katz (1963), and Smith (1973).

Although definitional issues are abundant, there seems to be agreement on one point: empathy involves a vicarious affective response on the part of the empathizer (Hoffman, 1978). The ability to empathize allows the perceiver to know and understand the feelings and thoughts of another (Buckley, Siegel, and Ness, 1979; Gove and Keating, 1979), to put one's self in the place of another (Kalish, 1973; Volpe, 1979). Psychotherapists (Ginott, 1965; Jourard, 1971; Shlien, 1961) posit an added dimension of empathy which involves not only sensitivity to another but also the capacity to communicate empathy. The ability "to communicate this perception in a language attuned to the client that allows him more clearly to sense and formulate his feelings is the essence of the communicative aspect of accurate empathy" (Truax and Carkhuff, 1967, p. 286). Rogers (1951) considered empathic understanding to be the therapist's primary goal.

While psychotherapists have been concerned with the practical need for empathy in the care of their clients, cognitive-developmental psychologists have delved into the underlying processes and functions of empathy. The attempt to understand empathy with respect to the stimuli producing empathy and the expression, acquisition, and operation of empathy have led to a dualistic view which emphasizes either cognitive or affective features of empathy. This distinction between cognitive and affective processes parallels the confusion of the terms empathy and sympathy. Empathy, as some have defined it (Borke, 1971; Chandler and Greenspan, 1972; Johnson and Matross, 1975), involves not only feeling the affective state of the other, but also cognitively representing and understanding the other's felt state. In her description of empathy, Dymond (1949, 1950) stresses the importance of insight and of intellectualizing the perspective of another. Krebs (1975) found that perceived similarity between subjects and those whom they observed increased subjects' empathy for the observees. The cognitive component of empathy may be required to enable the empathizer to be helpful in relating to the other's situation and needs.

The purely affective component appears to be more like sympathy than empathy. Aronfreed (1970) and others (Laird, 1974; Stotland, 1969) claim that the other's affective cues stimulate a similar affective state in the observer, a motor mimicry. Compelling results have been reported where affective stimuli were sufficient to produce affective responses in other individuals (Berger and Hadley, 1975; Sagi and Hoffman, 1976; Simner, 1971). Stotland and associates (Stotland, 1969; Stotland, Mathews, Sherman, Hansson, and Richardson, 1978; Stotland, Sherman, and Shaver, 1971) found that when the empathizer imagined himself/herself in the place of the other, the empathizer showed more palmar sweat and gave more verbal reports of feeling empathic. Feshbach and Roe (1968) limit empathy as an affective response but elaborate social comprehension as cognitive mediation between affective and situational cues.

Responding to affective signals with affect does not involve empathy as it has been defined here. Putting one's self in the place of the other requires a cognitive process. The affective dimension of empathy may be more akin to sympathy in which the observer identifies with another's emotional state because of similarities in their situations. In experiencing sympathy, observers lose their separate identities, take on the other's feelings and circumstances, and become preoccupied with their own feelings. Sympathy or a mere affective response to another's emotional state does not signify empathy because the element of objective understanding and the possibility of being helpful is missing. Katz (1963) developed this distinction between sympathy and empathy at length. Rogers (1957) clarifies the difference between these two concepts by stressing the "as if" quality of the observer's empathic response: "To sense the client's private world as if it were your own, but without ever losing the 'as if' quality . . . (p.99)."

Hoffman (1975a,b, 1977, 1978) offers a useful model interrelating cognitive and affective components of empathy. He describes acquisition stages of empathy which progress from an infant's reflexive crying in response to another infant's crying, through egocentrism and the distinction between self and other, to a role-taking ability, and finally, to sensing another as possessing a life space involving experiences and situations. Tomkins (1962) and others (Izard,.1971; Piaget and Inhelder, 1967) have also discussed the interplay between affective and cognitive components of empathy.

Social psychologists, in addition to developing measures of empathy to be discussed below, have been concerned with the role of empathy in social competence (Trower, Bryant, and Argyle, 1978; Berne, 1966). Being unable to take the role of another is a commonly reported symptom of psychiatric disorder (Meldman, 1967; Trower, Bryant, and Argyle, 1978) and chronic delinquency (Chandler, 1973; Ellis, 1982). Sensitivity training groups have been formed to help individuals cultivate essential social skills (Smith, 1973).

MEASURES OF EMPATHY

Verbal Behavior

Of the two major behavioral dimensions of communication, verbal and nonverbal behavior, verbal behavior has received more attention. This emphasis has occurred primarily because utterances have, until recently, been more readily perceivable, codeable, and interpretable than nonverbal or vocal behavior.

Empirical studies of rapport evolved from Rogerian client-centered psychotherapy, which emphasizes the quality of the interaction and components of empathy, warmth, and genuineness (Rogers, 1957). The Accurate Empathy Scale was developed by Truax and Carkhuff (1967) to assess the degree of empathy conveyed by therapists' verbal responses. Verbalizations are evaluated with respect to interest, regard, understanding, and clarification of patients' experiences and feelings. The scale has been widely used (Bergin and Solomon, 1970; Gurman, 1973; Kalish, 1973; Sanson-Fisher, 1978; Stetler, 1977), but questions have been raised about its content and validity (Caracena and Vicory, 1969; Rappaport and Chinsky, 1972; Wenegrat, 1976). Criticisms involve the lack of clear-cut objective criteria to assess empathy, methodological neglect in construction of the scale, and low or negative correlations with other empathy scales. Other measures of empathy using verbal material have also been developed (Carkhuff, 1969; Goodman, 1972) but used less extensively than the Accurate Empathy Scale.

Nearly all content analysis systems which examine the therapist's communications involve some measure of the therapist's warmth, empathy, interest, etc. (Strupp, 1960; see reviews in Kiesler, 1973; Marsden, 1965; Matarazzo, 1978). While most of these systems employ raters to judge the therapist's degree of empathy, other scales have been developed to take into account the client's perceptions of the therapist's empathy (Barrett-Leonard, 1962; Lorr, 1965). Fiedler's (1950) instrument measures therapists' perception of the "ideal therapeutic relationship."

In addition to measuring expressed empathy, research also has been concerned with assessing one's ability to be empathic (Cassell, 1963; Dymond, 1949; Gough, 1955; Kerr, 1947). For example, Hogan's scale (1969), based on personality characteristics and interpersonal attitudes from well-known inventories (CPI, MMPI, and items from testing forms from the Institute of Personality Assessment and Research), has been used to determine an individual's empathic disposition. This scale has been used to evaluate medical school applicants with respect to non-academic skills (Kupfer, Drew, Curtis, and Rubinstein, 1978). Streit-Forest (1982) found positive relationships between medical students' scores on the Hogan scale and their attitudes concerning the importance of doctor-patient interaction. Other scales assessing "empathic tendency" have also been developed (Mehrabian and Epstein, 1972).

Research has been conducted on the relationship between physicians' verbal behavior and diagnostic skills and patient variables such as satisfaction, compliance, and retention of information. While some investigators develop their own system for coding verbal behavior (Bain, 1976; Hess,

1969; Joyce, Caple, Mason, Reynolds, and Mathews, 1969), most of these studies have relied on an adaption of the Interaction Process Analysis System developed by Bales (1950). This system was evolved from systematic observations of task-oriented strategies and affective behavior within small groups. Bales' technique was instrumental in providing a framework for analyzing social interaction. Korsch and colleagues (Korsch, Gozzi, and Francis, 1968; Korsch and Negrete, 1974) and others (Adler and Enelow, 1966; Davis, 1968; Scott, Donnelly, Gallagher, and Hess, 1973) modified Bales' system to analyze doctor-patient communication during medical interviews. Information from these verbal categories is then correlated with patient outcome variables of satisfaction, compliance, information recall, and clinical recovery. Studies like these, while not directly measuring physicians' empathic responses, are valuable with respect to the information provided about non-psychotherapy doctor-patient interactions and about variables important in the establishment of rapport and the expression of physicians' concern and caring.

Recently, methods of discourse analysis used by linguists have been implemented in the study of doctor-patient communication. This linguistic perspective represents a new direction in medical interviewing research and an important shift in focus from evaluation to description. These structural studies involve systematic classification of verbalizations, based on grammar, syntax, and functions of the utterance in the interview (Byrne and Long, 1976; Coulthard and Ashby, 1976; Wadsworth, 1976). The resulting taxonomies permit objective and reliable distinctions among various forms of speech acts (i.e., questions, acknowledgment, reassurance, etc.) which can be correlated with other aspects of the consultation. For example, Stiles (1979, 1981) found significant relationships between specific "response modes" and phases (i.e., history taking, examination, etc.) of the interview. Patient satisfaction was positively correlated with the patients' being able to express complaints in their own words and receiving feedback and information from physicians at the conclusion of a visit (Stiles, Putnam, James, and Wolf, 1979). Tannen and Wallat (1983) examined doctors' and patients' "frames" (i.e., orientations and expectations within the interview) using linguistic and paralinguistic cues which were found to parallel the levels and types of involvement within the interaction (i.e., seeks reassurance; provides education). Cassell and Skopek (1977) have proposed the teaching of linguistics in medicine, and developed a system for organizing coded verbalizations using computer technology.

One final approach concerning empathy and doctor-patient communication is a program involving verbal and nonverbal behavior, and represents a point of transition from our discussion of verbal aspects of empathy to nonverbal dimensions of empathy. Kagan and associates (Kagan, 1975; Campbell, Kagan, and Krathwohl, 1971; Danish and Kagan, 1971; Kagan and Krathwohl, 1967) developed a technique (Interpersonal Process Recall) for focusing on the counselor-client communication process. This process allows the counselor to view and receive feedback about communicative behavior from trained counselors and from clients. Interpersonal Process Recall is a structured, well-researched method emphasizing the acquisition of a series of developmental skills. These skills involve the ability to recognize, identify, and respond to verbal, nonverbal, and vocal cues about a client's affect and attitude. Examples of such cues are: 1) abrupt shifts in theme during the interview, 2) changes in visual focus, especially glances at the counselor after the client has made a statement, and 3) changes in voice level, tone, or pace. Recently, this system has been modified to provide teaching of interpersonal relations to medical students and residents (Kagan, 1974). Students learn and practice specific "response modes" that effective interviewers consistently use. These response modes include exploration, listening, reacting to client/patient affect, and confrontation. During the feedback process, while reviewing a videotape, the student describes and discusses his or her thoughts, feelings, and reactions to the patient at various points in the interview. Interpersonal Process Recall is a self-learning model in that the instructor's task is to facilitate the student's learning and progressive awareness of communication patterns. Students are encouraged and helped to recognize their own areas of communication strength and difficulties. This technique represents a comprehensive component approach to the study of empathy in doctor-patient communication. Interpersonal Process Recall has been used in a variety of interpersonal skills training programs (Robbins, Kauss, Heinrich, Abrass, Dreyer, and Clyman, 1979; Werner and Schneider, 1974).

In our discussion of verbal behavior, we have described various methods of assessing empathy. Some of these are methods of evaluating one's ability to be empathic, while others involve appraisals of verbal responses with respect to expressed empathy. These latter measures provide information concerning an individual's encoding skills or effectiveness in communicating empathically. In the following section on nonverbal behavior we will consider measures and studies of both encoding and decoding empathy skills. There does not currently exist a method of measuring one's ability to decode empathy in verbal messages.

Nonverbal Behavior

Until recently, the bulk of research on doctor-patient communication has been focused on the verbal component, but the question of measuring empathy is more complex than a mere analysis of verbal responses. It has been suggested that empathy is not a unitary construct but a composite quality of several underlying variables (Kurtz and Grummon, 1972; Kalish, 1973). Cues from nonverbal channels have been shown to be significant factors in the expression of empathy (DiMatteo, 1979a,b; Friedman, 1979; Ekman and Friesen, 1969b; Stetler, 1977). Mansfield (1973) suggested that "nonverbal gestures, facial expressions, touching hands, and postural shifts conveyed a greater sense of empathy than could be captured with words alone on typed manuscripts or with voice tones on audio tapes" (p. 528).

Several instruments have been designed to measure an individual's ability to empathize by identifying or responding to affect expressed by a stimulus person(s): Behavioral Cognition Tests (O'Sullivan, Guilford, and DeMille, 1965); Brief Affect Recognition Test (Ekman and Friesen, 1974); Communication of Affect Receiving Ability Test (Buck, 1976); and the Social Interpretations Task (Archer and Akert, 1977). The two most commonly used scales will be discussed here: the Affect Sensitivity Scale and the Profile of Nonverbal Sensitivity Test.

The Affect Sensitivity Scale, devised by Kagan and colleagues (Kagan and Krathwohl, 1967; Campbell, Kagan, & Krathwohl, 1971), was designed to measure an individual's empathic ability—"the ability to detect and describe the immediate affective state of another . . . the ability to receive and decode affective communication" (Danish and Kagan, 1971, p. 51). This instrument consists of a series of videotaped vignettes of clients and counselors excerpted from actual counseling situations. Following exposure to each vignette, the subject chooses one of five alternatives to describe the client's or counselor's thoughts or reactions. The stimuli of the Affect Sensitivity Scale are presented verbally and nonverbally and consist of very complex statements about thoughts and feelings. Thus, the subject's task involves verbal evaluation as well as emotion recognition. This scale has been used most often as a pre-post test measure of interpersonal skills training (Robbins, Kauss, Heinrich, Abrass, Dreyer, and Clyman, 1979; Werner and Schneider, 1974) and counselor effectiveness (Campbell, Kagan, and Krathwohl, 1971).

The Profile of Nonverbal Sensitivity (PONS) Test, developed by Rosenthal, Hall, DiMatteo, Rogers, and Archer (1979), measures an individual's sensitivity to affect communicated by the sender's body, face, and voice. Two-second scenes are presented in auditory, visual, or audio-visual channels; after each scene is presented, the subject chooses one of two responses to describe the situation depicted. The audio segments have been electronically filtered or randomly spliced to remove input based on semantic content. The stimuli of the PONS Test, including the vocal ones, are nonverbal. The test has been widely used with subjects representing various ages, occupations, and levels of education and IQ, and coming from many different cultures. A fuller discussion of the PONS Test appears in Chapter 9.

The measures described so far represent techniques to evaluate an individual's ability to decode affect communicated both verbally and nonverbally. Encoding (transmitting) skills are likewise important in effective communication; that is, a person's ability to communicate empathically— through speech, tone of voice, and facial and body cues—is essential in establishing rapport.

Nonverbal behaviors, especially nonvocal ones, investigated with respect to empathy have multiple aspects. While verbal behavior is manifested in a single, sequential stream or channel of audible events, nonverbal behaviors are displayed simultaneously via several channels, including face, head, eyes, limbs, and trunk. Nonverbal units of behavior are difficult, if not impossible, to study in total isolation from one another. While the head is nodding, the trunk may be angled forward or back, the limbs may be still or moving, the face expressionless or animated, and the gaze steady, averted, or darting. Each unit of nonverbal behavior is interrelated in that each is capable of influencing the evaluation of another behavior. A further methodological dilemma involves the definition and coding of nonverbal behaviors. For example, a forward lean may vary from a 10° to a 40° angle from the upright posture, or a gesture may be recorded from onset through offset or only in relation to the type of movement involved. Analyses of verbal behavior are similarly problematic with respect to differentiating content.

Research on nonverbal components of empathy is more recent than research on empathic verbal behavior. Many more studies involve counselor-client interchanges than other therapeutic encounters (Gladstein, 1974), and few relate to physician-patient encounters. A majority of the research has dealt with observers' perceptions of empathic qualities; some has involved simulated and actual client perceptions, as well as measures of satisfaction and therapeutic outcome. There is a separate literature of experimental and descriptive clinical studies on patient nonverbal behavior related to diagnosis and therapy (Ekman and Friesen, 1974; Freedman, 1972; Mahl, 1968; Scheflen, 1964, 1965; Waxer, 1974, 1977). The following review of nonverbal encoding studies is not intended to be exhaustive but to highlight the major findings regarding empathy. The review emphasizes studies of therapeutic qualities: empathy, warmth, genuineness, trust, unconditional positive regard, facilitativeness, congruence, affiliation, liking, and attractiveness. Not all the studies mentioned here involve empathy in the therapeutic encounter. Research with similar objectives and using identical nonverbal behaviors is also included.

Using the Barrett-Lennard Relationship Inventory and scales for satisfaction and charisma, Fretz (1966) found that specific nonverbal behaviors (i.e., smiling, nodding, hand movements, etc.) by subjects performing the roles of "clients" and "counselors" were significantly correlated with empathy measures of the therapeutic relationship. Shapiro, Foster, and Powell (1968) reported that therapists' facial photographs, rather than body or face-body photographs, provide cues about the level of empathy, warmth, and genuineness. By systematically manipulating various combinations of nonverbal behaviors, Haase and Tepper (1972) showed that forward lean, eye contact, and maintaining close distance were the most important variables in communicating empathy. They concluded that, because the nonverbal components of the message accounted for twice as much variance as the verbal statements, "empathy is communicated in more than one channel . . . "(p. 421). In a later study Tepper and Haase (1978) demonstrated the dominant role of nonverbal behaviors (i.e., trunk lean, eye contact, vocal intonation, and facial expression) over verbal behavior in expression of empathy, genuineness, and respect. D'Augelli (1974) asked trained observers, helpers, and helpees to rate helpers on several therapeutic qualities (i.e., empathy, warmth, relaxed manner, openness, etc.). He found low but significant correlations between helpers' empathy attributes and nonverbal behaviors of smiling, nodding, and fidgeting. Smith-Hanen (1977) observed differences in judged empathy depending on the position of counselors' arms and legs. In a quasi-counseling analogue, Young (1980) reported significant differences in subjects' empathy ratings of interviewers who displayed nonverbal cues indicative of empathy (i.e., forward lean, direct orientation, nodding, backchannel responses, eye contact, paralinguistic cues) as against interviewers whose nonverbal cues indicated preoccupation (i.e., backward lean, folded arms, fiddling with objects, foot movements, decreased gaze, and decreased vocal inflection).

In addition to examining the effects of specific nonverbal acts on judgments of the positive qualities of the therapeutic interaction, research also has been focused on global aspects of nonverbal behavior. Charny (1966) and others (LaFrance, 1979; Trout and Rosenfeld, 1980) found significant correlations between rapport and posture-sharing by therapist and patient. Hill, Siegelman, Gronsky, Sturniolo, and Fretz (1981) found that the more consistently the counselor's affect was communicated in various channels (i.e., vocal, verbal, and nonverbal), the more congruent and facilitative the counselor was rated by clients. Studies of noncongruent or inconsistent verbal and nonverbal messages have shown that the nonverbal component is the principal determinant of the conveyed attitude (Bugental, Kaswan, and Love, 1970; Mehrabian, 1972; Mehrabian and Ferris, 1967). Domangue (1978) reported that confederates' nonverbal behaviors (i.e., eye contact, trunk lean, body orientation, nodding) had a stronger effect on subjects' decoding of an inconsistent message than did verbal behavior. Graves and Robinson (1976) found that when counselors present verbally and nonverbally inconsistent messages they were approached less closely and perceived to be less genuine by subjects.

Frequency of movement has been shown to have a significant impact on the evaluation of counselors. Strong, Taylor, Bratton, and Loper (1971) reported more positive judgments (i.e., warm, outgoing, energetic, etc.) for interviewers who were active rather than still during an interview. Smith (1972) found a correlation between differences in therapists' style (i.e., A = highly verbal, cautious, inhibited; B = affiliative, risk-taking) and frequency and variability of nonverbal behavior. Counselors have been rated more attractive and more facilitative—in addition to more empathic, congruent, and having a higher level of regard—when the counselor provides high versus low levels of eye contact, direct body orientation, and forward lean (Fretz, Corn, Tuemmler, and Bellett, 1979). Rosenfeld (1966a) found that approval-seeking subjects were twice as active nonverbally as approval-avoiding subjects.

Other qualities of the therapeutic relationship which have been investigated include the positive effects of nurses' touching of patients and patients' perception of rapport, correlated with desire to approach and engage in verbal interactions (Aguilera, 1967). Pattison (1973) noted that counselor-to-client touch increased clients' depth of self-exploration. Clients' evaluations of the degree of felt anxiety were found to differ as the result of varying proxemic distance between counselor and client (Dinges and Oetting, 1972). In addition to finding that affiliative counselors, (i.e., those exhibiting forward lean, gesturing, smiling, nodding, high degree of body contact, direct body orientation) were regarded as more attractive and persuasive than unaffiliative counselors (i.e., those exhibiting low eye contact, backward lean, less direct orientation, no smiling, nodding, or gesturing), LaCrosse (1975) noted that subjects most frequently reported influence by eye contact, smiling, and gesturing. Finally, Kelly (1972) found that client subgroups (e.g., acute paranoid schizophrenics, those with character disorders) and college student controls indicated more liking for counselors who sat closer, maintained more eye contact, leaned forward, and faced a client directly.

Research on the role of nonverbal behavior and ratings of interpersonal attributes in non-therapeutic interviews provides information that is important in clinical settings. In a series of experiments Rosenfeld (1966a, b) demonstrated that when subjects were asked to win, rather than avoid, approval from other interactants, more smiling, nodding, gesturing, and verbal recognition responses (i.e., "mhum," "yeah," etc.) were emitted. Similarly, Breed (1972) created conditions of high, medium, and low intimacy based on amount of gaze, trunk lean, and body orientation toward the other. As intimacy increased, subjects rated confederates as more interested and active, and as having a more positive attitude. Subjects also were more likely to lean toward confederates as intimacy increased. In studies of liking, status (Mehrabian, 1968; Mehrabian and Friar, 1969), and persuasiveness (Mehrabian and Williams, 1969), Mehrabian and co-workers found significant effects from several nonverbal behaviors: body orientation, trunk lean, nodding, gesturing, etc. Manipulations of warm or cold interviewer style (Pope and Siegman, 1968; Reece and Whitman, 1962) and increasing interviewer head nodding and listener responses such as "Mm-humm" (Matarazzo, Wiens, Saslow, Allen, and Weitman, 1964; Matarazzo and Wiens, 1967, 1977) have been found to affect significantly the speech patterns of interviewees.

A few studies are available of nonverbal behavior in physician-patient encounters. Larsen and Smith (1981) reported significant correlations between patients' satisfaction and understanding and physicians' nonverbal behaviors of immediacy (i.e., body orientation, forward lean, touching). Weinberger, Greene, and Mamlin (1981) found that several nonverbal cues influenced patient satisfaction: reduced distance between doctor and patient, and increased use of "nonverbal encouragement" (i.e., nods, gestures) by physicians. Hall, Roter, and Rand (1981) found that, when physicians' speech to patients appeared more angry and anxious, patients felt more content or satisfied with a medical visit. Using an observational approach, Byrne and Heath (1980) analyzed videotaped consultations between general practitioners and their patients. Their findings on postural shifts, gaze, trunk lean, distance, and orientation are described in relation to increasing the effectiveness of interviewing the patient and determining the patient's diagnosis. Mansfield (1973) reported the results of verbal and nonverbal behaviors associated with empathic communication between a psychiatric nurse and individual patients.

Finally, DiMatteo and colleagues (DiMatteo, 1979b; DiMatteo, Prince, and Taranta, 1979; DiMatteo, Taranta, Friedman, and Prince, 1980) analyzed the relationships among physicians' abilities to encode (perform) and decode (interpret) nonverbal behavior, patients' ratings of satisfaction, and the caring and sensitivity expressed by physicians. The PONS Test (Rosenthal, Hall, DiMatteo, Rogers, and Archer, 1979) was used to measure decoding abilities, and encoding skill was assessed by having the physicians communicate four different emotions while saying neutral, standard-content sentences. Doctors who demonstrated greater skill in interpreting and sending expressions of affect consistently received higher ratings by patients and "tended to establish more effective interpersonal relationships with their patients" (DiMatteo, 1979b, p. 127). Lee, Hallberg, Kocsis, and Haase (1980) used the PONS Test to select good and poor counselor decoders but were unable to demonstrate differences in decoder ability with respect to various nonverbal and verbal behaviors exhibited during interviews with clients.

The studies cited in this review provide evidence that several types of nonverbal behavior are important in the expression of empathy, warmth, and other positive qualities necessary for an effective therapeutic relationship. As in similar types of empirical research, many of these studies on the nonverbal aspects of empathy have been conducted with individuals enacting client-counselor or therapist-patient roles. A few investigations have involved actual client-patient (Charny, 1966; Fretz, 1966; Pattison, 1973) or physician-patient encounters (Larsen and Smith, 1981; Weinberger, Greene, and Mamlin, 1981). In reviews of nonverbal behavior (Harper, Wiens, and Matarazzo, 1978) and nonverbal behavior with respect to counseling/psychotherapy (Gladstein, 1974), the need for more research in naturalistic situations has been emphasized. The first study described below was designed in part to meet that need. In addition, this study was conducted with non-psychiatric physicians and patients as interactants because only two empirical studies had examined such interactions.

STUDY 1

Nine family-practice residents were videotaped in an interaction with both a new and a return-visit patient (Harrigan, Oxman, and Rosenthal, 1985). The first and middle minutes of the interviews were selected for analysis because the opening sequence is important in establishing doctor-patient communication and the middle minute was used as a standardized time frame for all residents. The experimenters coded the residents' nonverbal behaviors with a coding system developed in previous research (Harrigan, 1980). The physicians' body position and movement were coded as specific types of acts in various nonverbal categories (see Table 3.1). The 36 interactions (four minutes per doctor) were randomly edited onto a single tape and rated by a group of psychiatric nurses on 18 rating scales. The scales were bipolar adjectives ranging along a seven-point scale and were defined by the following endpoints: close-distant, positive-negative, yielding-tenacious, lenient-severe, interested-not interested, calm-excited, friendly-not friendly, accepting-rejecting, good-bad, open-closed, attentive-not attentive, dominant-submissive, hot-cold, active-passive, relaxed-tense, pleasant-unpleasant, strong-weak, and empathic-not empathic.

The physicians were divided into high and low rapport groups on the

Table 3.1 Nonverbal Behavior Categories

Behavioral Category	Description	Measurement Code
Proxemic	distance between doctor & patient	mean distance in feet mean* & percentage** of each category
Body orientation toward patient	forward 20° toward patient upright backward 20° angle away from patient	forward = 1 upright = 2 backward = 3 mean* & percentage** of each category
Trunk angle	directly facing—0° turned away from patient—45° perpendicular to patient—90°	0° = 3 45° = 2 90° = 1
Arm position	symmetrical open arms without hands touching symmetrical closed arms with hands touching asymmetric open with each arm in different posture asymmetric closed with each arm in different posture (NOTE: No folded arm postures were observed.)	percentage of each category**
Hand movement	gestures self-adaptors—hand-to-body contact for scratching, rubbing, grooming object adaptors—non-goal manipulation of objects involving chart (i.e., writing, reading)	percentage of each category**
Leg position	crossed—legs crossed at knee (i.e., knee over knee, ankle over knee)	percentage of each category**
Foot movement	not involved in positioning (i.e., flexing, kicking)	percentage of each category**

Table 3.1 continued

Behavioral Category	Description	Measurement Code
Head movement	nodding shaking cocked to side	percentage of each category**
Facial expression	smiling	percentage**
Gaze	eye-to-eye contact with patient doctor gazes at patient when patient not gazing at doctor doctor gazes at chart doctor gazes at other objects	percentage of each category**

*Mean position was determined by multiplying the percentage of time spent in each of the three measurement subsets for trunk lean or orientation by the assigned values of 1, 2, or 3, adding these three products, and dividing by 100 (e.g., 40 seconds or 67% in forward lean $\times$ 1 = 67; 15 seconds, 25%, in upright position $\times$ 2 = 50; and 5 seconds in backward lean 8% $\times$ 3 = 24; added together and divided by 100 = 1.41.

**Percentage refers to the amount of time (in seconds) during which the behavior occurred divided by the total number of seconds; e.g., mutual gaze occurred 33.6 seconds of the first minute (or 56%) of a return patient interview, $\times$ 100.

basis of their overall mean score on the 18 rapport variables. Mean scores in the high rapport group (N = 5) ranged between 5.08 and 4.42, and mean scores in the low rapport group (N = 4) ranged between 4.04 and 3.23. Discriminant analysis, using a stepwise method, was performed to determine which nonverbal behaviors would best predict membership in high and low rapport groups. (Table 3.2 lists the behaviors for which significant differences were demonstrated.) Four specific behaviors were shown to be the best predictors of rapport group membership: asymmetrical arm positions, crossed leg postures, degree of mutual gaze, and mean body orientation. Low rapport doctors spent more of the total time oriented away from the patient, in cross-legged and asymmetrical arm postures, and had higher rates of mutual gaze. Table 3.2 shows for each of these differences the t (on 7 df), the associated p levels (one-tailed), and the point-biserial correlations defining the degree of relationship between each of the four nonverbal behaviors and rapport group membership.

Open leg positions, with knees supporting the chart, tended to be associated with symmetrical arm positions in which the hands were not touching (open) or were lightly clasped or resting atop one another (closed). In this position high rapport doctors were more likely to use the chart, not as a central focus but with a readiness to refer to it when appropriate. It was perhaps not the open leg positions nor the symmetrical arm postures which were specifically regarded as more positive but rather the contribution of these positions in a general set of behaviors described by the raters as a reasonable degree of chart activity. While the physicians' use of the chart may be intuitively considered a negative behavior, it is likely that the effect of this activity was counter-balanced by behaviors rated more positively (open legs and arms, direct orientation, forward lean). Perhaps the critical variable is the extent to which physicians use the chart in relation to their response to the patient. For example, it would not be surprising to find a negative correlation between empathy ratings and near-constant use of the chart.

Table 3.2 Differences Between High and Low Rapport Groups on Nonverbal Behavior Variables*

Nonverbal Behavior	$t(7)$**	p(one-tailed)	Effect size (r)
Asymmetrical arms	2.50	.025	−.686
Crossed legs	2.22	.035	−.646
Mutual gaze	1.80	.06	−.562
Mean orientation (away)	1.75	.06	−.552

*Derived from discriminant analysis.
**Differences between high and low rapport groups.

"Immediacy" as described by Mehrabian (1972) refers to the degree of closeness between individuals and is regarded as an index of liking, attention, and openness to the encounter. It is displayed by direct orientation, close proximity, forward lean, bodily contact, open arm and leg postures, and mutual gaze. In our study high rapport doctors were more likely to be close, to face and lean toward the patient, and to arrange their arms and legs in open postures. Although significant differences (ps ranging from .025 to .06) between rapport groups were found only for orientation, mutual gaze, crossed legs, and asymmetrical arm postures, trends for closer proximity and forward lean were observed. This postural alignment was interpreted by the raters as more direct and open, and possibly reflects concern and interest in the patient. These results support those of Larsen and Smith (1981), who found significant correlations between patient satisfaction and physicians' overall immediacy measured by forward lean and direct, face-on orientation.

The second dimension described by Mehrabian, "relaxation," consists of asymmetrical arm and leg alignment, sideways or backward lean, hand relaxation, and less direct frontal orientation. These postures were adopted more often by the dominant subjects in Mehrabian's studies. Goffman (1961) also noted that high status individuals sit in more relaxed postures. In our study, doctors who were rated less favorably tended to position their arms asymmetrically, to be turned somewhat away from the patient, and to sit upright or leaning backward. Physicians who appear very relaxed during the interview possibly communicate a dominant attitude and are seen as less seriously concerned with the patient's needs.

Physicians who engaged in a high level of eye contact with the patient were judged as less empathic. While this result appears to contradict Mehrabian's (1972) findings for immediacy, two factors are relevant. Mehrabian's subjects were not involved in a task-oriented interaction as were the doctors in the present study. The task of the medical consultant is to diagnose the patient's difficulty and develop an appropriate treatment. While this goal involves social interaction, that is not the primary purpose of the patient visit. Although high rapport doctors maintained less eye contact, they engaged in more varied gaze patterns. These physicians were more likely to look at the patient when the patient was gazing away while talking. This sequence of behaviors corresponds with studies which have shown that listeners spend far more time looking at speakers than vice versa (Argyle and Ingham, 1972; Kendon, 1967; Nielsen, 1962). As mentioned earlier, high rapport doctors had more contact with the patient's chart, resulting in a greater amount of gaze at the chart. Perhaps there is a curvilinear relationship between use of the chart and positive evaluations. Quite possibly, physicians who use the chart to a reasonable extent are regarded more positively because they are seen as diligent, conscientious, and occupied in the task at hand, whereas physicians who use the chart very little are considered less industrious and less concerned with information provided by the patients. Physicians who use the chart throughout the interview possibly are ignoring the interactional needs of the patient.

In summary, this investigation was exploratory in nature and employed comprehensive categories of nonverbal behavior to study the relationship between body movement and physicians' rated rapport with their patients. Non-significant trends for some categories of nonverbal acts (e.g., nodding, self-adaptors, trunk lean) were also observed. The fact that significant findings resulted, given the small number of subjects, indicates the strong influence of these particular nonverbal behaviors on judgments of rapport.

STUDY 2

The second study was conducted to test hypotheses emerging from the first study (Harrigan and Rosenthal, 1983). In Study 1 physicians were evaluated significantly more positively when sitting directly facing the patient with legs uncrossed and engaging in moderate, though not extended, eye contact. Significant differences were found between symmetrical arm positions (arms parallel at opposite sides of the body, or lower arms and hands resting in the lap) and asymmetrical arm positions (each arm in a different posture or angle: e.g., one arm resting with elbow and hand on table, other arm at side with hand in lap). No significant differences were observed between the second defining feature of arm posture: closed (hands or arms in contact) and open (arms or hands not touching). Although results for trunk angle, head nodding, and open/closed arm posture were in the predicted direction, these behaviors did not reach significance. The present experiment was designed to test experimentally the effects of trunk angle, arm and leg position, and head nodding on perceptions of rapport in a medical context.

The available data on the selected behaviors indicated that, while there were generally positive findings with respect to trunk angle (Haase and Tepper, 1972; Tepper and Haase, 1978; Trout and Rosenfeld, 1980), some contradictory evidence also existed (Karger, 1975; Waldron, 1975). Leaning toward another was not always accompanied with warm motivations nor interpreted as such. For example, Herb and Elliott (1971) noted that high-authoritarian subjects adopted a forward leaning posture when playing subordinate roles, which the researchers hypothesized as an attempt to regain the leadership role. Studies on arm and leg postures were not entirely conclusive either. Some have been conducted with three-dimensional figures as stimulus items (Spiegel and Machotka, 1974) or with role-playing subjects pretending to interact with others while actually alone in a room (Mehrabian, 1969).

One of the aims of our study was to combine behaviors from four major areas of the body: trunk, arms, legs, and head. To our knowledge no study experimentally combining these specific behaviors has been published. We hypothesized specific results for the four dimensions of behavior with respect to judgments of rapport: that (1) positions of the trunk which brought the performer's body closer to the other participant (forward) would be regarded as more open, interested, warm, etc., that (2) scenes in which head nodding occurred would be rated more positively than those in which head nodding was absent, and that (3) open arm and (4) open leg postures would be judged significantly more positively than closed positions. In sum, the intent of the study was: (a) systematically to combine postural behaviors involving trunk, head, and limbs, in order to determine the effects of these behaviors on judgments of rapport, and (b) to assess the differential contributions of these body areas to perceptions of rapport.

One hundred and eighteen undergraduate psychology students were randomly assigned to either of two rating sessions labeled Sample 2a and Sample 2b. Two stimulus tapes were constructed; each tape was composed of 24 video segments randomly assigned to a pair of physicians from a total of four. Each of the 24 segments was thirty seconds in length and depicted each physician in all combinations of four dimensions of nonverbal behavior. These dimensions included three levels of trunk angle (forward, erect, backward), two levels of arm position (open with hands resting in lap; folded across chest), two levels of leg position (uncrossed; crossed ankle-on-knee), and two levels of head attitude (nodding, not nodding). In the forward-leaning position a doctor leaned toward the patient at an angle of approximately 30° from the vertical; the erect position involved sitting with back straight (0°); and the backward position involved leaning away from the patient at approximately 30° from upright. Observers were shown each scene and asked to rate each physician, using 14 seven-point bipolar adjective scales representing aspects of therapeutic rapport. The 14 scales were nearly identical to the 18 used in the previous study: positive-negative, interested-bored, friendly-not friendly, accepting-rejecting, good-bad, open-closed, dominant-submissive, warm-cold, active-passive, relaxed-tense, pleasant-unpleasant, strong-weak, empathic-not empathic, and sensitive-insensitive. Each of the 118 raters also completed a questionnaire assessing his/her health history (consultation frequency, types of illnesses experienced, and types of physician visited).

Preliminary Considerations Concerning Results

Results on the principal components analysis of the 14 rating scales showed such a strong first factor (unrotated) that a single supervariable labeled "rapport" was constructed by adding the ratings obtained on all 14 rating scales. The homogeneity of this supervariable was assessed by Armor's (1974) theta statistic; reliabilities were Sample 2a = .995 and Sample 2b = .992. Correlations among physicians' rapport ratings for each of the 24 scenes (r) ranged from .95 to .66 with a median of .85, showing that the results obtained for the four doctors were substantially similar. Because there were both significant effects for sample and interactions of sample with the nonverbal variables, the results are presented as a separate study for each sample.

Table 3.3 presents the basic results for Studies 2a and 2b. Since leg position made no difference in either study, the results are presented only for the remaining three hypotheses. Greater rapport was judged to occur

Table 3.3   Tests of Basic Hypotheses in Studies 2a and 2b

Study	Hypotheses		
	Trunk[a]	Arms[b]	Head[c]
Study 2a			
$F(1,56)$	311.67	19.73	278.10
p	.0001	.0001	.0001
r[d]	.92	.51	.91
Study 2b			
$F(1,60)$	117.03	11.96	210.92
p	.0001	.001	.0001
r	.81	.41	.88
Combined Studies			
Z	19.78	5.49	21.68
p	.0001	.0001	.0001
r	.87	.46	.90
Difference Between Studies			
p	.02	NS	NS

[a]Greater rapport for forward versus backward lean; the difference between backward lean and sitting straight was very much smaller and the sitting straight posture was not included in subsequent analyses of trunk position effects.
[b]Greater rapport for arms uncrossed, hands in lap.
[c]Greater rapport when head nodding occurred.

$$^d r = \sqrt{\frac{F}{F + df\ error}}$$

when physicians (a) leaned forward rather than backward, (b) had their arms uncrossed rather than crossed, and (c) engaged in head nodding rather than not nodding. For all three of these findings Samples 2a and 2b were in close agreement.

Replicated Interactions

Table 3.4 shows the table of means for the three interactions that were found to be significant in both Samples 2a and 2b. The trunk X legs position interaction showed that the main effect for trunk position was significantly greater when legs were uncrossed rather than crossed. The head X legs position interaction showed that the main effect of head position was significantly greater when legs were crossed rather than uncrossed. The head X arms position interaction showed that the main

Table 3.4 Means for Replicated Interactions

Interaction	Study 2a		Study 2b	
Trunk × Legs				
Trunk	Legs		Legs	
	Crossed	Uncrossed	Crossed	Uncrossed
Forward	4.42	4.88	4.48	4.87
Backward	3.40	3.28	3.87	3.62
Difference (Trunk Effect)	1.02*	1.60*	.61	1.25
Head × Legs				
Head	Legs		Legs	
	Crossed	Uncrossed	Crossed	Uncrossed
Nodding	4.56	4.50	4.64	4.48
Not Nodding	3.17	3.23	3.49	3.61
Difference (Head Effect)	1.39	1.27	1.15	.87
Head × Arms				
Head	Arms		Arms	
	Folded	Open	Folded	Open
Nodding	4.42	4.64	4.40	4.73
Not Nodding	3.15	3.25	3.58	3.53
Difference (Head Effect)	1.27	1.39	.82	1.20

*The interaction is defined as the difference between these two differences. Differences among the four means of each study define the *sum* of the row effect plus column effect plus interaction effect.

effect of head position was significantly greater when arms were open rather than folded.

Table 3.5 shows the tests for significance and effect size estimates (r) for all three interactions for Samples 2a and 2b. The combined p values are very significant for all three interactions and the effect size estimates are all quite substantial.

Questionnaire Results

Responses to the first three questions on the questionnaire revealed remarkable consistencies between the two study groups. The majority of observer-subjects visited physicians infrequently (two or fewer medical visits in the previous year, 54% of those in Sample 2a; 69% in Sample 2b). Most students (80%) sought medical advice for routine purposes or relatively minor illnesses (physical exams, flu, sprains), and usually the same physician was consulted (65%). The nine questions concerning attitudes about health care and satisfaction with physicians appeared to have few if any moderating effects on the results obtained.

Table 3.5 Interactions Replicated in Two Studies

	Interactions		
Study	Trunk* × Legs	Head × Legs	Head × Arms
Study 2a			
$F(1,56)$	54.47	4.00	4.84
p	.0001	.05	.03
r	.70	.26	.28
Study 2b			
$F(1,60)$	65.98	20.58	52.40
p	.0001	.0001	.0001
r	.72	.51	.68
Combined Studies			
Z	10.77	4.54	6.56
p	.0001	.0001	.0001
r	.71	.40	.51
Difference Between Studies			
p	NS	NS	.004

*Based only on the forward versus backward comparison.

Discussion

The results of these two studies show that physicians were regarded as significantly more positive when nodding their heads, leaning toward the patient, and sitting with hands resting in the lap rather than with arms folded across the chest. Leg positions, open or crossed, did not result in differences with respect to attributions of rapport. The results demonstrate that the positive consequences of head nodding and leaning forward are equally influential in observers' judgment of rapport.

Our research findings support earlier studies reporting positive effects for trunk angle (Haase and Tepper, 1972; Tepper and Haase, 1978; Trout and Rosenfeld, 1980). Leaning toward another seems to indicate a desire to be physically closer, and to communicate a more attentive and intimate orientation. Leaning away may appear more relaxed; it reduces close contact sensorily, and perhaps signals less involvement and less interest in being active. Because a forward lean communicates higher accessibility, attention, and readiness for action, this posture may be indicative of a dominant or challenging role, as Herb and Elliott (1971) hypothesized. Sometimes a dominant rather than a submissive attitude may be desired, necessary, or expected. Studies on the physician's role in health care have suggested that the traditional physicians' role as the active dominant figure may be essential in maintaining compliance with medical regimens or specific settings such as acute emergencies (Davis & Eichhorn, 1963; Szasz & Hollender, 1956).

Open arm postures, with hands resting on the lap lightly intertwined, were also rated as preferable. This position allows for greater ease of action for the performer and greater accessibility to the other participant than do folded arms. When the arms and hands are positioned in front of the upper body, a barrier is created, giving the impression of a closed, constrained, or defensive attitude. An unprotected frontal body surface may also communicate an interested, direct, and involved attitude. The same ratings could be hypothesized for open leg positions. However, open leg positions were not judged significantly more positive than crossed legs in this study. This contradicts results of other studies, but an explanation is posited. Ekman and Friesen (1969a) suggested that we are less aware of and less in control of the lower part of the body than of the upper part. Thus, the legs and feet are areas in which information about affect and attitude may be "leaked," while the upper body (face, arms, trunk) are controlled with respect to this information.

Two of the significant interactions—effect for nodding was greater with open arm postures, and effect of leaning forward was greater with open leg positions—can be viewed with respect to the concept of congruence (Condon and Ogston, 1967; Scheflen, 1966). Head nodding, open arm positions, and leaning forward by themselves were regarded as positive. When nodding or forward lean occurred with open arms, a congruent behavior pattern resulted that was also rated positive. A discrepant or incongruous pattern is one which a behavior rated as positive co-occurs with a behavior judged negative. Ratings may have been more negative for behaviors which were considered discrepant (nodding with folded arms; not-nodding with open arms) than those which are regarded as congruent (nodding with open arms; not-nodding with folded arms). Congruent scenes for trunk angle and arm position are leaning forward with open arms or leaning backward with folded arms; discrepant scenes involve forward lean and folded arms or backward lean and open arms. When the meaning carried by two body positions in a scene is similar (either positive or negative), a redundant message is conveyed and the meaning is interpreted without confusion. There is evidence that incongruent messages are interpreted negatively rather than positively, perhaps because of the inconsistency conveyed by dissimilar postures (Bugental, Kaswan, and Love, 1970; Mehrabian and Wiener, 1967). In this study it may be the redundancy of the two actions together and the congruence provided by these actions that result in relatively more positive ratings.

The difference observed between samples in the rating of scenes remains unexplained. The possibility that this rating difference was due to differences in the number of females and males in each sample was eliminated by the non-significant results for gender in each sample and in the samples combined. Correlations between every possible combination of doctors were also strongly significant, ruling out the likelihood that the sample difference could be attributed to dissimilarity among the physicians employed in each sample.

Rapport is an integral feature in the delivery of health care, both in medicine and in psychotherapy. Research has indicated that patients are more likely to be dissatisfied and to change physicians when little rapport exists and good communication is not established (DiMatteo, 1979b; Kasteler, Kane, Olsen, and Thetford, 1976). Nonverbal behavior plays a considerable role in doctor-patient communication in that facial and body movement convey information about affect and attitude, providing the backdrop for and conveyance of the verbal message. Research efforts which focus on determining the effect and meaning of the nonverbal components of the communicated message are essential for developing methods of effective communication. Results from such studies are of practical value in three ways: provision of information to health care practitioners, psychotherapists, and other helpers with respect to the nonverbal components of communicated rapport; development of interpersonal communication skills training programs for health care providers and other helpers; and development of more sophisticated selection procedures for applicants for training in the care-giving professions. Our current research is directed toward other dimensions of body position and movement, particularly actions involving the hands.

CURRENT RESEARCH

Several studies were designed as a result of our research on certain more static (i.e., trunk lean, arm and leg postures) and more mobile (i.e., head nodding) aspects of physicians' nonverbal behavior. These involved examination of a very common movement behavior in social interaction and one said to be indicative of underlying affect: self-touching. Self-touching refers to movements involving hand-to-body/head contact in which the performer scratches, rubs, picks, caresses, cleans, or grooms his/her own body or clothes. This behavior has been variously termed and studied (Ekman and Friesen, 1969a,b, 1974; Freedman, 1972; Freedman and Hoffman, 1967; Mahl, 1968; Rosenfeld, 1966a,b; Sainsbury, 1955). Self-touching behavior has been regarded as a sign of preoccupation, withdrawal, and conflict (Freedman, 1972); anxiety, guilt, hostility and discomfort (Ekman, 1977); deception (Knapp, Hart, and Dennis, (1974; O'Hair, Cody, and McLaughlin, 1981); and, in general, negative affect (Mehrabian, 1972). Recently, Freedman and colleagues have discussed self-touching with respect to interference in focus of attention (Grand, Freedman, Steingart, and Buchwald, 1975), language construction (Bucci and Freedman, 1978; Grand, 1977), and information processing (Barroso, Freedman, Grand, and van Meel, 1978; Freedman and Bucci, 1981).

In the first current study (Harrigan, Weber, and Kues, 1985), spontaneously performed and also posed self-touching movements of doctors and patients were rated by observers on a series of bipolar adjective scales and were compared with nearly identical control segments (i.e., same posture without self-touching) performed by the same doctors and patients. Results showed that scenes containing self-touching were judged more positively than control scenes. Physicians, whether performing self-touching or not, were always evaluated more positively than patients, and males were viewed more positively than females. The finding that self-touching scenes were judged more positively than control scenes was surprising in light of the fact that self-touching behavior has been considered indicative of negative affect states. Post-experimental inquiry suggested that the rating difference between self-touching and control scenes may have been the result of a movement-nonmovement discrepancy rather than a positive view of self-touching behavior. A second study (Harrigan, Kues, and Weber, 1985) was designed to distinguish among self-touching behaviors, hand gestures, and scenes in which neither behavior occurred. Results indicate that, as hypothesized, gestures were rated most positively, followed in order by self-touching and control scenes.

In another current study, not oriented toward a medical setting but more typical of empirical studies in social psychology, self-touching behavior was manipulated (Harrigan, Kues, Steffen, and Rosenthal, 1984). Eighty undergraduate psychology students participated in two separate interactions with each of the two confederates for purposes of "getting to know one another." During one of the conversations the confederate performed frequent self-touching, while in the other conversation the confederate did not engage in hand-to-body contact. Confederates who performed self-touching actions were rated more positively by subjects than confederates who did not. Videotapes of these interactions were analyzed with respect to subjects' and confederates' nonverbal behavior and subjects' responses on the PONS Test (Rosenthal, Hall, DiMatteo, Rogers, and Archer, 1979), Snyder's Self-Monitoring Scale (1974), Christie's Machiavellian Scale (Christie and Geis, 1970), and Eysenck's Introversion-Extraversion and Neuroticism Scales (1962).

Finally, one study is currently underway (Shreve, Harrigan, Kues and Kangas, 1985). Videotaped interviews between patients and physicians have been coded with respect to self-touching, hand gestures, and foot movement. These nonverbal behaviors offer a channel for detecting underlying affect and are considered indicators of "emotional leakage" outside the performer's conscious awareness (Ekman and Friesen, 1974). Two types of medical interviews are being studied. Control interviews are those in which the patient presents a single specific topic involving an organic problem. Experimental interviews are those where the patient presents a problem as a legitimate purpose (first agenda) for the consultation but also reveals a second though more salient reason for the visit (second agenda). This presentation of a second agenda is common in medical practice and is described by Balint (1973) and McWhinney (1972; Stewart, McWhinney, and Buck, 1975). Detection and treatment of second-agenda issues is problematic because these result from conflict and as such cannot be presented directly by the patient. Preliminary results of this study indicate that the amount of patient self-touching increases during the presentation of the second agenda. Higher rates of gesturing also occur during presentation of the second agenda and during presentation of the specific complaint in the control interviews. Low rates of gesturing, however, are associated with the first-agenda presentation of experimental interviews. Foot movements appear to be related to the severity of the complaint regardless of the mode of presentation (control, first or second agenda).

In conclusion, the studies of nonverbal behavior reviewed here lead one to conclude that interaction in the clinical setting involves considerably more than the verbal exchange of information. Ideally the therapeutic environment is characterized by a professional's expression of warmth and empathy such that rapport and trust develop between patient and clinician. Nonverbal channels offer a valuable medium for conveyance of these positive characteristics. More studies on nonverbal behavior as it relates to therapeutic settings are needed, particularly studies which analyze the interaction between verbal and nonverbal behaviors. Communication in the therapeutic setting is multichannel and bidirectional: both patient and clinician are simultaneously encoding and decoding nonverbal messages. Less is known about how patients and clinicians organize and understand one another's behavior, an important area for future research.

ACKNOWLEDGEMENTS

Preparation of this chapter was supported in part by grants from the Public Health Service, Department of Health and Human Service, Division of Medicine, for Dr. Harrigan and the National Science Foundation for Dr. Rosenthal.

REFERENCES

Adams, J. W. (1977). Patient discrimination against women physicians. *Journal of American Medical Women's Association, 32,* 255–61.

Adler, L. M. and Enelow, A. J. (1966). An instrument to measure skill in diagnostic interviewing: A teaching and evaluation tool. *Journal of Medical Education, 41,* 281–88.

Aguilera, D. C. (1967). Relationship between physical contact and verbal interaction between nurses and patients. *Journal of Psychiatric Nursing, 5,* 5–21.

Archer, D., and Akert, R. M. (1977). Words and everything else: Verbal and nonverbal cues in social interpretation. *Journal of Personality and Social Psychology, 35,* 443–49.

Argyle, M., and Ingham, R. (1972). Gaze, mutual gaze and proximity. *Semiotica, 6,* 32–49.

Armor, D. J. (1974). Theta reliability and factor scaling. In H. L. Costner (Ed.), *Sociological methodology, 1973–1974.* San Francisco: Jossey Bass.

Aronfreed, J. (1970). The socialization of altruistic and sympathetic behavior: Some theoretical and experimental analyses. In J. Macaulay and L. Berkowitz (Eds.), *Altruism and helping behavior.* New York: Academic Press.

Bain, D. J. G. (1976). Doctor-patient communication in general practice consultations. *Medical Education, 10,* 125–31.

Bales, R. F. (1950). *Interaction process analysis.* Cambridge, MA: Addison-Wesley.

Balint, M. (1964). *The doctor, his patient and the illness,* 2nd ed. New York: International Universities Press.

Balint, M. (1973). Research in psychotherapy. In E. Balint and J. S. Norrell (Eds.), *Six minutes for the patient: Interactions in general practice consultation.* London: Tavistock Publications.

Balint, M., and Balint, E. (1962). *Psychotherapeutic techniques in medicine.* London: Tavistock Publications.

Barbee, R. A., and Feldman, S. E. (1970). A three year longitudinal study of the medical interview and its relationship to student performance in clinical medicine. *Journal of Medical Education, 45,* 770–76.

Barrett-Lennard, G. T. (1962). Dimensions of therapist response as causal factors in therapeutic change. *Psychological Monographs, 76* (43 Serial No. 562).

Barroso, F., Freedman, N., Grand, S., and van Meel, J. (1978). The evocation of two types of hand movements in information processing. *Journal of Experimental Psychology: Human Perception and Performance, 4,* 321–29.

Becker, M. H., and Maiman, L. A. (1975). Sociobehavioral determinants of compliance with health and medical care recommendations. *Medical Care, 13,* 10–24.

Ben-Sira, Z. (1980). Affective and instrumental components in the physician-patient relationship: An additional dimension of interaction theory. *Journal of Health and Social Behavior, 21,* 170–80.

Berger, S. M., and Hadley, S. W. (1975). Some effects of a model's performance on an observer's electromyographic activity. *American Journal of Psychology, 88,* 263–76.

Bergin, A. E., and Solomon, S. (1970). Personality and performance correlates of empathic understanding in psychotherapy. In J. T. Hart and T. M. Tomlinson (Eds.), *New directions in client-centered therapy.* Boston: Houghton-Mifflin.

Bernarde, M. A., and Mayerson, E. W. (1978). Patient-physician negotiation. *Journal of American Medical Association, 239,* 1413–15.

Berne, E. (1966). *Games people play.* New York: Grove.

Bertakis, K. D. (1977). The communication of information from physician to patient: A method for increasing patient retention and satisfaction. *Journal of Family Practice, 5,* 217–22.

Blackwell, B. (1973). Patient compliance. *New England Journal of Medicine, 289,* 249–52.

Borke, H. (1971). Interpersonal perception of young children: Egocentrism or empathy? *Developmental Psychology, 5,* 263–69.

Breed, G. R. (1972). The effect of intimacy: Reciprocity or retreat? *British Journal of Social and Clinical Psychology, 11,* 135–42.

Bucci, W., and Freedman, N. (1978). Language and hand: The dimension of referential competence. *Journal of Personality, 46,* 594–622.

Buchheimer, A. (1963). The development of ideas about empathy. *Journal of Counseling Psychology, 10,* 61–70.

Buck, R. (1976). A test of nonverbal receiving ability: Preliminary studies. *Human Communication Research, 2,* 162–71.

Buckley, N., Siegel, L. S., and Ness, S. (1979). Egocentrism, empathy, and altruistic behavior in young children. *Developmental Psychology, 15,* 329–30.

Bugental, D. B., Kaswan, J. W., and Love, L. R. (1970). Perception of contradictory meanings conveyed by verbal and nonverbal channels. *Journal of Personality and Social Psychology, 16,* 647–55.

Byrne, P. S., and Heath, C. C. (1980). Practitioners' use of non-verbal behaviour in real consultations. *Journal of the Royal College of General Practitioners, 30,* 327–31.

Byrne, P. S., and Long, B. E. L. (1976). *Doctors talking to patients.* London: Department of Health and Social Security.

Campbell, R. J., Kagan, N., and Krathwohl, D. R. (1971). The development and validation of a scale to measure Affective Sensitivity (Empathy). *Journal of Counseling Psychology, 18,* 407–12.

Caracena, P. F., and Vicory, J. R. (1969). Correlates of phenomenological and judged empathy. *Journal of Counseling Psychology, 16,* 510–15.

Carkhuff, R. R. (1969). *Helping and human relations* (Vols. 1 & 2). New York, Holt, Rinehart & Winston.

Carroll, J. G., and Monroe, J. (1979). Teaching medical interviewing: A critique of educational research and practice. *Journal of Medical Education, 54,* 498–500.

Cassell, E. J., and Skopek, L. (1977). Language as a tool in medicine: Methodology and theoretical framework. *Journal of Medical Education, 52,* 197–203.

Cassell, R. N. (1963). *Test of social insight* (Rev. Ed.) New Rochelle, NY: Bruce.

Chandler, M. J. (1973). Egocentrism and antisocial behavior: The assessment and training of social perspective-taking skills. *Developmental Psychology, 9,* 326–32.

Chandler, M. J., and Greenspan, S. (1972). Ersatz egocentrism: A reply to H. Borke. *Developmental Psychology, 7,* 104–6.

Charney, E., Bynum, R., Eldredge, D., Frank, D., MacWhinney, J. B., McNabb, N., Scheiner, A., Sumpter, E. A., and Iker, H. (1967). How well do patients take oral penicillin? A collaborative study in private practice. *Pediatrics, 40,* 188–95.

Charny, E. J. (1966). Psychosomatic manifestations of rapport in psychotherapy. *Psychosomatic Medicine, 28,* 305–15.

Christie, R., and Geis, F. L. (1970). *Studies in Machiavellianism.* New York: Academic Press.

Clyne, M. B. (1973). The diagnosis. In E. Balint and J. S. Norell (Eds.), *Six minutes for the patient: Interactions in general practice consultation.* London: Tavistock Publications.

Comstock, L. M., Hooper, E. M., Goodwin, J. M., and Goodwin, J. S. (1982). Physician behaviors that correlate with patient satisfaction. *Journal of Medical Education, 57,* 105–12.

Condon, W. S., and Ogston, W. D. (1967). A segmentation of behavior. *Journal of Psychiatric Research, 5,* 221–35.

Congalton, A. A. (1969). Public evaluation of medical care. *Medical Journal of Australia, 24,* 1165–71.

Coulthard, M., and Ashby, M. (1976). A linguistic description of doctor-patient interviews. In M. Wadsworth and D. Robinson (Eds.), *Studies in everyday medical life.* London: Martin Robertson.

Danish, S. J., and Kagan, N. (1971). Measurement of Affective Sensitivity: Toward a valid measure of interpersonal perception. *Journal of Counseling Psychology, 18,* 51–54.

Davis, M. S., (1968). Variations in patients' compliance with doctors' advice: An empirical analysis of patterns of communication. *American Journal of Public Health, 58,* 274–88.

Davis, M. S. (1971). Variation in patients' compliance with doctors' orders: Medical practice and doctor-patient interaction. *Psychiatry in Medicine, 2,* 31–54.

Davis, M. S. and Eichhorn, R. L. (1963). Compliance with medical regimens: A panel study. *Journal of Health and Human Behavior, 4,* 240–49.

D'Augelli, A. R. (1974). Nonverbal behavior of helpers in initial helping interactions. *Journal of Counseling Psychology, 21,* 360–63.

DiMatteo, M. R., (1979a). A social-psychological analysis of physician-patient rapport: Toward a science of the art of medicine. *Journal of Social Issues, 35,* 12–33.

DiMatteo, M. R. (1979b). Nonverbal skill and the physician-patient relationship. In R. Rosenthal (Ed.), *Skill in Nonverbal Communication Individual Differences,* Cambridge, MA: Oelgeschlager, Gunn and Hain.

DiMatteo, M. R. and DiNicola, D. D. (1982). *Achieving patient compliance: The psychology of the medical practitioner's role.* New York: Pergamon.

DiMatteo, M. R., Prince, L. M., and Taranta, A. (1979). Patients' perceptions of physicians' behavior: Determinants of patient commitment to the therapeutic relationship. *Journal of Community Health, 4,* 280–90.

DiMatteo, M. R., Taranta, A., Friedman, H. S., and Prince, L. M. (1980). Predicting patient satisfaction from physicians' nonverbal communication skills. *Medical Care, 18,* 376–87.

Dinges, N. G., and Oetting, E. R. (1972). Interaction distance anxiety in the counseling dyad. *Journal of Counseling Psychology, 19,* 146–49.

Domangue, B. B. (1978). Decoding effects of cognitive complexity, tolerance of ambiguity, and verbal-nonverbal inconsistency. *Journal of Personality, 46,* 519–35.

Dymond, R. F. (1949). A scale for the measurement of empathic ability. *Journal of Consulting Psychology, 13,* 127–33.

Dymond, R. F. (1950). Personality and empathy. *Journal of Consulting Psychology, 14,* 343–50.

Ekman, P. (1977). Biological and cultural contributions to body and facial movement. In J. Blacking (Ed.), *The anthropology of the body.* London: Academic Press.

Ekman, P., and Friesen, W. V. (1969a). Nonverbal leakage and clues to deception. *Psychiatry, 32,* 88–105.

Ekman, P., and Friesen, W. V. (1969b). The repertoire of nonverbal behavior: Categories, origins, usage, and coding. *Semiotica, 1,* 49–98.

Ekman, P., and Friesen, W. V. (1974). Nonverbal behavior and psychopathology. In R. J. Friedman and M. M. Katz (Eds.), *The psychology of depression: Contemporary theory and research.* Washington, D. C.: Winston and Sons.

Ellis, P. L. (1982). Empathy: A factor in antisocial behavior. *Journal of Abnormal Child Psychology, 10,* 123–34.

Engel, G. L. (1973). Enduring attributes of medicine relevant for the education of the physician. *Annals of Internal Medicine, 78,* 587–93.

Engleman, E. G. (1974). Attitudes toward women physicians: A study of 500 clinic patients. *Western Journal of Medicine, 120,* 95–100.

Engler, C. M., Saltzman, G. A., Walker, M. L., and Wolf, F. M. (1981). Medical student acquisition and retention of communication and interviewing skills. *Journal of Medical Education, 56,* 572–79.

Eysenck, H. J. (1962). *The Maudsley personality inventory.* San Diego: Educational and Industrial Testing Service.

Feshbach, N. D., and Roe, K. (1968). Empathy in six- and seven-year-olds. *Child Development, 39,* 133–45.

Fiedler, F. E. (1950). The concept of an ideal therapeutic relationship. *Journal of Consulting Psychology, 14,* 239–45.

Fisher, A. W. (1971). Patients' evaluation of outpatient medical care. *Journal of Medical Education, 46,* 238–44.

Flavell, J. H., Botkin, P. T., Fry, C. L., Wright, J. W., and Jarvis, P. E. (1968). *The development of role-taking and communication skills in children.* New York: John Wiley and Sons.

Freedman, N. (1972). The analysis of movement behavior during the clinical interview.

In A. Seigman and B. Pope (Eds.), *Studies in dyadic communication.* New York: Pergamon.

Freedman, N., and Bucci, W. (1981). On kinesic filtering in associative monologue. *Semiotica, 34,* 225–49.

Freedman, N., and Hoffman, S. P. (1967). Kinetic behavior in altered clinical states: Approach to objective analysis of motor behavior during clinical interviews. *Perceptual and Motor Skills, 24,* 527–39.

Friedman, H. S. (1979). Nonverbal communication between patients and medical practitioners. *Journal of Social Issues, 35,* 82–99.

Fretz, B. R. (1966). Postural movements in a counseling dyad. *Journal of Counseling Psychology, 13,* 335–43.

Fretz, B. R., Corn, R., Tuemmler, J. M., and Bellet, W. (1979). Counselor nonverbal behaviors and client evaluations. *Journal of Counseling Psychology, 26,* 304–11.

Gillum, R. F., and Barsky, A. J. (1974). Diagnosis and management of patient noncompliance. *Journal of American Medical Association, 228,* 1563–67.

Ginott, H. G. (1965). *Between parent and child.* New York: Macmillan.

Gladstein, G. A. (1974). Nonverbal communication and counseling/psychotherapy: A review. *Counseling Psychologist, 4,* 34–52.

Glassman, M., and Glassman, N. (1981). A marketing analysis of physician selection and patient satisfaction. *Journal of Health Care Marketing, 1,* 25–31.

Goffman, E. (1961). *Asylums.* Garden City, New York: Anchor.

Goodman, G. (1972). *Companionship therapy.* San Francisco: Jossey-Bass.

Gorlin, R., and Zucker, H. D. (1983). Physicians' reactions to patients. *New England Journal of Medicine, 308,* 1059–63.

Gough, H. G. (1955). *The assessment of social acuity.* (Project no. 7730; Contract no. AF 18 600-8). Berkeley: University of California Institute of Personality Assessment and Research.

Gove, F. L., and Keating, D. P. (1979). Empathic role-taking precursors. *Developmental Psychology, 15,* 594–600.

Grand, S. (1977). On hand movements during speech: Studies of the role of self-stimulation in communication under conditions of psychopathology, sensory deficit, and bilingualism. In N. Freedman and S. Grand (Eds.), *Communicative structures and psychic structures.* New York: Plenum.

Grand, S., Freedman, N., Steingart, I., and Buchwald, C. (1975). The relation of adaptive styles to kinetic and linguistic aspects of interview behavior. *Journal of Nervous and Mental Disease, 161,* 293–306.

Graves, J. R., and Robinson, J. D. (1976). Proxemic behavior as a function of inconsistent verbal and nonverbal messages. *Journal of Counseling Psychology, 23,* 333–38.

Gurman, A. S. (1973). Instability of therapeutic conditions in psychotherapy. *Journal of Counseling Psychology, 20,* 16–24.

Haase, R. F., and Tepper, D. T. (1972). Nonverbal components of empathic communication. *Journal of Counseling Psychology, 19,* 417–24.

Hall, J. A., Roter, D. L. and Rand, C. S. (1981). Communication of affect between patient and physician. *Journal of Health and Social Behavior, 22,* 18–30.

Hall, R. (1979). Helping patients take their medicine. *Australian Family Physician, 8,* 1081–85.

Harper, R. G., Wiens, A. N., and Matarazzo, J. D. (1978). *Nonverbal communication: The state of the art.* New York: John Wiley and Sons.

Harrigan, J. A. (1980). The relationship between the auditors' nonverbal behavior and turn-taking in social conversation. *Dissertation Abstracts International, 40,* 5867B (University Microfilm) No. 8012231.

Harrigan, J. A., Kues, J. R., Steffen, J. J., and Rosenthal, R. (1984). Effects of self-touching on observers' attributions of others. Manuscript submitted for publication.

Harrigan, J. A., Kues, J. R., and Weber, J. G. (1985). Attributions of self-touching and gestures. Manuscript submitted for publication.

Harrigan, J. A., Oxman, T. E., and Rosenthal, R. (1985). Rapport expressed through nonverbal behavior. *Journal of Nonverbal Behavior*, in press.

Harrigan, J. A., and Rosenthal, R. (1983). Physicians' head and body positions as determinants of perceived rapport. *Journal of Applied Social Psychology, 13*, 496–509.

Harrigan, J. A., Weber, J. G., and Kues, J. R. (1985). Observers' judgments of self-touching by physicians and patients. *Journal of Clinical and Social Psychology*, in press.

Haug, M. R., and Lavin, B. (1979). Public challenge of physician authority. *Medical Care, 17*, 844–58.

Hayes-Bautista, D. E. (1976). Modifying the treatment: Patient compliance, patient control, and medical care. *Social Science and Medicine, 10*, 233–38.

Haynes, R. B., Taylor, D. W., and Sackett, D. L. (Eds.). (1979). *Compliance in health care*. Baltimore: Johns Hopkins University Press.

Herb, T. R., and Elliott, R. F., Jr. (1971). Authoritarianism in the conversation of gestures. *Kansas Journal of Sociology, 7*(3), 93–101.

Hess, J. W. (1969). A comparison of methods for evaluating medical student skill in relating to patients. *Journal of Medical Education, 44*, 934–38.

Hill, C. E., Siegelman, L., Gronsky, B. R., Sturniolo, F., and Fretz, B. R. (1981). Nonverbal communication and counseling outcome. *Journal of Counseling Psychology, 28*,203–12.

Hoffman, M. L. (1975a). Developmental synthesis of affect and cognition and its implications for altruistic motivation. *Developmental Psychology, 11*, 607–22.

Hoffman, M. L. (1975b). The development of altruistic motivation. In D. J. DePalma and J. M. Foley (Eds.), *Moral development: Current theory and research*. Hillsdale, N. J.: Lawrence Erlbaum.

Hoffman, M. L. (1977). Empathy, its development and prosocial implications. In B. Keasy (Ed.), *Nebraska symposium on motivation* (Vol. 25). Lincoln: University of Nebraska Press.

Hoffman, M. L. (1978). Toward a theory of empathic arousal and development. In M. Lewis and L. A. Rosenblum (Eds.), *The Development of affect*. New York: Plenum Press.

Hogan, R. (1969). Development of an empathy scale. *Journal of Consulting and Clinical Psychology, 33*, 307–16.

Hornsby, J. L., and Payne, F. E. (1979). A model of communication skills development for family practice residents. *Journal of Family Practice, 8*, 71–76.

Hulka, B. S., Kupper, L. L., Cassel, J. C., and Mayo, F. (1975). Doctor-patient communication and outcomes among diabetic patients. *Journal of Community Health, 1*, 15–27.

Izard, C. E. (1971). *The face of emotion*. New York: Appleton-Century-Crofts.

Jensen, P. S. (1981). The doctor-patient relationship: Headed for impasse or improvement? *Annals of Internal Medicine, 95*, 769–71.

Johnson, D. W., and Matross, R. P. (1975). Attitude modification methods. In F. H. Kanfer and A. P. Goldstein (Eds.), *Helping people change: A textbook of methods*. New York: Pergamon.

Jourard, S. M. (1971). *The transparent self*, 2nd ed. New York: Van Nostrand Reinhold.

Joyce, C. R. B., Caple, G., Mason, M., Reynolds, E., and Mathews, J. A. (1969). Quantitative study of doctor-patient communication. *Quarterly Journal of Medicine, 38*, 183–94.

Kagan, N., and Krathwohl, D. R. (1967). *Studies in human interaction: Interpersonal process recall simulated by videotape.* (Project No. 5-0800; Grant No. OE 7-32-0410-270.) East Lansing, MI: Michigan State University, Office of Education, U. S. Department of Health, Education, and Welfare.

Kagan, N. I. (1974). Teaching interpersonal relations for the practice of medicine. *Lakartidningen, 71,* 4758–60.

Kagan, N. (1975). Influencing human interaction–Eleven years with IPR. *Canadian Counsellor, 9,* 74–97.

Kahn, G. S., Cohen, B., and Jason, H. (1979). The teaching of interpersonal skills in U. S. medical schools. *Journal of Medical Education, 54,* 29–35.

Kalish, B. J. (1973). What is empathy? *American Journal of Nursing, 73,* 1548–52.

Karger, K. (1975). The relationship of nonverbal counselor behavior to client and rater perceptions of empathy. *Dissertation Abstracts International, 35,* 4161A. (University Microfilms No. 74-19, 921.)

Kasteler, J., Kane, R. L., Olsen, D. M., and Thetford, C. (1976). Issues underlying prevalence of "doctor-shopping" behavior. *Journal of Health and Social Behavior, 17,* 328–39.

Katz, R. L. (1963). *Empathy: Its nature and uses.* London: The Free Press of Glencoe.

Kauss, D. R., Robbins, A. S., Abrass, I., Bakaitis, R. F., and Anderson, L. A. (1980). The long-term effectiveness of interpersonal skills training in medical schools. *Journal of Medical Education, 55,* 595–601.

Kelly, F. D. (1972). Communicational significance of therapist proxemic cures. *Journal of Consulting and Clinical Psychology, 39,* 345.

Kendon, A. (1967). Some functions of gaze direction in social interaction. *Acta Psychologica, 26,* 22–63.

Kerr, W. A. (1947). *The empathy test.* Chicago: Psychometric Affiliates.

Kiesler, D. J. (1973). *The process of psychotherapy.* Chicago: Aldine.

Knapp, M. L., Hart, R. P., and Dennis, H. S. (1974). An exploration of deception as a communication construct. *Human Communication Research, 1,* 15–29.

Korsch, B. M., Gozzi, E. K., and Francis, V. (1968). Gaps in doctor-patient interaction and patient satisfaction. *Pediatrics, 42,* 855–71.

Korsch, B. M., and Negrete, V. F. (1974). Doctor-patient communication. *Scientific American, 7,* 66–74.

Krebs, D. (1975). Empathy and altruism. *Journal of Personality and Social Psychology, 32,* 1134–46.

Kupfer, D. J., Drew, F. L., Curtis, E. K., and Rubinstein, D. N. (1978). Personality style and empathy in medical students. *Journal of Medical Education, 53,* 507–9.

Kurtz, R. R., and Grummon, D. L. (1972). Different approaches to the measurement of therapist empathy and their relationship to therapy outcomes. *Journal of Consulting and Clinical Psychology, 39,* 106–15.

LaCrosse, M. B. (1975). Nonverbal behavior and perceived counselor attractiveness and persuasiveness. *Journal of Counseling Psychology, 22,* 563–66.

LaFrance, M. (1979). Nonverbal synchrony and rapport: Analysis by the cross-lag panel technique. *Social Psychology Quarterly, 42,* 66–70.

Laird, J. D. (1974). Self attribution of emotion: The effects of expressive behavior on the quality of emotional experience. *Journal of Personality and Social Psychology, 29,* 475–86.

Larsen, D. E., and Rootman, I. (1976). Physician role performance and patient satisfaction. *Social Science and Medicine, 10,* 29–32.

Larsen, K. M., and Smith, C. K. (1981). Assessment of nonverbal communication in the patient-physician interview. *Journal of Family Practice, 12,* 481–88.

Lee, D. Y., Hallberg, E. T., Kocsis, M., and Haase, R. F. (1980). Decoding skills in nonverbal communication and perceived interviewer effectiveness. *Journal of Counseling Psychology, 27,* 89–92.

Ley, P. (1977). Psychological studies of doctor-patient communication. In S. Rachman (Ed.), *Contributions to medical psychology (Vol. 1).* New York: Pergamon.

Lorr, M. (1965). Client perceptions of therapists: A study of the therapeutic relationship. *Journal of Consulting Psychology, 29,* 146–49.

Mahl, G. F. (1968). Gestures and body movements in interviews. In J. M. Shlien, H. F. Hunt, J. D. Matarazzo, and C. Savage (Eds.), *Research in psychotherapy.* Washington, D. C.: American Psychological Association.

Mansfield, E. (1973). Concept and identified psychiatric nursing behavior. *Nursing Research, 22,* 525–30.

Marsden, G. (1965). Content-analysis studies of therapeutic interviews: 1954 to 1964. *Psychological Bulletin, 63,* 298–321.

Marston, M. (1970). Compliance with medical regimens: A review of the literature. *Nursing Research, 19,* 312–23.

Matarazzo, J. D., Wiens, A. N., Saslow, G., Allen, B. V., and Weitman, M. (1964). Interviewer Mm-hmm and interviewee speech durations. *Psychotherapy: Theory, Research, and Practice, 1,* 109–14.

Matarazzo, J. D., and Wiens, A. N. (1967). Interviewer influence on durations of interviewee silence. *Journal of Experimental Research in Personality, 2,* 56–69.

Matarazzo, J. D., and Wiens, A. N. (1977). Speech behavior as an objective correlate of empathy and outcome in interview and psychotherapy research. *Behavior Modification, 1,* 453–80.

Matarazzo, R. G. (1978). Research on the teaching and learning of psychotherapeutic skills. In A. E. Bergin and S. L. Garfield (Eds.), *Handbook of psychotherapy and behavior change: An empirical analysis.* New York: John Wiley and Sons.

McWhinney, I. R. (1972). An approach to the integration of behavioral science and clinical medicine. *New England Journal of Medicine, 287,* 384–87.

Mehrabian, A. (1968). Relationship of attitude to seated posture, orientation, and distance. *Journal of Personality and Social Psychology, 10,* 26–30.

Mehrabian, A. (1969). Significance of posture and position in the communication of attitude and status relationships. *Psychological Bulletin, 71,* 359–72.

Mehrabian, A. (1972). *Nonverbal communication.* Chicago: Aldine-Atherton.

Mehrabian, A., and Epstein, N. (1972). A measure of emotional empathy. *Journal of Personality, 40,* 525–43.

Mehrabian, A. and Ferris, S. R. (1967). Inference of attitudes from nonverbal communication in two channels. *Journal of Consulting Psychology, 31,* 248–52.

Mehrabian, A., and Friar, J. T. (1969). Encoding of attitude by a seated communicator via posture and position cues. *Journal of Consulting and Clinical Psychology, 33,* 330–36.

Mehrabian, A., and Wiener, M. (1967). Decoding of inconsistent communications. *Journal of Personality and Social Psychology, 6,* 108–14.

Mehrabian, A., and Williams, M. (1969). Nonverbal concomitants of perceived and intended persuasiveness. *Journal of Personality and Social Psychology, 13,* 37–58.

Meldman, M. J. (1967). Verbal behavior analysis of self-hyperattentionism. *Disorders of the Nervous System, 28,* 469–73.

Moore, B. S., Underwood, B., and Rosenhan, D. L. (1973). Affect and altruism. *Developmental Psychology, 8,* 99–104.

Nielsen, G. (1962). *Studies in self confrontation.* Copenhagen: Monksgaard.

O'Hair, H. D., Cody, M. J., and McLaughlin, M. L. (1981). Prepared lies, spontaneous lies, machiavellianism, and nonverbal communication. *Human Communication Research, 7,* 325–39.

O'Sullivan, M., Guilford, J. P., and DeMille, R. (1965). *The measurement of social intelligence*. (Reports from the psychological laboratory No. 34.) Los Angeles: University of Southern California.

Pattison, J. E. (1973). Effects of touch on self-exploration and the therapeutic relationship. *Journal of Consulting and Clinical Psychology, 40,* 170–75.

Pendleton, D., and Hasler, J. (Eds.). (1983). *Doctor-patient communication*. London: Academic Press.

Piaget, J., and Inhelder, B. (1967). *The child's conception of space*. New York: W. W. Norton.

Platt, F. W., and McMath, J. C. (1979). Clinical hypocompetence: The interview. *Annals of Internal Medicine, 91,* 898–902.

Pope, B., and Siegman, A. W. (1968). Interviewer warmth in relation to interviewee verbal behavior. *Journal of Consulting and Clinical Psychology, 32,* 588–95.

Quirk, M., and Babineau, R. A. (1982). Teaching interviewing skills to students in clinical years: A comparative analysis of three strategies. *Journal of Medical Education, 57,* 939–41.

Rappaport, J., and Chinsky, J. M. (1972). Accurate empathy: Confusion of a construct. *Psychological Bulletin, 77,* 400–4.

Reece, M. M., and Whitman, R. N. (1962). Expressive movements, warmth, and verbal reinforcement. *Journal of Abnormal and Social Psychology, 64,* 234–36.

Robbins, A. S., Kauss, D. R., Heinrich, R., Abrass, L., Dreyer, J., and Clyman, B. (1979). Interpersonal skills training: Evaluation in an internal medicine residency. *Journal of Medical Education, 54,* 885–94.

Rogers, C. R. (1951). *Client-centered therapy*. Boston: Houghton Mifflin.

Rogers, C. R. (1957). The necessary and sufficient conditions of therapeutic personality change. *Journal of Consulting Psychology, 21,* 95–103.

Rosenfeld, H. M. (1966a). Approval-seeking and approval-inducing functions of verbal and nonverbal responses in the dyad. *Journal of Personality and Social Psychology, 4,* 597–605.

Rosenfeld, H. M. (1966b). Instrumental affiliative functions of facial and gestural expressions. *Journal of Personality and Social Psychology, 4,* 65–72.

Rosenthal, R., Hall, J. A., DiMatteo, M. R., Rogers, P. L., and Archer, D. (1979). *Sensitivity to nonverbal communication: The PONS test*. Baltimore: The Johns Hopkins University Press.

Sagi, A., and Hoffman, M. L. (1976). Empathic distress in the newborn. *Developmental Psychology, 12,* 175–76.

Sainsbury, P. (1955). Gestural movement during the psychiatric interview. *Psychosomatic Medicine, 17,* 458–69.

Sanson-Fisher, B. (1978). A multidimensional scaling analysis of empathy. *Journal of Clinical Psychology, 34,* 971–77.

Sanson-Fisher, R. W., and Poole, A. D. (1978). Training medical students to empathize: An experimental study. *Medical Journal of Australia, 1,* 473–76.

Scheflen, A. E. (1964). The significance of posture in communication systems. *Psychiatry, 27,* 316–31.

Scheflen, A. E. (1965). Quasi-courtship behavior in psychotherapy. *Psychiatry, 28,* 245–57.

Scheflen, A. E. (1966). Natural history method in psychotherapy: Communication research. In L. A. Gottschalk and A. H. Auerbach (Eds.), *Methods and research in psychotherapy*. New York: Appleton-Century-Crofts.

Schmidt, D. D. (1977). Patient compliance: The effect of the doctor as a therapeutic agent. *Journal of Family Practice, 4,* 853–56.

Schneider, H. W. (Ed.). (1948). *Adam Smith's moral and political philosophy*. New York: Hafner.

Schüffel, W. (1977). The doctor-patient relationship in the practice of medicine. In Z. L. Lipowsky, D. R. Lipsitt, and P. C. Whybrow (Eds.), *Psychosomatic medicine: Current trends and clinical applications.* New York: Oxford University Press.

Scott, N. C., Donnelly, M. B., Gallagher, R., and Hess, J. W. (1973). Interaction analysis as a method for assessing skill in relating to patients: Studies on validity. *British Journal of Medical Education, 7,* 174–78.

Shapiro, J. G., Foster, C. P., and Powell, T. (1968). Facial and body cues of genuineness, empathy and warmth. *Journal of Clinical Psychology, 24,* 233–36.

Shlien, J. M. (1961). A client-centered approach to schizophrenia: First approximation. In A. Burton (Ed.), *Psychotherapy of the psychoses.* New York: Basic Books.

Shreve, E. G., Harrigan, J. A., Kues, J. R., and Kangas, D. (1985). Self-touching as an expression of patient's affective concerns. Manuscript in preparation.

Simner, M. L. (1971). Newborn's response to the cry of another infant. *Developmental Psychology, 5,* 136–50.

Smith, E. W. L. (1972). Postural and gestural communication of A and B "therapist types" during dyadic interviews. *Journal of Consulting and Clinical Psychology, 39,* 29–36.

Smith, H. C. (1973). *Sensitivity training: The scientific understanding of individuals.* New York: McGraw-Hill.

Smith-Hanen, S. S. (1977). Effects of nonverbal behaviors on judged levels of counselor warmth and empathy. *Journal of Counseling Psychology, 24,* 87–91.

Snyder, M. (1974). Self-monitoring of expressive behavior. *Journal of Personality and Social Psychology, 30,* 526–37.

Spiegel, J., and Machotka, P. (1974). *Messages of the body.* New York: The Free Press.

Stetler, C. B. (1977). Relationship of perceived empathy to nurses' communication. *Nursing Research, 26,* 432–38.

Stewart, M. A., McWhinney, I. R., and Buck, C. W. (1975). How illness presents: A study of patient behavior. *Journal of Family Practice, 2,* 411–14.

Stiles, W. B. (1979). Verbal response modes and psychotherapeutic technique. *Psychiatry, 42,* 49–62.

Stiles, W. B. (1981). Classification of intersubjective illocutionary acts. *Language in Society, 10,* 227–49.

Stiles, W. B., Putnam, S. M., James, S. A., and Wolf, M. H. (1979). Dimensions of patient and physician roles in medical screening interviews. *Social Science and Medicine, 13,* 335–41.

Stimson, G. V. (1974). Obeying doctor's orders: A view from the other side. *Social Science and Medicine, 8,* 97–104.

Stone, G. C. (1979). Patient compliance and the role of the expert. *Journal of Social Issues, 35,* 34–59.

Stotland, E. (1969). Exploratory investigations of empathy. In L. Berkowitz (Ed.), *Advances in experimental social psychology* (Vol. 4). New York: Academic Press.

Stotland, E., Mathews, K. E., Sherman, S. E., Hansson, R. O., and Richardson, B. Z. (1978). *Empathy, fantasy and helping.* Beverly Hills, CA: Sage.

Stotland, E., Sherman, S. E., and Shaver, K. G. (1971). *Empathy and birth order: Some experimental explorations.* Lincoln: University of Nebraska Press.

Streit-Forest, U. (1982). Differences in empathy: A preliminary analysis. *Journal of Medical Education, 57,* 65–67.

Strong, S. R., Taylor, R. G., Bratton, J. C., and Loper, R. G. (1971). Nonverbal behavior and perceived counselor characteristics. *Journal of Counseling Psychology, 18,* 554–61.

Strupp, H. H. (1960). *Psychotherapists in action: Explorations of the therapist's contributions to the treatment process.* New York: Grune and Stratton.

Szasz, T. S., and Hollender, M. H. (1956). A contribution to the philosophy of medicine: The basic models of the doctor-patient relationship. *Archives of Internal Medicine, 97*, 585–92.

Tannen, D., and Wallat, C. (1983). Doctor/mother/child communication: Linguistic analysis of a pediatric interaction. In S. Fisher and A. D. Todd (Eds.), *The social organization of doctor/patient communication.* Washington, D. C.: Center for Applied Linguistics.

Tepper, D. T., and Haase, R. F. (1978). Verbal and nonverbal communication of facilitative conditions. *Journal of Counseling Psychology, 25*, 35–44.

Tomkins, S. S. (1962). *Affect, imagery, consciousness* (Vol. 1), *The positive affects.* New York: Springer.

Trout, D. L., and Rosenfeld, H. M. (1980). The effect of postural lean and body congruence on the judgment of psychotherapeutic rapport. *Journal of Nonverbal Behavior, 4*, 176–90.

Trower, P., Bryant, B., and Argyle, M. (1978) *Social skills and mental health.* Pittsburgh: University of Pittsburgh Press.

Truax, C. B., and Carkhuff, R. R. (1967). *Toward effective counseling and psychotherapy.* Chicago: Aldine.

Vaccarino, J. M. (1977). Malpractice: The problem and perspective. *Journal of American Medical Association, 238*, 861–63.

Volpe, R. (1979). Developing role taking activity. *Child Study Journal, 9*, 61–68.

Vuori, H., Aaku, T., Aine, E., Erkko, R., and Johansson, R. (1972). Doctor-patient relationship in the light of patients' experiences. *Social Science in Medicine, 6*, 723–30.

Wadsworth, M. (1976). Studies of doctor-patient communication. In M. Wadsworth and D. Robinson (Eds.), *Studies in everyday medical life.* London: Martin Robertson.

Waitkin, H. (1984). Doctor-patient communication. *Journal of American Medical Association, 252*, 2441–46.

Waldron, J. (1975). Judgment of like-dislike from facial expression and body posture. *Perceptual and Motor Skills, 41*, 799–804.

Ware, J. E., Davies-Avery, A., and Stewart, A. L. (1980) *The measurement and meaning of patient quality of care assessment.* Santa Monica, CA: Rand Corporation.

Waxer, P. (1974). Nonverbal cues for depression. *Journal of Abnormal Psychology, 83*, 319–22.

Waxer, P. (1977). Nonverbal cues for anxiety: An examination of emotional leakage. *Journal of Abnormal Psychology, 86*, 306–14.

Weinberger, M., Greene, J. Y., and Mamlin, J. J. (1981). The impact of clinical encounter events on patient and physician satisfaction. *Social Science in Medicine, 15*, 239–44.

Wenegrat, A. (1976). Linguistic variables of therapist speech and Accurate Empathy ratings. *Psychotherapy: Theory, Research, and Practice, 13*, 30–33.

Werner, A., and Schneider, J. M. (1974). Teaching medical students interactional skills: A research-based course in the doctor-patient relationship. *New England Journal of Medicine, 290*, 1232–37.

Wilson, J. T. (1973). Compliance with instructions in the evaluation of therapeutic efficacy. *Clinical Pediatrics, 12*, 333–40.

Wolinsky, F. D., and Steiber, S. R. (1982). Salient issues in choosing a new doctor. *Social Science and Medicine, 16*, 759–67.

Woolley, F. R., Kane, R. L., Hughes, C. C., and Wright, D. D. (1978). The effects of doctor-patient communication on satisfaction and outcome of care. *Social Science and Medicine, 12*, 123–28.

Young, D. W. (1980). Meanings of counselor nonverbal gestures: Fixed or interpretive? *Journal of Counseling Psychology, 27*, 447–52.

4 Nonverbal Communication in the Medical Context: The Physician-Patient Relationship

M. Robin DiMatteo, Louise M. Prince, and Ron Hays

The doctor was a lady doctor and she looked a little bit like a hawk . . . she was a little bit fiendish looking. She said "I think we have a problem here." And my head flashed . . . I knew something was disastrously wrong but I ignored my own warning. Just the look in her eyes . . . she was blinking . . . you know the way people look when they have something disastrous to tell you? And she said "We have a bit of a problem here." And I asked quite naively, "Well, what do you mean?" but my heart was racing when she said that. And she said, "Well, uh, you have acute leukemia."—Ted Rosenthal, *How Could I Not Be Among You?* Benchmark Films, 1970

Under the weight of tremendous uncertainty, the patient was gripped by fear. In considerable pain, she waited and cooperated as her physicians hunted the elusive diagnosis. "B.U.N. and Creatinine are elevated," said the handsome young intern, aloof and oblivious to her presence. "Let's go for an I.V.P. and a Renal Ultrasound." Vacillating between courage and terror, she helplessly watched the baby-faced intern and his resident deep in discussion at the foot of her bed. The intensity of her focus on the minute changes in their facial muscles was like the intense concentration of the commodities broker watching a computer screen with second-by-second price changes that signal the gain or loss of millions of dollars. She was looking for clues not to dollars but to the condition of her body and the future course of her life. She was hesitant about relying on the facial expressions of the intern and resident for the information she craved. After all, the doctors might be hungry or fatigued and their expressions might have no relation to her condition. But no other cues were available. So her hopes rose and fell with their smiles and frowns. In her hypervigilant state, she simply could not take her eyes off their faces.

The physician-patient relationship has begun to receive considerable attention from professionals concerned with the process of medical care. Whether one looks at consumer satisfaction or at patient adjustment to and benefit from treatment, the interpersonal behavior of the physician is found to have a prominent place in determining the outcome. Evidence is growing that patients who are satisfied with the affective behavior of their physicians are more likely to comply with prescribed treatment regimens (cf. DiMatteo & DiNicola, 1982a) and, as a result, have a greater chance of recovering from their physical ills.

It is a common observation that patients tend to gravitate toward physicians who satisfy them and that some physicians are simply more popular than others. When given a choice, patients seek out their favorite physicians and remain loyal to them (DiMatteo & Hays, 1980; DiMatteo, Prince, & Taranta, 1979). Factors related to the delivery of medical services (such as cost and convenience) are relevant, of course, and patients' choices certainly depend in part upon these factors. Doyle and Ware (1977) have shown, however, that although cost, convenience, and other such "practical" factors do exert some influence on responses to and evaluation of medical care, *physician behavior is the most important determinant of patients' satisfaction with the medical treatment they receive.*

HISTORICAL BACKGROUND

Although the literature to date on physicians' interpersonal skills and the relationship of these to issues of health care is relatively sparse (Maguire, 1981), psychologists and other social scientists have begun to focus research attention on the interpersonal and social skills of medical providers (DiMatteo & Friedman, 1982a; Friedman & DiMatteo, 1982). The interpersonal skills that have been delineated encompass: (a) effective verbal communication (Korsch, Gozzi & Francis, 1968; Stiles, Putnam, Wolf, & James, 1979a, 1979b); (b) nonverbal sensitivity and expressiveness (Friedman, 1979, 1982); and (c) related (albeit somewhat more nebulous) interpersonal factors such as reassurance (Cassell, 1974) and the capacity to instill positive expectations in the patient (Beecher, 1955, 1959; Shapiro, 1960). Global assessments of patients' perceptions of their practitioners' warmth and friendliness have been examined as well (Gray & Cartwright,

1953; Kasteler, Kane, Olsen, & Thetford, 1976), although studies have lacked the operational definitions necessary for in-depth examination. Precise operational definitions of physicians' interpersonal skills are in general still limited. Such limitations have impeded the progress of research.

A clear understanding of physician conduct as it relates to patients' responses to medical care is necessary for both theoretical and practical reasons. The special characteristics of the physician-patient relationship provide the opportunity to examine issues of social power and influence as well as of nurturance and therapeutic transference. Further, the study of components of physician conduct as these relate to outcome variables (e.g., patient compliance, the outcome of treatment) sheds light on the role of psychological factors in the process of healing. Finally, efforts to teach interpersonal skills to physicians in training can be developed only with a clear picture of the specific components of these skills. See chapter 5 for a discussion of efforts to teach interpersonal skills to clinicians.

One promising line of research on physician behavior in the therapeutic relationship has been the study of physicians' nonverbal communication skill (DiMatteo, 1979). This skill includes two components: (1) the capacity to understand or decode the emotion conveyed through others' nonverbal cues of facial expression, body movement, and/or voice tone; and (2) the capacity to express or encode emotion (so that other people understand) through nonverbal cues. Some empirical evidence has linked physicians' nonverbal communication skills with patients' expressed satisfaction with care (DiMatteo, Taranta, Friedman, & Prince, 1980). These findings support the view of Hippocrates as early as the 4th century B.C.:

> [The physician must] bear in mind [his] manner of sitting, reserve, arrangement of dress, decisive utterance, brevity of speech, composure, bedside manners, care, replies to objections, calm self-control . . . his manner must be serious and humane; without stooping to be jocular or failing to be just, he must avoid excessive austerity; he must always be in control of himself. [1923 translation]

The effect of physician nonverbal skill on *behavioral* measures such as patient commitment to treatment or the actual choice of a physician—in contrast to *attitudinal* measures such as verbally expressed satisfaction—has not yet been studied. Such relationships are of major importance, however, particularly to those for whom practical outcomes are a necessary fact of administrative or academic curriculum concern. Indirect evidence is available supporting the importance of nonverbal skills to behavioral outcomes. For example, nonverbal skill has been shown to influence satisfaction, which in turn is significantly related to patient commitment (that is, stated intention) to return to the physician (DiMatteo et al., 1979). This stated intention is, of course, an attitudinal measure. An empirical relationship between physicians' nonverbal skill and actual patient behavior has yet to be established.

This chapter describes attempts to establish that link by examining measures of physician workload (in this study, an indication of the physician's popularity among patients) and patient behavior (appointment keeping). It is hypothesized that physicians with greater nonverbal communication skill (those who score high on objective measures of sensitivity and/or expressiveness) will be chosen more often by patients and will enjoy a higher degree of patient compliance with appointments. General theoretical support for these predictions is not difficult to find. It can be argued, for example, that in a social-exchange framework, physicians "trade" social skills for patient loyalty (cf. Thibaut & Kelley, 1959). Further, since physician-patient interactions are typically brief (fifteen minutes on the average: Feller, 1979), nonverbal cues may be necessary (and in fact relied upon for the exchange of both factual and affective information). In addition, studies suggest that more than 50% of patient visits in routine primary care settings are for psychosocial problems (Baker and Cassata, 1978). Certainly nonverbal aspects of communication are highly salient when the issues of concern are psychosocial in nature. The necessary "nonspecific" aspects of healing are best communicated through nonverbal channels (Friedman, 1979, 1982), and physicians whose skill is well developed are likely to enjoy the greatest therapeutic success.

The nonspecific aspects of healing are as old as medicine itself. From the time of Hippocrates in the fourth century B.C., medical healers have held the *art* of medicine in high esteem. Interpersonal behavior toward patients, sensitivity to patients' emotional needs, and a pleasing bedside manner have been lauded by physicians in every age. The remedies of the early physicians practicing prior to 1900 were, for the most part, ineffective in technical terms, although they often achieved desired results in that patients were cured of their ills (Sigerist, 1951). According to Shapiro (1960), the entire history of medicine is little more than the history of the therapeutic effect of the physician's behavior. During this century, the proliferation of medical technology and therapeutic advances has tended to relegate interpersonal concerns to a less prominent place in the care of patients. However, the central role of the art of medicine has continued to be recognized and called for by prominent and influential medical educators:

It is . . . curious that dissatisfaction with medicine in America is at its most vociferous just at a time when doctors have at their disposal the most powerful medical technology the world has yet seen. The "old fashioned" general practitioner, with few drugs that really worked and not much surgery to recommend, is for some reason looking good to many people—in retrospect, at least. . . . Present-day disenchantment with physicians, at a time when they can do more than ever in history to halt and repair the ravages of serious illness, probably reflects the perception by people that they are not being cared for. . . . The patient wants time, sympathetic attention, and concern for himself as a person (Eisenberg, 1977, pp. 235, 238).

The central role played by nonverbal communication in the art of medicine is seen in the contribution of nonverbal aspects of physician behavior to patients' therapeutic outcome. As noted by Friedman (1982), the typical face-to-face interaction in the medical care encounter is highly charged emotionally, and nonverbal cues are very often the focus of a great deal of attention. Encounters with unfamiliar medical terminology and technology, coupled with separation from supportive loved ones, often leave the patient exceptionally vulnerable to the subtle expressive cues of the practitioner. Patients often search the faces of their physicians for clues that relevant information is being withheld from them or that their situation is graver than the physician admits. Finally, because in many ways patients are in a position of low power vis-à-vis their medical professionals (because of less knowledge and often lower socio-economic status), patients are motivated to gain information indirectly rather than directly—even about how well they are doing as patients. Such factors make physicians' control over their own expressive (nonverbal) behavior critically important.

Patients' nonverbal expressions are equally significant in the patient care encounter, and physician sensitivity to these cues plays a central role in the art of medicine. In the medical care situation, patients experience a large number of emotions that need to be recognized by practitioners if patients' needs are to be met effectively. Patients express feelings of pain, fear, confusion, and anger through their nonverbal cues. These feelings are not readily described in words, but they can be detected rather easily in nonverbal cues. The usual question asked by the physician following a treatment recommendation, "Do you have any questions?" is often coupled with his or her averted gaze, pleased acknowledgment of the patient's unconvincing "I don't think so," and quick scurry out the door of the examining room. The physician who is sensitive to nonverbal cues will notice the hesitation in the patient's voice tone, the tension in the patient's body, and the patient's averted glance. The sensitive physician will probe further and perhaps find that the patient is one of the 60% of medical patients who come away from their treatment visits with virtually no idea of what they are expected to do (DiMatteo & DiNicola, 1982a). Nonverbal communication skill comprises an important part of the non-specific aspects of healing.

METHODS OF THE PRESENT STUDY

The setting of the research was the family practice clinic of a university-affiliated West Coast county hospital's family practice residency program. Fifty-seven members of the house staff (residency), 51 males and 6 females, participated in the study, as did 329 ambulatory patients cared for by these residents (although not all physicians participated in all aspects of the study). The physician-patient relationship was, for the most part, an ongoing one since the family practice clinic program emphasized continuity of care.

The Predictive Measures

Personality. Three self-report measures of personality or relatively enduring communication style were filled out by the physicians: (1) the Hogan Empathy Scale (Hogan, 1969), measuring empathy or the ability/tendency to place oneself in another's position; (2) the Self-Monitoring Scale (Snyder, 1974), measuring an individual's tendency to be sensitive to social appropriateness considerations and social expectations and to monitor his or her own behavior to fulfill them; and (3) the Affective Communication Test (Friedman, Prince, Riggio, & DiMatteo, 1980), measuring self-reported nonverbal expressiveness.

Decoding. The nonverbal decoding skills of 28 of the residents, 24 males and 4 females, were measured with the Short Profile of Nonverbal Sensitivity Test (the short PONS Test: Rosenthal, Hall, DiMatteo, Rogers, & Archer, 1979). This test has two parts: a 15-minute, 16mm film test of an individual's ability to decode the emotion communicated by another through facial expressions and body movements; and a 10-minute audiotape test measuring sensitivity to voice tone. High scores on the PONS Test reflect the respondent's sensitivity to the nonverbally communicated feelings of another, as noted in chapter 3. An extensive series of successful convergent and discriminant validity studies is reported by Rosenthal et al. (1979). Research by these authors has produced evidence supporting the validity of the PONS Test in measuring interpersonal success in the therapeutic relationship (see chapter 9 for details). These investigations measured nonverbal sensitivity of counselors and psychotherapists (practicing and in-training) to facial expressions, body movements and postures, and voice tone. Within each of six samples, there was a trend for individuals rated high by their superiors in therapeutic skills and effectiveness to be more sensitive to nonverbal information—particularly body-movement and postural cues to emotion. Important as well are empirical findings by Ekman and Friesen (1969, 1974) showing that people may "leak" their true feelings through body cues. Hence, a practitioner's communication with patients is likely to be enhanced by his or her skill at reading body-movement cues. Though it might be predicted that physicians who are skillful at reading nonverbal cues will be correspondingly more successful interpersonally with their patients, a more precise prediction would involve practitioners' specific sensitivity to bodily communication. We anticipated that skill at reading body cues of emotion would be the most strongly correlated with criterion measures of physician success.

The PONS Test yields scores for four distinct kinds of nonverbal stimuli: (1) *face channel* (20 items), consisting of silent motion picture recordings of a woman's face expressing emotion; (2) *body channel* (20 items), consisting of silent motion picture recordings of a woman's body from neck to knees, expressing emotion through postural and movement cues; (3) *randomized-spliced voice tone* (20 items), consisting of recorded speech unaltered in pitch and amplitude but altered in sequence (because the tape has been physically cut and spliced together in a random order); and (4) *content-filtered voice tone* (20 items), consisting of recorded speech altered by stripping off the highest and lowest frequencies in the voice so that it sounds muffled (as though coming from behind a wall), although the sequence and pacing of speech are preserved.

Encoding. Physicians were asked to communicate each of three verbally neutral sentences to an experimenter (who was simulating a patient) while expressing (encoding) four different emotions: happiness, sadness, anger, and surprise. Each physician encoded a total of twelve communications using this standard-content procedure. Each communication was sound-film recorded, using a Sankyo 40 S XL sound movie camera on a tripod with an attached ECM-16 microphone. Ektachrome 160A sound film was used. The camera was focused on the face of each of 28 (24 male and 4 female) physicians from about ten feet away. The Kodak-processed films were transferred to Sony 3/4 inch cassette videotape using a Kodak Videoplayer. The recorded communications were edited, with specific counterbalancing schemes for the position of a segment on the composite tape. Each segment of the composite tape was preceded by a number: a six-second rating pause followed each segment. For the composite tape of HAPPINESS, SADNESS, ANGER, and SURPRISE three samples of judges were used. The videotape containing *audiovisual* segments was judged by 25 undergraduate college students; 25 additional undergraduates judged only the *audio* portion of the segments; and another 25 undergraduates judged only the *visual* track of the videotape (which contains standard-content vocal communication). The judges listened and/or looked at the composite tapes and on an answer sheet circled Happiness, Sadness, Anger, or Surprise according to which emotion they thought was being communicated by the physician in each segment. The proportion of the total sample of judges that accurately identified the emotion intended by a physician was used as the encoding accuracy score for that physician for that segment. The use of untrained raters to decode intentionally encoded emotion from videotaped segments has been shown to be a valid measurement of nonverbal encoding skill (Zuckerman, Hall, DeFrank, & Rosenthal, 1976). Three types of encoding scores were derived: (1) voice tone (audio) and face and shoulders (video) cues combined; (2) audio alone; and (3) video alone. The sum of the accuracy scores for all twelve communications constituted the total encoding scores. The percentage of communications that were intended by the physician to be positive (happiness or surprise) but were perceived by the judges as negative (anger or sadness) comprised the "posneg" scores.

The nonverbal communication examined here consists of "posed" emotions rather than spontaneous emotions. Some past research has shown a moderate to high correlation between "posed" encoding and spontaneous expressiveness in situations such as the research reported here (Zuckerman et al., 1976). More importantly, however, posed affect was considered to be more representative of physician-patient communication than spontaneous affect since medical practitioners are typically engaged in fulfilling certain role requirements when caring for their patients. For example, consider the family medicine specialist who, while making rounds at the hospital one day, visits three patients: the first recovering from a successful surgery, the second dying of cancer, and the third resting after the birth of a healthy baby. In less than an hour, the physician must change demeanor drastically at least three times if the affect of the patient is to be acknowledged and to some extent matched by the physician. Such matching is considered the ideal condition in the communication of empathy to the patient (cf. Truax & Carkhuff, 1967). To some extent, the physician can certainly be himself/herself and express what he/she is feeling. However, while a lighthearted, somewhat jovial disposition may be very appropriate for the third patient, seriousness, nurturance, and some saddened affect may be more appropriate for the second patient. Such sharp swings of emotional expression demand the physician's skill at encoding posed affect. Because the family medicine residents in the present sample were engaged in just such interpersonally demanding aspects of patient care, skill at encoding posed affect was considered essential.

The Criterion Measures

Two criterion domains of physician interpersonal success were employed: attitudinal and behavioral.

Attitudinal Measures: Patient Satisfaction. Evaluations of the physicians' performance were obtained from their patients by means of questionnaires. An average of six of each physician's patients filled out a questionnaire immediately after a visit with the physician in the family practice clinic. Patients were chosen randomly for the survey (within the constraints of the schedules of the residents and staff). The physician-patient relationship was an ongoing one in this clinic, which emphasized continuity of care.

Questionnaires were distributed by four trained student assistants (two females and two males). A student approached a patient after his or her visit with a physician and asked the patient to participate in this voluntary and anonymous survey. Assistants were given no information about nonverbal skill scores of the physicians.

The patients were, on the average, 44 years old (*SD* = 20.0). They had an average of eleven years of education (*SD* = 2.7) and 26% of them were male. Only 22% of the patients were employed; this low percentage was partly due to the high proportion of older and female patients. Of the patients with jobs, the average occupational status (measured by O. D. Duncan's scale, 1961) was approximately that of a semi-skilled worker. The patient population was 74.0% Anglo (Caucasian), 12.7% Black, 11.8% Chicano, and 1.5% of other ethnic groups. Patients had been coming to the family practice clinic an average of 30 months and had been seen by the respective physicians they rated an average of 11 months. Using the scale developed by Wyler, Masuda, and Holmes (1968) for the rated seriousness of patients' illnesses, it was found that the average seriousness was 55 with a possible range from 1 to 126 (the least serious illnesses being such things as colds, the most serious being cancer). More extensive information on the patient sample is reported by DiMatteo and Hays (1980).

Aspects of patient satisfaction with care were measured with a questionnaire consisting of 25 statements each requiring an agree-disagree response on a five-point Likert scale. Scales were developed by theoretical grouping of the items based upon previous work with such measures (Ware, Davies-Avery, & Stewart, 1978; Wolf, Putnam, James, & Stiles, 1979). These scales represent 1) *communication*—patients' perception of the physician as having given sufficient information to them (an eight-item scale); 2) patients' perception of the physician's *affective* behavior (a nine-item scale); and 3) patients' perception of the physician's *technical competence* (a three-item scale). Examples of items appearing on the questionnaire for each of the scales are: 1) communication scale: "During the examination, this doctor hardly ever tells me what he or she is doing" (reversed item); 2) affective scale: "This doctor acts like I don't have any feelings" (reversed item); 3) technical scale: "I have some doubts about the ability of the doctor" (reversed item). In order to prevent acquiescence response, half the items were reversed. The items from the three scales were also randomly intermixed in the questionnaire.

Behavioral Measures: Physician Popularity and Patient Compliance. The physician popularity measure consisted of the average number of patients a physician saw per day in the clinic. Physicians were assigned to the clinic for the same daily work period (one half-day—four hours). The number of patients seen during that time was obviously somewhat a function of the physician's efficiency, although the time allotted each patient was ample (one-half hour or one hour depending on medical condition). However, the number of patients seen depended more than anything on the physician's own ability to fill the appointment hours. Patients were not assigned to the resident by a superior or by a clerk. Rather, all residents were encouraged to take on family practice patients for the duration of their residency (as part of their own "clinic practice"). A physician would initially see a particular patient (or patient family) and arrange by mutual consent to have the individual (or family) become member(s) of the practice. An unpopular physician would have difficulty recruiting patients and might see no more than one or two patients in an afternoon clinic assignment, whereas a physician in demand might see seven or eight. Popularity was measured, then, by the density of the physician's clinic appointments because all efforts were made to assign each patient to a physician he or she chose, and to reassign the patient if he or she was unhappy with the physician. The number of patients a physician saw in one month divided by the number of days the physician worked in the clinic that month, summed over a six-month period, was used as a measure of popularity. This six-month period immediately preceded the collection of the personality, nonverbal skill, and patient satisfaction measures. Summing over the six-month period provided greater measurement stability than would the data for only one month. This sum was calculated from each physician's appointment records for those months and involved all the patients the physician saw, not only those who filled out questionnaires. A physician's "popularity" could, of course, also be labeled "workload." It was hypothesized that the more expressive and/or sensitive the physician, the more popular that physician would be with patients—that is, the more patients would choose that physician and the greater would be his or her workload. This prediction was proposed despite the fact that treating more patients would give the physician more work to do and might result in fatigue and possibly diminished attention. Such difficulties are likely to interfere with, rather than enhance, communication. Thus, if a positive correlation between popularity (workload) and nonverbal communication skill is found, it can be argued that there is a rather strong relationship between the two variables.

Patient noncompliance was assessed by four measures of appointment keeping. The first measure, cancellation total, consisted of the total number of cancelled appointments (cancelled with no reappointment plus cancelled with reappointment) divided by the number of patients a physician was scheduled to see in one month, summed over the six–month period. Two other noncompliance measures may be regarded as subsets of the first measure: (1) the number of cancelled appointments in a month for which *reappointment* was made divided by the number of patients a physician was scheduled to see in one month, summed over the six-month period; and (2) the number of cancelled appointments per month for which *no reappointment* was made, calculated in the same way. The former is labeled "cancellation-reappointment" and the latter, "cancellation—no reappointment" in Table 4.1. A final criterion measure, "cancellation–no reappointment by cancellation-reappointment," was computed by dividing the second measure in the above subset by the first measure.

The assessment of patient compliance is a complex undertaking. Four measures were included in this study to enhance interpretation of the associations between compliance and other variables. Conclusions about the relationship between compliance and the other variables in the study require a consideration of the pattern of correlations across the four measures. We expected that the individual measurements would relate differently to other variables and that an interpretation of the pattern of intercorrelations would be necessary to provide insights about the entire process.

HYPOTHESES

Theoretical writings suggest the importance of empathy to physician-patient relationships. Carl Rogers' (1957) formulation of the three conditions necessary for effective counseling and psychotherapy includes empathy, which he defines as the *understanding of the patient's feeling and a communication of that understanding*. The other two conditions involve the communication of unconditional warmth and positive regard to the client and the communication of genuineness and sincerity (see also Truax & Carkhuff, 1967). Thus, it was expected that the Hogan Empathy Scale (HES) would predict in a positive way both the attitudinal appraisals by patients and patients' compliance behaviors. However, since the construct of importance may in fact be nonverbal sensitivity and/or expressive *behavior* and not empathy as an attitude or desire to feel what others feel, this prediction was made with somewhat less confidence than the others. No specific predictions were made about the Self-Monitoring Scale (SMS). Because it is an indirect measure, it was not expected to be as accurate as the direct encoding and decoding measures in predicting patients' attitudes and behavior. The Affective Communication Test (ACT), a simplified paper and pencil test of nonverbal encoding skill, was predicted to correlate positively with patient satisfaction and significantly with the compliance measures because of its established association with film measures of nonverbal encoding skill.

Based on previous research suggesting the importance of nonverbal communication in patient satisfaction with medical care, it was hypothesized that physicians who scored high on measures of nonverbal decoding skill on the PONS Test and/or on measures of encoding skill would receive higher ratings of satisfaction from their patients, particularly on the affective and communication dimensions. It was also hypothesized that a physician's capacity to recognize and understand his or her patient's subtle, unintended emotional reaction may be a significant component in influencing physician popularity with patients and their patients' commitment to them (appointment compliance).

Since previous research (see DiMatteo et al., 1980) has found the Body channel of the PONS to be the most valid predictor of patient satisfaction (body cues are suggested as those in which cues to "true feelings" are encoded), it was hypothesized in this study that Body scores on the PONS Test would correlate highest with patient satisfaction and other criterion measures. By recognizing cues of dissatisfaction and negative affect in the body language of patients, the physician may, it has been suggested, become aware of each patient's emotional distress and confront it before the patient terminates the treatment relationship, attenuates treatment effects by lack of cooperation, or retaliates with malpractice litigation (DiMatteo & DiNicola, 1982b). In particular, it was expected that the more generally expressive and/or sensitive the physician, the smaller would be the ratio of lost (unreappointed) patients to patients scheduled. Patients cancel appointments for many legitimate reasons, but if they are complying with medical treatment or have a commitment to a physician, patients will make new appointments. If a patient is dissatisfied with a physician or in some manner rebellious, however, he/she will likely avoid encountering that physician again. Gray and Cartwright (1953) found that patients' dissatisfaction with physicians' interpersonal treatment was the most important factor in patients' decisions not to return to their physicians. Successful encoding is necessary in order to instill patients' confidence in a physician and enhance patients' perceptions of a physician's caring and concern (cf. DiMatteo, 1979). Social psychological theories of social influence suggest, also, that physicians' nonverbal expressiveness is essential because patients look to their physicians for cues as to how they should respond to medical situations and how they should interpret their own emotional arousal. Physicians can communicate calm and a hopeful attitude to patients rather than panic, fear, and hopelessness (Friedman, 1979; Rodin & Janis, 1979).

Before considering the results of our study, one final note is in order. Variations in sample size among the measures, and indeed the relatively small sample size itself, are at best less than ideal in this research. While every effort was made to schedule and reschedule appointments for testing, unexpected emergencies, patient responsibilities, and overwhelming fatigue prevented some physicians from participating in some or all aspects of the study. Because of such frustrations and the nature of the field setting (in which the outsider/researcher is asking for time and attention from those who have little of either to spare), research such as this must often press ahead despite smaller-than-desired sample sizes if important questions are to be addressed.

RESULTS

Descriptive Statistics and Reliabilities

Table 4.1 contains the number of cases, means, standard deviations, number of items, and alpha reliability coefficients for the personality, nonverbal sensitivity, nonverbal encoding, and criterion variables.

Table 4.1 Reliabilities of Predictor and Criterion Variables

Variable	N	Scale Mean	SD	n	Alpha Reliability
Personality					
1. Hogan empathy scale	29	40.64	4.05	64	.31
2. Self-monitoring scale	29	11.83	3.90	25	.67
3. Affective communication test	29	75.10	14.34	13	.79
Nonverbal Sensitivity (PONS)					
4. Face	29	15.38	1.76	20	.21
5. Body	29	14.90	1.54	20	.00
6. Video total	29	30.28	2.90	40	.40
7. Random spliced	29	12.34	2.24	20	.28
8. Content filtered	29	14.21	1.72	20	.01
9. Audio total	29	26.55	2.78	40	.15
Nonverbal Encoding					
10. Audio plus video total	25	743.92	145.00	4	.65
11. Audio plus video posneg	25	109.15	72.21	12	.59
12. Audio total	25	633.25	108.32	4	.29
13. Audio posneg	25	140.19	84.53	12	.64
14. Video total	25	648.12	133.57	4	.00
15. Video posneg	25	187.37	105.01	12	.67
Criterion					
16. Satisfaction with communication	53	35.76	3.72	8	.75
17. Satisfaction with affective	53	41.26	3.75	9	.79
18. Satisfaction with technical	53	13.76	1.70	3	.65
19. Popularity (or workload)	47	18.02	5.58	6	.88
20. Cancellation total	47	0.44	0.21	6	.36
21. Cancellation-reappointment	47	0.20	0.13	6	.25
22. Cancellation-no reappointment	47	0.23	0.14	6	.32
23. Cancellation-no reappointment by cancellation-reappointment	46	0.53	0.22	—	—

NOTE: The internal consistency estimate for cancellation total is based on the ratio of cancelled appointments per patients scheduled, over *six* months. The reliability estimate for cancellation-reappointment is based on the ratio of cancelled appointments *for which a reappointment was made* per patients scheduled, over *six* months. Likewise, the reliability estimate for cancellation-no reappointment is based on the ratio of cancelled appointments *for which no reappointment* was made per patients scheduled, over *six* months.

While the HES exhibited relatively low reliability, both the SMS and ACT measures were adequate in this regard. The PONS measures (of nonverbal sensitivity)—perhaps because they were taken from the short form of the test—were disappointing in their reliability. The posneg nonverbal encoding measures were internally consistent, but the total encoding measures had low alpha reliability. Although, the three measures of patient satisfaction and the measure of physician popularity (or workload) were reliable, the appointment noncompliance measures displayed low internal consistency across the six months they were collected.

Intercorrelations Among the Variables

Table 4.2 presents the intercorrelations among the personality, nonverbal sensitivity, and nonverbal encoding variables.

Predictor Variables. The personality measures were correlated positively with one another, although the magnitude of the relationships was small. Correlations among the PONS measures reflected some degree of independence between the audio and video channels (video total with audio total: $r = .21$, $p > .05$) and within the audio channel (random spliced with content filtered: $= -.03$, $p > .05$). The face and body dimensions of the video channel were significantly correlated with one another ($r = .54$, $p \leq .01$). A substantial degree of covariance was found among the different types of encoding total scores, but less commonality was found among the posneg measures. Audio plus video total correlated .77 and .79 (p's $\leq .01$) with audio total and video total, respectively. Audio total correlated .62 with video total. In contrast, audio posneg correlated .26 and $-.10$(p's $> .05$) with audio plus video posneg and video posneg, respectively. Audio plus video posneg correlated .78 with video posneg.

The personality measures were, for the most part, relatively independent of the nonverbal skill scores. There was a tendency for the HES to be correlated with PONS in a negative fashion and to bear modest though nonsignificant correlations with the encoding scores. The SMS correlated negatively with the video PONS measures and positively with the audio PONS measures. The ACT scale, conceptually an outgrowth of the more cumbersome assessments of nonverbal expressiveness, was not significantly ($p > .05$) correlated with any of the measures of nonverbal encoding.

Correlations between nonverbal sensitivity scores and nonverbal encoding scores were uniformly weak and bidirectional. These two skills were relatively independent of each other in this sample of physicians.

Table 4.2 Intercorrelations Among Personality, Nonverbal Sensitivity, and Nonverbal Encoding Variables (decimals omitted)

Variable	1	2	3	4	5	6	7	8	9	10	11	12	13	14	15
Personality															
1. Hogan empathy scale (HES)	—														
2. Self-monitoring scale (SMS)	28	—													
3. Affective communication test (ACT)	24	30	—												
Nonverbal Sensitivity (PONS)															
4. Face	-13	-16	-05	—											
5. Body	-20	-39*	-00	54**	—										
6. Video total	-18	-30	-03	89**	86**	—									
7. Random spliced (RS)	-14	12	-09	15	11	15	—								
8. Content filtered (CF)	-30	14	03	14	13	15	-03	—							
9. Audio total	-30	18	-05	20	17	21	79**	59**	—						
Nonverbal Encoding															
10. Audio plus video total	20	25	37†	-13	-07	-11	12	17	20	—					
11. Audio plus video posneg	14	-14	-26	-28	00	-17	05	-17	-06	-37†	—				
12. Audio total	15	29	17	-13	-16	-17	-04	20	09	77**	-05	—			
13. Audio posneg	01	-11	-21	-16	-09	-14	08	-22	-07	-27	26	-53**	—		
14. Video total	17	04	27	-18	-13	-18	-04	-00	-03	79**	-47*	62**	-37†	—	
15. Video posneg	07	05	-12	-13	06	-05	15	04	14	-20	78**	15	-10	-47*	—

†p ≤ .10
*p ≤ .05
**p ≤ .01

NOTE: Correlations are based on different number of cases, ranging from $n = 25$ for the associations involving the nonverbal encoding variables to $n = 29$ for the associations among the measures of personality and nonverbal sensitivity.

Criterion Variables. Table 4.3 provides the intercorrelations among the criterion variables. The three measures of patient satisfaction (communication, affective, and technical) were very highly correlated with one another, reflecting, perhaps, the tendency for patients to avoid making completely independent judgments of their physicians' performance on various dimensions (DiMatteo & Hays, 1980). In addition, the satisfaction measures were positively correlated with physician popularity, cancellation total, cancellation-reappointment, and cancellation-no reappointment. The satisfaction measures were negatively correlated with cancellation-no reappointment by cancellation-reappointment. As expected, satisfaction with communication and affective care were more strongly linked to the criterion variables than was satisfaction with technical care. Physician popularity was positively correlated with cancellation-reappointment and negatively correlated with cancellation-no reappointment by cancellation-reappointment.

Between Predictor and Criterion Variables. Table 4.4 contains the correlations between the predictor and criterion variables. Of the personality measures, only the ACT was a significant predictor of any of the criterion variables (the ACT was positively correlated with physician popularity). Similarly, the nonverbal sensitivity measures were not consistently related to the criterion variables. However, nonverbal sensitivity did tend to be negatively related to cancellation total and cancellation-reappointment. In addition, the video sensitivity measures were positively correlated, and the audio sensitivity measures were negatively correlated or uncorrelated, with cancellation-no reappointment and cancellation-no reappointment by cancellation-reappointment.

The nonverbal encoding measures were clearly the best predictors of the criterion variables. As hypothesized, total sending scores (combining the accuracy of all emotions sent), whether for audio or video channels separately or combined, were positively associated with patient satisfaction. Furthermore, the total encoding scores were positively correlated, and the posneg scores were negatively correlated, with physician popularity. The nonverbal posneg measures reflect the tendency of the physician to express negative emotion (i.e., be perceived as encoding negative emotion) when his/her intention was to express positive emotion. Thus, physicians who were more likely to make such expressive "errors" were less popular with patients (and thus had fewer patients). Although there was a trend for the sending scores to predict patient compliance, the relationships were modest. Nonetheless, it is noteworthy that total encoding scores were positively associated and posneg encoding scores were negatively associated with cancellation-reappointment. These results suggest that patients of more nonverbally expressive physicians may be more

Table 4.3 Intercorrelations among the Criterion Variables (decimals omitted)

Criterion	16	17	18	19	20	21	22	23
16. Satisfaction with communication	—							
17. Satisfaction with affective care	90**	—						
18. Satisfaction with technical care	81**	81**	—					
19. Popularity (or workload)	19	15	07	—				
20. Cancellation total	26†	38**	21	21	—			
21. Cancellation-reappointment	36*	48**	15	25†	73**	—		
22. Cancellation–no reappointment	04	11	17	07	79**	16	—	
23. Cancellation by cancellation-reappointment	-26†	-26†	-06	-12	-02	-63**	55**	—

†p ≤ .10
*p ≤ .05
**p ≤ .01

NOTE: Correlations are based on different number of cases, ranging from $n = 43$ for the associations between the last criterion variable and the satisfaction measures to $n = 53$ for the associations among the satisfaction measures.

Table 4.4 Personality, Nonverbal Sensitivity, and Nonverbal Encoding as Predictors of Patient Satisfaction, Physician Popularity/Workload, and Patient Compliance (decimals omitted)

	Personality Measures			Nonverbal Sensitivity						Nonverbal Encoding					
										Audio & Video		Audio		Video	
	HES	SMS	Act	Face	Body	Video Total	RS	CF	Audio Total	Total	Posneg	Total	Posneg	Total	Posneg
	1	2	3	4	5	6	7	8	9	10	11	12	13	14	15
16. Satisfaction with communication	06	01	−14	09	07	09	−16	13	−05	34†	−14	37†	−17	39†	−04
17. Satisfaction with affective care	−00	00	−13	09	08	10	−09	19	04	39*	−12	41*	−21	41*	03
18. Satisfaction with technical care	−04	09	−17	01	−07	−03	−18	14	−06	34†	−16	40*	−40*	36†	05
19. Popularity (or workload)	−05	12	52**	17	26	24	−05	12	04	42*	−43*	38†	−50*	40†	−27
20. Cancellation total	05	−15	04	−01	−07	−04	−48**	−14	−47*	01	−31	18	−40†	32	−19
21. Cancellation-reappointment	14	02	08	−24	−16	−24	−24	−07	−23	25	−31	24	−23	45*	−25
22. Cancellation-no reappointment	−04	−22	−00	18	03	13	−49**	−13	−47*	−23	−22	06	−44*	09	−07
23. Cancellation-no reappointment by cancellation-reappointment	−09	−14	−18	47*	17	38†	−07	05	−02	−33	05	−10	−12	−19	08

†p ≤ .10
*p ≤ .05
**p ≤ .01

NOTE: Correlations are based on different number of cases, ranging from $n = 23$ for the associations involving the nonverbal encoding variables to $n = 28$ for the associations between the personality and nonverbal sensitivity variables and the satisfaction measures.

inclined to make a reappointment after cancellation of a scheduled appointment.

The fact that most of the correlations between the encoding posneg measures and the criterion measures were negative is particularly interesting in the light of some recent empirical findings (Friedman, 1979). Friedman (1979) operationally defined genuineness and sincerity (one of the three therapeutic conditions proposed by Carl Rogers) as consistency between verbal and nonverbal cues. While posneg is not directly a measure of verbal-nonverbal cue combinations, it does assess the physician's tendency to send negative nonverbal cues while trying to say a neutral sentence in a positive manner. It is likely that some positive and some negative cues are communicated under such conditions, making the overall effect *more* negative than if the intention and the result were consistent—that is, to send negative emotion. (In fact, accuracy of communication—that is, consistency between intention and resultant communication—was positively related to outcome measures.)

DISCUSSION

The present study adds to a growing body of recent research that points to the centrality of the physicians' nonverbal communication skills to the process of medical treatment (cf. DiMatteo, 1979). Specifically, previous research on this topic has found that patient's expressed (attitudinal) satisfaction with their physicians can be predicted on the basis of the nonverbal skills of these physicians. The nonverbal skills have involved both encoding success and decoding ability—particularly sensitivity to nonverbal cues in the body channel (DiMatteo et al., 1980). No studies to date, however, have extended the criterion measures to include behavioral outcomes such as patients' actual choice of their physician and compliance with appointment scheduling.

The findings of this research provide further information about the importance of nonverbal communication in the physician-patient relationship. Despite the considerable "noise" invariably found in behavioral measures from field studies such as this, the relationships between the nonverbal communication variables and the criterion variables were encouraging. In addition, it was found that patients' attitudes and behavior provide somewhat independent perspectives on patients' responses to the physician-patient relationship.

Validity of the criterion measures used in research is sometimes questionable in medical settings because of the complex nature of the social psychological processes taking place there. One can never be quite sure what the variables measured really mean. For example, "physician workload" is a criterion assessing the number of patients seen by the physician in a given period of time. While clinic scheduling and pressures of the treatment situation make it highly likely that this measure reflects simply the number of patients who have chosen come to a particular physician (and hence measure his/her popularity), certainly it is possible that the physician's efficiency and energy have something to do with how many patients he/she is able to see in a given period of time. (The physician, for example, may always take only one-half hour or less to see a patient and never use a one-hour time block.) Since this measure is correlated rather substantially with the nonverbal expressiveness of the physicians, one wonders to what extent *both* nonverbal expressiveness and workload (popularity) might reflect a third variable—the physician's energy level (or even more specifically, physiological adaptation to the unavoidable sleep deprivation of residency training!). Certainly such issues need further exploration.

Despite these questions, the importance of nonverbal cues in the clinical context should not be underestimated. The results of this research suggest that physicians' "acting ability" (i.e., ability successfully to communicate posed emotion) has important implications for *both* patient attitudinal satisfaction and behavioral commitment to the physician. Whether this is the result of specific skill in controlling facial expressions and voice tone or simply the energy to engage such control may be initially a less critical question than determining that nonverbal expressiveness *does* have clinical implications. The next steps involve determining precisely how and why. For example, does nonverbal encoding skill of the physician promote more positive therapeutic results because the physician is able to control leakage of his or her own feelings and reactions to the patient or the therapeutic situation? Does a physician's skill in controlling his or her spontaneous affect contribute as much to therapeutic outcome as his or her ability to send posed affect? To what extent might the encouragement of acting ability in physicians actually detract from the genuineness of the physician-patient relationship—increasing rather than decreasing the interpersonal distance between the two? These and many other important theoretical and practical questions need to be answered before the precise role of nonverbal encoding skill in the therapeutic relationship can be understood.

Naturally, the correlational nature of these results prompts questions about the causal inferences in the present study. Although implicit in our arguments are inferences regarding physician communication skill as a cause of patient satisfaction, it is certainly possible that patient satisfaction, and particularly such behaviors as compliance with appointments, may eventually influence physicians' emotional expressivity. There may be nothing more encouraging than initial interpersonal success with patients to prompt further efforts by physicians.

The relatively greater success of nonverbal expressiveness over nonverbal sensitivity variables in predicting attitudinal and behavioral aspects of patient satisfaction is not altogether clear, although it does tend to be consistent with previous research (see DiMatteo et al., 1980). In earlier studies, sending variables on the whole have been somewhat stronger predictors than receiving (sensitivity) variables in general (although, in earlier studies, sensitivity to body cues has proven to be substantially related to attitudinal satisfaction). The use of a short version of the PONS Test in the present study may explain the attenuated relationships with sensitivity scores. Compared with the full 220-item version of the PONS Test, the short version has considerably lower reliability, and thus may account for attenuated correlations with other variables. (Clearly the longer, more reliable test is preferable to the shortened version, but time constraints for data collection are particularly acute when subjects are physicians-in-training.) This result may, however, not be a methodological artifact at all but rather may reflect the relatively greater importance of encoding skill versus decoding skill. While it is important for a physician to understand a patient's feelings, for example, the only way for the patient to perceive that he or she is understood is from the physician's own communication of that understanding. Also, it is possible that even without fully understanding the patient's concerns, the physician may still be able to communicate calm assurance and a sense of deep caring that is so important to the patient.

IMPLICATIONS

The results of this study add to a growing body of evidence in support of the role of nonverbal skill in successful therapeutic interaction. Particularly in the medical context, where patients may experience a distressing information deficit, the nonverbal cues of practitioners may take on heightened importance. Further, because patients are likely to be verbally constrained by the medical care context and/or their own fear, practitioners may need to depend heavily on their own nonverbal sensitivities in order to understand both the psychological and medical conditions of their patients (Friedman, 1979, 1982).

In the past decade, some leaders in medical education (e.g., Eichna, 1980; Eisenberg, 1977) have begun to turn their attentions back to the interpersonal aspects of patient care. Two avenues have been explored in attempting to enhance the level of humanism in today's physicians: selection and training. To date, no acceptable psychological measurements have been developed that are capable of reliably and validly screening applicants for medical school or residency positions based upon their interpersonal skills (see DiMatteo & DiNicola, 1982b). Perhaps measures of nonverbal skill such as those described in this chapter might someday be used to enhance predictions of clinical success (which now are typically based on personal interviews with their attendant subjective biases). Because of the ethical and methodological problems inherent in using such selection devices, however, training may be a more acceptable approach. Courses dealing with the many psychosocial components of medicine (e.g., DiMatteo & Friedman, 1982b) and interpersonal skills training programs (see review by Hays & DiMatteo, in press) are being developed and implemented in medical as well as nursing training. Although most instructors have a clear idea of the content issues they consider central (indeed most will have their own strong preferences), questions of "process" often remain unresolved. That is, in teaching how to "get along" with patients—e.g., how to satisfy them interpersonally and help them to feel less anxious—what precisely does one teach? (See chapter 5 of this book.) Certainly, the classical microcounseling skills are likely to be relevant (cf. Ivey, 1977). Yet such skills as active listening and reflecting have a strong verbal component to them and as such are limited in scope. So much of what goes on between health professionals and patients occurs on a nonverbal level. Thus, a precise understanding of the workings of nonverbal communication in medical settings is crucial. More refined specification of the precise skills needed for successful physician-patient relationships, such as that offered by the present research, is necessary to further develop effective training methods for direct patient care.

ACKNOWLEDGMENTS

This research was funded by an NIMH Small Grant (#R03-MH31421) to the first author. Thanks are due to Marianne Archambault, Carl Eklund, Jann Gumbiner, Dan Takeda, and Amy Tsubota for assistance in data collection and tabulation.

REFERENCES

Baker, R. M., & Cassata, D. M. (1978). The physician-patient relationship. In R. B. Taylor (Ed.), *Family medicine: principles and practice.* New York: Springer-Verlag.

Beecher, H. K. (1955, December 24). The powerful placebo. *Journal of the American Medical Association,* pp. 1602–6.

Beecher, H. K. (1959). *Measurement of subjective responses.* New York: Oxford University Press.

Cassell, E. J. (1974). *The healer's art: a new approach to the doctor-patient relationship.* New York: Penguin Books.

DiMatteo, M. R. (1979). Nonverbal skill and the physician-patient relationship. In R. Rosenthal (Ed.), *Skill in nonverbal communication.* Cambridge, MA: Oelgeschlager, Gunn & Hain.

DiMatteo, M. R., & DiNicola, D. D. (1982a). *Achieving patient compliance.* Elmsford, New York: Pergamon Press.

DiMatteo, M. R., & DiNicola, D. D. (1982b). Social science and the art of medicine: From Hippocrates to Holism. In H. S. Friedman and M. R. DiMatteo (Eds.), *Interpersonal issues in health care.* New York: Academic Press.

DiMatteo, M. R., & Friedman, H. S. (1982a). *Social psychology and medicine.* Cambridge, Mass.: Oelgeschlager, Gunn & Hain.

DiMatteo, M. R., & Friedman, H. S. (1982b). A new undergraduate course in Social Psychology and Health. *Health Psychology, 1(2),* 181–93.

DiMatteo, M. R., & Hays, R. (1980). The significance of patients' perceptions of physician conduct: A study of patient satisfaction in a family practice center. *Journal of Community Health, 6,* 18–33.

DiMatteo, M. R., Prince, L. M., & Taranta, A. (1979). Patients' perceptions of physicians' behavior: Determinants of patient commitment to the therapeutic relationship. *Journal of Community Health, 4,* 280–90.

DiMatteo, M. R., Taranta, A., Friedman, H. S., & Prince, L. M. (1980). Predicting patient satisfaction from physicians' nonverbal communication skills. *Medical Care, 18,* 376–87.

Doyle, B. J., & Ware, J. E. (1977). Physician conduct and other factors that affect consumer satisfaction with medical care. *Journal of Medical Education, 52,* 793–801.

Duncan, O. D. (1961). Socioeconomic index for occupations in the detailed classification of the Bureau of the Census, 1950 (transformed to NORC scale). In A. J. Reiss, O. D. Duncan, & P. K. Hatt (Eds.), *Occupation and Social Status.* Glencoe, IL: The Free Press.

Eichna, L. W. (1980). Medical school education, 1975–79: A student's perspective. *New England Journal of Medicine, 303,* 727–34.

Eisenberg, L. (1977). The search for care. *Daedalus, 106,* 235–46.

Ekman, P., & Friesen, W. V. (1969). Nonverbal leakage and clues to deception. *Psychiatry, 32,* 88–106.

Ekman, P., & Friesen, W. V. (1974). Detecting deception from the body or face. *Journal of Personality and Social Psychology, 29,* 288–98.

Feller, B. A. (1979). *Characteristics of general internists and the content of care of their patients.* Washington, D. C.: U.S. Dept. of Health, Education, and Welfare, HRA-79-652.

Friedman, H. S. (1979). Nonverbal communication between patients and medical practitioners. *Journal of Social Issues, 35(1),* 85–99.

Friedman, H. S. (1982). Nonverbal communication in medical interaction. In H. S. Friedman & M. R. DiMatteo (Eds.), *Interpersonal issues in health care.* New York: Academic Press.

Friedman, H. S., & DiMatteo, M. R. (Eds.). (1982). *Interpersonal issues in health care.* New York: Academic Press.

Friedman, H. S., Prince, L. M., Riggio, R. E., & DiMatteo, M. R. (1980). Understanding and assessing nonverbal expressiveness: The affective communication test. *Journal of Personality and Social Psychology, 39,* 333–51.

Gray, P. G., & Cartwright, A. (1953, December 19). Choosing and changing doctors. *The Lancet, 1308.*

Hays, R., & DiMatteo, M. R. (in press). Toward a more therapeutic physician–patient relationship. In S. Duck (Ed.), *Personal relationships 5: Repairing personal relationships.* New York: Academic Press.

Hippocrates (1923). *Volume II: On Decorum and the Physician* (W. H. S. Jones, Trans.). London: William Heinemann.

Hogan, R. (1969). Development of an empathy scale. *Journal of Consulting and Clinical Psychology, 33,* 307–16.

Ivey, A. (1977). *Microcounseling: interviewing skills manual,* 2nd ed. Springfield, IL: Charles C. Thomas.

Kasteler, J., Kane, R. L., Olsen, D. M., & Thetford, C. (1976). Issues underlying prevalence of "doctor-shopping" behavior. *Journal of Health and Social Behavior, 17,* 328–39.

Korsch, B. M., Gozzi, E. K., & Francis, V. (1968). Gaps in doctor-patient communication. I: Doctor-patient interaction and patient satisfaction. *Pediatrics, 42,* 855–71.

Maguire, P. (1981). Doctor-patient skills. In M. Argyle (Ed.), *Social skills and health.* London: Methuen.

Rodin, J., & Janis, I. L. (1979). The social power of health-care practitioners as agents of change. *The Journal of Social Issues, 35,* 60–81.

Rogers, C. R. (1957). The necessary and sufficient conditions of therapeutic personality change. *Journal of Consulting Psychology, 21,* 95–103.

Rosenthal, R., Hall, J. A., DiMatteo, M. R., Rogers, P. L., & Archer, D. (1979). *Sensitivity to nonverbal communication: the PONS test.* Baltimore: Johns Hopkins University Press.

Shapiro, A. K. (1960). A contribution to a history of the placebo effect. *Behavioral Science, 5,* 109–35.

Sigerist, H. E. (1951). *A history of medicine.* London: Oxford University Press.

Snyder, M. (1974). The self-monitoring of expressive behavior. *Journal of Personality and Social Psychology, 39,* 526–37.

Stiles, W. B., Putnam, S. M., Wolf, M. H., & James, S. A. (1979a). Verbal response mode profiles of patients and physicians in medical screening interviews. *Journal of Medical Education, 54,* 81–89.

Stiles, W. B., Putnam, S. M., Wolf, M. H., & James, S. A. (1979b). Interaction exchange structure and patient satisfaction with medical interviews. *Medical Care, 17,* 667–79.

Thibaut, J. W., & Kelley, H. H. (1959). *The social psychology of groups.* New York: Wiley.

Truax, C. B., & Carkhuff, R. R. (1967). *Toward effective counseling and psychotherapy.* Chicago: Aldine.

Ware, J. E., Davies-Avery, A., & Stewart, A. L. (1978). The measurement and meaning of patient satisfaction. *Health and Medical Care Services Review, 1,* 3–15.

Wolf, M. H., Putnam, S. M., James, S. A., & Stiles, W. B. (1979). The medical interview satisfaction scale: Development of a scale to measure patient perceptions of physician behavior. *Journal of Behavioral Medicine, 1,* 391–402.

Wyler, A. R., Masuda, M., & Holmes, T. H. (1968). Seriousness of illness rating scale. *Journal of Psychosomatic Research, 11,* 363–73.

Zuckerman, M., Hall, J., DeFrank, R., & Rosenthal, R. (1976). Encoding and decoding of spontaneous and posed facial expressions. *Journal of Personality and Social Psychology, 34,* 966–77.

5 Talking To and About Patients: The Therapist's Tone of Voice

Peter David Blanck, Robert Rosenthal, and Marsha Vannicelli

Investigators have long been intuitively aware of the influence which expressive cues in speech have on the psychotherapeutic process. Almost two generations ago, Snyder (1946) stated: "Our experience suggests that, try as we may, a counselor shows by subtle cues of voice and facial expressions the basic attitudes which he may think he is nicely disguising. . ." (p. 492). In recent years, the literature on tone of voice and other nonverbal aspects of communication has been systematically related to the general functions of social behavior (for a review see Scherer, 1982), as well as to the specific qualities of therapeutic interaction (Duncan, Rice, & Butler, 1968). Indeed, tone of voice has been implicated as an important nonverbal channel for communicating emotional and expressive feelings and states in the therapeutic process.

This chapter reports a systematic investigation of the therapist's tone of voice with special emphasis on five areas of analysis: (1) descriptive (i.e., delineating the major dimensions of the therapist's tone of voice), (2) psychometric (i.e., assessing the reliability, validity, and consistency of measures of the therapists' tone of voice), (3) interactional (i.e., examining the therapist's tone of voice as a predictor of psychotherapeutic processes), (4) competence (i.e., measuring the relationship between therapists' competence and therapists' tone of voice), and (5) trans-situational (i.e., observing the degree to which talking *about* patients simulates, or dissimulates, talking *to* those same patients). For each of these five areas of analysis, we first discuss related research reports, next describe our findings on the therapist's tone of voice, and finally speculate about future research directions and questions in the area. We begin with an overview of our research program, including our overall strategy and our general methods for studying both speech about and speech to patients.

RESEARCH ON THE THERAPIST'S TONE OF VOICE: OVERVIEW

Research Objectives

The long-term goal of our research program has been to increase understanding of unintentional interpersonal influence in social interaction. As part of this research program, for example, we have attempted to further our understanding of the social pscyhology of interpersonal expectancy effects in social interaction. The earliest studies in this area demonstrated that experimenters' expectations could function as self-fulfilling prophecies with both human and animal research subjects for a variety of dependent variables. Later studies investigated the factors serving to increase or decrease these interpersonal expectancy effects and began to investigate the process of experimenter-subject communication that served to mediate these expectancy effects (Rosenthal, 1969, 1976, in press). The mediating processes were found to be, to a large extent, nonverbal in nature (Blanck, Rosenthal, 1984; Rosenthal, 1981; Rosenthal, Hall, DiMatteo, Rogers, & Archer, 1979), and in particular expressed via tone of voice.

A second goal of our research program has been to further understanding of the role of nonverbal and verbal cue communication in social interaction in general and in the mediation of naturally occurring and experimentally induced interpersonal expectancy effects in particular (Blanck, Rosenthal, & Cordell, in press; Rosenthal, in press). For example, we recently have examined the nonverbal variables in tone of voice (e.g., warmth and hostility) serving to mediate the operation of interpersonal expectancy effects. We also have integrated Babad, Inbar, and Rosenthal's (1982a, b) findings on the relationship between personality styles and susceptibility to biasing information through nonverbal mediation (specifically tone of voice) of interpersonal expectancy effects (Blanck & Rosenthal, 1984). The latter study was the first successfully to distinguish nonverbal correlates (via tone of voice) of susceptibility to biasing information. Perhaps the most compelling and most general conclusions to be drawn from these findings are that human beings do engage in highly effective and presumably unintended communication (e.g., via tone of voice) with one another, and that such communication is in part responsible for the self-fulfilling prophecies we see in interpersonal relationships.

A final aim of our research efforts has been to further understanding of the implications of the operation of nonverbal communication in social interaction, for research methodology, clinical practice, and social relations in general. As a start toward the goal of more completely specifying the accuracy of sending and receiving nonverbal cues in social interaction, an instrument was designed to measure sensitivity to various channels of nonverbal communication: the Profile of Nonverbal Sensitivity, or PONS (for detailed description of the PONS see chapter 9 and Rosenthal et al., 1979). Many special groups have been tested with the PONS, and those scoring best have been actors and students of nonverbal communication. Interestingly, clinical psychologists, psychiatrists, and other clinicians scored no higher than college students, but clinicians rated as more effective by their supervisors scored significantly higher than did clinicians rated as less effective by their supervisors. Other uses of the PONS are reported in chapters 3, 4, and 9.

More recently, we have developed the Measure of Verbal and Nonverbal Sensitivity (MOVANS) test, designed to provide a standardized instrument for the assessment of sensitivity to discrepant and consistent social messages in the verbal and nonverbal channels (for a detailed description of the MOVANS test see Blanck and Rosenthal, 1982). The preliminary groups of adults and children tested with the MOVANS have shown that the advantages of age were especially great for the decoding of discrepant verbal-nonverbal messages. These results were encouraging, given that most clinical theorizing about discrepant or "double-bind" communications has emphasized the discrepancy between verbal and nonverbal modalities (i.e., Bateson, Jackson, Haley, & Weakland, 1956; see also chapter 2 in the present book). In a more clinically relevant context, our group working with J. Masling gave the MOVANS to a group of high oral subjects and a group of low oral subjects (as determined by Rorschach scores). Preliminary results suggested that those subjects scoring high on orality were relatively more accurate at decoding discrepant verbal and nonverbal communications. These results are consistent with a series of studies which suggest that high levels of orality may be associated with increased social awareness and social concern (Masling, O'Neil, & Katkin, 1982).

The research described in this chapter continues our interest in understanding the methodological, practical, and clinical implications of the operation of nonverbal communication in social interaction.

Research Strategy

Our general research strategy for the examination of tone of voice and other aspects of nonverbal communication, including the series of studies described in this chapter, has been to employ a mix of experimental and observational studies conducted in contexts some of which are more laboratory-like and some of which are more field-like. The aim of this strategy has been to reap the benefits of both the greater precision and internal validity of more experimental and laboratory-like studies and also the greater external or ecological validity of more observational and field-like studies (for a review of conducting judgment studies see Rosenthal, 1982 and for a discussion of field-based observational and experimental studies see Blank and Turner, in press).

Our method for studying tone of voice and emotion in speech has been the "content-filtering" of tape-recorded samples of speech. Content-filtering involves the re-recording of an audiotape through a low-pass filter, thus removing from the tape the high frequencies on which word recognition depends but preserving the sequence and rhythm of natural speech (for a more detailed description of the content-filtering process see Rogers, Scherer, and Rosenthal, 1971 and Rosenthal et al., 1979). Although no norms exist for the proportion of words that can still be understood after content-filtering, two recent studies found that proportion to be .17 (Green, DePaulo, & Rosenthal, 1981) and .11 (Blank & Rosenthal, 1984).

Several studies have examined tone of voice (both as an independent and a dependent variable) employing content-filtered speech segments. Recently, Caporael, Lukaszewski, and Culbertson (1983) have demonstrated that a care-giver's tone of voice (i.e., the use of soothing "baby-talk") was related to general expectations for patients' prognosis. Similarly, Milmoe, Rosenthal, Blane, and Chafetz (1967) have shown that doctors' hostility, assessed from tone of voice while speaking of patients, was related to patient outcome. In their study, Milmoe and her colleagues showed that there was a significant negative relationship between judges' ratings of hostility (or anger) in tone of voice and doctors' effectiveness in the referral of alcoholic patients (for reviews of nonverbal communication in the doctor-patient relationship, see chapters 3 and 4 in the present book; for a practitioner's view, see R. H. Blanck, 1985). Finally, Blank and Rosenthal (1984) have shown that less competent and more ineffective camp counselors were more prone to biasing effects as reflected in their tone of voice when talking about their campers, while counselors who displayed more competent and more effective attributes generally did not show differential expectancy effects as reflected in their tone of voice. The results of these studies are especially dramatic if we recall that the judges used were "blind" both to the experimenters' purpose and to the speakers' verbal content and topic of discussion.

In each of the studies described in this chapter, groups of judges rated all the content-filtered samples of speech on the following global nonverbal variables:

1. warm-not warm
2. anxious-not anxious
3. hostile-not hostile
4. empathic-not empathic
5. liking-not liking

6. professional-not professional
7. competent-not competent
8. optimistic-not optimistic
9. dominant-not dominant
10. honest-not honest

These variables were selected for several reasons. First, many of them have been employed in a variety of studies of nonverbal communication and interpersonal expectancy effects and have been found to be related to the mediation of these effects in laboratory contexts and to the mediation of clinical outcomes in physician-patient interaction (e.g., Milmoe et al., 1967; and Rosenthal, 1974, 1976, which reviews many of these studies). Second, these variables correspond to the domains found in a variety of studies to be necessary for describing adequately the communication of affect (Abelson & Sermat, 1962; Argyle, 1975; Dawes & Dramer, 1966; Frijda & Philipszoon, 1963; Mehrabian, 1970; Osgood, 1966; Scherer, 1974; Sweeny, Tinling, & Schmale, 1970; Williams & Tolch, 1965; Wish, Deutsch, & Kaplan, 1976). The primary lesson of these studies is that, while different factor solutions emerge in different studies, one almost always finds an evaluative factor as most important and one or more additional factors tapping activity, potency, or related factors. In short, especially for the first factor, but also to some degree for the next one or two, Osgood's three-dimensional space of evaluation, activity, and potency holds up quite well.

Research Design

In the first stage of the studies described in this chapter, 21 psychotherapists (10 males and 11 females) conducted interviews with three or four male or female inpatients or outpatients who had participated in an intensive 5-week program for alcohol (and drug) abusers. These interviews were audiotaped and then content-filtered. Judges rated brief segments of each therapist's tone of voice from three phases of these interviews (beginning, middle, and end) and on the ten global nonverbal dimensions.

The second stage of the studies was exactly analogous to the first stage except that the therapists were talking not *to* but *about* the same patients, and that 20-second clips rather than 10-second clips were used. Our interest was focused on the similarities and differences between the nonverbal variables in the therapist's tone of voice in situations in which therapists were directly interacting with their patients (first stage) and those in which they were merely talking about those same patients (second stage). Specifically, in this second stage the same twenty-one male and female therapists as in stage one (plus three additional female therapists) spoke about 218 patients who had participated in the alcohol treatment program. In reviewing the interviews, we found that 10-second clips generally captured the essence of a therapist's verbal comments to patients, whereas 20-second clips more accurately represented a therapist's verbal comments about patients. We therefore decided to sample 10-second clips of therapists speaking to patients and 20-second clips of therapists speaking about patients.

In the final stage of our studies we addressed the important question of the degree to which talking about people simulates (or dissimulates) talking to those same people. In fact, 98 of the 101 patients interviewed in the first stage (talking to) were also talked about in the second stage of our studies. As we will discuss, our examination of the judges' ratings of the content-filtered tapes (from the beginning, middle, and end) of the therapist's utterances yielded correlations between communication patterns found while they talked to particular patients and communication patterns found while they talked about those same patients. We will argue that an understanding of these correlations provides a great advantage to researchers in clinical (and other applied) contexts. Since there are serious logistic and sometimes ethical problems associated with studying interactions of clinicians with their patients, it is extremely useful to know under what conditions, if any, talking about a patient could be a useful substitute for talking to a patient. Selection programs, training programs, and basic research programs would all benefit through an understanding of variations in tone of voice when therapists talk to and about patients.

In sum, each stage of our research program was designed to provide a comprehensive examination of the therapist's tone of voice. Unlike previous research in this area, our program eliminated the potential confounding effects of the verbal content of the interviews by studying the content-filtered speech of therapists. Additionally, extremely brief segments of speech (10- or 20-second clips) were sampled from longer interviews as compared with the trend in this area of research to sample at least three to five minutes of therapists' speech (Bachrach, Curtis, Escoll, Graff, Huxster, Ottenberg, & Pulver, 1981). Pittenger, Hockett, and Danehy's (1960) classic study showed the verbal and nonverbal richness of the first five minutes of the therapeutic interview; we were interested in describing the type and amount of information (expressed only via the therapist's tone of voice) in just *10 or 20 seconds* of the therapeutic interaction. Recent research on tone of voice had suggested that important information can indeed be communicated even in segments lasting only a few seconds (Rosenthal, Blanck, & Vannicelli, 1984; Rosenthal, et al., 1979).

GENERAL METHOD: RATING SPEECH TO PATIENTS

Therapists and Patients

Twenty-one (10 male and 11 female) psychologists, psychiatrists, counselors, and social workers at a hospital treatment center (both inpatient and outpatient staff) asked 101 patients to make an oral evaluation of an intensive 5-week program for alcohol and drug abusers in which they had participated. The 43 male and 58 female patients consisted of 49 inpatients and 52 outpatients.

Supervisor's Ratings of Therapists' Competence

The head clinical supervisor at the treatment center rated all of the therapists in this study on a dimension of general therapeutic competence. The endpoints of the 9-point scale for this dimension were: not competent . . . very competent.

The Interview Context

Therapists were asked to name and rank order approximately eight patients with whom they were currently working or with whom they had recently worked, ranking them from those for whom they held the highest expectations for favorable outcome to those for whom they held the lowest expectations. Outcome expectations were defined in terms of drinking-related behavior and also global improvement in overall life functioning.

Patients were told that this was a special study of the alchohol and drug treatment program at the hospital—one aim of which was to gather impressions of the program from participating patients. Toward this end, patients were asked to talk to a staff member for fifteen minutes about their impressions of the following: 1) the setting (buildings, grounds, etc.), 2) scheduling of activities, 3) therapy groups, 4) involvement of family members, 5) hall meetings, and 6) whether or not they would recommend the program to a relative or friend.

The Interview Recording

The 101 interviews were audiotape-recorded and ranged in length from 4 to 37 minutes with mean length of 17 minutes. For purposes of the present study three different tapes were derived from the original recording, employing the following method: From each interview, the first 10 seconds of the therapist's speech was assembled and re-recorded onto one tape; 10 seconds of the therapist's midmost speech was assembled and re-recorded onto a second tape; finally, the last 10 seconds of the therapist's speech was assembled and re-recorded onto a third tape. The order of the 101 clips on each of the three tapes was randomized. Because we were interested only in therapist's tone of voice in this study, the patient's speech was excluded from the derived tapes.

The final result was three tapes containing 101 ten-second segments or clips of speech from the beginning, middle, and ending portions of each interview. These master tapes were then content-filtered (Rogers, Scherer, and Rosenthal, 1971).

Judges and Ratings

Twelve (6 male and 6 female) undergraduates at Harvard University were paid to rate the three tapes (beginning, middle, and ending segments). Judges were randomly assigned to any one of three counter-balanced conditions representing the order in which they would rate the three tapes. Judges were told that they would hear therapists talking and would be able to understand only the speakers' tone of voice. All judges rated all the segments (101 beginning, 101 middle, and 101 ending) on the ten dimensions discussed above—warm-not warm, hostile-not hostile, anxious-not anxious, dominant-not dominant, empathic-not empathic, competent-not competent, optimistic-not optimistic, professional-not professional, honest-not honest, and liking-not liking. Each segment was played once, and all judges were given 15 seconds to make the ten ratings. In general, judges had no problem in understanding the task or making the ratings.

GENERAL METHOD: RATING SPEECH ABOUT PATIENTS

Therapists and Patients

The same 21 male and female therapists just described and three additional female therapists spoke about 218 patients who had participated in the alcohol and drug treatment program. The male ($n=94$) and female ($n=124$) patients consisted of 76 inpatients and 142 outpatients. (Ninety-eight of these 218 patients had been interviewed [spoken to] by the therapists in the previous study.) As before, the supervisor at the treatment center rated all of the therapists in this study on the dimension of general therapeutic competence.

The Interview Context

Each therapist spoke about three or more patients (up to 21) for approximately three to five minutes each. As in the previous study, therapists were asked to name a group of approximately eight patients with whom they had recently worked and to rank order them with regard to the therapists' expectations of their likelihood of recovery.

Staff members were instructed to discuss anything that came to mind about each of the patients, or about their experiences with particular patients that led them to feel a certain way about them. The sequence of the therapists' discussions of the patients (i.e., whether the patient to be discussed would be of high or low expectancy, female or male) was determined by a pre-arranged randomization schedule which differed for each therapist.

The Interview Recording

As in the first study, three different tapes were derived from the original recordings (from the beginning, middle, and final portions of the interviews), but 20-second segments (instead of 10-second segments) were used.[1] Also as before, the order of the 218 clips on each of the three tapes was randomized and the master tapes were content-filtered.

Judges and Ratings

Twelve (6 male and 6 female) undergraduates at Harvard University were paid to rate the three tapes. None of these judges had participated in the previous study. Judges were randomly assigned among three counterbalanced conditions representing the order in which they would rate the three tapes. They were told that they would hear therapists talking and would be able to understand only the speakers' tone of voice. Each judge rated all the segments (218 beginning, 218 middle, 218 ending segments) on the same 10 dimensions employed earlier—warm-not warm, hostile-not hostile, etc. Each segment was played once, and all judges were given 15 seconds to make the ten ratings. Once again, judges had no problem in understanding the task or making the ratings.

ANALYSIS 1—DESCRIPTIVE ASPECTS OF THERAPIST'S TONE OF VOICE: A FACTOR-ANALYTIC STUDY

Background

The research described here was aimed at delineating the major dimensions of the therapist's tone of voice (Blanck, Rosenthal, Vannicelli, & Lee, in press). Our interest was in studying the interpersonal manner of therapists (expressed via tone of voice), or what Schaffer (1982) and Orlinsky and Howard (1978) have referred to as the manner in which the therapist relates to the patient (i.e., talks to and talks about patients). The therapist's interpersonal manner or behavior has been shown to communicate a wide range of affect and emotional meaning: for example warmth, empathy, and genuineness (Rogers, 1957); the optimal-empathic relationship (Mintz, Luborsky, & Auerbach, 1971); or the warmth and friendliness of the therapeutic relationship (Gomes-Schwartz, 1978; Gomes-Schwartz & Schwartz, 1978).

Unlike the earlier work of Mintz et al. (1971) or Gomes-Schwartz (1978), our research was aimed at describing and delineating the major dimensions of only the therapist's tone of voice when talking both to and about patients. An analysis of principal components with varimax rotation was performed on the intercorrelations among the means of all judges' ratings of the ten variables for (a) the therapists' tone of voice when talking to patients, and for (b) the therapists' tone of voice when talking about patients.

Findings

The varimax-rotated factor matrix for the therapists' tone of voice when talking to patients is presented in Table 5.1. This analysis yielded four interpretable factors after rotation. We subsequently confirmed the four-factor solution by means of a cluster analysis in which the mean within cluster r was .72 compared to a mean between cluster r of .25. As Table 5.1 shows, a first factor of therapist "warmth" in tone of voice clearly emerged. This first dimension was comprised (after reflecting, i.e., multiplying by -1) of the judges' ratings of warm, not hostile, not dominant, empathic, and liking. The dimension of warmth in tone of voice seems to embody the *nonverbal* qualities of the "optimal-emphatic relationship" described by Mintz and his colleagues, the "optimal therapist relationship style" suggested by Fiedler's classic work in the area, and of course, the therapeutic dimensions of warmth, empathy, and unconditional regard as discussed by the Rogerian research group (Bergin, 1966; Rogers, Gendlin, Kiesler, & Truax, 1967; Truax, 1963). The dimension of warmth in tone of voice is also clearly related to the evaluative dimension of Osgood, Suci, and Tannenbaum's (1957) semantic differential, given the strong loadings of the liking and warm variables.

Table 5.1   Four-Factor Solution: Varimax Rotated Factor Loadings of Principal Components Analysis on Mean Judges' Ratings of Therapists' Tone of Voice When Talking To Patients

Nonverbal Variable	Component (Factor)			
	Warmth	Professional	Anxious	Honest
Warm	$-.956$[a]	$-.020$	$-.103$	$-.077$
Hostile	$.851$[a]	.101	.454	$-.033$
Anxious	.309	$-.032$	$.925$[a]	$-.023$
Dominant	$.739$[a]	.392	.477	.004
Empathic	$-.933$[a]	.024	$-.084$	.175
Competent	.162	$.913$[a]	$-.065$	.188
Optimistic	$-.358$	$.830$[a]	.257	$-.172$
Professional	.152	$.910$[a]	$-.084$	.244
Honest	$-.466$	.330	$-.018$	$.792$[a]
Liking	$-.916$[a]	.018	$-.140$	.245

[a]Loadings serving to define each of the factors.

A second factor of "professional" in the therapist's tone of voice when talking to patients can be seen in Table 5.1. The professional factor is comprised of the ratings of competent, optimistic, and professional. The nonverbal qualities of professional in the therapist's tone of voice may parallel Mintz and his colleagues's "directive mode" of therapeutic interaction, and Gomes-Schwartz and Schwartz's (1978) description of "therapist directiveness." Rogers (1942) describes the professional or directive mode of treatment as one of providing "advice and persuasion." As Mintz and his colleagues point out, the emphasis of the professional or directive dimension is on the therapist's role in structuring, leading, and advising. The professional or directive role has also been compared to Osgood et al.'s (1957) activity dimension (Mintz et al., 1971). Whether our *nonverbal* professional factor parallels the *verbal* directive factor awaits further study.

The third and fourth dimensions, anxiety and honesty, describe the last two factors of the four-factor solution. These appear to be separate dimensions, unrelated to the warmth or profesional factors described earlier (or to the potency factor which forms the third leg of Osgood's semantic differential).

Overall, our description of the therapists' tone of voice when talking *to* patients, based on purely *nonverbal* stimuli, parallels both earlier descriptions of the factor structure of therapists' interactions with patients based on the *verbal content* of interviews, and also Osgood's and his colleagues' semantic differential ratings.

The varimax-rotated factor matrix for the therapists' tone of voice when talking about patients is presented in Table 5.2. This analysis yielded seven interpretable factors after rotation. The determination of this seven-factor solution was influenced by a basic working rule of thumb. We decided to define each of these factors in a manner consistent with the factor solution of the therapist's tone of voice when talking *to* patients. Thus, while it would seem that the variable "dominant" should help to define the professional factor, because it did not do so in the first set of factors, it is shown as a new dimension in the second set. In line with the same principle, the optimistic dimension was not included in the warmth factor and was conceptualized as a separate dimension. Subsequent cluster analyses of the seven factors supported these conceptual distinctions (i.e., dominant and optimistic were defined as separate factors). The mean within cluster r was .88 compared to a mean between cluster r of .56.

Table 5.2 shows a first factor of therapist "warmth" in tone of voice when talking about patients. The warmth dimension was comprised of the judges' ratings of warm, empathic, and liking. This dimension of warmth in tone of voice when talking about patients embodies the cen-

Table 5.2 Seven-Factor Solution: Varimax Rotated Factor Loadings of Principal Components Analysis on Mean Judges' Ratings of Therapists' Tone of Voice When Talking About Patients

Nonverbal Variable	Component (Factor)					
	Warmth	Professional	Anxious	Honest	Hostile	Optimistic
Warm	.869[a]	-.120	-.178	.239	.150	-.172
Hostile	-.372	-.086	.440	-.137	-.797[a]	.065
Anxious	-.057	.027	.956[a]	-.044	.224	.029
Dominant	-.119	-.881[b]	.379	-.009	-.124	-.098
Empathic	.947[a]	-.144	.005	.093	.186	.052
Competent	.464	-.782[a]	-.270	.197	.068	-.072
Optimistic	.651	-.415	-.041	.082	.102	-.593[a]
Professional	.434	-.771[a]	-.308	.228	.029	.091
Honest	.587	-.273	-.062	.727[a]	.160	-.056
Liking	.776[a]	-.165	-.146	.333	.188	-.308

[a]Loadings serving to define each of the factors.
[b]Not included in this factor and defined as a separate factor (see text).

tral nonverbal qualities described earlier by the warmth dimension in tone of voice when talking to patients. Interestingly, in talking about patients the warmth factor loses the relatively more active and potent dimensions (i.e., dominant and not hostile) and retains the purely evaluative components.

As in talking to patients, a second factor, "professional," emerged—comprised (after reflecting) of the ratings of professional and competent. Finally, as Table 5.2 shows, anxious, honest, hostile, optimistic, and dominant dimensions completed the seven-factor solution, with the last two reflected (i.e., multiplied by -1).

Overall, our description of therapists' tone of voice when talking about patients parallels conceptually the factor structure of therapists' interactions while talking *to* their patients. However, a more differentiated factor structure emerged in the non-interactive interview context. It may be that the interactional quality of talking to patients relatively inhibits the differentiation of nonverbal processes. The non-interactive context, on the other hand, may allow for a more refined description of patients.

Most encouraging overall was the finding that the factor structure of talking to patients and the factor structure of talking about patients were conceptually very similar.[2] Each solution provided information concerning therapists' basic styles (expressed via tone of voice) in relating to patients. Our description of the nonverbal qualities of therapists' tone of voice was also congruent with earlier discussions of the major dimensions of the psychotherapeutic process. The interpersonal manner of the therapist (expressed via tone of voice) remains an interesting area for future research.

ANALYSIS 2—PSYCHOMETRIC ASPECTS OF ASSESSING THE THERAPIST'S TONE OF VOICE: RELIABILITY AND CONSISTENCY

Background

There is a growing concern about the reliability and utility of various lengths of segments from audiotapes recording therapeutic interaction. Important questions have been raised regarding how much of the clinical process needs to be studied (Blanck, Rosenthal, Vannicelli, & Lee, in press). Mintz and Luborsky (1971) have addressed this question by demonstrating that brief segments (i.e., in their study, 4 minutes) of the therapeutic hour can be a useful research unit for many of the verbal and nonverbal process variables of psychotherapy (e.g., therapist empathy, directiveness, and warmth), while many of the qualities of the therapist-patient interaction (e.g., their composite measure of the "optimal-empathic relationship") are not captured by the brief segments.

More recently, Bachrach et al. (1981) have also found that judgments about the major dimensions of the therapeutic relationship (e.g., transference) based on brief segments *did not* correlate with the judgments based on the entire sessions. However, judgments of brief segments based on such verbal and nonverbal variables as activity, empathy, warmth, and directiveness *did* correlate with judgments based on the 50-minute session. These communicative process variables appeared to a large extent to be nonverbal in nature and were implicitly expressed in the therapists' tone of voice. It is evident that sampling decisions concerning the psychotherapeutic process need to be related to the types of variables of interest and to the rating system employed. The present study specifically attempted to document the reliability and utility of ultra-brief segments (10–60 seconds) of nonverbal behavior in capturing important dimensions of the therapeutic process.

A second purpose of the present study was to access the consistency of therapists' tone of voice across three phases of the psychotherapeutic session (beginning, middle, and end). Gurman (1973) found that therapists varied considerably in their level of facilitative therapeutic functioning (e.g., levels of empathy, warmth, and genuineness) both across and within sessions with the same patients. In the present study, the methodological question addressed was whether or not the dimensions of the therapeutic process specifically related to therapist's tone of voice can be equivalently assessed from different phases of the interaction.

In sum, the general question of interest was whether the interactive interviews (talking to patients) and the non-interactive interviews (talking about patients) can be measured reliably (over judges) and consistently (over time) from brief tone-of-voice segments.

Reliability of Judges' Ratings of Therapists' Tone of Voice When Talking To Patients

To determine the reliability of the judges' ratings of therapists' tone of voice in speaking to patients, intraclass correlations were computed. (For a discussion of this application of intraclass correlation see Rosenthal, 1982). The simple reliability of a single judge, the simple reliability for an extrapolated 50-minute session, the effective reliability for the mean of the 12 judges (Spearman-Brown corrected reliabilities), and the effective reliability for an extrapolated 50-minute session (Spearman-Brown corrected reliabilities) for the four ratings of tone of voice are presented in Table 5.3.

The simple reliability of a single judge (identical to the reliability between any two judges) for the full 30-second clips on the four nonverbal variables ranged from .023 to .276. The most general finding here is that single judges vary considerably in their assessment of the nonverbal dimensions in tone of voice. These results suggest that clinical researchers interested in assessing nonverbal variables in tone of voice would be well advised to employ either several judges, or longer clips, or both, to achieve any desired level of reliability (Rosenthal, 1982). Interestingly, warmth in tone of voice, perhaps the central dependent variable in the nonverbal literature, was the most reliable nonverbal measure for any single judge. This result could be expected, given that the warmth supervariable was based on five separate ratings of tone of voice.

The simple reliability for a single judge extrapolated to a 50-minute therapeutic session ranged from .702 to .974. Such extrapolation would require 100 times more ratings by the single judge since there are 100 clips of 30 seconds each in a "50 minute hour" (Rosenthal, 1982). These results suggest that any single judge can reliably assess these four nonverbal dimensions of tone of voice over the course of a 50-minute session, given the standard Spearman-Brown assumptions for this situation of relatively homogeneous reliabilities from judge to judge and from time period to time period (Rosenthal, 1982). In general, clinical researchers can be relatively confident that these nonverbal variables in tone of voice can be reliably extracted from a 50-minute session by the typical single naive judge.

The effective or actual reliability of the *mean* of the 12 judges' ratings for the 30-second clips ranged from .220 to .821. These estimated reliabilities for this set of 12 judges indicate a high level of inter-rater agreement for the four nonverbal ratings in tone of voice. It seems that 12 judges are able reliably to understand the nonverbal dimensions in tone of voice for these brief 30-second clips.

The effective reliability for the mean of the 12 judges extrapolated to a 50-minute session ranged from .965 to .998. It is evident that 12 judges can very reliably assess the nonverbal variables in the therapist's tone of voice over the course of a 50-minute therapeutic session.

Table 5.3 Reliability of Judges' Ratings of 30-Second Clips of Tone of Voice: Speaking To Patients

Variables	Simple Reliability		Effective Reliability[a]	
	Reliability of a single judge	Extrapolated reliability for a 50-minute session	Reliability of the mean of 12 judges	Extrapolated reliability for a 50-minute session
Professional-Competence[b]	.064	.872	.451	.988
Warmth[c]	.276	.974	.821	.998
Anxious	.181	.957	.726	.996
Honest	.023	.702	.220	.965

[a]Effective reliability is computed by applying the Spearman-Brown correction for the number of judges employed (Rosenthal, 1982).
[b]Comprised of competent, optimistic, and professional.
[c]Comprised of warm, not hostile, not dominant, empathic, and liking.

Consistency of Ratings of Therapists' Tone of Voice When Talking To Patients

To determine the consistency over time of assessment of therapists' tone of voice in speaking to patients, intraclass correlations averaged over the 12 judges were again computed. Table 5.4 presents the simple reliability of a single 10-second phase for the beginning, middle, and end portions of the interview, the simple reliability for the 10-second phases extrapolated to a 50-minute session, the effective reliability of the mean of the three phases (Spearman-Brown corrected reliabilities), and the effective reliability of the mean of the three 10-second phases (Spearman-Brown corrected reliabilities) extrapolated to a 50-minute session for the four tone-of-voice ratings.

The simple reliability of a single 10-second phase for assessing the four nonverbal variables in tone of voice ranged from .115 to .508. Therapists' tone of voice may not be uniformly consistent across the three phases of the interview process. Nevertheless, when we consider that these findings are based on only 10-second clips of the interview, the results take on added impact. In particular, assessment of the warmth-nonverbal variable, with a simple reliability of .508, is strikingly consistent across the three phases of the interview. Evidently warmth in therapists' tone of voice is fairly reliably assessed from the first 10 seconds of the therapist-patient interaction, as it is from the middle or ending 10 seconds for this set of 12 judges.

When we examine the simple reliability of a single phase extrapolated to a 50-minute session, the consistency in ratings of therapists' tone of voice during the three individual phases of speaking to patients is especially dramatic. These reliabilities range from .929 to .990.

The effective reliability of the mean of the three 10-second phases (i.e., the reliability of 30 seconds) ranged from .280 to .756. Again, these findings are especially exciting, given that each segment represents only 10 seconds of the interaction. As would be expected, the results become even more dramatic when we estimate the effective reliability of the sum of the three phases extrapolated to the 50-minute session. The range of these results was from .975 to .997 and constitute the best estimate of the reliability of a full 50-minute session as a basis for assessment.

Reliability of Judges' Ratings of Therapists' Tone of Voice When Talking About Patients

To determine the reliability of the judges' ratings of the therapists' tone of voice in speaking about patients, intraclass correlations were computed exactly as in the previous study. The simple reliability of a single judge,

Table 5.4 Consistency of Ratings of Tone of Voice for Beginning, Middle, and Ending Phases (10-Second Segments): Speaking To Patients

Variables	Simple Reliability		Effective Reliability[a]	
	Reliability of a single phase	Extrapolated Reliability for a 50-minute session[b]	Reliability of the mean of the 3 phases	Extrapolated reliability for a 50-minute session[c]
Professional-Competence[d]	.115	.929	.280	.975
Warmth[e]	.508	.990	.756	.997
Anxious	.368	.983	.636	.994
Honest	.146	.945	.339	.981

[a]Effective reliability is computed by applying the Spearman-Brown correction for the number of phases employed (Rosenthal, 1982).
[b]Based on extrapolation of a single phase, i.e., beginning, middle, or end.
[c]Based on extrapolation of the mean of the three phases.
[d]Comprised of competent, optimistic, and professional.
[e]Comprised of warm, not hostile, not dominant, empathic, and liking.

the simple reliability for an extrapolated 50-minute discussion of patients, the effective reliability for the mean of the 12 judges (Spearman-Brown corrected reliabilities), and the effective reliability for an extrapolated 50-minute discussion of patients (Spearman-Brown corrected reliabilities) for the seven tone-of-voice ratings are presented in Table 5.5.

The simple reliability of a single judge for the full 60-second clips on the seven nonverbal variables ranged from .069 to .284. Again, individual judges seem to vary considerably in their assessment of the nonverbal dimensions in tone of voice. Consistently with the results of the previous study, use of several judges or longer experimental clips seems to be warranted for the reliable assessment of tone of voice in therapists' speaking about patients. When the simple reliability of a single judge is extrapolated to a 50-minute session, the results range from .787 to .952. Overall, during the course of a 50-minute discussion of a patient, judges should be able reliably to assess these seven nonverbal variables based on therapists' tone of voice.

The effective reliability of the mean of the 12 judges' ratings for the 60-second clips ranged from .471 to .826. Thus, judgments based on the ratings of the mean of 12 judges show a high level of agreement in rating the seven nonverbal variables in therapists' tone of voice. These results become even more striking when they are extrapolated to a 50-minute discussion of patients (range of reliabilities, .978 to .996).

Consistency of Ratings of Therapists' Tone of Voice When Talking About Patients

As in the previous study, intraclass correlations based on the 12 judges' ratings were computed to determine the consistency over time of assessment of therapists' tone of voice in speaking about patients. Table 5.6 presents the simple reliability of a single 20-second phase for the beginnings, middle, and end portions of the discussion, the simple reliability for the 20-second phases extrapolated to a 50-minute discussion, the effective reliabillity of the mean of the three 20-second phases (Spearman-Brown corrected reliabilities), and the effective reliability of the mean of the three 20-second phases (Spearman-Brown corrected reliabilities) extrapolated to a 50-minute discussion for the seven tone-of-voice ratings.

The simple reliability of a single 20-second phase for the seven nonverbal variables in tone of voice ranged from .130 to .489. As in the previous study, the therapist's tone of voice in talking about patients may not be uniformly consistent across the course of a discussion. However, in view of the brief length of these segments, the results are quite encouraging.

Table 5.5 Reliability of Judges' Ratings of 60-Second Clips of Tone of Voice: Speaking About Patients

Variables	Simple Reliability		Effective Reliability[a]	
	Reliability of a single judge	Extrapolated reliability for a 50-minute session	Reliability of the mean of 12 judges	Extrapolated reliability for a 50-minute session
Professional-Competent[b]	.190	.921	.738	.993
Warmth[c]	.131	.883	.644	.989
Not Hostile	.069	.787	.471	.978
Anxious	.146	.895	.672	.990
Dominant	.284	.952	.826	.996
Optimistic	.097	.843	.563	.985
Honest	.098	.845	.566	.985

[a]Effective reliability is computed by applying the Spearman-Brown correction for the number of judges employed (Rosenthal, 1982).
[b]Comprised of competent and professional.
[c]Comprised of warm, empathic, and liking.

Table 5.6 Consistency of Tone of Voice for Beginning, Middle, and Ending Phases (20-Second Segments): Speaking About Patients

Variables	Simple Reliability		Effective Reliability[a]	
	Reliability of a single phase	Extrapolated reliability for a 50-minute session[b]	Reliability of the mean of the 3 phases	Extrapolated reliability for a 50-minute session[c]
Professional-Competent[d]	.383	.969	.651	.989
Warmth[e]	.358	.965	.626	.988
Not Hostile	.130	.882	.310	.957
Anxious	.360	.966	.628	.988
Dominant	.489	.980	.742	.993
Optimistic	.268	.948	.523	.982
Honest	.303	.956	.566	.985

[a]Effective reliability is computed by applying the Spearman-Brown correction for the number of phases employed (Rosenthal, 1982).
[b]Based on extrapolation of a single phase, i.e., beginning, middle, or end.
[c]Based on extrapolation of the mean of the three phases.
[d]Comprised of competent and professional.
[e]Comprised of warm, empathic, and liking.

Of the seven nonverbal variables, dominance in tone of voice seems to be most consistently expressed during the phases of the discussion. When we examine the simple reliability of a single phase extrapolated to a 50-minute session, the reliabilities range from .882 to .980. Evidently over the course of a 50-minute discussion of a patient, judges should be able reliably to agree about the nonverbal qualities in the therapist's tone of voice.

The effective reliability of the mean of the three phases, averaged over the 12 judges, ranged from .310 to .742. Again, in view of the brevity of these clips, the results take on added impact. Finally, the estimates of the effective reliability for the mean of the three phases extrapolated to a 50-minute session ranged from .957 to .993. Clearly, researchers who are interested in assessing the consistency of the nonverbal qualities of the therapist's tone of voice in speaking about patients would be well advised to examine several phases and longer segments in the therapists' discussion.

Discussion

Our first general purpose was to assess the inter-judge reliability and to estimate the longer segment reliabilities of our psychotherapeutic process variables. Consistently with Bachrach et al.'s (1981) suggestion, we do not believe that brief segments of the therapy hour can be naively substituted for entire 50-minute session assessments. However, our findings add to the growing literature suggesting that psychotherapeutic process variables can be reliably measured from brief segments of a therapeutic session. In fact, several of our nonverbal process variables could be reliably assessed from only 10 or 20 seconds of an interview by only one judge. Evidently the stylistic variables associated with the therapist's social and nonverbal skills can be reliably measured from very brief segments. On the other hand, as Bachrach et al. (1981) and Mintz and Luborsky (1971) have concluded, brief segments of the psychotherapeutic process do not reliably capture the richness of the therapist-patient interaction—even when the focus is solely on the therapist, as in our study.

Our second general purpose was to assess the consistency of the therapist's tone of voice across the three phases of the psychotherapeutic process (beginning, middle, and end). Gurman (1973) found that therapists seem to vary considerably during the course of their sessions in their facilitative therapeutic functioning (e.g., as measured by the Truax scales of nonexpressive warmth and genuineness [Truax and Carkhuff, 1967]). In particular, employing the Truax content-analysis technique, Gurman found a trend for maximal within-session therapeutic conditions to occur in the middle and later segments of the therapeutic hour. Gurman attributed this pattern to the therapist's need to have a "warming-up" period (i.e., the beginning phase) in the therapy hour.

In the two studies in this section, therapists' tone of voice was equivalently assessed across the three phases of the therapeutic interview. Our findings suggest that the stylistic process variables associated with the therapist's tone of voice can be reliably estimated from different phases in the therapeutic interview. Most dramatically, the consistency of the therapist's tone of voice could be assessed from 10 to 60 seconds of content-filtered speech by these sets of twelve judges. In general, these analyses also support Mintz, Luborsky, and Auerbach's (1971) conclusion that there is a substantial degree of consistency in the qualities of a therapist's style in relating to many different kinds of patients.

ANALYSIS 3—INTERACTIONAL ASPECTS OF THE THERAPIST'S TONE OF VOICE: PREDICTORS OF ASPECTS OF PSYCHOTHERAPEUTIC PROCESSES

Background

Here we examine the therapist's tone of voice as a predictor (or postdictor or paridictor) of the psychotherapeutic process. More specifically, our aim was to see what information can be inferred from the therapist's tone of voice alone about the patient's inpatient vs. outpatient status, the therapist's sex, and the therapist's expectations for the patient's recovery (Blanck, Rosenthal, Vannicelli, & Lee, in press).

There have been several reviews of studies examining the relationship between therapist behavior and therapeutic outcome (for reviews see Parloff, Waskow, & Wolfe, 1978; Pope, 1977; Schaffer, 1982). The most general conclusion to be drawn from these reviews is that the quality of therapist behavior has more influence on the outcome of therapy than does the quantity of therapist behavior (see also chapter 3 in this book). In examining the therapist's tone of voice as a predictor of psychotherapeutic processes we were concerned with the "nonverbal quality" of the therapist's behavior.

Other investigators have examined measures of therapist or patient verbal behavior as predictors of therapy outcome (for a review see chapter 4). For example, Rice (1965) and Rice and Wagstaff (1967) have demonstrated that the therapist's verbal style of participation is related to both the therapist's level of experience and to the patient's outcome. Gomes-Schwartz's (1978) analyses of verbal behavior during therapy sessions showed that patient involvement even more than therapist variables most consistently predicted therapy outcome.

The present study was designed to refine the classification of information concerning the therapeutic interview process that can be inferred from the therapist's tone of voice. More specifically, this part of our research program attempted to further our understanding of unintentional social influence (expressed via tone of voice) in social interaction in general, and to further our understanding of the influence which the therapist's tone of voice may have on the therapy process in particular.

Predicting Therapist Tone of Voice When Talking To Patients

The correlations between therapist tone of voice when speaking to patients and inpatient versus outpatient status are presented in Table 5.7. These correlations are presented to answer the following question: What can we infer or predict about patient status (inpatient versus outpatient) from therapists' tone of voice in speaking to patients in these brief content-filtered clips?

From Table 5.7 it is apparent that therapists were significantly more

Table 5.7 Relationship Between Therapist Tone of Voice and Inpatient versus Outpatient Status[a]: Speaking To Patients

Variables	Phases			Total (30 seconds)
	Beginning (10 seconds)	Middle (10 seconds)	End (10 seconds)	
Professional-Competence[b]	.04	−.02	−.02	−.00
Warmth[c]	.04	.12	.16	.14
Anxious	−.17	−.23*	−.32**	−.31**
Honest	−.13	−.02	.07	−.04

[a]A positive correlation means that tone of voice was more professional-competent, warmer, more anxious, and more honest when speaking to outpatients.
[b]Comprised of competent, optimistic, and professional.
[c]Comprised of warm, not hostile, not dominant, empathic, and liking.
*$p < .05$
**$p < .01$

anxious when talking to inpatients than when talking to outpatients. Indeed, it is possible significantly to predict to the future, postdict to the past, or paridict to the current situation, the patient's status by examining only the first 10 seconds of the therapist's tone of voice for the nonverbal dimension of anxiety. Overall, anxiety in the therapist's tone of voice when talking to patients seems to be the most effective predictor of patient status, with the therapist's tone of voice displaying more anxiety when talking to inpatients than when talking to outpatients. We find it remarkable that a 10-second clip of therapists' content-filtered speech can so increase the accuracy of prediction (or postdiction, or paridiction) of the type of patient to whom the therapist is speaking. (For example, a correlation of .20 is equivalent to increasing the accuracy of prediction from 40% to 60%; for a fuller discussion see Rosenthal and Rubin, 1982.) Clearly, important aspects of the therapeutic situation can be inferred from ultra-brief samples of therapists' tone of voice.

Table 5.8 shows the relationship between therapist tone of voice when speaking to patients and therapist sex. Here we wanted to learn whether therapist sex could be inferred from the therapist's tone of voice in speaking to patients for just 10 seconds. As Table 5.8 clearly shows, female therapists' tone of voice in speaking to patients was rated as less professional and competent (Blanck, Rosenthal, & Cordell, in press; Krasner, Snodgrass, & Rosenthal, 1983; but see also Steckler & Rosenthal, 1985). In addition, female therapists' tone of voice was rated as significantly warmer, more anxious, and more honest when talking to patients than

Table 5.8   Relationship Between Therapist Tone of Voice and Therapist Sex[a]: Speaking To Patients

	Phases			
Variables	Beginning (10 seconds)	Middle (10 seconds)	End (10 seconds)	Total (30 seconds)
Professional-Competence[b]	−.15	−.13	−.29**	−.32**
Warmth[c]	.43***	.41***	.36***	.47***
Anxious	.24*	.01	.22*	.20*
Honest	.16	.19	.13	.24*

[a] A positive correlation means that tone of voice was more professional-competent, warmer, more anxious, and more honest when female therapists were speaking to patients.
[b] Comprised of competent, optimistic, and professional.
[c] Comprised of warm, not hostile, not dominant, empathic, and liking.
*p < .05
**p < .01
***p < .001

was male therapists' tone of voice. Consistent with a socialization hypothesis of the development of sex differences in nonverbal communication skills and styles (Blanck & Rosenthal, 1982; Blanck, Rosenthal, Snodgrass, DePaulo, & Zuckerman, 1981, 1982; Hall, 1979), these results suggest that therapists' tone of voice in talking to patients may be consistent with traditional sex-role standards. It is important to note, however, that these results may be influenced by basic differences in pitch or tone of voice for males and females, and by a rating bias on the part of the judges who seemingly ascribed sex-appropriate characteristics to "female"-sounding voices (e.g., warmth) and to "male"-sounding voices (e.g., professional).

Finally, we examined how a therapist might nonverbally communicate (via tone of voice) expectations for patient outcome. This analysis investigated the role of tone of voice as a possible factor in the mediation of naturally occurring (rather than experimentally produced) interpersonal expectancy effects. Judges rated the therapists' tone of voice as significantly more professional-competent when talking to high versus low expectancy patients during the middle of the interviews ($r = .25$, $p < .05$ for the entire cluster and for its individual variables; $r = .20$, $p < .05$ for competence; $r = .25$, $p < .05$ for professional; and $r = .20$, $p < .05$ for optimistic. It appears, then, that a professional, competent quality in tone of voice may be an important mediator of interpersonal expectancy effects in the clinical context.

Predicting Therapist Tone of Voice When Talking About Patients

The correlations between therapist tone of voice when speaking about patients and inpatient versus outpatient status are presented in Table 5.9. As in the previous study, our aim was to investigate predicting or inferring patient status (inpatient versus outpatient status) from the therapist's tone of voice in speaking about patients from brief content-filtered clips. Several interesting results emerged. First, when talking about patients, therapists' tone of voice was rated (combining the results from the three segments) as significantly less hostile, less anxious, and less dominant when talking about outpatients than about inpatients. Consistently with the results of the previous study, therapists' tone of voice seems to be clearly implicated in the mediation of feelings and attitudes concerning patient status. Additionally, by examining the tone-of-voice dimensions of warm, not hostile, anxious, dominant, and optimistic we can predict (or postdict, or paridict) patient status from only the first 20 seconds of a

Table 5.9   Relationship Between Therapist Tone of Voice and Inpatient versus Outpatient Status[a]: Speaking About Patients

	Phases			
Variables	Beginning (20 seconds)	Middle (20 seconds)	End (20 seconds)	Total (60 seconds)
Professional-Competent[b]	.03	−.08	−.02	−.03
Warmth[c]	.16*	−.10	.05	.05
Not Hostile	.22***	.13*	.18**	.28***
Anxious	−.21**	−.20**	−.10	−.22***
Dominant	−.20**	−.23***	−.17*	−.25***
Optimistic	.16*	−.16*	−.04	−.02
Honest	.08	−.04	.02	.03

[a]A positive correlation means that tone of voice was more professional-competent, warmer, less hostile, more anxious, more dominant, more optimistic, and more honest when speaking about outpatients.
[b]Comprised of competent and professional.
[c]Comprised of warm, empathic, and liking.
*$p < .05$
**$p < .01$
***$p < .001$

Table 5.10   Relationship Between Therapist Tone of Voice and Therapist Sex[a]: Speaking About Patients

	Phases			
Variables	Beginning (20 seconds)	Middle (20 seconds)	End (20 seconds)	Total (60 seconds)
Professional-Competent[b]	−.22***	−.16*	−.26***	−.28***
Warmth[c]	.24***	.26***	.07	.25***
Not Hostile	.03	−.00	.09	.05
Anxious	.19**	.26***	.17*	.27***
Dominant	−.36***	−.31***	−.39***	−.43***
Optimistic	.07	−.03	−.09	−.02
Honest	.15*	.10	.06	.14*

[a]A positive correlation means that tone of voice was more professional-competent, warmer, less hostile, more anxious, more dominant, more optimistic, and more honest when female therapists were speaking about patients.
[b]Comprised of competent and professional.
[c]Comprised of warm, empathic, and liking.
*$p < .05$
**$p < .01$
***$p < .001$

therapist's discussion. Finally, it is interesting to note that anxiety in tone of voice can be useful in inferring patient status when therapists are talking both *to* and *about* their patients.

Table 5.10 displays the relationship between therapist tone of voice when speaking about patients and therapist sex. Consistently with the findings of the previous study, therapist sex can clearly be inferred from judges' ratings of the therapist's tone of voice in speaking about patients for 20-second clips. The results for speaking about patients parallel the earlier results of speaking to patients, suggesting that the sex-role standards discussed earlier may operate in both the interactive (speaking to) and the non-interactive (speaking about) context.

Finally, unlike the positive findings relating therapist expectancy to therapist tone of voice when speaking to patients, tone of voice when speaking about patients was not implicated in the mediation of interpersonal expectancy effects. As discussed in the next section, this result may be due to relatively less therapeutic involvement in talking about patients.

Discussion

In this study we examined therapists' tone of voice as a predictor of aspects of the psychotherapeutic process. In view of the extremely brief length of the interview segments (10- or 20-second clips) and the purely nonverbal nature of the segments (tone of voice only), the results are surprisingly striking and encourage further work employing ultra-brief segments of nonverbal behavior in psychotherapy process research.

Our interest was to examine the type of information that can be inferred or predicted from only therapists' tone of voice. In both the interactional context (talking to patients) and the non-interactional context (talking about patients), therapists' tone of voice was significantly related to patient status and therapist sex. These results are particularly encouraging in light of the orthogonality of our nonverbal variables as defined by the principal components factor analyses. That is, our relatively uncorrelated factor-based variables were independently able to account for a proportion of the unique variance in tone of voice from which we can infer patient status or therapist sex.

In talking to and talking about patients, therapists' tone of voice was rated as more anxious when dealing with inpatients than when dealing with outpatients. These results are consistent with a series of studies which suggest that there may be a tendency for individuals to "leak" or send their true underlying affects about other people in nonverbal channels, especially in tone of voice (Blanck & Rosenthal, 1982; Blanck,

Rosenthal, & Cordell, in press; Ekman & Friesen, 1969; Ekman, Friesen, & Scherer, 1976; Rosenthal & DePaulo, 1979a, 1979b; Zuckerman, DePaulo, & Rosenthal, 1981), as discussed in chapter 2. Interestingly, the results suggest that therapists' tone of voice was more likely to leak certain underlying feelings when talking about inpatients rather than when talking to inpatients. More specifically, when therapists talked about inpatients, their tone was rated as more hostile, more anxious, and more dominant. It may be that the interactional quality of talking to patients inhibits to some extent the "nonverbal leakage" processes. Most encouraging overall was that for a majority of the nonverbal dimensions, patients' status could be inferred from only 10 or 20 seconds of a therapist's tone of voice.[3]

The relationship between therapist tone of voice and therapist sex when talking to and about patients must be interpreted with some caution. Our results indicate that female therapists' tone of voice is generally rated as warmer, less dominant, less professional-competent, more anxious, and more honest than male therapists' tone of voice. Indeed, these results are consistent with the literature on sex differences in nonverbal communication skills and styles (for a review see Hall, 1978, 1979, 1984). Various explanations for these sex differences in nonverbal skills have been set forth and have ranged from socioemotional hypotheses (e.g., differing levels of empathy in males and females or sex differences in adaptation to asymmetrical social power) to biological hypotheses (e.g., hemispheric differences between males and females). Despite the consistency of our findings with previous work, it is important to point out that our findings could be confounded by the sex role socialization of our judges (i.e., when a female tone of voice is recognized, certain "feminine" voice qualities are ascribed, and the reverse for a "male" sounding voice), or by fundamental differences in the pitch of male and female voices. The nature of sex differences in tone of voice, and what can generally be inferred from male and female voices, requires further attention.

The specific type of information about the therapeutic interaction that can be inferred from the nonverbal and verbal behavior of the therapist and the patient remains an interesting subject for future research. The next step will be to apply the resulting understanding to therapist selection and training techniques, patient therapy programs, and perhaps even, as Gomes-Schwartz (1978) has suggested, to the "matching" of optimal therapist-patient pairs. We believe that it is possible to study the outcomes of "nonverbally matched" therapists and patients (e.g., pairing a good receiving therapist with a poor sending patient) and that the similarity and complementarity of the nonverbal and verbal communication styles and skills of dyads may dramatically influence social outcomes

(Blanck & Rosenthal, 1981; Blanck & Rosenthal, 1982; Blanck, Rosenthal, & Cordell, in press; Blanck, Zuckerman, DePaulo, & Rosenthal, 1980; Rosenthal, et al., 1979).

ANALYSIS 4—THERAPISTS' COMPETENCY AND THERAPISTS' TONE OF VOICE

Background

Babad, Inbar, and Rosenthal (1982a, 1982b) and Blanck and Rosenthal (1984) have shown the relevance of individual difference variables to an understanding of the effects of interpersonal expectancies. Blanck and Rosenthal (1984), for example, demonstrated that differential expectancy effects were a function of individual competencies, as operationalized by indices of experts' ratings of counselor competence and interpersonal skill. Specifically, less competent and less effective counselors were more prone to biasing effects, talking more negatively about campers of perceived low potential and more positively (i.e., more warmly) about campers of perceived high potential. More competent and interpersonally more effective counselors treated campers of perceived high and low potential more equally.

Therapists' Competency and Tone of Voice When Talking To Patients

We have seen that anxiety in therapists' tone of voice when talking to patients relates significantly to patient status. Anxiety in therapists' tone of voice when talking to patients also seems to be an effective predictor of therapist competence, as determined by supervisors' ratings (Blanck, Rosenthal, Vannicelli, & Lee, in press). Here our results demonstrate that therapists' tone of voice displayed significantly less anxiety when talking to patients when the therapist was rated as more competent by their supervisor ($r = -.22$, $p < .05$). Interestingly, more competently rated therapists also became less anxious in talking to patients over the course of the therapeutic interview (linear contrast for competence rating by interview phase interaction: $F(1,86) = 4.59$, $p < .04$, $r = .23$).

An even more interesting finding was that our general indication of overall therapeutic competence (i.e., supervisors' ratings) was significantly related to the professional-competent dimension in tone of voice when talking to patients. Specifically, in the beginning of the interview more competently rated therapists spoke more professionally and competently to patients ($r = .25$, $p < .05$). However, over the course of the entire therapeutic interview more competently rated therapists spoke less and less professionally and competently to patients compared to less competently rated therapists (linear contrast for competence rating by interview phase interaction: $F(1,86) = 3.86$, $p = .05$, $r = .21$), but spoke more and more warmly to patients compared to less competently rated therapists (linear contrast for competence rating by interview phase interaction: $F(1,86) = 6.00$, $p < .02$, $r = .26$).

Therapists' Competency and Tone of Voice When Talking About Patients

The correlations between therapists' tone of voice when talking about patients and supervisors' ratings of competence present a different picture. More competently rated therapists were less warm, less professional-competent, and less honest in tone of voice when talking about patients (for the warmth supervariable, especially during the middle of the interview, $r = -.23$, $p < .001$, and for the empathy component, in particular throughout the interview, $r = -.16$, $p < .05$; for the professional-competent supervariable, especially during the middle of the interview, $r = -.14$, $p < .05$; and for honest, especially during the middle of the interview, $r = -.16$, $p < .05$).

These results are obviously different from those obtained when the therapists' tone of voice was analyzed in talking *to* patients. However, it is important to consider that the supervisors' ratings of competence largely reflected a specific "interactional" therapeutic competency that would be expected to relate more closely to nonverbal qualities of the therapists' tone of voice in the interactive context (speaking to patients) than in the noninteractive context (speaking about patients). Alternatively, it could be that the more competent therapists felt less need to "act" in a professionally appropriate way and were more relaxed when talking to the interviewer about their patients—whereas less competent therapists were more likely to worry about seeming to exhibit a professionally appropriate manner even in this context.

Discussion

The most compelling conclusions to be drawn from the present findings are that supervisors' ratings of therapists' interactional competence significantly predict therapists' tone of voice in talking to and about patients. Again, in view of the extremely brief length of the voice segments, the purely nonverbal nature of the segments, and the relative orthogonality of our nonverbal variables as defined by factor analysis of the principal components, the results are surprisingly encouraging.

While these results extend earlier research on the relationship between interpersonal competence, susceptibility to biasing information, and the process of nonverbal communication, they do not specifically replicate earlier findings demonstrating that more competent counselors showed smaller differential expectancy effects, as reflected in their tone of voice, than did less competent counselors (Blanck & Rosenthal, 1984).

More generally, the present findings may have considerable importance for increasing understanding of how to assess specific therapeutic competencies in talking to and about patients across the phases of the interview process. Future research might suggest the value to clinical supervisors of systematically assessing the tone of voice in which student clinicians, supervisees, or applicants for training speak to and about their patients.

ANALYSIS 5—TRANS-SITUATIONAL ASPECTS: THE DEGREE TO WHICH TALKING ABOUT PATIENTS SIMULATES (OR DISSIMULATES) TALKING TO PATIENTS

Background

In the final stage of our studies on the therapist's tone of voice we addressed the important question of the degree to which talking *about* people simulates (or dissimulates) talking *to* those same people (Rosenthal, Blanck, & Vannicelli, 1984). We employed three types of analyses: (a) simple correlations, (b) multiple regressions, and (c) canonical correlation.

Simple Correlations

For our first analysis we correlated each of the 10 variables that had been rated by judges while therapists talked to patients with each of the corresponding 10 variables that had been rated by judges while therapists talked about patients. The first column of correlations of Table 5.11 shows the results of this analysis. All of the correlations were positive, most were significant at $p < .05$ and half were significant at $p < .01$. The median effect size (r) of .236 was also significant at $p < .01$ and was equivalent in practical magnitude to increasing the accuracy of prediction from 38% to 62% by means of the binomial effect size display (BESD; Rosenthal & Rubin, 1982). These correlations provide strong evidence for the hypothesis that therapists' tone of voice in talking about patients can be used to predict significantly, and with practical benefit, the tone of voice therapists are likely to employ in talking to patients. This finding is remarkable when we recall that the total length of the speech sample of talking to patients was only 30 seconds and that of talking about patients was only 60 seconds. Furthermore, the speech samples of therapists talking to patients were rated by a diffferent group of 12 judges than were those of talking about patients.

Table 5.11   Predicting Therapist Tone of Voice While Talking To 98 Patients from Therapist Tone of Voice While Talking About Same 98 Patients: Simple Correlations

Nonverbal Variable	Correlation With Predictor Variable	Median Correlation With Nonpredictor Variables	Difference
Warm	.311***	.127	.184
Hostile	.094	.079	.015
Anxious	.083	.066	.017
Dominant	.270***	.008	.262
Empathic	.225*	.052	.173
Competent	.253**	.045	.208
Optimistic	.276***	.137	.139
Professional	.248**	.003	.245
Honest	.048	.175	−.127
Liking	.154	.020	.134
Median	.236**	.059	[a]

[a]The difference between the medians is .177; the median of the 10 differences is .156.
*$p \leq .025$ one-tailed
**$p \leq .01$ one-tailed
***$p \leq .005$ one-tailed

In addition to the predictive validities, we wanted to investigate the differential or discriminant validities of our predictor variables. For example, suppose that warmth while talking to a patient not only correlated .311 with warmth while talking about a patient but also that warmth while talking to a patient correlated approximately .311 with hostility, anxiety, dominance, etc., while talking about the patient. The predictive validity of warmth while talking about a patient would not thereby be impugned, but the differential or discriminant validity would be. Accordingly, for each criterion variable, we computed correlations with the nine nonpredictor variables that should *not* have predicted the criterion variable very well. For example, for the criterion variable warm (while talking to patients), we computed its correlations with hostile, anxious, dominant, etc., (while talking about patients). If there is differential or discriminant validity, these correlations, on the average, will be lower than the specifically predictive correlations. The second column of correlations in Table 5.11 shows the median correlation of these "nonpredictive" variables with the criterion variable. None of these median correlations was significant; their median value was only .059; and only one of these, that for the criterion variable of honest (while talking to), was larger than the corresponding predictive correlation. This finding adds substantial construct validity to the predictive validity we have established.

Multiple Regressions

After establishing the basic predictive and discriminant validity of therapists' nonverbal behaviors while talking about patients as predictors of nonverbal behaviors while talking to patients, we checked our findings by employing multiple regression rather than just simple correlation. Since it seemed unnecessarily cumbersome to check 10 predictors against 10 dependent variables, we employed as our dependent variables the four supervariables based on our principal components analysis of the "talking to" segments. The supervariable of professional-competence was made up of the mean of the variables competent, optimistic, and professional. The supervariable of warmth was made up of the mean of the variables warm, not hostile, not dominant, empathic, and liking. The remaining two variables (anxious and honest) stood alone. We employed as our predictor variables the seven supervariables based on our principal components analysis of the "talking about" segments. The supervariable of professional-competent was made up of the mean of those two variables (professional, competent). The supervariable of warmth was made up of the mean of the variables warm, empathic, and liking. The remaining five variables (not hostile, anxious, dominant, optimistic, and honest) stood alone. These seven variables were employed as the predictor battery for each of the four dependent variables, in turn.

Table 5.12 shows the results of the regression analysis. Two variables significantly predicted professional-competence in therapists' tone of voice in talking to their patients: talking about them in a dominant and an

Table 5.12   Predicting Therapist Tone of Voice While Talking To 98 Patients from Therapist Tone of Voice While Talking About Same 98 Patients: Multiple Regression

Predictor Variable	Unique Variance	$t(95)$	p	effect size (r)[a]	Multiple R
Predicting Professional Competence					
Dominant	.074	2.85	.006	.281	
Optimistic	.036	1.99	.050	.200	.356*

$^*F(2,95) = 6.89, p = .002.$

Predictor Variable	Unique Variance	$t(94)$	p	effect size (r)[a]	Multiple R
Predicting Warmth					
Dominant	.098	−3.35	.002	−.327	
Anxious	.091	3.23	.002	.316	
Warm[b]	.042	2.19	.032	.220	.425*

$^*F(3,94) = 6.92, p < .001.$

Predictor Variable	Unique Variance	$t(95)$	p	effect size (r)[a]	Multiple R
Predicting Anxiety					
Honest	.041	2.01	.048	.202	
Not Hostile	.026	−1.60	.113	−.162	.211*

$^*F(2,95) = 2.20, p = .116.$

Predictor Variable	Unique Variance	$t(94)$	p	effect size (r)[a]	Multiple R
Predicting Honesty					
Warm[b]	.125	3.74	.001	.360	
Honest	.045	−2.26	.027	−.227	
Anxious	.042	2.16	.034	.217	.404*

$^*F(3,94) = 6.13, p < .001.$

[a]Computed as $\sqrt{\dfrac{t^2}{t^2 + df}}$

[b]Comprised of warm, empathic, and liking.

optimistic tone of voice. The multiple R was not only significant statistically ($p = .002$) but substantial in magnitude as well (.356; see Rosenthal & Rubin, 1982).

The supervariable warmth while talking to patients was significantly predicted by the variables of speaking about the patients in a tone of voice that was not dominant, but anxious, and warm. The last of these predictors, warm, was a supervariable comprised of the variables warm, empathic, and liking. The multiple R of .425 was significant at $p < .001$.

Anxiety in the therapist's tone of voice in talking to patients was not significantly predicted by any battery of predictor variables. Table 5.12 shows that honesty in talking about a patient was significantly related to anxiety while talking to patients only when hostility was also entered into the regression equation. The trend, though not significant, was for therapists' anxiety in talking to patients to be predicted from their talking about patients in an honest but hostile manner.

Honesty in the therapist's tone of voice in talking to patients was significantly predicted by a battery of three predictors: talking about their patients in a way that was warm, *not* honest, and anxious. The multiple R of .404 was significant at $p < .001$.

The results of the four multiple regressions showed that three of the four dependent supervariables describing therapists' tone of voice in talking to patients could be predicted significantly from knowing how therapists talked about patients as measured on five predictor variables— warmth, anxiety, dominance, optimism, and honesty. The remaining two predictor variables of hostility and professional-competence in talking about patients did not contribute significantly to the prediction of the four factor-based dependent variables.

Figure 5.1 summarizes the four regression equations graphically. The four dependent variables are shown in boxes, while the five significant predictors are shown on the perimeter of the diagram. This form of display of a set of multiple regression equations has the advantage that it not only shows for each dependent variable its successful predictors but also shows for each predictor the various dependent variables to which it makes a predictive contribution. The single substantive conclusion that seems clearest is that therapists who speak about their patients with warmth and anxiety (interpreted in this context as concern and caring) and not in a dominant manner are likely to treat their patients with warmth and honesty as judged from their tone of voice in speaking to their patients.

Additional, more tentative conclusions from Figure 5.1 are (a) that therapists speaking of patients in a dominant but optimistic manner tend to talk to those patients in a professionally competent manner, (b) that honesty in talking about a patient may be associated with anxiety in

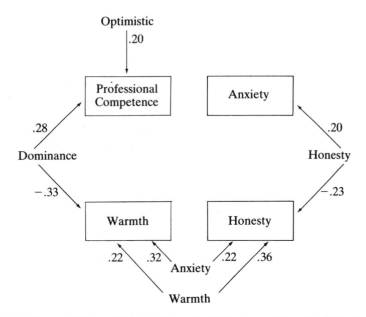

Fig. 5.1. Tone of Voice While Talking To 98 Patients (Four Variables) as Predicted from Tone of Voice While Talking About Same 98 Patients (Five Variables). *Note:* The four criterion variables are enclosed in boxes; the five predictor variables are arrayed around the perimeter.

talking to that patient, and (c) that honesty *after correction for any component of warmth* (see Table 5.2) may predict dishonesty in tone of voice while talking to patients. Honesty corrected for warmth may be akin to brutal frankness, a kind of "honesty" that may not be of therapeutic benefit.

Canonical Correlation

In our final analysis we examined the overall relationship between the same seven predictor variables and four criterion variables. The resulting canonical correlation R was .584, $p = .00022$, showing that the information in the predictor set significantly predicted the information in the criterion set. Of the four canonical correlations that could be computed, only the first was significant.

Table 5.13 shows the loadings on the first canonical variate for the predictor and the criterion variables. The pattern of loadings on the predictor variables suggest that therapists scoring high on this canonical vari-

Table 5.13 Predicting Therapist Tone of Voice While Talking To 98 Patients from Therapist Tone of Voice While Talking About Same 98 Patients: Canonical Correlation

Predictor Variables		Criterion Variables	
Variables	Loadings	Variables	Loadings
Professional-Competent	.343	Professional-Competence	.392
Warm	−.427	Warm	−.719
Not Hostile	.081	Anxious	−.082
Anxious	−.490	Honest	−.516
Dominant	.490		
Optimistic	−.044		
Honest	−.131		

ate manifest a tone of voice in talking about patients that is cold, uncaring (unanxious), perhaps overly professional, and dominating—a pattern that appears "coldly autocratic." These "coldly autocratic" speakers about patients when speaking to patients are characterized by being cold, dishonest, and again, perhaps overly professional or "coldly professional." In short, therapists who speak of patients in a coldly autocratic way tend to speak to those patients in a coldly professional way.

The canonical correlation of .584 is the correlation between the canonical variates, not the original variables considered as sets. To obtain the correlation between the two sets of variables, an index called $\sqrt{\text{redundancy}}$ (Stewart & Love, 1968; Tucker & Chase, 1980) is computed. For the present data that correlation was .388 considering all four canonical variates and .284 considering only the first canonical variate. The magnitudes of relationship found in the present clinical context are quite comparable to those found in other clinical contexts such as psychotherapy outcome research (Smith & Glass, 1977; Smith, Glass, & Miller, 1980) and in other areas assessing the effects of nonverbal processes of social influence such as the effects of interpersonal expectations (Rosenthal, 1966; Rosenthal & Jacobson, 1968; Rosenthal & Rubin, 1978).

CONCLUSION

In this chapter we first summarized our research program on the therapist's tone of voice, including our long-term goals: (1) to further understanding of the social psychology of unintentional interpersonal influence in social interaction; (2) to further understanding of the role of nonverbal *and* verbal cue communication in general and in the clinical context in particular (Blanck, Rosenthal, Vannicelli, & Yerrell, 1985); and (3) to further understanding of the implications for research methodology, clinical practice, and social relations of the operation of nonverbal communication in the clinical context.

We next described our research strategy and research design, presenting a systematic approach for studying nonverbal communication in the clinical context. We showed, for example, how content-filtered speech samples can be employed by clinical researchers, and suggested some of the nonverbal dimensions which may tap the expression and communication of emotion in tone of voice.

Finally, we discussed a series of studies aimed at the systematic investigation of therapists' tone of voice. The first study was designed to delineate and describe the major dimensions in therapists' tone of voice. The factor structures for studying therapists talking to patients and talking about patients were conceptually quite similar. Each factor solution provided information concerning the dimensions of basic interpersonal styles of therapists (expressed via tone of voice) in relating to patients and in talking about them. In the second study we documented the reliability, validity, and consistency of using ultra-brief segments (10–60 seconds) of the therapeutic process for rating purely nonverbally communicated cues in a therapist's tone of voice. Here we saw that the stylistic variables associated with therapists' clinical interactions can be reliably measured from very brief segments, and that these stylistic variables can be equivalently assessed from different phases of the therapeutic interview. Next we examined therapists' tone of voice as a predictor of aspects of the psychotherapeutic process. In both the interactional context and the non-interactional context, the brief clips of the therapists' tone of voice were significantly related to patient status and therapist sex. We then examined how specific therapeutic competencies affect how therapists talk to and about their patients. For example, therapists rated as more competent by their supervisors were less anxious in talking to patients. Finally, we provided data on the degree to which therapists' talking about patients simulates talking to those same patients. Examination of the resulting correlations showed that, for example, therapists who talked *about* patients in a coldly autocratic manner (expressed via tone of voice) talked *to* those same patients in a coldly professional manner.

The research described in this chapter is part of a larger program of research aimed at understanding the social psychology of interpersonal behavior and social communication. Our future interests include a more detailed understanding of the types of communicative process variables (both verbal and nonverbal) employed by different schools of therapists with patients of varying types and degrees of disturbance; for examples see chapter 6. We also are studying how "judicial bias," or unfairness by a trial judge during an actual trial, can be manifested in both explicit as well as subtle verbal and nonverbal cues, and how these cues can affect the due process rights of defendants (Blanck, Rosenthal, & Cordell, in press). Most importantly, in all these studies we hope to begin to understand the role of nonverbal and verbal communication in ongoing social interaction and in the clinical context.

ACKNOWLEDGMENT

This research was supported in part by the National Science Foundation. Requests for reprints should be sent to Peter David Blanck, Department of Psychology and Social Relations, Harvard University, William James Hall, 33 Kirkland Street, Cambridge, MA 02138.

NOTES

1. For one of the 20-second clips of the therapists speaking about patients (beginning), a 40-second clip was inadvertently substituted. This 40-second clip was comprised of the therapist speaking of two different outpatients (a male and a female patient), both in the low expectancy condition. However, patient sex was not significantly predicted by any of our nonverbal variables.

2. Our research on the nonverbal qualities of children's tone of voice and of the executive's tone of voice interestingly parallel the factor structure of the therapist's tone of voice. The factor solution for the children's tone of voice (7–9 years old) yielded three major dimensions after rotation: warmth, dominance, and control (Blanck & Rosenthal, 1985a). The solution for the executive's tone of voice also yielded three major dimensions: warmth, dominance, and expressiveness (Blanck & Rosenthal, 1985b). These solutions provide further information confirming the individual's general nonverbal style, expressed via tone of voice, in relating to others.

3. Because there was a significant relationship between level of therapist training and seeing outpatients rather than inpatients ($r's$ = .43 and .36 for speaking to and speaking about, respectively), we also computed partial correlations removing the effects of therapist training from the significant relationships between patient status and therapist tone of voice. The median change in the absolute value of these $r's$ was only from .26 to .25, so that therapist level of training was not a plausible explanation of the obtained significant relationships.

REFERENCES

Abelson, R. P., & Sermat, V. (1962). Multidimensional scaling of facial expressions. *Journal of Experimental Psychology, 63*, 546–54.

Argyle, M. (1975). *Bodily communication.* New York: International Universities Press.

Babad, E. Y., Inbar, J., & Rosenthal, R. (1982a). Teachers' judgment of students' potential as a function of teachers' susceptibility to biasing information. *Journal of Personality and Social Psychology, 42*, 541–47.

Babad, E. Y., Inbar, J., & Rosenthal, R. (1982b). Pygmalion, Galatea, and the Golem: Investigations of biased and unbiased teachers. *Journal of Educational Psychology, 74*, 459–74.

Bachrach, H., Curtis, H., Escoll, P., Graff, H., Huxster, H., Ottenberg, P. & Pulver, S. (1981). Units of observation and perspectives on the psychoanalytic process. *British Journal of Medical Psychology, 54*, 25–33.

Bateson, G., Jackson, D. D., Haley, J., & Weakland, J. (1956). Toward a theory of schizophrenia. *Behavioral Science, 1*, 251–64.

Bergin, A. (1966). Some implications of psychotherapy research for therapeutic practice. *Journal of Abnormal Psychology, 71*, 235–46.

Blanck, P. D., & Rosenthal, R. (1981). Nonverbal styles and skills in best-friend relationships. Presentation at the meeting of the New England Psychological Association Convention, Brandeis University.

Blanck, P. D., & Rosenthal, R. (1982). Developing strategies for decoding "leaky" messages: On learning how and when to decode discrepant and consistent social communications. In R. S. Feldman (Ed.), *Development of nonverbal behavior in children.* New York: Springer-Verlag.

Blanck, P. D., & Rosenthal, R. (1984). The mediation of interpersonal expectancy effects: The counselor's tone of voice. *Journal of Educational Psychology, 76*, 418–26.

Blanck, P. D. & Rosenthal, R. (1985a). Children's tone of voice. Unpublished data, Harvard University.

Blanck, P. D. & Rosenthal, R. (1985b). The executive's tone of voice. Unpublished data, Harvard University.

Blanck, P. D., Rosenthal, R., & Cordell, L. H. (in press). Judges' verbal and nonverbal behavior in criminal jury trials. *Stanford Law Review, 38*, 89–164.

Blanck, P. D., Rosenthal, R., Snodgrass, S. E., DePaulo, B. M., & Zuckerman, M. (1981). Sex differences in eavesdropping on nonverbal cues: Developmental changes. *Journal of Personality and Social Psychology, 41*, 391–96.

Blanck, P. D., Rosenthal, R., Snodgrass, S. E., DePaulo, B. M., & Zuckerman, M. (1982). Longitudinal and cross-sectional age effects in nonverbal decoding skill and style. *Developmental Psychology, 18*, 491–98.

Blanck, P. D. Rosenthal, R., Vannicelli, M., & Lee, T. D. (in press). Therapists' tone of voice: Descriptive, psychometric, interactional, and competence analyses. *Journal of Social and Clinical Psychology.*

Blanck, P. D., Rosenthal, R., Vannicelli, M., & Yerrell, P. (1985). Verbal and nonverbal aspects of the therapist's voice: Preliminary findings. Manuscript in preparation.

Blanck, P. D., & Turner, A. N. (in press). Gestalt research: Clinical field research approaches to studying organizations. In J. Lorsch (Ed.), *The handbook of organizational behavior.* New York: Prentice-Hall.

Blanck, P. D., Zuckerman, M., DePaulo, B. M., & Rosenthal, R. (1980). Sibling resemblances in nonverbal skill and style. *Journal of Nonverbal Behavior, 4*, 219–26.

Blanck, R. H. (1985). Doctor-patient relationship: The importance of history taking. *M.S. Newsletter*, April.

Caporael, L. R., Lukaszewski, M. P., & Culbertson, G. H. (1983). Secondary baby talk: Judgments by institutionalized elderly and their caregivers. *Journal of Personality and Social Psychology, 44*(4), 746–54.

Dawes, R. M., & Dramer, E. (1966). A proximity analysis of vocally expressed emotion. *Perceptual and Motor Skills, 22,* 571–74.

Duncan, S., Jr., Rice, L. N., & Butler, J. M. (1968). Therapists' paralanguage in peak and poor psychotherapy hours. *Journal of Abnormal Psychology, 73*(6), 566–70.

Ekman, P., & Friesen, W. V. (1969). Nonverbal leakage and clues to deception. *Psychiatry, 32,* 88–106.

Ekman, P., Friesen, W. V., & Scherer, K. R. (1976). Body movement and voice pitch in deceptive interaction. *Semiotica, 16,* 23–27.

Frijda, N. H., & Philipszoon, E. (1963). Dimensions of recognition of expression. *Journal of Abnormal and Social Psychology, 66,* 45–51.

Gomes-Schwartz, B. (1978). Effective ingredients in psychotherapy: Prediction of outcome from process variables. *Journal of Consulting and Clinical Psychology, 46,* 1023–35.

Gomes-Schwartz, B., & Schwartz, J. M. (1978). Psychotherapy process variables: Distinguishing the "inherently helpful" person from the professional psychotherapist. *Journal of Clinical and Consulting Psychology, 46,* 196–97.

Green, C. R., DePaulo, B. M., & Rosenthal, R. (1981). On decoding noisy talk about women. Presentation at the meeting of the American Psychological Convention, Los Angeles.

Gurman, A. S. (1973). Instability of therapeutic conditions in psychotherapy. *Journal of Counseling Psychology, 20*(1), 16–24.

Hall, J. A. (1978). Gender effects in decoding nonverbal cues. *Psychological Bulletin, 85,* 845–57.

Hall, J. A. (1979). Gender, gender roles, and nonverbal communication skills. In R. Rosenthal (Ed.) *Skill in nonverbal communication: Individual differences.* Cambridge, MA: Oelgeschlager, Gunn & Hain.

Hall, J. A. (1984). *Nonverbal sex differences.* Baltimore: Johns Hopkins Univ. Press.

Karl, N. J., & Abeles, N. (1969). Psychotherapy process as a function of the time segment sampled. *Journal of Consulting and Clinical Psychology, 33*(2), 207–12.

Krasner, S. Q., Snodgrass, S. E., & Rosenthal, R. (1983). Is the executive woman an oxymoron?: Tone of voice and the evaluation of executive competence. Manuscript submitted for publication.

Masling, J., O'Neil, R., & Katkin, E. S. (1982). Autonomic arousal, interpersonal climate, and orality. *Journal of Personality and Social Psychology, 42,* 529–34.

Mehrabian, A. (1970). A semantic space for nonverbal behavior. *Journal of Consulting and Clinical Psychology, 35,* 248–57.

Milmoe, S., Rosenthal, R., Blane, H. T., Chafetz, M. E., & Wolf, I. (1967). The doctor's voice: Postdictor of successful referral of alcoholic patients. *Journal of Abnormal Psychology, 72,* 78–84.

Mintz, J., & Luborsky, L. (1971). Segments versus whole sessions: Which is the better unit for psychotherapy process research? *Journal of Abnormal Psychology, 78*(2), 180–91.

Mintz, J., Luborsky, L., & Auerbach, A. H. (1971). Dimensions of psychotherapy: A factor-analytic study of ratings of psychotherapy sessions. *Journal of Consulting and Clinical Psychology, 36* (1), 106–20.

Orlinsky, D. E., & Howard, K. I. (1978). The relation of process to outcome in psychotherapy. In S. L. Garfield & A. E. Bergin (Eds.), *Handbook of psychotherapy and behavior change,* 2nd ed. New York: Wiley.

Osgood, C. E. (1966). Dimensionality of the semantic space for communication via facial expressions. *Scandinavian Journal of Psychology, 7,* 1–30.

Osgood, C. E., Suci, G. J., & Tannenbaum, P. H. (1957). *The measurement of meaning.* Urbana: University of Illinois Press.

Parloff, M. B., Waskow, I. E., & Wolfe, B. E. (1978). Research on therapist variables in relationship to process and outcome. In S. L. Garfield & A. E. Bergin (Eds.), *Handbook of psychotherapy and behavior change,* 2nd ed. New York: Wiley.

Pittenger, R. E., Hockett, C. F., & Danehy, J. J. (1960). *The first five minutes.* Ithaca: Matineau Press.

Pope, B. (1978). Research on therapeutic style. In A. S. Gurman & A. M. Razin (Eds.), *Effective psychotherapy: A handbook of research.* New York: Pergamon Press.

Rice, L. N. (1965). Therapist's style of participation and case outcome. *Journal of Consulting Psychology, 29,* 155–60.

Rice, L. N., & Wagstaff, A. K. (1967). Client voice quality and expressive style as indexes of productive psychotherapy. *Journal of Consulting Psychology, 31,* 557–63.

Rogers, C. (1942). *Counseling and psychotherapy.* Boston: Houghton-Mifflin.

Rogers, C. (1957). The necessary and sufficient conditions of therapeutic personality change. *Journal of Consulting Psychology, 21,* 95–103.

Rogers, C., Gendlin, E., Kiesler, D., & Truax, C. (Eds.) (1967). *The therapeutic relationship and its impact: A study of psychotherapy with schizophrenics.* Madison: University of Wisconsin Press.

Rogers, P. L., Scherer, K. R., & Rosenthal, R. (1971). Content-filtering human speech. *Behavioral Research Methods and Instrumentation, 3,* 16–18.

Rosenthal, R. (1969). Interpersonal expectations. In R. Rosenthal & R. L. Rosnow (Eds.), *Artifact in behavioral research.* New York: Academic Press.

Rosenthal, R. (1974). *On the social psychology of the self-fulfilling prophecy.* New York: MSS Modular Publication, Mod. 53.

Rosenthal, R. (1976). *Experimenter effects in behavioral research* (enl. ed.). New York: Irvington.

Rosenthal, R. (1981). Pavlov's mice, Pfungst's horse, and Pygmalion's PONS: Some models for the study of interpersonal expectancy effects. In T. A. Sebeok and R. Rosenthal (Eds.), *The Clever Hans phenomenon.* Annals of the New York Academy of Sciences, No. 364.

Rosenthal, R. (1982). Conducting judgment studies. In K. R. Scherer & P. Edman (Eds.), *Handbook of methods in nonverbal behavior research.* New York: Cambridge University Press.

Rosenthal, R. (in press). Nonverbal cues in the mediation of interpersonal expectancy effects. In A. W. Siegman & S. Feldstein (Eds.), *Nonverbal communication.* Hillsdale, N.J.: Lawrence Erlbaum Associates.

Rosenthal, R., Blanck, P. D., & Vannicelli, M. (1984). Speaking to and about patients: Predicting therapists' tone of voice. *Journal of Clinical and Consulting Psychology, 52,* 679–86.

Rosenthal, R., & DePaulo, B. M. (1979a). Sex differences in accommodation in nonverbal communication. In R. Rosenthal (Ed.), *Skill in nonverbal communication: Individual differences.* Cambridge, MA: Oelgeschlager, Gunn & Hain.

Rosenthal, R., & DePaulo, B. M. (1979b). Sex differences in eavesdropping on nonverbal cues. *Journal of Personality and Social Psychology, 37,* 273–85.

Rosenthal, R., Hall, J. A., DiMatteo, M. R., Rogers, P. L., & Archer, D. (1979). *Sensitivity to nonverbal communication: The PONS test.* Baltimore: The Johns Hopkins University Press.

Rosenthal, R., & Rubin, D. B. (1982). A simple, general purpose display of magnitude of experimental effect. *Journal of Educational Psychology, 74,* 166–69.

Schaffer, N. D. (1982). Multidimensional measures of therapist behavior as predictors of outcome. *Psychological Bulletin, 92,* 670–81.

Scherer, K. R. (1974). Acoustic concomitants of emotional dimensions: Judging affect from synthesized tone sequences. In S. Weitz (Ed.), *Nonverbal communication.* New York: Oxford University Press. (Also 2nd edition, 1979).

Scherer, K. R. (1982). Methods of research on vocal communication: Paradigms and parameters. In K. R. Scherer & P. Ekman (Eds.), *Handbook of methods in nonverbal behavior research.* New York: Cambridge University Press.

Smith. M. L., & Glass, G. V (1977). Meta-analysis of psychotherapy outcome studies. *American Psychologist, 32,* 752–60.

Smith, M. L., Glass, G. V, & Miller, T. I. (1980). *The benefits of psychotherapy.* Baltimore: The Johns Hopkins University Press.

Snyder, W. V. (1946). "Warmth" in nondirective counseling. *Journal of Abnormal and Social Psychology, 41*(4), 491–95.

Steckler, N., & Rosenthal, R. (1985). Sex differences in nonverbal and verbal communication with bosses, peers, and subordinates. *Journal of Applied Psychology, 70*(1), 157–63.

Stewart, D., & Love, W. (1968). A general canonical correlation index. *Psychological Bulletin, 70,* 160–63.

Sweeny, D. R., Tinling, D. C., & Schmale, A. H., Jr. (1970). Dimensions of affective expression in four expensive modes. *Behavioral Science, 15,* 393–407.

Truax, C. (1963). Effective ingredients in psychotherapy: An approach to unraveling the patient-therapist interaction. *Journal of Counseling Psychology, 10,* 256–63.

Truax, C. B., & Carkhuff, R. R. (1967). *Toward effective counseling and psychotherapy: Training and practice.* Chicago: Aldine.

Tucker, R. K., & Chase, L. J. (1980). Canonical correlation. In P. R. Monge & J. N. Capella (Eds.), *Multivariate techniques in human communication research.* New York: Academic Press.

Williams, F., & Tolch, J. (1965). Communication by facial expression. *Journal of Communication, 15,* 17–27.

Wish, M., Deutsch, M., & Kaplan, S. J. (1976). Perceived dimensions of interpersonal relations. *Journal of Personality and Social Psychology, 33,* 409–20.

Zuckerman, M., DePaulo, B. M., & Rosenthal, R. (1981). Verbal and nonverbal communication of deception. In L. Berkowitz (Ed.), *Advances in experimental social psychology,* Vol. 14. New York: Academic Press.

6 Nonverbal Cues, the Type A Behavior Pattern, and Coronary Heart Disease

Judith A. Hall, Howard S. Friedman, and Monica J. Harris

An observable pattern of behavior, characteristic of modern lifestyles, is linked to heart disease. If we think about a highly stressed business executive who talks fast, interrupts and hurries his colleagues in conversations, barks at his secretary, gulps down lunch while shifting restlessly in his seat, and often clenches his teeth and shakes his fist, most of us would not be surprised to hear that this person is likely to have a heart attack. This observable style of behaving has been termed the "Type A behavior pattern" or TABP, and has indeed been shown to predict coronary heart disease.

As is apparent in the description above, the construct of Type A behavior is intimately connected with nonverbal cues. The nonverbal expressive style of an extremely Type A individual can be noticed by even a casual observer. Although there has been speculation for over 100 years about the possibility of a link between an intense, emotional style of living and the development of heart disease, programmatic research on this topic did not begin until the 1950s (M. Friedman & Rosenman, 1959). Cardiologists Meyer Friedman and Ray H. Rosenman pioneered the empirical assessment of TABP as a consequence of their extensive clinical experience with heart patients. In 1974, in their important book *Type A Behavior and Your Heart,* they outlined not only their definition of TABP but also some of the clues that alerted them to TABP in the first place. One such clue came when an upholsterer noted that the chairs in their reception room were worn in an unusual way: only at the front edge. What this implied about the heart patients who occupied those chairs—that they were tense, alert, and impatient—became major elements in the definition of the Type A personality.

TABP has been conceived to be a constellation of attributes, most of which are overtly observable in everyday life, in stressful interviews, or in laboratory experiments. These attributes include time urgency, competitive drive, hostility (possibly denied), and a style of interpersonal interaction that consists, either explicitly or by implication, of a variety of nonverbal expressive behaviors. These nonverbal behaviors are generally considered to reflect and embody the alertness, vigor, impatience, and aggressiveness of the Type A individual. Their absence is the mark of the Type B individual. Type B individuals are less likely to develop heart disease.

The centrality of nonverbal behavior (NVB) in the diagnosis of TABP has been recognized from the start. In describing the Structured Inverview (SI), the chief method of TABP assessment, M. Friedman and his colleagues wrote:

> Our own method . . . has consisted primarily of a personal interview during which time a series of specially structured questions are asked, and the motor reactions and the quality of the voice of the interviewee also are observed as he responds to the questions asked of him. The assessment of the behavior pattern actually is determined far more by the stylistics in which the interviewee responds than by the content of his responses. [M. Friedman et al., 1969, p. 829]

The first goal of TABP research was to demonstrate the behavior pattern's association with coronary heart disease (CHD). Many prospective and retrospective studies have now related TABP to heart disease (heart attack, for example) or to associated factors such as hypertension. There is an indisputable connection (for a review of the TABP-CHD relationship, see Jenkins, 1975; Surwit et al., 1982). One prospective study, the Western Collaborative Group Study (Rosenman et al., 1975), led a review panel established by the National Heart, Lung and Blood Institute to conclude that Type A behavior is associated with an increased risk of clinically apparent coronary heart disease and that this increased risk is independent of that resulting from age, high blood pressure, and smoking (Cooper et al., 1981).

The second goal of TABP research has been, and still is, to specify more exactly what the TABP is and how it, or its components, might be causally related to heart disease. The multidimensional nature of the TABP construct is very evident in the many studies that have compared different assessment instruments. The two major instruments are the Structured Interview or SI (Rosenman, 1978), which results in a categorical diagnosis by the interviewer or by other observers, and the Jenkins Activity Survey or JAS (Jenkins et al., 1979), a self-administered paper-and-pencil instrument. Factor analyses have demonstrated three factors of the JAS: speed and impatience, hard drivingness, and job involvement. The SI and the JAS (as well as other analogous paper-and-pencil instruments) are only moderately associated with each other, at best (MacDougall et al., 1979; Matthews, 1982), and differ somewhat in the strength with which they predict health outcomes, though both the SI and JAS are generally considered to be valid predictors of heart disease (Jenkins, 1978; Jenkins et al., 1978). One important reason for the difference seems to be that nonverbal behavior is explicitly included as a diagnostic criterion in the SI but is not in the JAS (or is included only implicitly, as in items that inquire about the respondents' level of impatience).

All current writers seem to agree that TABP needs further specification. Chesney et al. (1980), for example, call the SI a "behavioral assessment in the rough." Various components and conceptualizations of TABP have recently been discussed in a review paper by Matthews (1982). One element of consensus is that the Type A net is cast too broadly. Matthews et al. (1982) write: "Whereas evidence consistently indicates that the Type B pattern is related to low incidence of heart disease, large numbers of persons who will not suffer from heart disease are falsely being classified as coronary-prone [i.e., Type A] by the interview" (p. 312).

GOALS OF THIS CHAPTER

Although the conceptual significance of nonverbal behavior (NVB) in TABP is universally recognized, the extent of empirical research on NVB's role is limited. The form that this research usually takes is to see if the diagnosis of Type A from the SI is, in fact, based to some extent on NVB. Our first goal in this chapter is to document both the claims that have been made about NVB and the available empirical evidence relating NVB to TABP and to heart disease and related physiological states. Our second goal is to describe our point of view on how investigators of TABP may be misidentifying which individuals are actually at risk. We would argue that the kinds of NVB used for diagnostic purposes are inadequately specified, and that some individuals who are actually healthy are falsely called coronary-prone because of superficial expressive similarities to truly coronary-prone individuals. Our third goal is to describe some of our own research on expressive style and TABP.

CLAIMS ABOUT NVB AND TABP

Writers on TABP, especially those with the greatest clinical experience, are not reluctant to describe the expressive style of the Type A person.[1] Table 6.1 contains a list of such descriptions. Rarely are such descriptions accompanied by references to empirical literature. In fact, much of the relevant empirical research was done *after* these descriptions were offered. It is important to note that we are not implying that the descriptions are false. They are based on extensive observation by serious investigators of TABP. But they are based largely on informal, or at least undocumented, observation and therefore represent, in our view, hypotheses to be tested. Of course, one must acknowledge that those who defined TABP in the first place have every right to state what behaviors are part of the definition. But it is still useful to separate definitional and informally observed attributes from attributes that have been empirically linked to the Type A diagnosis and to health outcomes.[2]

The theoreticians of TABP emphasize that characteristic behaviors of the Type A person emerge mainly under environmental challenge—for example, irritation is aroused by being kept waiting, hostility is aroused by interaction with another Type A individual. But perusal of Table 6.1, as well as the tone of various authors' statements, suggest that the characteristic behaviors are, to some extent at least, general traits of the Type A person. "Walks briskly," for example, does not sound exclusively like a response to environmental challenge, though certainly under stress the Type A person might walk even faster than usual. (If, of course, the Type A person perceives him/herself to be under *continual* environmental challenge, then the distinction becomes meaningless.) As the research summarized below shows, some behaviors said to be characteristic of the Type A person do, in fact, emerge in situations that are not obviously challenging or stressful.

EMPIRICAL RELATIONSHIP OF NVB AND TABP

What is actually known about the relationship of NVB to TABP? Table 6.2 summarizes the empirical literature. Several comments must be made about the studies and data presented. First, the basis on which Type A was diagnosed differs, and is indicated in the last column of the table. Second, the coding of NVB was not always done blind to the diagnosis of

Table 6.1   Nonverbal Behaviors Said to be Characteristic of Type A Individuals

Source	Behaviors
M. Friedman & Rosenman (1959)	excessively rapid body movements, tense facial and body musculature, explosive conversational intonations, hand or teeth clenching, excessive unconscious gesturing, general air of impatience
M. Friedman (1964)	desk-pounding, facial grimacing, "keyed up" body movements, no simple or flaccid movements, strong voice, various words unduly emphasized, attempts to hurry or condense speech of others
M. Friedman et al. (1969)	aggressive timbre in voice
M. Friedman & Rosenman (1974)	easily aroused hostility and irritation (especially when temporarily frustrated), accelerates ends of sentences, pounds fist into palm of other hand, corners of mouth jerk backwards spasmodically in tic-like way to expose teeth, grinds teeth
Rosenman (1978)	walks briskly, face is extraordinarily alert (eyes alive, quickly seeking to take in the situation at a glance), smile is a lateral extension and not an oval, laugh is rarely a "belly laugh," looks at others straight and unflinchingly, sits poised on edge of chair, rarely do hands hang limply with fingers widely spaced, never whines, rarely whispers, rarely pauses in middle of sentence, hostile face (especially eyes; never "wistful"), firm handshake, loud and/or vigorous voice, clipped speech, rapid speech, frequent interruptions of others' speech, frequent pointing of finger at other in emphasis, frequent sighing (especially when asked about work), frequent emphatic one-word responses
Jenkins (1975)	gestures with abrupt and assertive movements, posture and concentration show intense involvement, vigilant in expression and posture, looks ready to move, abrasive in trying to get own way, fails to register details of social environment or own impact on others, exudes bravado and self-confidence, staccato speech, speaks with certainty, explosive laughs, often acts out anger when telling about it, motorizes while seated, overflow of energy, quick tense smiles, uneven breathing
Price (1982, quoting M. Friedman, 1979)	rapid horizontal eyeball movements during ordinary conversaton, rapid eye blinking, knee jiggling or rapid tapping of fingers, clicks with tongue to front teeth while talking, hostile and jarring laugh

NOTE: The authors cited included more descriptions than are listed here. We chose not to repeat a description if it seemed completely redundant with earlier descriptions on list.

Type A (e.g., Matthews et al., 1982), though in the great majority of studies it was. Third, the NVB that was observed was not always elicited under challenge (e.g., Guggisberg et al., 1981), though in most cases it was, the challenge being either the SI itself or a stressful experimental task. Fourth, not all of the entries in Table 6.2 are independent; it is obvious that investigators often gave more than one A/B diagnostic instrument and often coded multiple variables for a single sample of subjects. Fifth, the correlations and *p*-values given in the table were not always provided in the original reports but were sometimes calculated by us on the basis of data provided in those reports. Sixth, some categories of NVB have many studies, while others have few. The most extensively studied categories pertain to speech behavior and the least studied pertain to facial behavior and nonverbal communication skills. This imbalance in what cues have been studied is most likely due to the ease with which audiotapes can be obtained, and the eagerness of investigators to replicate the strong results that emerged early for the voice channel. Indeed, some behaviors listed in Table 6.1 appear not to have been studied at all (e.g., tic-like smiles and brisk walk).

In Table 6.2, the overall median correlation within a behavior category is given whenever the variables included in the category are similar enough to warrant calculation of the median. In addition, separate median correlations are given for the SI and JAS whenever sufficient data were available.

On the basis of the work summarized in Table 6.2, it is possible to reach several conclusions. Most strongly related to Type A diagnosis are fast and/or accelerated speech, uneven speech rate, short speech latencies, loud and/or explosive voice, uneven loudness, hard or staccato voice, body movements suggesting restlessness, and cues suggesting energy, hostility, and annoyance. Also related, though to a weaker degree, are number of interruptions, repeated words, percussive sounds, and gross body movement. In addition, several variables that have not been extensively studied show encouraging results worthy of further study: alert look, amount of gaze, head nods, and poor nonverbal decoding skill. Finally, several variables that also have been infrequently studied show weak or inconclusive results but because of their theoretical interest seem also to deserve further research: hurrying the interviewer, backchanneling,[3] clipped words, sighs, laughter and type of smiles, clenched jaw, hand movements, strong handshake, and clenched fists.

As discussed earlier, raters and interviewers who diagnose people as Type A or B from SI-type situations are trained to look for certain kinds of NVB. It would therefore be surprising if such behaviors were not actually related to Type A diagnosis. At least one study (Bortner & Rosenman, 1967) found nonverbal signs to be not only related to Type A diagnosis but more strongly related than variables based on answer con-

Table 6.2   Nonverbal Correlates of Type A Behavior

Nonverbal Variables	r	p	Test
I. Voice			
A. Rate			
1. Fast speech and/or acceleration			
DeFrank, 1980 (rate)	.33	.003	JAS
Dembroski et al., 1978 (rapid			
and accelerating)	.71	.001	SI
H. Friedman et al., 1985 (rate)	−.03	n.s.	JAS
Guggisberg et al., 1981 (rate)	.14	n.s.	BPI
Hecker et al., 1981 (rate)	.24	.05	SI
Hecker et al., 1981 (accelerating)	.27	.05	SI
Heller, 1980 (rate)	.59	.0005	SI
Lovallo & Pishkin, 1980 (rate)	.17	n.s.	SI
Matthews et al., 1982 (sample 1)			
(rapid and accelerating)	.66	.01	SI
	.22	.01	JAS
Matthews et al., 1982 (sample 2)			
(rapid and accelerating)	.70	.01	SI
	.25	.01	JAS
Scherwitz et al., 1977 (rate)	.32	.007	SI
	?	n.s.	JAS
Schucker & Jacobs, 1977 (rate)	.40	.05	SI
Sparacino et al., 1979 (rate)	+	.05	SI
Median	.30		
SI Median	.40		
JAS Median	.24		
2. Uneven speech rate			
Guggisberg et al., 1981	.51	.002	BPI
Schucker & Jacobs, 1977	.38	.05	SI
Median	.44		
B. Latency			
1. Short latency			
Dembroski et al., 1978	.65	.001	SI
H. Friedman et al., 1985	−.05	n.s.	JAS
Guggisberg et al., 1981	−.33	.02	BPI
Howland & Siegman, 1982	.45	.01	SI
Matthews et al., 1982 (sample 1)	.67	.01	SI
Matthews et al., 1982 (sample 2)	.62	.01	SI
	.21	.01	JAS
Scherwitz et al., 1977	.14	.03	SI
	?	n.s.	JAS
Schucker & Jacobs, 1977	.29[a]	.05	SI
Sparacino et al., 1979	+	n.s.	SI
Median	.28		
SI Median	.54		
JAS Median	.08		
2. Interruptions			
H. Friedman et al., 1985	−.19	n.s.	JAS
Guggisberg et al., 1981	−.08	n.s.	BPI

Table 6.2 continued

Howland & Siegman, 1982	.09	n.s.	SI
Matthews & Angulo, 1980[b]	.16	.10	TR
Matthews et al., 1982 (sample 1)	.38	.01	SI
	.11	n.s.	JAS
Matthews et al., 1982 (sample 2)	.63	.01	SI
	.28	.01	JAS
Schucker & Jacobs, 1977	.21	.05	SI
Sparacino et al., 1979	+	.03	SI
Median	.16		
SI Median	.30		
JAS Median	.11		
C. Loudness			
1. Loud voice			
DeFrank, 1980	.19	.09	JAS
Guggisberg et al., 1981	.10	n.s.	BPI
Hecker et al., 1981	.27	.05	SI
Howland & Siegman, 1982	.25	.05	SI
Schucker & Jacobs, 1977	.56	.05	SI
Sparacino et al., 1979	+	.001	SI
Median	.25		
SI Median	.27		
JAS Median	.19		
2. Explosive words			
H. Friedman et al., 1985			
(number of loud words)	−.15	n.s.	JAS
Guggisberg et al., 1981	.46	.003	BPI
Hecker et al., 1981 (explosive			
start)	.31	.01	SI
Matthews et al., 1982 (sample 1)	.68	.01	SI
	.19	.05	JAS
Scherwitz et al., 1977 (emphasis)	.48	.0001	SI
	?	n.s.	JAS
Schucker & Jacobs, 1977	.43	.05	SI
Sparacino et al., 1979	+	.001	SI
Median	.43		
SI Median	.46		
JAS Median	.02		
3. Loud and explosive			
Dembroski et al., 1978	.68	.001	SI
M. Friedman et al., 1969	.52[c]	.001	SI
Matthews et al., 1982 (sample 2)	.76	.01	SI
	.31	.01	JAS
Median	.60		
SI Median	.68		
JAS Median	.31		
4. Uneven loudness			
Guggisberg et al., 1981	.38	.01	BPI
Hecker et al., 1981 (syllabic			
emphasis)	.50	.01	SI
Howland & Siegman, 1982	−.12	n.s.	SI
Median	.38		

Table 6.2   continued

D. Hurrying the Interviewer			
H. Friedman et al., 1985	.04	n.s.	JAS
Hecker et al., 1981	−.03	n.s.	SI
Median	.005		
E. Back Channeling			
Matthews et al., 1982 (sample 1)			
(affirmations during interviewer's			
speech)	.07	n.s.	SI
	−.02	n.s.	JAS
Sparacino et al., 1979 (mainly			
affirmations)	+	.02	SI
Median	.02		
F. Repeated Words			
Guggisberg et al., 1981	.10	n.s.	BPI
Schucker & Jacobs, 1977	.30	.05	SI
Sparacino et al., 1979 (stutters			
and repetitions)	+	.01	SI
Median	.20		
G. Percussive Sounds			
Hecker et al., 1981 (strident			
inhalation)	.10	n.s.	SI
Hecker et al., 1981 (tongue clicks			
or lip smacks)	.16	n.s.	SI
Matthews & Angulo, 1980 (tongue			
clicks)[b]	.19	.06	TR
Matthews et al., 1982 (sample 1)			
(tongue clicks)	.10	n.s.	SI
	.01	n.s.	JAS
Matthews et al., 1982 (sample 1)			
(hissing)	.20	.01	SI
Median	.13		
SI Median	.13		
JAS Median	.01		
H. Sighs			
Hecker et al., 1981	.08	n.s.	SI
Matthews & Angulo, 1980[b]	.28	.01	TR
Matthews et al., 1982 (sample 1)	.06	n.s.	SI
	.11	n.s.	JAS
Sparacino et al., 1979	?	n.s.	SI
Median	.10		
SI Median	.07		
JAS Median	.11		
I. Laughter			
Hecker et al., 1981 (forced laugh)	−.06	n.s.	SI
Sparacino et al., 1979	?	n.s.	SI
J. Voice Quality			
Hecker et al., 1981 (hard voice)	.39	.01	SI
Hecker et al., 1981 (staccato)	.21	.10	SI
Median	.30		
K. Filled Pauses			
H. Friedman et al., 1985	.03	n.s.	JAS
Sparacino et al., 1979	+	n.s.	SI

Table 6.2   continued

L. Other

H. Friedman et al., 1985 (speech disturbances other than filled pauses)	−.21	n.s.	JAS
Howland & Siegman, 1982 (pause duration)	−.09	n.s.	SI
Schucker & Jacobs, 1977 (clipped words)	.18	n.s.	SI

II. Body

A. Gross Body Movement

H. Friedman et al., 1985 (posture shifts)	.22	.09	JAS
H. Friedman et al., 1985 (leg movements)	.18	n.s.	JAS
Glass et al., 1974 (expt. 1) (tense and hyperactive)	.38	.09	JAS
Matthews & Angulo, 1980 (squirming)[b]	.24	.02	TR
Matthews & Angulo, 1980 (restlessness)[b]	.17	.08	TR
Matthews et al., 1982 (sample 1) (motor pace)	−.06	n.s.	SI
Matthews et al., 1982 (sample 1) (rhythmic movement of hands and feet)	.07	n.s.	SI
Median	.18		
SI Median	.00		
JAS Median	.22		

B. Hands

1. Illustrators and pointing

DeFrank, 1980 (pointing and gesturing)	?	n.s.	JAS
H. Friedman et al., 1985 (nonemphatic illustrators)	.08	n.s.	JAS
Heller, 1980 (illustrators)	.25	.05	SI
Matthews & Angulo, 1980 (emphatic pointing)[b]	?	n.s.	TR
Median	.16		

2. Manipulators

H. Friedman et al., 1985 (body)	−.15	n.s.	JAS
H. Friedman et al., 1985 (props)	−.12	n.s.	JAS
Heller, 1980 (face)	.12	n.s.	SI
Heller, 1980 (props)	−.12	n.s.	SI
Heller, 1980 (body)	.07	n.s.	SI
Median	−.12		
SI Median	.07		
JAS Median	−.14		

3. Clenched fists

H. Friedman et al., 1985	.18	n.s.	JAS
Heller, 1980	.11	n.s.	SI
Matthews & Angulo, 1980[b]	?	n.s.	TR

Table 6.2   continued

Matthews et al., 1982 (sample 1)	.09	n.s.	SI
Median	.11		
SI Median	.10		
JAS Median	.18		
4. Other hand and body movements			
H. Friedman et al., 1985 (parallel gestures)	−.30	.02	JAS
H. Friedman et al., 1985 (picking)	.03	n.s.	JAS
H. Friedman et al., 1985 (hand-to-hand)	.14	n.s.	JAS
H. Friedman et al., 1985 (hand clasp)	.07	n.s.	JAS
H. Friedman et al., 1985 (hand-to-head)	.05	n.s.	JAS
Heller, 1980 (shrugs)	−.04	n.s.	SI
Matthews et al., 1982 (sample 1) (strong handshake)	−.05	n.s.	SI
III. Face and Head			
A. Facial Behavior			
H. Friedman et al., 1985 (smiles)	.02	n.s.	JAS
H. Friedman et al., 1985 (mouth movements)	−.14	n.s.	JAS
Matthews et al., 1982 (sample 1) (clenched jaw)	.18	n.s.	SI
Matthews et al., 1982 (sample 1) (lateral smile)	.09	n.s.	SI
Matthews et al., 1982 (sample 1) (alert look)	.22	.01	SI
B. Gaze at Interactant			
DeFrank, 1980	.28	.02	JAS
H. Friedman et al., 1985	.23	.08	JAS
Median	.26		
C. Head Nods			
DeFrank, 1980	.25	.03	JAS
H. Friedman et al., 1985	−.11	n.s.	JAS
Median	.07		
D. Other Head Movements			
H. Friedman et al., 1985 (shakes)	−.21	.10	JAS
H. Friedman et al., 1985 (movements)	.01	n.s.	JAS
IV. Nonverbal Communication Skills			
A. Encoding Skill			
DeFrank, 1980	?	n.s.	JAS
B. Decoding Skill			
DeFrank, 1980	−.23[d]	.03	JAS
V. Global Ratings and Composites			
A. Exhibited Hostility			
Dembroski et al., 1978	.68	.001	SI

Table 6.2   continued

	Magnitude		
Gilbert & Reynolds, 1984 (head			
shakes, negative facial emotion)	.27[g]	.05	JAS
	.25	.05	FRAM
Hecker et al., 1981	.25	.05	SI
Matthews et al., 1982 (sample 1)	.64	.01	SI
	.36	.01	JAS
Matthews et al., 1982 (sample 2)	.53	.01	SI
	.28	.01	JAS
Median	.32		
SI Median	.58		
JAS Median	.28		
B. Other			
Bortner & Rosenman, 1967 ("fist-			
clenching, sighing, etc.")	.29	.05	SI
Gilbert & Reynolds, 1984 (smiles,			
head nods, and body shifting)	−.04	n.s.	JAS
	.00	n.s.	FRAM
Gilbert & Reynolds, 1984 (fidgeting/			
manipulating, abrupt downward head			
movement, and "attentional orienta-			
tion")	.01	n.s.	JAS
	−.23	.05	FRAM
Glass et al., 1974 (expt. 2) (ner-			
vous touching of body, tapping			
table, facial annoyance)	.33[e]	.05	JAS[f]
Matthews et al., 1982 (sample 1)			
(exhibited energy)	.51	.01	SI
	.27	.01	JAS

NOTE: Positive values in "Magnitude" column indicate that the stated nonverbal variable is more characteristic of Type A than Type B individuals. These values are correlation coefficients or standardized regression coefficients. SI=Structured Interview or adaptation of it. JAS=Jenkins Activity Survey. BPI=Bortner Personality Inventory. TR=teacher ratings. FRAM=Framingham Type A scale. ?=relationship unknown. +=direction of relationship positive but magnitude unknown. −=direction of relationship negative but magnitude unknown. n.s.=not significant.

Some nonsignificant results from Matthews et al. (1982) were generously supplied by personal communication from K. A. Matthews. Results identified as H. Friedman et al., 1985, are mainly unpublished results from that study.

[a]Average of two latency variables; $p < .05$ for each.
[b]Children.
[c]Average of results for baseline and hortatory readings; $p < .001$ for each.
[d]Median of three significant correlations between Type A and decoding of nonverbal cues expressing dominance in both visual and auditory channels. Overall decoding skill showed no significant relationship with Type A.
[e]Baseline data; for change as function of experimentally induced aggression, $p < .06$.
[f]Speed and Impatience factor; no significant difference for JAS total score.
[g]Average of Job Involvement and Hard-driving subscales; no significant difference for JAS total score.

tent. In light of the tautology implied by relating observed NVB to Type A diagnosis based on the SI, it is important to examine relationships of observed NVB to *different* methods of Type A diagnosis. Table 6.2 includes a number of studies in which diagnosis was based on the JAS, an instrument that does not focus on nonverbal behavior and which is based on self-report rather than direct observation. These studies show NVB-Type A correlations that are definitely smaller than those yielded by the SI, as shown by the median correlations in the table. But many of the JAS-NVB relationships are credible nevertheless, and generally consistent with the interview-based results.[4] Several other results in the table that are based on paper-and-pencil instruments also showed encouraging relationships.

Though TABP is most often said to appear under challenge, evidence from several studies indicates this is not necessarily so (DeFrank, 1980; H. Friedman et al., 1985; Glass et al., 1974; Guggisberg et al., 1981; M. Friedman et al., 1969). In these studies, subjects' NVB was coded from nonstressful interviews or interpersonal tasks, or baseline conditions in challenge experiments. Table 6.2 shows that several of these studies found credible relationships between Type A diagnosis and NVB.

In addition to the explicitly nonverbal behaviors that have been coded in this research area, some traits that probably have nonverbal manifestations also have been shown to be related to TABP. Among these are (1) aggression, anger, or hostility (e.g., Chesney et al., 1981; Dimsdale et al., 1978); (2) competitiveness, (3) impatience, (4) dominance (e.g., Chesney et al., 1981); and (5) expressiveness, liveliness, or exhibition (e.g., Caffrey, 1968; Chesney et al., 1981). These traits have been assessed mainly by self-report. The last category, consisting of implied nonverbal expressiveness and related behaviors, is especially relevant to theoretical issues presented later in this chapter.

RELATIONSHIP OF NVB TO CHD

Naturally what one really wants to know is whether the nonverbal component of TABP is related to health outcomes. If it is not, then the whole pursuit described thus far is misguided. The relevant literature for this important question is limited because of the obvious difficulty and expense of mounting research that includes health outcomes, especially prospective studies. The evidence does suggest, however, that NVB is related to CHD or to related physiological variables. M. Friedman and

Rosenman (1960) found that fidgeting, contracting and relaxing the jaw muscles, clenching the fists, and making unpleasant grimaces distinguished heart patients from normals. In M. Friedman et al. (1969), explosive speech distinguished angina and infarct patients from normals. Matthews et al. (1977) found in a prospective study that heart victims were distinguished from normals on explosive speech, exhibited hostility, and vigor of answers. In Dembroski et al. (1978), loud and explosive speech, rapid and accelerated speech, short speech latency, and exhibited hostility were related to heart rate variability and blood pressure changes in a laboratory task. And Manuck et al. (1979) found that higher voice volume and emphasis were associated with elevated pulse pressure on an experimental task. Thus, the nonverbal elements alone are related to CHD or to its suspected precursors.

In addition to these explicitly nonverbal behaviors, as above, some writers focus on personality traits that may be reflected in NVB but that also imply other kinds of behaviors. For example, the trait of aggression might be manifested in nonverbal expressive style but also in destruction of objects, rude or obscene language, or way of dealing with the world that is offensively competitive or manipulative. The trait of aggression, anger, or hostility has in fact been shown to be related to CHD (Diamond, 1982; Matthews et al., 1977).

The exact causal relationship of NVB to CHD is unknown. Dembroski (1978) presents a model in which "psychological reactions and behaviors" are connected to CHD via physiological processes. In such a view NVB would have an indirect (i.e., mediated) causal relationship to CHD. It is possible, for example, that the arousal and irritation of the Type A individual, either as a constant state or alternating with other states, causes physiological deterioration (Schneiderman, 1983). Matthews (1982) presents other hypotheses. One is that NVB is merely a symptom of other traits such as competition and time urgency. In such a view NVB would have no causal relationship to CHD but might still be useful diagnostically. Another possibility put forth by Matthews (1982) is that Type A individuals are highly reactive to a challenge situation such as the SI. Thus their NVB would reflect unconscious mimicry or reciprocation of the interviewer's own behavior. In this case, NVB itself could have either some causal relationship to CHD or could, again, be simply a sign that the person is in a damaging physiological state. Actually, since NVB is related to other ways of diagnosing TABP, it is unlikely that the NVB characteristic of Type A individuals is solely a product of reacting to the behavior of a difficult interviewer.

Another hypothesis, implied by Dembroski's (1978) model, is that Type A individuals alienate others to the point that important social and emotional supports degrade over time, putting such persons at higher health risk (Suls et al., 1981; Surwit et al., 1982). This condition could come about through some combination of general obnoxiousness and competitiveness, and of poorly developed communication skills. Not only have inadequate communication skills been proposed as a Type A trait (Jenkins, 1975), but, as shown in Table 6.2, such a relationship has been demonstrated empirically (DeFrank, 1980). People who are poor at reading the nonverbal expressions of others could certainly do themselves harm, both because they lack important interpersonal contact and because they may have more suspicious, resentful, and generally stressful experiences when they do interact with others. Research on correlates of nonverbal decoding skills does indeed indicate that poor decoders are, among other things, less popular, less skilled as teachers and therapists, and less well adjusted than are good decoders (Rosenthal et al., 1979).

Regardless of whether NVB is related causally to CHD, we would argue that its study is important for several reasons. First, NVB is obviously a major part of Type A diagnosis and therefore has a demonstrated significance from a purely practical standpoint. Second, the careful assessment of NVB may permit a closer definition of which "Type A" individuals are actually at risk. And third, to the extent that NVB has physiological feedback functions (see Part II of this book), is related to major traits such as time urgency, and has social impact, interventions designed to alter NVB could be extremely useful.

OUR CONCEPTUAL APPROACH

Theory, clinical report, and published studies clearly suggest that Type A personality is manifested in a constellation of nonverbal expressive tendencies such as loud, fast, and explosive speech, short speech latency, tendency to squirm, and a general expression of vigor. It is also clear that the Type A label is too inclusive, in that it identifies a larger group of people than is actually at risk. One problem, we submit, is that nonverbal analysis has not been detailed enough nor sufficiently theoretically developed, with the consequence that prediction is poorer than it could be.

Recent research by one of us indicates that some people are naturally nonverbally expressive and can best be termed "charismatic" (H. Friedman et al., 1980; H. Friedman & Riggio, 1981; Riggio & H. Friedman, 1982). Charisma can be measured by the Affective Communication Test (ACT). Two items of the ACT are: "My laugh is soft and subdued" (reversed item) and "I can easily express emotion over the telephone."

(It is interesting to note that the SI is also concerned with laughter and vocal expression.) The ACT has been validated in terms of friends' ratings, social characteristics, personality variables, and nonverbal social skills. People who are charismatic (nonverbally expressive) have been shown to be high on dominance, exhibition, extraversion, and impulsivity. These people are easily noted by others, are popular, and wind up in positions of leadership and social influence. They seem emotionally healthy and are not necessarily concerned with control, manipulation, or self-monitoring. They may appear "animated." Thus, they share certain characteristics with people who would be labeled Type A by the SI, but these charismatic people do not appear to fit the overall description of the coronary-prone personality. They are just naturally expressive rather than characterized by excessive striving and competition.

We would refine the measurement of coronary proneness by introducing specific factors of verbal and nonverbal expressiveness into the prediction battery. We hypothesize that some individuals who are labeled Type A but who are not actually coronary-prone are misidentified because of gross behavioral similarities between "true" Type As and healthy individuals who also are very confident, dominant, and active in their expressive style. This latter group we would call "healthy expressives." We predict that the expressive style as well as the personality structure of these two groups will be found to differ in subtle yet measurable ways. Similarly, we hypothesize that some individuals labeled Type B who actually are coronary-prone or prone to other diseases are mislabeled because of gross behavioral similarities between "true" Type Bs, who are healthy, unexpressive, quiet, and relaxed, and unhealthy individuals who also are quiet, slow to speak, and unaggressive on the surface but who actually may be tense, overcontrolled, and filled with repressed hostility. We predict that the expressive style and personality structure of these two groups will be found to differ as well.

A related matter concerns research on successfully coping with stress. The overworked, overstressed business executive was the stereotypic image motivating research on TABP, but it has been shown that many hardworking executives have good health. Healthy executives know how to cope with stress. They have a personality variously termed "hardy," "coherent," or "competent" (Antonovsky, 1979; Cohen, 1979; Kobasa, 1979). Therefore, from our standpoint as researchers of expressive style, we see an interesting parallel between two research traditions. To the extent that Type A behavior is seen as related to other personality traits, it is typically viewed as involving a mixture of positive and negative traits, for example, extraversion, dominance, aggressiveness, achievement-striving, and desire for control. It is important, in our view, to distinguish the healthy expressiveness termed charisma from an unhealthy aggressiveness and excessive desire for control. Hence, we concluded that we should apply our knowledge of a healthy nonverbal expressive style to a fine-grained analysis of assessment of TABP.

BRIEF DESCRIPTION AND RESULTS OF OUR RESEARCH

Subjects in this study were 60 men in the Harvard site of the Multiple Risk Factor Intervention trial (MRFIT), a national experiment on heart disease prevention (Paul, 1976). These men were originally selected for the MRFIT study because of high values on the coronary disease risk factors of smoking, blood pressure, and serum cholesterol. For these subjects, Type A/B classification using the JAS, expressive style assessment using the ACT, health data during participation in MRFIT, and a four-minute videotape of the subject in interpersonal interaction were obtained. This interaction was a standard interview administered by a MRFIT staff member as part of the project's termination. It was nonstressful and simply involved a series of questions about the subject's evaluation of the MRFIT project and its benefit to him. Half the subjects for our study were selected from among those scoring highest on the JAS (6 and above) and half were selected from among the lowest scoring (−6 and below).

From the videotapes, a wide range of nonverbal expressive behaviors were counted and/or rated, including the following:

Face, head, and body movement: head shakes and nods; smiles;
    eye movements; movements of the body, arms, hands, and legs.
Vocal behavior: speed of speech; speech latency; interruptions;
    speech emphasis; speech disturbances; amount of speech.
Judges' global ratings of aggressive, tense, dominant, alert,
    expressive, friendly, active, and healthy demeanor (in five
    conditions: video and full audio, video only, full audio,
    transcript, and content-masked, i.e., filtered, audio).

Intercoder (N=2) and interrater (N=8–12) reliabilities for these measures were generally excellent.

A main finding to emerge from our study is clear evidence that there are indeed systematic relationships among nonverbal cues, expressive style, Type A behavior, and health. In this chapter, we focus on the relationship between coded nonverbal cues and TABP. For further information on our empirical method and results, the reader may consult Friedman, Hall, and Harris (1985).

We operationalized overall expressiveness as subjects' scores on the Affective Communication Test (ACT), described earlier; high scorers on this instrument are charismatic and extraverted. By cross-classifying subjects on the ACT and JAS we created the four groups mentioned above and shown in Table 6.3: "healthy" and "unhealthy" Type As (high and low ACT, respectively), and "healthy" and "unhealthy" Type Bs (low and high ACT, respectively). The terms healthy and unhealthy, as used here, refer to a priori predictions based on our theoretical model and not to the actual health of the individuals; actual health is a separate, important empirical issue which our study addressed but only in a preliminary way since variation in health status was very limited. (For details on physical health outcomes, see H. Friedman et al., 1985.)

To simplify presentation of our results, we shall discuss three comparisons using the nonverbal cues we coded. First, we related nonverbal cues to Type A versus B classification. Second, we related nonverbal cues to the *kind of Type A person*—healthy (high ACT) Type As versus unhealthy (low ACT) As. Third, we related nonverbal cues to our classifications of healthy (high ACT As and low ACT Bs) versus unhealthy (low ACT As and high ACT Bs). This last comparison is easily recognized as the statistical interaction of A/B classification with low/high ACT.

The results for overall Type A/B classification—the first comparison described above—are included in Table 6.2, with the designation "H. Friedman et al. (1985)." Not surprisingly, considering that our diagnostic instrument was the JAS, the overall magnitude of the NVB-Type A correlations is weaker than analogous correlations based on the SI. The vocal channels produced particularly weak results. This outcome is proba-

Table 6.3   Predicted Health of Four Groups as Function of Type A/B and Charisma

ACT	JAS	
	Low (Type B)	High (Type A)
Low (not charismatic)	healthy relaxed	unhealthy aggressive
High (charismatic)	unhealthy tense	healthy popular

NOTE: JAS = Jenkins Activity Survey. ACT = Affective Communication Test.

bly in part because our videotaped clips were short, only four minutes maximum, leading to very low frequencies for most of the coded vocal behaviors. Behaviors in the visual channels showed stronger results in line with analogous results from other studies summarized in Table 6.2 for gross body movements, hand manipulators, clenched fists, and gaze.

Table 6.4 shows the results for the remaining two comparisons described—low versus high ACT As, and the two unhealthy groups versus the two healthy groups. Shown in Table 6.4 are the results for two groups of nonverbal behaviors. First are the nonverbal cue *factors* derived from a factor analysis of all the nonverbal behaviors we coded, and second are the single coded behaviors that were entered into the factor analysis. In the case of single behaviors, only those variables that showed at least one result of $p < .20$, two-tailed test, are presented.

The nonverbal cue factors, defined in the notes to Table 6.4, showed no significant overall relationship to Type A/B classification. Only one, the defensive hostility factor, showed a marginally significant relationship, with Type As scoring higher than Type Bs ($r(58) = .22, p = .09$). This result is mainly due to the contribution of posture shifts, leg movements, and clenched fists (see Table 6.2).

However, Table 6.4 shows that the repression factor significantly differentiated low ACT from high ACT Type As, with the high ACT As (predicted to be healthy) appearing less repressed than low ACT As. This effect was mainly due to the high ACT As showing less leg crossing, less body-focused gesturing, and more hand-to-hand contact (Table 6.4, part II). Low and high ACT As also differed significantly on the talkative factor, with high ACT As scoring higher on all the variables making up this factor (Table 6.4, part II). The "defensive/hostile" factor (e.g., fists) also seemed related to being a "true" Type A person (see H. Friedman et al., 1985, for details on further analyses of this factor).

Table 6.4 also shows that the repression factor differentiated the two groups predicted to be healthy from the two groups predicted to be unhealthy, with the two "healthy" groups (high ACT As and low ACT Bs) appearing less repressed than the two "unhealthy" groups (low ACT As and high ACT Bs). This effect was mainly due to less leg crossing in the two healthy groups (Table 6.4, part II).

Importantly, in this study the Type A/B classification was a much weaker predictor of nonverbal behavior than was the ACT within the Type A group alone. Approximately three-quarters of the correlations for individual behaviors were weaker for the former than for the latter comparison. Though to some extent the correlations between ACT and NVB within the Type A group reflect main effects of ACT on NVB—effects which are not surprising, given that the ACT's items tap aspects of nonverbal expressiveness—it still has a strong implication for researchers of TABP. It indicates that one reason why the Type A label is overinclusive

Table 6.4 Further Results from the Study of Coded Nonverbal Cues

Nonverbal Variables	Unhealthy As versus Healthy As $(N=26)$[a]		Unhealthy versus Healthy Groups $(N=52)$[b]	
	r	p	r	p
I. Nonverbal Cue Factors				
Repressed[c]	−.51	.007	−.28	.05
Defensive hostility[d]	−.24	n.s.	−.16	n.s.
Animation[e]	.23	n.s.	.12	n.s.
Face/head movement[f]	.14	n.s.	.04	n.s.
Talkative[g]	.54	.005	.08	n.s.
Directness[h]	.20	n.s.	.12	n.s.
Impatience[i]	.05	n.s.	.04	n.s.
Disturbed speech[j]	−.17	n.s.	−.08	n.s.
II. Individual Behaviors				
Body-focused (freq.)	−.35	.08	−.23	.10
Body-focused (dura.)	−.39	.05	−.01	n.s.
Leg cross (dura.)	−.56	.003	−.33	.02
Hand-to-hand (freq.)	.54	.004	.25	.08
Hand-to-hand (dura.)	.48	.01	.09	n.s.
Hand clasp (dura.)	.29	.16	.05	n.s.
Posture shifts	−.15	n.s.	−.24	.09
Leg movements	.29	.15	.17	n.s.
Hand-to-head (freq.)	−.36	.07	−.17	n.s.
Hand-to-head (dura.)	−.54	.004	−.21	.14
Emphatic object-focused (freq.)	−.41	.04	−.23	.11
Parallel gestures (freq.)	.21	n.s.	.20	.17
Eye contact (dura.)	.38	.05	.09	n.s.
Syllables/sec.	−.28	.16	−.17	n.s.
Average length of turns	.29	.15	.00	n.s.
Percentage of time speaking	.53	.006	.09	n.s.

[a]Positive correlation means healthy (high ACT) Type As score higher on the cue than unhealthy (low ACT) Type As.
[b]Positive correlation means that the two groups defined as healthy score higher on the cue than the two groups defined as unhealthy (see text).
[c]The repression factor is based on standardized leg cross (+), prop manipulators (+), body-focused gestures (+), hand clasp (−), and hand-to-hand contact (−).
[d]The defensive-hostility factor is based on standardized posture shifts (+), leg movements (+), hand-to-head contact (+), fists (+), and emphatic object-focused gestures (+).
[e]The animation factor is based on standardized nods (+), head shakes (+), speech rate (+), parallel gestures (+), and frequency of eye contact (+).
[f]The face/head movements factor is based on standardized head movements (+), mouth movements (+), frequency of eye contact (+), and parallel gestures (+).
[g]The talkative factor is based on standardized average length of utterances (+), percentage of segment the subject spoke (+), and duration of eye contact (+).
[h]The directness factor is based on standardized frequency of smiles (+), duration of eye contact (+), nonemphatic gestures (+), and picking and scratching (−).
[i]The impatience factor is based on standardized speech hurrying (+), interruptions (+), number of speaking turns (+), "ah's" (−), and speech latencies (−).
[j]The disturbed speech factor is based on standardized non-"ah" speech disturbances (+), loud words (+), "ah's" (+), and speech hurrying (+).

is that it puts together two groups of individuals who differ sharply in their behavioral style. The healthier group, the high ACT As, are more forthcoming and less repressed nonverbally.

Finally, though our exploration of actual health outcomes was limited in scope, our results for one important health variable were highly supportive of the theoretical approach described in this chapter. For physician-diagnosed signs of peripheral artery disease, the two groups designated a priori as healthy did indeed score significantly lower (healthier) than the two groups designated a priori as unhealthy.

CONCLUSIONS

The description of the Type A behavior pattern is one of the major achievements in health psychology. It has great potential significance for our understanding of the psychological mechanisms leading to heart disease, as well as for our ability to prevent heart disease by lifestyle intervention. But this field of research is also at an important turning point. The global nature of the Type A construct must be refined into component constructs and causal models developed and applied.

Our effort is to refine the Type A construct by applying rigorous methods of nonverbal cue analysis and by drawing on theoretical concepts from the nonverbal communication and personality areas. Our prediction that the Type A and Type B groups, as currently defined, each include subtypes that differ in nonverbal expression has received preliminary support.

In future research testing our theoretical model, inclusion of solid health outcome data is essential, including not only variables indicative of CHD but also a range of possible psychosomatic disorders and other symptoms of stress. It will be particularly important to explore the health status of the subgroup of Type Bs who, according to our model, are repressed, conflicted, and predicted to be unhealthy. This group appeared conflicted in two ways. First, there is an implied contradiction in attributing "Type B" traits to oneself and yet describing oneself as extraverted and charismatic. Second, though they described themselves as charismatic, their nonverbal behavior did not correspond. That a group of "Type Bs" may have problems with emotional adjustment and/or physical health is a possibility that has been ignored in the TABP literature. Pursuing this possibility will help place TABP research within the broader context of research on stress and psychosomatic disease, where it belongs.

ACKNOWLEDGMENTS

This research has been supported by the American Heart Association, California Affiliate, Riverside Chapter; by the Milton Fund of Harvard University; by the Center for Social and Behavioral Science Research at the University of California, Riverside; by a UCR Intramural Research Grant; by the Biomedical Research Support Grant Program of NIH; and by a University of California President's Fellowship. Part of the research was conducted while the first author was supported by the Andrew Mellon Foundation as a research fellow in Interdisciplinary Programs in Health, Harvard School of Public Health, and while the third author was an NIMH Social Ecology Trainee. We wish to thank Liz Blozan and Nancy R. Katz for research assistance, and the staff and participants of the Harvard MRFIT Center for their patience and cooperation. The help of Debbie Kousch of the Harvard MRFIT Center was especially important.

NOTES

1. One can also describe attributes of the Type B person, but since they are usually the converse of the Type A attributes, we shall not do so here.

2. There is some inevitable ambiguity about which behaviors should be called "nonverbal" and which "verbal." We have decided to identify most of the speech variables that have been discussed in the TABP literature as nonverbal. Major exceptions are total speech production (e.g., length of answers to questions) and number of self-references (e.g., personal pronouns); we have not reviewed either of these.

3. Hurrying the interviewer and back-channeling may actually be synonymous since the inserted affirmations (uh-huh, etc.) most often coded as back-channel responses may serve the subject's desire to hurry the speaker along.

4. The extreme differences found by Matthews et al. (1982) between correlations based on the SI and the JAS may be due to the fact that some of the NVB ratings and Type A diagnosis from the SI were apparently made by the same coders, a method that could easily create spuriously large NVB-SI Type A correlations. Consistent with this hypothesis, the latter correlations are, in fact, almost always the highest obtained in their respective categories.

REFERENCES

Antonovsky, A. (1979). *Health, stress and coping.* San Francisco: Jossey-Bass.

Bortner, R. W., & Rosenman, R. H. (1967). The measurement of Pattern A behavior. *Journal of Chronic Diseases, 20,* 525–33.

Caffrey, B. (1968). Reliability and validity of personality and behavioral measures in a study of coronary heart disease. *Journal of Chronic Diseases, 21,* 191–204.

Chesney, M. A., Eagleston, J. R., & Rosenman, R. H. (1980). The Type A Structured Interview: A behavioral assessment in the rough. *Journal of Behavioral Assessment, 2,* 255–72.

Chesney, M. A., Black, G. W., Chadwick, J. H., & Rosenman, R. H. (1981). Psychological correlates of the Type A behavior pattern. *Journal of Behavioral Medicine, 4,* 217–29.

Cohen, F. (1979). Personality, stress, and the development of illness. In G. C. Stone, F. Cohen, & N. E. Adler (Eds.), *Health psychology: A handbook.* San Francisco: Jossey-Bass.

Cooper, T., Detre, T., & Weiss, S. M. (1981). Coronary prone behavior and coronary heart disease: A critical review. *Circulation, 63,* 1199–1215.

DeFrank, R. S. (1980). Interactive, verbal and nonverbal aspects of the coronary-prone behavior pattern. Unpublished doctoral dissertation, University of Rochester.

Dembroski, T. M. (1978). Reliability and validity of methods used to assess coronary-prone behavior. In T. M. Dembroski, S. Weiss, J. Shields, S. G. Hanes, & M. Feinleib (Eds.), *Coronary-prone behavior.* New York: Springer-Verlag.

Dembroski, T. M., MacDougall, J. M., Shields, J. L., Petitto, J., & Lushene, R. (1978). Components of the type A coronary-prone behavior pattern and cardiovascular responses to psychomotor performance challenge. *Journal of Behavioral Medicine, 1,* 159–76.

Diamond, E. L. (1982). The role of anger and hostility in essential hypertension and coronary heart disease. *Psychological Bulletin, 92,* 410–33.

Dimsdale, J. E., Hackett, T. P., Block, P. C., & Hutter, A. M. (1978). Emotional correlates of the Type A behavior pattern. *Psychosomatic Medicine, 40,* 580–83.

Friedman, H. S., Hall, J. A., & Harris, M. J. (1985). Type A behavior, nonverbal expressive style, and health. *Journal of Personality and Social Psychology, 48,* 1299–1315.

Friedman, H. S., Prince, L. M., Riggio, R. E., & DiMatteo, M. R. (1980). Understanding and assessing nonverbal expressiveness: The Affective Communication Test. *Journal of Personality and Social Psychology, 39,* 333–51.

Friedman, H. S., & Riggio, R. E. (1981). The effect of individual differences in nonverbal expressiveness on the transmission of emotion. *Journal of Nonverbal Behavior, 6,* 96–104.

Friedman, M. (1964). Behavior pattern and its pathogenetic role in clinical coronary artery disease. *Geriatrics, 19,* 562–67.

Friedman, M. (1979). The modification of Type A behavior in post-infarction patients. *American Heart Journal, 97,* 551–60.

Friedman, M., Brown, A. E., & Rosenman, R. H. (1969). Voice analysis test for detection of behavior pattern: Responses of normal men and coronary patients. *Journal of the American Medical Association, 208,* 828–36.

Friedman, M., & Rosenman, R. H. (1959). Association of specific overt behavior pattern with blood and cardiovascular findings. *Journal of the American Medical Association, 169,* 1286–96.

Friedman, M., & Rosenman, R. H. (1960). Overt behavior pattern in coronary disease: Detection of overt behavior pattern A in patients with coronary disease by a new psychophysiological procedure. *Journal of the American Medical Association, 173,* 1320–5.

Friedman, M., & Rosenman, R. H. (1974). *Type A behavior and your heart.* New York: Alfred A. Knopf.

Gilbert, D. G., and Reynolds, J. H. (1984). Type A personality: Correlations with personality variables and nonverbal emotional expressions during interpersonal competition. *Personality and Individual Differences, 5,* 27–34.

Glass, D. C., Snyder, M. L., & Hollis, J. F. (1974). Time urgency and the Type A coronary-prone behavior pattern. *Journal of Applied Social Psychology, 4,* 125–40.

Guggisberg, R., Laederach, K., & Adler, R. (1981). Formal speech stylistics and type A behavior in 38 subjects during nonstress interviews. *Psychotherapy and Psychosomatics, 36,* 86–91.

Hecker, M. H. L., Chesney, M. A., Black, G. W., and Rosenman, R. H. (1981). Speech analysis of Type A behavior. In J. Darby (Ed.), *Speech evaluation in medicine.* New York: Grune & Stratton.

Heller, B. W. (1980). Nonverbal behavior and coronary-prone behavior: Hand movement and the Type A pattern. Unpublished doctoral dissertation, University of California, Davis.

Howland, E. W., & Siegman, A. W. (1982). Toward the automated measurement of the Type-A behavior pattern. *Journal of Behavioral Medicine, 5,* 37–54.

Jenkins, C. D. (1975). The coronary-prone personality. In W. D. Gentry & R. B. Williams (Eds.), *Psychological aspects of myocardial infarction and coronary care.* St. Louis: Mosby.

Jenkins, C. D. (1978). A comparative review of the interview and questionnaire methods in the assessment of the coronary-prone behavior pattern. In T. M. Dembroski, S. Weiss, J. Shields, S. G. Hanes, & M. Feinleib (Eds.), *Coronary-prone behavior.* New York: Springer-Verlag.

Jenkins, C. D., Zyzanski, S. J., & Rosenman, R. H. (1978). Coronary-prone behavior: One pattern or several? *Psychosomatic Medicine, 40,* 25–43.

Jenkins, C. D., Zyzanski, S. J., & Rosenman, R. H. (1979). *Jenkins Activity Survey.* New York: The Psychological Corporation.

Kobasa, S. C. (1979). Stressful life events, personality, and health: An inquiry into hardiness. *Journal of Personality and Social Psychology, 37,* 1–11.

Lovallo, W. R., & Pishkin, V. (1980). Type A behavior, self-involvement, autonomic activity, and the traits of neuroticism and extraversion. *Psychosomatic Medicine, 42,* 329–34.

MacDougall, J. M., Dembroski, T. M., & Musante, L. (1979). The structured interview and questionnaire methods of assessing coronary-prone behavior in male and female college students. *Journal of Behavioral Medicine, 2,* 71–82.

Manuck, S. B., Corse, C. D., & Winkelman, P. A. (1979). Behavioral correlates of individual differences in blood pressure activity. *Journal of Psychosomatic Research, 23,* 281–88.

Matthews, K. A. (1982). Psychological perspectives on the Type A behavior pattern. *Psychological Bulletin, 91,* 293–323.

Matthews, K. A., & Angulo, J. (1980). Measurement of the type A behavior pattern in children: Assessment of children's competitiveness, impatience-anger, and aggression. *Child Development, 51,* 466–75.

Matthews, K. A., Glass, D. C., Rosenman, R. H., & Bortner, R. W. (1977). Competitive drive, Pattern A, and coronary heart disease: A further analysis of some data from the Western Collaborative Group Study. *Journal of Chronic Diseases, 30,* 489–98.

Matthews, K. A., Krantz, D. S., Dembroski, T. M., & MacDougall, J. M. (1982). Unique and common variance in Structured Interview and Jenkins Activity Survey measures of the Type A behavior pattern. *Journal of Personality and Social Psychology, 42,* 303–13.

Paul, O. (1976). The Multiple Risk Factor Intervention Trial (MRFIT): A national study of primary prevention of coronary heart disease. *Journal of the American Medical Association, 235,* 825–27.

Price, V. A. (1982). *Type A Behavior Pattern: A model for research and practice.* New York: Academic Press.

Riggio, R. E., & Friedman, H. S. (1982). The interrelationships of self-monitoring factors, personality traits, and nonverbal social skills. *Journal of Nonverbal Behavior, 7,* 33–45.

Rosenman, R. H. (1978). The interview method of assessment of the coronary-prone behavior pattern. In T. M. Dembroski, S. Weiss, J. Shields, S. G. Hanes, & M. Feinleib (Eds.), *Coronary-prone behavior.* New York: Springer-Verlag.

Rosenman, R. H., Brand, R. J., Jenkins, C. D., Friedman, M., Straus, R., & Wurm, M. (1975). Coronary heart disease in the Western Collaborative Group Study: Final follow-up experience of 8½ years. *Journal of the American Medical Association, 233,* 872–77.

Rosenthal, R., Hall, J. A., DiMatteo, M. R., Rogers, P. L., & Archer, D. (1979). *Sensitivity to nonverbal communication: The PONS test.* Baltimore: Johns Hopkins University Press.

Scherwitz, L., Berton, K., & Leventhal, H. (1977). Type A assessment and interaction in the behavior pattern interview. *Psychosomatic Medicine, 39,* 229–40.

Schneiderman, N. (1983). Animal behavior models of coronary heart disease. In D. Krantz, A. Baum, & J. E. Singer (Eds.), *Handbook of psychology and health,* vol. 3. Hillsdale, NJ: L. Erlbaum.

Schucker, B., & Jacobs, D. R., Jr. (1977). Assessment of behavioral risk for coronary disease by voice characteristics. *Psychosomatic Medicine, 39,* 219–28.

Sparacino, J., Hansell, S., & Smyth, K. (1979). Type A (coronary-prone) behavior and transient blood pressure change. *Nursing Research, 28,* 198–204.

Suls, J. M., Becker, M. A., & Mullen, B. (1981). Coronary-prone behavior, social insecurity, and stress among college-aged adults. *Journal of Human Stress, 7,* 27–34.

Surwit, R. S., Williams, R. B., Jr., & Shapiro, D. (1982). *Behavioral approaches to cardiovascular disease.* New York: Academic Press.

PART II
Brain Functions and Nonverbal Communication in the Clinical Context

Part II is devoted to the analysis of the brain mechanisms underlying nonverbal communication, and the clinical evidence for, and implications of, this analysis. In chapter 1 we presented a hierarchical view of human nature and communication, in which spontaneous nonverbal communication is seen to be based upon subcortical and paleocortical mechanisms that have remained relatively unchanged over the course of evolution. These "reptilian" and "old mammalian" systems interact with the "new mammalian" neocortical structures which, in humans, involve linguistic control. We also noted in chapter 1 that, in addition to this "higher/lower" neocortical-subcortical dimension, there are left/right and anterior/posterior dimensions that must be considered in analyzing the brain's role in emotion, cognition, and communication. Part II presents the results of four recent research programs devoted to this analysis.

In Part I we used *One Flew Over the Cuckoo's Nest* to illustrate the themes covered in the chapters. Kesey's book is a cautionary tale about the control of human behavior, illustrating how Billy Bibbit is controlled *through communication* by his mother and Miss Ratched, and how the Chief maintains his inner freedom only by refusing such communication while outwardly acquiescing to the demands of the institution. The institution similarly cannot control the behavior of McMurphy, so it resorts to a more draconian measure—prefrontal lobotomy—to accomplish this purpose. The lobotomy has the effect of severing the connections between the emotional centers in the subcortical/paleocortical regions of McMurphy's brain and the higher structures, so that his former spontaneous expressiveness is cut off from its source and irretrievably lost.

No responsible professional desires this kind of control. Control of human behavior by drugs, while being less permanent and more reversible, has its own undesirable side effects. The challenge to brain research is to achieve control over human behavior in ways that are consistent with the well-being of the patient, that preserve rather than destroy the human spirit which remains so elusive. The best way to accomplish this objective may often be through communication—but humane and loving communication.

We noted in chapter 1 that nonverbal behavior can have specific physiological effects which are objectively similar to the effects of drugs. In Part II, we believe it will be useful to "unpack" that assertion and to give some specific examples and explanations.

COMMUNICATION AND BIOREGULATION

There is evidence from a wide variety of sources that the individual organism is open to social influences that are qualitatively different from those previously recognized. Specifically, it appears that social stimuli participate directly in the physiological regulation of the individual—in the basic process of homeostasis and adaptation. This fact has very important implications for the understanding of human nature.

Love as an Addiction

When an infant mouse is separated from its mother, it emits a peculiar, high-pitched chirping sound. Jaak Panksepp (1982) has investigated the neurological mechanism of this behavior and reports that a minute quantity of a substance called naloxone quiets the mouse's cry. Here is one of the few effects of naloxone on naturally occurring behavior that has yet been identified. This finding is significant because naloxone is an opiate antagonist which binds to synapses activated by the naturally occurring opiates—the endorphins—negating their effects. Thus naloxone reverses the pain-killing effects of opium, and is given in cases of heroin and morphine overdose. Why does it also quiet the cry of an orphaned mouse?

Panksepp's answer to this question has important implications indeed. He suggests that social attachment is based upon endorphinergic neural systems at the level of the hypothalamus (Panksepp, 1981; 1982). If this is the case, social attachment must involve drives as basic as those for food and water, drives mediated by naturally occurring morphine. This process would explain the solitary nature of the morphine addict—his or her needs for other persons are satisfied by the drug. Panksepp's hypothesis also implies that in normal persons the existence of close relationships with others may be associated with increased levels of endogenous morphines—that we are in a sense addicted to close personal attachments with others. In the words of a popular song, love may well be, in this sense, an addiction.

There is plentiful evidence that deprivation of normal social experience in infancy has widespread negative consequences in both animals and humans. Hofer (1984) recently has demonstrated that the syndrome of maternal separation is not caused by the generalized stress associated with separation, as had often been supposed, but rather is caused by the elimination of a variety of *specific* regulatory social stimuli. By systematically providing some stimuli associated with the mother's presence but withholding others, Hofer was able to demonstrate the specific function of each of them. For example, a lack of growth hormone and subsequent slowed growth is associated with a lack of activity normally provided by the mother, and the lack of the warmth of the mother's body appears to interfere with the normal levels of norepinepherine and dopamine in the infant's nervous system. Thus, deprivation of *specific aspects* of the mother-infant interaction appears to cause *specific biological deficits* in the infant. This finding suggests in turn that the infant's homeostatic system does not function independently but rather is open to social influence. In Hofer's terms, "biologic regulation is delegated in part to the mother" (p. 186).

Hofer notes that there is evidence for the social regulation of biological functions in humans as well as animals. He discusses the phenomenon of separation and bereavement from this point of view, noting that the physiological responses to bereavement in humans parallel the responses to separation in animals. Supportive social relationships are a powerful buffer against stress in both humans and animals (Bovard, 1959; Cobb, 1976), and separation from those supports has widespread negative impact upon the body, leading to muscular, cardiovascular, endocrine, and immune system changes and increased susceptibility to stress and disease (Hofer, 1984). Hofer concludes that bereavement involves the withdrawal of "multiple regulators woven into the fabric of the relationship." He goes on: "Independent self-regulation may not exist, even in adulthood. Social interactions continue to play an important role in the everyday regulation of internal biologic systems throughout life" (p. 194). He also suggests that these bioregulating functions of social relationships are mediated by nonverbal signals that are outside the awareness of the participants—facial expressions, gesture, touches, smells—in short, by nonverbal communication.

The Other as a Biofeedback Device

Findings such as Hofer's and Panksepp's imply that social stimuli have previously unrecognized bioregulatory functions. The nonverbal feedback received from the other, or others, in the context of an ongoing social relationship may be an important aspect of this bioregulatory process. Thus, the presence of others may function in ways analogous to a biofeedback device. With such a device, a relatively inaccessible physiological response is rendered more "accessible" because of its association with a feedback signal. If nonverbal behavior functions as an interpersonal feedback device, the expressiveness of the individuals involved, their patterns of attention to the signals conveyed, and their past experience in the same or similar relationships must determine the efficiency of that device—just as the sensitivity and clarity of a feedback signal and the subject's experience with it determine the efficiency of any biofeedback instrument.

The net result of experience in a social relationship is that an individual learns to respond effectively in that context, controlling his or her displays appropriately while the social relationship performs important bioregulatory functions in its own right. This behavioral pattern can be seen to occur in animals as well as humans. In humans, an additional level of complexity is added by the capacity for language. Humans appear to be unique in their abilities to encode experiences into words, allowing the contemplation of experiences that one has not had or that indeed are impossible. Humans use the resulting verbal and logical abilities in their exploration of the external physical environment, a process of cognitive development that has been long acknowledged and is much studied. At the same time, humans must make connections between, on one hand, verbal labels and reasoning and, on the other, the internal environment of their own bodies—the environment of feelings and desires. The resulting process of *emotional education* has received much less attention than cognitive development (Buck, 1983). Moreover, it is clear that nonverbal communication must play a major role in the former process.

If the foregoing argument is correct, it would follow that persons and situations that enrich and clarify one's knowledge of internal reality would be as intrinsically interesting and rewarding as are persons and situations that enrich and clarify one's knowledge of external reality. The ability of a leader to elicit and label feelings may be the basis of so-called charisma. The ability of a novel or play, a film or song to elicit and label strong emotions may determine their success. Such appears to be the case even for "negative" emotions like fear, anger, and sadness, as horror shows, "tear-jerkers," and novels like *One Flew Over the Cuckoo's Nest* are testament.

Attention to the internal environment has clear implications for the clinical context, for it is in this context that a very important and focused sort of emotional education occurs. In medical contexts, the patient faces coping with events in the internal milieu—the symptoms of illness—that are new and frightening (Reardon & Buck, 1984). In the context of psychotherapy, the patient is striving to understand feelings and desires that are difficult to control, or difficult to experience, or difficult to express and share with others. The ability of the therapist to elicit, label, and aid in understanding these feelings will determine the effectiveness of the therapist as a biofeedback device and the patient's enthusiasm for the therapy. Much of this outcome will in turn be determined by the therapist's skills at nonverbal communication. The effects upon the patient will be not merely psychological. The therapist will be an important bioregulator for the patient, altering his or her physiological functioning in subtle but powerful ways by a glance, a touch, a tremor in the voice.

BRAIN MECHANISMS AND NONVERBAL COMMUNICATION

The idea of communication as a bioregulatory process emphasizes the importance of understanding the brain mechanisms of nonverbal communication, for it implies that human relationships can have therapeutic—or destructive—biological effects analogous to those of purely biological manipulations. Part II brings together the results of four programs of research dedicated to this goal.

Chapter 7, by Esther Strauss, focuses upon the different cognitive abilities of the left and right hemispheres. Strauss summarizes the considerable evidence that the right hemisphere is best at tasks requiring complex nonverbal spatial integration, while the left hemisphere is superior at linguistic and analytic tasks. She goes on to describe the changes in emotional expression and reported mood that occur subsequent to injury and malfunctioning in the temporal lobes in humans. The temporal lobes are closely tied to the "old mammalian" structures of the limbic system. Strauss suggests that hemispheric differences are important in emotional behavior to the degree that such behavior demands cognitive activity requiring neocortical mediation. Emotional behavior involving only the lower structures is less likely to be lateralized. She notes that, in intact subjects, emotion invariably involves the contribution of both systems, and the value of studying brain-damaged persons is that their abnormal brain activity can potentially provide a clearer picture of how the higher and lower systems operate. Strauss's chapter involves phenomena that are relatively low in the hierarchy of structures controlling human emotion and communication.

Chapter 8, by Joan Borod, Elissa Koff, and Ross Buck, considers the phenomenon of facedness: the tendency of emotion to be expressed differently on the right versus the left side of the face. The right hemisphere controls the left half of the lower face, while the left hemisphere controls the right lower face. Many emotional expressions are left-sided, perhaps indicating relative right hemisphere activation (or left hemisphere inhibition). Borod and her colleagues' position implies that the extent of facedness could be an index of cognitive involvement in emotion: if there is relatively little cognitive involvement, the expression should be less lateralized. This issue is considered, together with the possibility that the facedness of an expression may be an important clue to whether the responder is intensifying or masking his or her "real" feelings. Such clues can be critically important in a clinical setting, where determining the "true feelings" of the client can be crucial in the clinician's ability to help.

Chapter 9, by Robert Rosenthal and Larry Benowitz, focuses upon "nonverbal sensitivity"—the ability to use such nonverbal clues in making accurate predictions about another person. Studies in normal subjects and patient groups suggest that right-hemisphere-damaged patients are almost completely incapable of decoding certain nonverbal cues, while left-hemisphere-damaged patients function at an essentially normal level. This chapter thus suggests that right hemisphere functioning is particularly important in the reception as well as the expression of nonverbal communiques.

The final chapter is a major integrative effort by Don Tucker, which considers his and others' work on the cognitive abilities of the left and right hemispheres and the implications of this work for the analysis of both voluntary (symbolic) and spontaneous (nonverbal) communication. Tucker also considers the anterior-posterior and cortical-subcortical distinctions. The result is a comprehensive neurophysiological model which encompasses not only communication but also the general process of self-control. After dividing the brain, Tucker reunites it in a discussion of whole brain functions. Much of this chapter is based upon studies from the clinic, and at the end Tucker returns to a consideration of the clinical implications of his analysis.

REFERENCES

Bovard, E. (1959). Effects of social stimuli on the response to stress. *Psychological Review,* *66,* 267–77.

Buck, R. (1983). Emotional development and emotional education. In R. Plutchik and H. Kellerman (Eds.), *Emotion: Theory, Research and Experience*, Volume 2, *Emotions in Early Development*. New York: Academic Press.

Hofer, M. A. (1984). Relationships as regulators: A psychobiologic perspective on bereavement. *Psychosomatic Medicine, 46*, 183–92.

Panksepp, J. (1981). Brain opiods: A neurochemical substrate for narcotic and social dependence. In S. Cooper (Ed.), *Theory in Psychopharmacology*, Vol. 1. New York: Academic Press.

Panksepp, J. (1982). Toward a general psychobiological theory of emotions. *The Behavioral and Brain Sciences, 5*, 407–67.

Reardon, K., and Buck, R. (1984). Emotion, reason, and communication in coping with cancer. Paper presented at the International Communication Association convention, San Francisco.

7 Cerebral Representation of Emotion

Esther Strauss

Evidence regarding functional hemispheric specialization has been well established for over a century. The early data (e.g., Broca, 1861; Wernicke, 1874) showed the left hemisphere to be specialized for language. Damage to specific zones within that hemisphere produce different, but characteristic, linguistic disturbances (see Goodglass & Kaplan, 1972, for a review). The observation that language disorders rarely occur following right hemisphere damage suggested that the right hemisphere's role in higher cognitive functions was relatively minor. Closer examination of people with right hemisphere disease and studies with neurologically intact people, however, have revealed that the right hemisphere, rather than being minor, plays a critical role in the perception of spatial relations and material for which a verbal label can only be applied with difficulty (see Milner, 1974; Moscovitch, 1979, for reviews). More recently, the left hemisphere has also been characterized as analytic, whereas the right hemisphere has been described as a holistic or gestalt processor (Bradshaw & Nettleton, 1981).

In the last few years, intense interest has focused on the nature of the contributions of both hemispheres to emotion. A major debate is whether the right hemisphere is dominant for all emotions (e.g., Bryden & Ley, 1983) or whether the left hemisphere handles positive affect while the right hemisphere is dominant for negative emotion (e.g., Sackeim et al., 1982). This issue is addressed through three lines of work: (1) studies on the perception of emotional auditory information, (2) studies on the perception of visually presented emotional stimuli, and (3) studies on the alterations in affective behavior seen subsequent to brain injury. Before consideration of these investigations, some techniques for examining functional localization in humans are reviewed.

COMMENTS ON TECHNIQUES

The oldest and richest source of data regarding functional hemispheric specialization derives from observing and reporting the consequences of accidental injury or deliberate surgery. It is important to note that the study of such patients can only indicate that a particular site is implicated in some facets of a mental process. It cannot claim that the area "houses" the process. The major limitation of lesion studies involves the population available for investigation. Naturally occurring lesions rarely result in well-localized damage. In patients who have undergone neurosurgical procedures, such as for the relief of seizure activity, there usually is a long history of neurological abnormalities predating the operative procedures. In such cases, structural plasticity and functional reorganization may be confounding variables in the determination of the normal pattern of lateralization.

Another major approach involves lateralized presentation of stimuli in different modalities (e.g., divided visual field, dichotic listening; see figure 7.1). In principle, these tools can be employed on normal or brain-

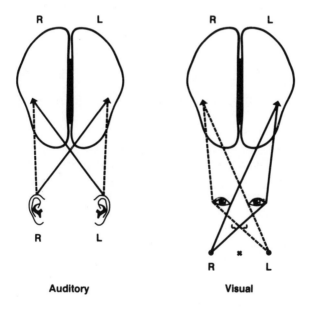

Auditory   Visual

Fig. 7.1 Schematic representation showing auditory and visual pathways.

damaged people. In practice, however, they have been used generally with normal people. The rationale underlying these techniques derives from the fact that each cerebral hemisphere receives information primarily from the opposite side of the body. Thus, the visual cortex receives input from only the contralateral visual half field. A stimulus projected to the left visual field (LVF) will be received first by the right hemisphere, whereas a stimulus presented to the right visual field (RVF) will be received first by the left hemisphere. Laterality effects exist in divided-visual-field studies because one hemisphere is more proficient than the other at dealing with certain types of material or at carrying out certain operations. For the auditory modality, using the dichotic listening paradigm, stimuli are presented simultaneously to both ears. Since contralateral projections from the ears to the hemispheres are stronger and more direct than ipsilateral ones, material is directed primarily to the opposite hemisphere and is perceived best in the ear contralateral to the hemisphere specialized in processing that information. While the logic underlying these techniques may be simple, a major and unresolved issue concerns the validity of perceptual tests as indices of brain lateralization (e.g., Beaumont, 1982; Strauss, Wada & Kosaka, 1985).

Because of the limitations of clinical and "normal" approaches, this chapter emphasizes research from both areas. Fortunately, as we shall see, the fit between data deriving from perceptual laterality tasks and from clinical studies is relatively good.

PERCEPTION OF EMOTIONAL AUDITORY STIMULI

A number of recent studies in the auditory domain have indicated that the right hemisphere, in the normal right-handed person, plays an important role in the processing of emotional tones of speech. Haggard and Parkinson (1971) presented emotionally intonated sentences to one ear and verbal babbling to the other ear. Normal people had to report, by ticking a response sheet, both the affective tone (angry, bored, happy, distressed) and the verbal content (e.g., "Put it down there") of the sentences. A left ear advantage (LEA), suggesting right hemisphere dominance, was obtained for judging the emotional tone. However, the expected right ear advantage (REA), suggesting left hemisphere dominance, for judging the sentence content was not found.

Ley and Bryden (1982), on the other hand, were able to demonstrate a LEA for judging the affective tone (happy, sad, angry, neutral) and a simultaneous REA for recognizing the verbal content (e.g., "The game ended at four o'clock") of emotionally intoned sentences dichotically paired with monotone sentences.

Children, aged 5 to 14 years, also show a LEA for judging the emotional tone of sentences and a REA for identifying the content of the sentences (Saxby & Bryden, 1984). These findings suggest that the right hemisphere mechanisms for the recognition of affective tone are operational in childhood, and do not alter significantly with age (Bryden & Ley, 1983).

Additional support for the idea that the right hemisphere plays an important role in the judgment of the emotional tone of spoken passages comes from a somewhat different type of study. Safer and Leventhal (1977) presented passages varying in emotional tone and emotional content (positive, negative, neutral) to normal adults. They were instructed to listen with either the left or right ear and then rate the emotion expressed in the passages. The majority of subjects who listened with the left ear rated the passages by the tone-of-voice cues, whereas most of those listening with the right ear used the content cues.

The recognition of nonverbal speech sounds, such as laughing, crying, and sighing, has been studied by King and Kimura (1971). They presented dichotic pairs of sounds, and the subjects had to recognize these pairs from four successive binaural sounds, two of which were identical with the two dichotic sounds. This delayed recognition technique yielded a LEA. Carmon and Nachshon (1973) used laughs, shrieks, and cries as stimuli. Subjects listened to a dichotic pair and responded by pointing at appropriate drawings of characters from a multiple choice display. A significant LEA was found, with the majority of subjects being more accurate reporting stimuli presented to the left, as opposed to the right, ear. Finally, a dichotic listening experiment with normal right-handed adults has shown a LEA for the judgment of the emotional tone (positive, negative, neutral) of musical passages (Bryden, Ley & Sugarman, 1982).

Studies with neurologically impaired people provide some support for the view that the right hemisphere plays a role in the judgment of emotional auditory stimuli. Heilman, Scholes, and Watson (1975) asked patients to judge the emotional mood (happy, sad, angry, indifferent) and content (e.g., "The man is showing the boys the horseshoes") of tape-recorded sentences. Line drawings containing facial expressions of the emotions or line drawings corresponding with the contents were displayed with each sentence, and a patient responded by pointing to the appropriate drawing. All patients made perfect scores on the content portion of the test. Patients with right hemisphere lesions, mainly temporal-parietal, were more impaired on the tone task than patients with analogous left hemisphere lesions. Finally, Ross (1981) has described right-handed patients with focal lesions of the right hemisphere who had difficulty comprehending the affective tone of speech. Unfortunately, in the study by Heilman et al. (1975), normal controls were not tested, while in the study by Ross (1981), normals and patients with left hemisphere damage were not evaluated. Consequently, one cannot rule out the possibility that deficits in affective tone recognition may also result from damage to the left hemisphere.

Regarding the controversy mentioned at the outset of this chapter, these investigations in the auditory domain provide no support for the suggestion that the left hemisphere handles positive affect whereas the right hemisphere processes negative emotion. In general, the right hemisphere superiority was found for both positive and negative affective stimuli. Thus, the evidence is compatible with the claim that there are special mechanisms in the right hemisphere for handling emotional material (Bryden & Ley, 1983). On the other hand, it is equally possible that the findings reflect the right hemisphere's more general role in processing complex patterns that are difficult to code verbally. According to this view, material that requires linguistic analysis, even emotional material, should call upon the special abilities of the left hemisphere. In this regard, the study by Safer and Leventhal (1977) is important. Recall that subjects listening with the left ear rated the affective value of passages in terms of the nonverbal tone-of-voice cues, whereas subjects listening with the right ear used the verbal content cues. It would be interesting to have normal subjects judge emotional words presented dichotically. A left hemisphere advantage in such a task would strengthen the proposal that both hemispheres contribute to the analysis of emotional material, albeit in different ways. Examination of studies conducted in the visual modality might shed further light on this issue.

PERCEPTION OF VISUALLY PRESENTED EMOTIONAL STIMULI

The majority of research in the visual domain has centered on the nature of the contributions of both hemispheres to the processing of facial expressions. For example, Strauss and Moscovitch (1981, Experiment 3) used a memory paradigm in which right-handed men and women had to indicate, by pressing a button, whether test faces presented to either the right or left visual field displayed the same affect (happy, sad, surprised) as a target retained over a prolonged time interval. The responses of the subjects were faster in the left, than in the right, visual field, regardless of the type of emotion (see Table 7.1). Similar memory paradigms have been used in other investigations (Suberi & McKeever, 1977; Ley & Bryden, 1979; Ladavas et al., 1980; Hansch & Pirozzola, 1980; McKeever & Dixon, 1981). All these studies, like ours, have reported a LVF–right hemisphere superiority for both positive (e.g., happy) and negative (e.g., sad) emotions, with either accuracy or reaction time as the dependent measure.

A somewhat different memory technique was used by Campbell (1978) and Heller and Levy (1981). Photographs of facial composites, half the face smiling and the other half neutral, were presented tachistoscopically. On each trial, a pair of stimuli was shown with a brief delay separating the presentation of each pair member. In one member of each pair, the smiling half-face was in the LVF and in the other pair member, the smiling half-face was in the RVF. Right- but not left-handed adults judged faces as happier when the smiling half-face was in the LVF and a neutral expression in the RVF.

Recently, I used the chimeric technique described above to extend the scope of investigation to one other distinct emotion, fear. My method was similar to that of Campbell (1978) and Heller and Levy (1981). Sets of composite photographs were prepared, in which half the face had a frightened expression and the other half had a neutral expression. On each tachistoscopic trial, a pair of stimuli was shown; the first member of the pair displayed for 150 milliseconds in midline, followed by a 1000 msec blank field, and then the other pair member for 150 msec in midline. In one pair member the frightened half-face was in the LVF and in the other pair member, the frightened half-face was in the RVF. On each trial, subjects were asked to specify which member of the pair looked more frightened. Eighty (40 men, 40 women) right-handed and 40 (20 men, 20 women) left-handed adults judged the set of composites. In line with the findings of Campbell (1978) and Heller and Levy (1981), I found that the majority of right-handed adults (64%) perceived faces as more frightened when the frightened half-face was in the left visual field. Twenty-six percent showed a right-sided bias and only 10% demonstrated no bias. This

Table 7.1   Time Required to Identify Facial
Expressions of Emotion (in seconds)

	LVF	RVF
Happy	.668	.686
Sad	.616	.632
Surprised	.644	.659

SOURCE: Strauss & Moscovitch, 1981, Experiment 3

pattern was significantly different from that seen in left-handers (Chi square = 7.52, $df = 2$, $p = .02$). In this latter group, 37.5% showed a LVF bias, 47.5% a RVF bias, and 15% showed no difference in LVF and RVF judgments. (See Table 7.2.)

The studies employing a memory paradigm are important for at least two reasons. First, the failure to observe a significant visual field bias for left-handers is consistent with neurological evidence that left-handers are he-terogeneous in their patterns of lateralization, and provides support for the suggestion that the visual field advantage found in right-handers derives from cerebral asymmetry of function (Heller & Levy, 1981). Second, these studies show that among right-handers, a perceptual asymmetry emerges in favor of one of the hemispheres (the right) for both positive and negative emotions. Thus, as was true in the auditory domain, there is little evidence in these visual experiments that the left and right hemispheres mediate positive and negative affect, respectively (but see below).

Again, there are two possible interpretations of these data. First, it may well be that processing any emotional task requires special mechanisms located in the right hemisphere. Alternatively, it is possible that these right hemispheric effects occurred because subjects handled their tasks in a non-verbal manner. Recent studies from our own and others' laboratories support the latter position: that is, both hemispheres contribute to the analysis of emotional material, albeit in different ways. The right hemi-sphere is dominant in affective tasks that require complex non-verbal analysis, whereas the left hemisphere assumes the prominent role in emo-tional tasks that place strong demands on linguistic or analytical processes.

In one of our studies (Strauss, 1983), a left hemisphere–RVF superiority emerged in the processing of linguistic information, even when that informa-tion included emotional words. Positive (e.g., "love"), negative (e.g., "hate"), and nonsense words were presented to the right and left visual fields simultaneously. Thus, each stimulus contained two four-letter strings, one in the LVF, one in the RVF. Half the stimuli consisted of two nonsense strings, half contained one emotional word and one nonsense string. Right-handed men and women pressed a lever whenever "a real English word was seen." In males, positive and negative emotional words were recognized especially well when shown to the RVF-left hemisphere. Females showed a similar, albeit non-significant, trend in the same direction.

Table 7.2 Bias in Perception of Facial Expressions of Fear

	LVF Bias	RVF Bias	No Bias
Right-handers	64%	26%	10%
Left-handers	37.5%	47.5%	15%

On the other hand, Graves, Landis, and Goodglass (1981) argue that the right hemisphere possesses some ability to read emotional words. In their study, emotional (e.g., love), non-emotional (e.g., time), and nonsense words (e.g, etim) were presented to the right and left visual field simultaneously. Half the stimuli contained one word and one non-word, and half the stimuli contained two non-words. The subject had to indicate, by pressing a lever, if any of the words were real English ones. Males showed an overall RVF superiority, but in the LVF, recognition accuracy for emotional words was significantly higher than that for non-emotional words. In the RVF, accuracy levels did not differ significantly. Scores for females were more variable, and there was no overall visual field effect. These findings are important because they suggest that in men there are special processors in the right hemisphere that are particularly concerned with processing emotion.

I tried (Strauss 1983) to replicate the findings of Graves and his colleagues (1981). In addition to the accuracy data, which were of primary interest, latency data, not reported by Graves et al., were examined. For both males and females, emotional and non-emotional words were recognized more accurately when the words were presented in the right, as opposed to the left, visual field. In contrast to the results reported by Graves et al., the emotional quality of words did not improve recognition of the tachistoscopically presented words in the LVF. Analysis of the reaction-time data showed that none of the effects involving visual field reached statistical levels of significance. In short, my study does not indicate that the right hemisphere is uniquely adapted to deal with emotional information. Rather, the results suggest that it is the left hemipshere that handles the linguistic analysis of information, even when that information includes emotional material.

Additional support for the view that the left hemisphere evaluates linguistic aspects of emotional material, whereas the right hemisphere is dominant in affective tasks that require complex spatial analysis, comes from a study by Hansch and Pirozzola (1980). They presented both neutral and emotional words and neutral and emotional faces tachistoscopically. Right-handed normal men and women were cued orally with the name of the emotion or neutral name and were asked to determine whether the stimulus matched the cue. A LVF-right hemisphere superiority was found for the recognition of neutral and emotional faces, whereas a RVF-left hemisphere advantage emerged for the neutral and emotional words.

A similar picture emerges from studies of neurologically impaired people. Gardner, Ling, Flamm, and Silverman (1975) gave a test of humor to a population of brain-damaged and control patients. The subject had to choose the funniest of four cartoons. All brain-damaged patients were impaired on this test, but there was an asymmetry in the pattern of errors. Patients with right hemisphere lesions performed better on items with captions, whereas patients with left hemisphere damage performed better on captionless items.

Kolb and Taylor (1981) examined patients with unilateral focal lesions, using both facial-expression and sentence-matching tests. In the facial-expression test, the subject was first shown seven key photographs, depicting sadness, fear, happiness, anger, disgust, surprise, and interest. The subject was then shown a series of 24 photographs and was asked to match each of them with the key photograph that most clearly expressed the same emotion. In the sentence-matching test, the subject was given the verbal categories of emotion listed above and was asked to indicate the emotion of a person portrayed in each of 48 sentences describing an event. Patients with lesions of the right hemisphere were significantly impaired on the photograph-matching task, whereas patients with lesions of the left hemisphere were significantly impaired on the verbal task.

Berent (1977) tested patients on two tasks, both before and after they were administered a single, unilateral electroconvulsive (ECT) treatment. In task I, the patients were shown a photograph of a face, and following a 5-second delay, were asked to indicate from among three pictures the one most similar to that originally presented. The three test faces were all photographs of the same person, though not the person whose photograph was shown previously. In one of these test photographs, however, the person displayed a facial expression similar to that of the person in the stimulus picture. In task II, the patients were asked to remember a face. They were then shown three pictures and asked to pick the one they had seen originally. In this case, the test pictures included the one originally seen and two people not previously seen. All three pictures displayed facial expressions similar to one another but different from that conveyed in the stimulus phase. Left, but not right, ECT resulted in a significant deterioration in performance on task I, whereas right, but not left, ECT was disruptive to task II. Berent suggested that successful performance on task I was dependent on encoding a labeled expression, whereas in task II configuration was central to successful recognition, thereby accounting for the opposite laterality effects between the two tasks.

Thus, the picture that emerges from these studies with normal and neurologically impaired people is that the right hemisphere is dominant in affective tasks requiring complex nonverbal spatial analysis, whereas the left hemisphere evaluates linguistic aspects of emotional material. At this juncture, however, a set of experiments with normal people by Reuter-Lorenz and her colleagues (Reuter-Lorenz & Davidson, 1981; Reuter-Lorenz, Givis & Moscovitch, 1983) deserves mention. An emotional face (happy, sad) was presented to one visual half field and a neutral face to the other. Each subject's task was to indicate the side on which the emotional face was presented. For right-handers, a right hemisphere advantage emerged for sad faces, whereas a left hemisphere advantage was found for happy faces. One explanation for the results is that the left and right hemispheres are differentially specialized for positive and negative affect, respectively. The investigators, however, point out an alternative explanation. The discrimination of happy and sad faces may be accomplished by utilizing different cognitive strategies. Happy faces may be detected on the basis of a limited portion of the face (e.g., mouth), an analytic task for which the left hemisphere is presumably specialized (Bradshaw & Nettleton, 1981). Identifying sad faces may require that information from various parts of the face be related to each other, a holistic process that presumably requires the right hemisphere. Additional studies are needed to decide between these alternatives.

To summarize, the evidence reviewed in this section, both that of others and that of our own, does not indicate a general right hemisphere superiority for the processing of emotional information (Bryden & Ley, 1983) or only negative affective material (but see Reuter-Lorenz & Davidson, 1981; Reuter-Lorenz, Givis & Moscovitch, 1983; Sackeim et al., 1982). Rather, the data suggest that emotional material is processed no differently than non-emotional information. Accordingly, both the left and right hemispheres contribute to the analysis of emotional information, albeit in different ways. The right hemisphere assumes the prominent role in emotional tasks where complex nonverbal configurations have to be evaluated, whereas the left hemisphere is dominant in affective tasks that place strong demands on linguistic or analytic processes.

Finally, to end this section on a clinical note, we have seen that patients with left hemisphere damage may not be able to comprehend the affective content of linguistic utterances, whereas patients with right hemisphere lesions may experience difficulty in interpreting extralinguistic cues such as tone of voice or facial expression. In short, patients' communication of affect in its broadest sense is likely to be abnormal when they have damage to either hemisphere.

ALTERATIONS IN AFFECTIVE BEHAVIOR SUBSEQUENT TO BRAIN INJURY

Gainotti (1969, 1972) was the first to record systematically the emotional reactions associated with unilateral hemispheric lesions. He reported that in patients undergoing routine neuropsychological tests, anxiety reactions, bursts of tears, imprecations, sharp refusals, or depressed abandonments of the task were significantly associated with left hemisphere lesions, whereas indifference reactions, a tendency to joke, anosognosia, and minimization of the disability were more common in patients with right hemisphere damage. These findings confirmed earlier observations (e.g., Goldstein, 1948) of an association between "catastrophic" reactions and left hemisphere damage and between "indifference" reactions and right brain damage.

Bear and Fedio (1977) compared the emotional behavior occurring in seizure-free periods (interictal behavior) of patients with unilateral temporal lobe epileptic foci. Eighteen traits (e.g., sadness, paranoia, guilt, anger, elation) were assessed in equivalent questionnaires completed by both patients and observers. Right temporal epileptics exhibited "denial," while left temporal epileptics demonstrated a "catastrophic" overemphasis of dissocial behavior.

Strauss, Risser, and Jones (1982) used a self-report questionnaire—a fear inventory—to compare the interictal emotional behavior of patients with right and left temporal lobe epilepsy. In order to explore whether the behavioral features were unique to temporal lobe epilepsy as opposed to disorders arising from other brain sites or from physical insults in general, the following control groups were also given the fear inventory: patients with generalized seizures, patients with peripheral nerve disorders, and healthy individuals. Subjects were asked to evaluate their non-ictal (i.e., not seizure-related) fears of animals/insects (e.g., fear of big dogs or ants), threatened physical injury (e.g., fear of being in a fire), social situations (e.g., fear of speaking to a group of people), and sexual situations (e.g., fear of sexual arousal). They were instructed to respond to each item on a three-point forced-choice scale: never, sometimes, or always afraid. We found that fears of animals and situations causing physical injury did not show consistent group differences. Differential patterns, however, did appear in self-reports of social and sexual situations. While healthy adults, individuals with peripheral nerve disorders, and those with generalized seizures showed similar sexual and social fear reports, patients with foci in the left temporal lobe reported greater social and sexual fearfulness, while patients with foci in the right temporal lobe reported the least social fearfulness. In short, aberrant levels of reported fear appeared to be specific to epilepsies of the temporal-limbic system and were confined to a subtype of stimuli rather than overall fearfulness per se. In line with the studies discussed above, patients with left hemisphere dysfunction were more likely than their right-sided counterparts to report negative feelings.

Recently, Hurwitz and his associates (Hurwitz, Wada, Kosaka & Strauss, in press) observed a 53-year-old right-handed female with independent left and right temporal lobe discharges whose post-ictal mood varied with the side of seizure discharge. Following left-sided discharge, she exhibited an agitated, depressed state while, subsequent to right-sided seizures, she appeared euphoric.

To summarize, dysphoric or negative affect is seen following some left hemisphere disturbances, whereas indifference or euphoria is common with right hemisphere dysfunction. The situation is, however, more complicated than this summary statement suggests. Recent findings with patients who suffered cerebral vascular accidents (strokes) suggest that the location of the lesion within one hemisphere, and not only the laterality of the brain lesion, is an important determinant of mood. Depression is common accompanying damage to the more anterior portions of the left hemisphere but may also occur in mild form accompanying damage to the more posterior portion of the right hemisphere (Lipsey et al., 1983; Robinson et al., 1984). Indifference may occur accompanying anterior right hemisphere damage but can also be seen accompanying a limited lesion to the more posterior portion of the left hemisphere (Benson, 1973; Geschwind, 1981; Robinson & Benson, 1981; Lipsey et al., 1983; Robinson et al., 1984). These findings, if generalizable to other patients with neurological disorders, argue against the simple notion that the left and right hemispheres subserve positive and negative emotions, respectively.

The etiology of the mood alterations is not known. Some researchers have suggested that the mood changes are related to abnormalities in neurotransmitter activity (e.g., Robinson et al., 1984; Lipsey et al., 1983; and Tucker, chapter 10 of this volume). More specifically, alterations in the biogenic amine pathways are thought to underlie the mood changes. A different possibility is that the distinctive patterns can be traced to the patients' cognitive impairments associated with damage to specific brain sites (see preceding sections and Tucker, chapter 10). Thus, the affective disturbances may be due to a patient's misinterpretation of verbal or nonverbal cues. On the other hand, psychological reactions (e.g., grief) to the impairments (e.g., speech disturbance) cannot be ruled out by the current data. Depression in patients wth left hemisphere damage is often correlated with the presence of specific subtypes of aphasia and may appear after repeated failures in communication (Benson, 1973; Kolb & Whishaw, 1980). The indifference reactions of patients with right hemisphere damage may be correlated with the presence of neglect of part of the body and/or space contralateral to the lesion (Kolb & Whishaw, 1980).

Interpretation is made more difficult by the fact that some studies of emotional behaviors show left-right differences, while others do not. The key to this difference may lie in the nature of the behaviors themselves. It is worth noting that, in general, the distinctive hemispheric patterns reviewed above were demonstrated in situations requiring considerable cognitive activity on the part of the patient. Thus, one possibility is that hemispheric differences emerge only under conditions where a cognitive component, requiring *cortical* mediation, is operational. Emotional behavior that is determined by *subcortical* processes (e.g., limbic system, extrapyramydal system, hypothalamus) is unlikely to be lateralized (see Rinn, 1984, for a similar view).

Consistent with this notion are some studies on uncontrolled (spontaneous) emotional displays. Strauss, Risser, and Jones (1982) looked at ictal emotions. These are brief states that are *unusual* in that they generally are not directly associated with anything or anyone. Case reports of 73 patients with right or left temporal lobe epilepsy were examined for the incidence and type of affect felt as part of the epileptic experience. In line with previous studies (Gloor, 1972; Williams, 1956), fear was the most common ictal emotion, reported in 22% of our population. Ictal fear was found equally with right- and left-sided foci, independent of sex and hand preference. There were too few cases of other types of ictal emotions for analysis. It is noteworthy that Gloor (1972) and Williams (1956) have also found that the incidence and nature of uncontrollable moods are not related differentially to ictal processes involving either one of the hemispheres.

Strauss, Wada, and Kosaka (1983) have investigated uncontrollable facial expressions occurring at the onset of focal electrical discharge. The ictal events were documented by simultaneous EEG and videotape recording. The origin of seizure activity was left-sided in 38 patients and right-sided in 39 patients. Since seizure activity may spread from the point of origin, only those facial expressions occurring at the onset of the seizures, as determined by the EEG record, were examined. Each patient's facial expression was scored as reflecting the emotion of happiness, sadness, surprise, anger, fear, or disgust. Blank expressions were scored as neutral. Thus, for each patient, only one expression, the one occurring at seizure onset, was scored. Two judges analyzed the tapes independently.

In the sample as a whole, no association was found between the origin of seizure focus (left, right) and incidence or type of facial expression displayed. There was also no relation between origin of seizure discharge and type of facial expression when males and females were examined separately and when only those with left hemisphere speech dominance (as determined via carotid Amytal tests) were evaluated. The patients in this study had their seizures induced by drugs, and possibly this manipulation interfered with the normal operation of brain mechanisms and thus obscured clinical ictal reflection of hemispheric asymmetries that may exist. In order to clarify this issue, it is necessary to obtain recordings of spontaneous (that is, not drug-induced) seizure activity. At present, the results of this experiment are similar to those from our study on ictal moods. Both suggest that when uncontrollable emotional displays are involved, left-right hemispheric mechanisms do not play their usual roles.

Studies by other researchers point to the same conclusion. Milner and her associates (Milner, 1967; Kolb & Milner, 1981) recorded the frequency of spontaneous facial movements (e.g., brows raised, smiles, lips tight, etc.) in epileptic patients undergoing routine neuropsychological tests. They found that patients with limited cortical excisions of either the right or left frontal lobe exhibit a reduction in spontaneous facial expression (movements?), as compared to patients with unilateral parietal- or temporal-lobe lesions. Kolb and Milner also report no difference in mood (rated by patients and observers) or in frequency or type of facial expressions (movements?) following pharmacological inactivation by carotid Amytal injections of the left and right hemispheres, respectively.

A number of investigators have found, however, that hemispheric differences exist when uncontrolled emotional behaviors are involved. Sackeim and his colleagues (1982) reviewed case reports of uncontrollable emotional outbursts observed during epileptic seizures. Regardless of lateralization, there were few reports of seizure-induced crying. Of the cases of ictal laughing episodes, the epileptic focus was twice as likely to be predominantly left-, as opposed to right-, sided. Assuming that seizure manifestation is associated with activation of the area of the seizure focus, Sackeim et al. interpret these findings as indicating left hemisphere mediation of positive affect and right hemisphere dominance of negative affect.

Pharmacological inactivation of the left and right hemispheres has been found to result in different emotional reactions. Carotid Amytal studies, conducted by Rossi and Rossadini (1967) and Terzian (1965), reveal that depression is associated with left-sided injection, whereas euphoria is more common after right-sided injection. These findings conflict with those of Tsunoda and Oka (1976), who report euphoria with left-sided injection, and with those of Milner (1967; Kolb & Milner, 1981), who observed no consistent relation between emotional behavior and side of injection. The reason for the conflicting observations is as yet unknown, but may reflect procedural differences. Milner and her associates examined the mood of the patient while the drug was still active in the injected hemisphere. However, Rossi and Rossadini (1967) reported that, in general, the emotional reactions occurred as the drug was wearing off. Consequently, it would be important to assess mood a) following pharmacological inactivation of a hemisphere and b) once there is no clinical evidence of drug effects and there is dissipation of marked EEG asymmetry.

In summary, several points deserve emphasis. First of all, we should be skeptical of the argument that the two hemispheres are polar opposites emotionally (see also Geschwind, 1981). There is evidence that both the side of the brain lesion (right, left) and the location of the disturbance within the hemisphere (anterior, posterior) are critical determinants of affective behavior. One should also note that a major unresolved issue is whether the distinctive patterns are due to alterations in neurotransmitter activity, or to cognitive defects associated with injury to specific brain sites, or are secondary reactions to cognitive or sensorimotor loss. In addition, there is reason to suggest that hemispheric differences emerge only under conditions that involve cortically mediated cognitive activity. Uncontrolled or other emotional behavior that is determined by subcortical systems is unlikely to be lateralized. Intact emotional states involve the contributions of both the cortical and subcortical systems, although their contributions are not always equal. The value of studying brain-damaged people, however, is that such complex processes can be fractionated into their constituent components. Such research might ultimately provide a clearer picture of how the systems operate and the nature of their interaction.

SUMMARY AND IMPLICATIONS

The research reported in this chapter, both our own and that of others, suggests several conclusions regarding the lateralization of emotion. Many of these conclusions can be translated into guidelines for future research in the field.

First, there is little evidence in the perceptual literature that positive and negative emotions are lateralized differently (but see Reuter-Lorenz & Davidson, 1981; Reuter-Lorenz, Givis & Moscovitch, 1983; Sackeim et al., 1982). When ear asymmetries or visual field differences emerge, both types of emotion typically show the same perceptual bias. Studies on the alterations in affect seen subsequent to unilateral brain insult also argue against the simple notion that the left and right hemispheres subserve positive and negative affect, respectively. Dysphoric or negative mood may occur following anterior left and possibly posterior right hemisphere damage, whereas indifference or euphoria can be seen with anterior right and posterior left hemisphere lesions.

Second, the claim that the right hemisphere is uniquely adapted for processing emotional information (e.g., Bryden & Ley, 1983) is also not supported by research of the kind reported in this chapter. Processing of emotional material in some instances results in a right hemisphere superiority. In different circumstances, a left hemisphere advantage emerges. The general principle to be extrapolated from studies on visual perceptual asymmetries is that both hemispheres contribute in different ways to the analysis of emotional information. The right hemisphere assumes the prominent role in affective tasks that require analysis of complex nonverbal configurations, whereas the left hemisphere is dominant in emotional tasks that place demands on linguistic or analytic processes. It will be. interesting to see whether this view is upheld in later research on the visual system and also in other sensory domains, such as audition.

One point deserving emphasis is that disturbances to distinct regions of the left and right hemispheres have different effects on emotional behavior. However, the changes in affect produced by damage to the frontal, parietal, and temporal regions in each hemisphere need further clarification. For example, different lesion sites have been associated with euphoria (right anterior, left posterior), yet the actual patterns of euphoria might be quite different. Geschwind (1981) reports that, in his personal experience, the patient with Wernicke's aphasia often laughs and shows unconcern about his speech disorder but does not manifest the more widespread unconcern often observed in the right hemisphere patient: i.e., loss of personal modesty, incontinence of urine, and social inappropriateness. This clinical impression requires more systematic investigation. Similarly, studies are needed to determine whether qualitative differences exist in the patterns of depressive symptomatology associated with different lesion sites.

Another critical issue concerns the cause (or causes) of these affective behaviors. It may be that the abnormal emotional behaviors result from disturbances in neurotransmitter systems. Another possibility is that the behaviors are due to cognitive defects associated with injury to specific brain sites. Yet a different possibility is that the alterations in affective behavior reflect secondary reactions to cognitive or sensorimotor loss. As a preliminary step, it would be important to determine whether the abnormal emotional responses (e.g., depression) are indeed linked with specific cognitive disturbances (e.g., degree of verbal impairment) (see also Lipsey et al., 1983, Buck & Duffy, 1980). If a linkage does exist, then future research may reveal whether treatment in one sphere (e.g., antidepressant medication) results in improvement in another domain (e.g., cognition).

Another point to be emphasized is the desirability of separating emotional behavior that is cortically mediated from that which relies primarily on subcortical circuits (see also Rinn, 1984). A review of the research on behavior change following brain damage suggests that hemispheric differences are observed more readily in situations that require considerable cognitive activity on the part of the patient. Uncontrolled (spontaneous), or other emotional behavior that is mediated by subcortical processes, is unlikely to be lateralized. These ideas, however, remain to be tested.

The familial stress that could arise from emotional changes subsequent to brain injury is also a topic that merits further study. Finally, this chapter has dealt with a rather limited set of affective behaviors in a generally right-handed adult population. Research on other behaviors, such as voluntary emotional expressions and individual differences, is active and likely to become even more so in the future.

Given the many questions that remain to be answered, what guidelines can be given to the clinician for whom recognition and appropriate diagnosis is a considerable challenge? First, one should not lose sight of the fact that distinctive hemispheric patterns have been uncovered. For example, patients with certain left hemisphere lesions are at greater risk for feelings of isolation, low self-esteem, and fear of interpersonal interactions than are patients with damage to homologous regions in the right hemisphere. In short, the approach suggested here requires that the clinician have a sound knowledge of brain-behavior relations and the clinical manifestations associated with various disorders.

Second, every patient should undergo a thorough assessment of perceptual/cognitive abilities since such an examination may provide the key to a patient's abnormal emotional response (Ruckdeschel-Hibbard et al., 1984). For example, a patient with a perceptual deficit may appear indifferent because he misreads cues conveyed through tone of voice or facial expression. The aphasic patient may withdraw, angry and depressed, if a situation challenges his language capacities. A paranoid reaction may occur in the patient with a comprehension defect who falsely believes others are talking about him, possibly using a special code to keep him from understanding (Benson, 1973).

Finally, standard measures of mood (e.g., Beck Depression Inventory, 1961) should be given to document each patient's self-report of affective state. In many cases, it will be necessary to read the questions aloud in order to ensure that patients understand the questions. Ruckdeschel-Hibbard, Gordon, and Diller (1984) suggest that observer ratings of mood should be used concurrently with self-report indices so that any discrepancies can be documented. In this way, issues of denial and exaggeration of affective state can be evaluated.

This chapter has considered both experimental and clinical evidence regarding the brain mechanisms underlying the communication of affect. While a number of questions remain to be answered, researchers and clinicians can gain useful insights from the discovery that distinctive hemispheric patterns exist.

ACKNOWLEDGMENTS

The research conducted and reported in this chapter was supported by grant MA-6973 from the Canadian Medical Research Council and by grant A7933 from the Natural Sciences and Engineering Research Council of Canada.

REFERENCES

Bear, D., & Fedio, P. (1977). Quantitative analysis of interictal behavior in temporal lobe epilepsy. *Archives of Neurology, 34*, 454–67.

Beaumont, G. (1982). *Divided visual field studies of cerebral organization.* London: Academic Press.

Beck, A., Ward, C., Mendelson, M., Mock, J., & Erbargh, J. (1961). An inventory for measuring depression. *Archives of Psychiatry, 4*, 561–67.

Benson, D. F. (1973) Psychiatric aspects of aphasia. *Br. J. Psychiatry, 123*, 555–66.

Berent, S. (1977). Functional asymmetry of the human brain in the recognition of faces. *Neuropsychologia, 15*, 829–31.

Bever, T. G., & Chiarello, R. J. (1974). Cerebral dominance in musicians and nonmusicians. *Science, 185*, 137–39.

Borod, J. C., Koff, E., & White, B. (1983). Facial asymmetry in posed and spontaneous expressions of emotion. *Brain and Cognition, 12*, 165–75.

Bradshaw, J. L., & Nettleton, N. C. (1981). The nature of hemispheric specialization in man. *The Behavioral and Brain Sciences, 4*, 51–91.

Bradshaw, J. L., & Sherlock, D. (1982). Bugs and faces in the two visual fields: Task order, difficulty, practice and the analytic/holistic dichotomy. *Cortex, 18*, 211–26.

Broca, P. (1865). Sur la faculté langage articulé. *Bulletin de la Société d'Anthropolgie de Paris, 6.* 493–94.

Bryden, M. P., Ley, R. G., & Sugarman, J. H. (1982). A left-ear advantage for identifying the emotional quality of tone sequences. *Neuropsychologia, 20*, 3–87.

Bryden, M. P., & Ley, R. G. (1983). Right hemisphere involvement in the perception and expressions of emotion in normal humans. In K. Heilman & P. Satz (Eds.), *The neuropsychology of emotion.* New York: Academic Press.

Buck, R., & Duffy, R. J. (1980). Nonverbal communication of affect in brain-damaged patients. *Cortex, 16*, 351–62.

Campbell, R. (1978). Asymmetries in interpreting and expressing a posed facial expression. *Cortex, 14*, 327–42.

Carmon, A., & Nachshon, I. (1973). Ear asymmetry in perception of emotional non-verbal stimuli. *Acta Psychologica, 37*, 351–57.

Cohen, G. (1972) Hemispheric differences in a letter classification task. *Perception and Psychophysics, 11*, 139–42.

Gainotti, G. (1969). Reactions 'catastrophiques' et manifestations d'indifference au cours des atteintes cerebrales. *Neuropsychologia, 7*, 174–87.

Gainotti, G. (1972). Emotional behavior and hemispheric side of the lesion. *Cortex, 8*, 41–55.

Gardner, H., Ling, P. K., Flamm, L., & Silverman, J. (1975). Comprehension and appreciation of humorous material following brain damage. *Brain, 98,* 395–412.

Geschwind, N. (1981). The significance of lateralization in non-human species. *Behav. Brain Sci., 4,* 26–27.

Gloor, P. (1972). Temporal lobe epilepsy: Its possible contribution to the understanding of the functional significance of the amygdala and its interaction with neocortical-temporal mechanisms. In B. E. Eleftheriou (Ed.), *The neurobiology of the amygdala.* New York: Plenum Press.

Goldstein, K. (1948). *The organism.* New York: American Book.

Goodglass, H., & Kaplan, E. (1972). *The assessment of aphasia and related disorders.* Philadelphia: Lea & Febiger.

Graves, R., Landis, T., & Goodglass, H. (1981). Laterality and sex differences for visual recognition of emotional and non-emotional words. *Neuropsychologia, 19,* 95–102.

Haggard, M. P., & Parkinson, A. M. (1971). Stimulus and task factors in the perceptual lateralization of speech signals. *Quarterly Journal of Experimental Psychology, 23,* 168–77.

Hansch, E. C., & Pirozzola, F. J. (1980). Task relevant effects on the assessment of cerebral specialization for facial emotion. *Brain and Language, 10,* 51–59.

Heilman, K. M., Scholes, R., & Watson, R. T., (1975). Auditory affective agnosia: disturbed comprehension of affective speech. *Journal of Neurology, Neurosurgery and Psychiatry, 38,* 69–72.

Heller, W., & Levy, J. (1981). Perception and expression of emotion in right-handers and left-handers. *Neuropsychologia, 19,* 263–72.

Hurwitz, T. A., Wada, J. A., Kosaka, B. D., & Strauss, E. H. (in press). Cerebral organization of affect suggested by temporal lobe seizures. *Neurology.*

King, F. L., & Kimura, D. (1972). Left-ear superiority in dichotic perception of vocal nonverbal sounds. *Canadian Journal of Psychology, 26,* 111–16.

Kolb, B., & Milner, B. (1981). Observations on spontaneous facial expresson after focal cerebral excisions and after intracarotid injection of sodium Amytal. *Neuropsychologia, 19,* 505–14.

Kolb, B., & Taylor, L. (1981). Affective behavior in patients with localized cortical excisions: Role of lesion site and side. *Science, 214,* 89–91.

Kolb, B., & Whishaw, I. Q. (1980). *Fundamentals of human neuropsychology.* San Francisco: W.H. Freeman & Co.

Ladavas, E., Umilta, C., & Ricci-Bitti, P. E. (1980). Evidence for sex differences in right-hemisphere dominance for emotions. *Neurospychologia, 18,* 316–66.

Ley, R. G., & Bryden, M. P. (1979). Hemispheric differences in recognizing faces and emotions. *Brain and Language, 7,* 127–38.

Ley, R. G., & Bryden, M. P. (1982) A dissociation of right and left hemispheric effects for recognizing emotional tone and verbal content. *Brain and Cognition, 1,* 3–9.

Lipsey, J. R., Robinson, R. G., Pearlson, G. D., Rao, K., & Price, T. R. (1983). Mood change following bilateral hemisphere brain injury. *Brit. J. Psychiat. 143,* 266–73.

Mckeever, W. F., & Dixon, M. S. (1981). Right-hemisphere superiority for discriminating memorized from nonmemorized faces: Affective imagery, sex, and perceived emotionality effects. *Brain and Language, 12,* 246–60.

Milner, B. (1967). In C. Millikin & F. Darley (Eds.), *Brain mechanisms underlying speech and language.* New York: Grune & Stratton.

Milner, B. (1972). Hemispheric specialization: Scope and limits. In F. O. Schmitt & F. G. Worden (Eds.), *The neurosciences: Third study program.* Cambridge, MA: MIT Press.

Moscovitch, M. (1979). Information processing and the cerebral hemispheres. In M. Gazzaniga (Ed.), *Handbook of behavioral neurobiology,* Vol. II, *Neuropsychology.* New York: Plenum.

Reuter-Lorenz, P., & Davidson, R. J. (1981). Differential contributions of the two cerebral hemispheres to the perception of happy and sad faces. *Neuropsychologia, 15,* 609–14.

Reuter-Lorenz, P. A., Givis, R. P., & Moscovitch, M. (1983). Hemisphere specialization and the perception of emotion: evidence from right-handers and from inverted and non-inverted left-handers. *Neuropsychologia, 21,* 687–92.

Rinn, W. E. (1984). The neuropsychology of facial expression: A review of the neurological and psychological mechanisms for producing facial expressions. *Psych. Bull. 95,* 52–77.

Robinson, R. G., & Benson, D. F. (1981). Depression in aphasic patients: frequency, severity, and clinical-pathological correlation. *Brain and Language, 14,* 282–91.

Robinson, R. G., Kubos, K. L., Starr, L. B., Rao, K., & Price, T. R. (1984). Mood disorders in stroke patients: importance of lesion location. *Brain, 107,* 81–93.

Ross, E. D. (1981). The aprosodias: functional-anatomic organization of the affective components of language in the right hemisphere. *Archives of Neurology, 38,* 561–63.

Rossi, G., & Rossadini, G. (1967). Experimental analysis in cerebral dominance in man. In C. Millikan & F. Darley (Eds.), *Brain mechanisms underlying speech and language.* New York: Grune & Stratton.

Ruckdeschel-Hibbard, M., Gordon, W. A., & Diller, L. (1984). Affective disturbances associated with brain damage. In S. Filskov & T. Boll (Eds.), *Handbook of neuropsychology,* Vol. 2. New York: John Wiley & Sons.

Sackeim, H., Weiman, A., Gur, R. C., Greenberg, M., Hungerbuhler, J., & Geschwind, N. (1982). Functional brain asymmetry in the experience of positive and negative emotions: Lateralizaton of insult in cases of uncontrollable emotional outbursts. *Archives of Neurology, 39,* 210–18.

Safer, M. A. (1981). Sex and hemisphere differences in access to codes for processing emotional expressions and faces. *Journal of Experimental Psychology: General, 110,* 86–100

Safer, M., & Leventhal, H. (1977). Ear differences in evaluating emotional tones of voice and verbal content. *JEP: Human Perception and Performance, 3,* 75–82.

Saxby, L., & Bryden, M. P. (1984). Left-ear superiority in children for processing auditory emotional material. *Dev. Psych., 20,* 72–80.

Strauss, E. (1983). Perception of emotional words. *Neuropsychologia, 21,* 99–104.

Strauss, E., & Moscovitch, M. (1981). Perception of facial expressions. *Brain and Language, 13,* 308–32.

Strauss, E., Risser, A., & Jones, M. (1982). Fear responses in patients with epilepsy. *Archives of Neurology, 39,* 626–30.

Strauss, E., Wada, J., & Kosaka, B. (1983). Spontaneous facial expressions occurring at onset of focal seizure activity. *Archives of Neurology, 40,* 545–47.

Strauss, E., Wada, J., & Kosaka, B. (1985). Visual laterality effects and cerebral dominance for speech determined by the carotid amytal test. *Neuropsychologia, 23,* 567–70.

Suberi, M., & Mckeever, W. F. (1977). Differential right hemispheric memory storage of emotional and non-emotional faces. *Neurospychologia, 5,* 757–68.

Terzian, H. (1965). Behavioral and EEG effects of intracarotid sodium Amytal injection. *Acta Neurochirurgia, 12,* 230–39.

Tsunoda, T., & Oka, M. (1976). Lateralization for emotion in the human brain and auditory cerebral dominance. *Proc. Japan Academy, 52,* 528–31.

Wernicke, C. (1874). *Der Aphasiche Symptomen Komplex.* Breslau: Cohn & Weigert.

Williams, D. (1956). The structure of emotions reflected in epileptic experiences. *Brain, 79,* 29–67.

8 The Neuropsychology of Facial Expression: Data from Normal and Brain-Damaged Adults

Joan C. Borod, Elissa Koff, and Ross Buck

The research described in this chapter focuses on the neurospychology of emotional expression, using the face as a behavioral index of emotion. We began with the observation that the two sides of the face often demonstrate striking asymmetries for extent of movement and for intensity of expression. We wondered whether these asymmetries were systematic, and if so, what their relationship to other lateralized functions might be. Further, since the lower portion of the face appears to be predominantly innervated by the contralateral cerebral hemisphere (Brodal, 1957; Kuypers, 1958), we thought that this could be exploited to study the implications of such asymmetries for laterality. Since voluntary facial expression and movement presumably involve cortical control, we thought that facial asymmetry might constitute another index of lateral dominance, and provide a window onto brain/behavior relationships. Also, if facial asymmetry proved to be a reliable phenomenon, it would provide a method for the study of emotional expression in the normal subject.

Darwin (1872) seems to have been the first to document the phenomenon of facial asymmetry during social communication. His discussion, entitled "Sneering and Defiance," contains an assessment of facial asymmetry. Intrigued by reports that Australian natives, when angry, drew the upper lip to one or the other side, Darwin instructed four subjects to uncover the canine tooth on one side of the face during the act of sneering. Two of the subjects could expose the canine only on the left side, one only on the right side, and the fourth on neither side. This distribution, albeit based on a sample of four, foreshadows the findings from contemporary studies of facial asymmetry.

The first systematic study of facial asymmetry for extent of movement was conducted by Lynn and Lynn in 1938 at McLean Hospital. Around the same time, Wolff (1933) pioneered the study of facial asymmetry for emotional quality, using composite photographs. Wolff suggested that the right hemiface projects the social facade while the left hemiface reveals the unconscious self. Since these early reports, a handful of studies have concentrated on facial asymmetry for emotional quality (Karch & Grant, 1978; Lindzey, Prince, & Wright, 1952; Seinen & Van Der Werff, 1969; Stringer & May, 1980), but only in the last five years have studies addressed the more quantitative aspect of facial asymmetry, i.e., the relative extent or intensity of expression on the right and left sides of the face.

In this chapter, we describe four sets of studies relevant to the phenomenon of facial asymmetry, and conclude with a theoretical discussion about the neuropsychology of facial expresson. In the first study, we examined facial asymmetry during posed expression of emotion (Borod & Caron, 1980) and then related those asymmetries to traditional measures of lateral dominance (Borod, Caron, & Koff, 1981a). The second set of studies was designed to rule out the possible confounding effects of hemiface mobility and hemiface size on observed facial asymmetries (Koff, Borod, & White, 1981; Borod & Koff, 1983). In the third study, we compared facial asymmetries observed during posed expression to those seen during spontaneous expression, and examined their relationship to the emotional valence (positive or negative) of the expression (Borod, Koff, & White, 1983). In the final studies, we examined facial emotional expression in brain-damaged patients with unilateral lesions in an attempt to verify the findings observed in normals; both posed (Borod, Koff, Perlman, & Nicholas, 1983) and spontaneous (Borod, Koff, Perlman Lorch, & Nicholas, in press; Buck & Duffy, 1980) expressions were studied.

STUDY I: FACIAL ASYMMETRY DURING POSED EXPRESSION IN NORMALS

When we began our work on facial asymmetry in the mid-seventies, we were primarily interested in determining which side of the face was more involved during posed emotional expression. At that time, there were two separate literatures which led us to opposite predictions about the direction of facial asymmetry. The first prediction, based on the lateral dominance literature, was that facial asymmetry might be another instance of a lateralized motoric function like handedness and footedness, controlled by the dominant cerebral hemisphere. Were this the case, facial expression would be *right*-sided for right-handers and *left*-sided for left-handers. An alternative prediction, based on the emotional-processing literature

(Gainotti, 1972; Gardner, 1975; Heilman, Scholes, & Watson, 1975) was that the facial expression of emotion might be mediated by the right hemisphere. In this event, facial expression would be *left*-sided in right-handers. Assumptions about left-handers were not yet warranted, since most of the studies on emotion had used right-handed subjects.

Method

Fifty-one right- and left-handed normal adults were coached with verbal imagery and visual examples to deliberately produce eight different facial emotional expressions (see Table 8.1), ranging in affective valence from positive to negative (Borod & Caron, 1980). Subjects were videotaped while posing each expression. Later, judges viewed and rated each of the expressions for facial asymmetry, operationally defined as the extent of muscular involvement in the lower face on a fifteen-point scale from extreme left-sided to extreme right-sided. Slow-motion replay was used to locate the film frame that demonstrated maximum or peak expression.

Results

The facial asymmetry scores were analyzed for direction of asymmetry and for their relationship to lateral dominance and emotional valence.

Direction. Overall, the left hemiface was significantly more involved in facial expression than the right hemiface. When subjects were characterized as left- or right-sided according to the direction of the majority of the eight expressions (see Figure 8.1), significantly more subjects were left-sided (N=30) than were right-sided (N=13); only eight subjects showed no consistent asymmetry for expression (for details, see Borod, Koff, & Caron, 1983). The finding of greater left hemiface involvement in

Table 8.1 Facial Expressions

GREETING (mild smiling)
FLIRTATION ("come hither")
CLOWNING (silly—to amuse a child)
CONFUSION (perplexed)
DISAPPROVAL (scolding)
HORROR (terrified)
GRIEF (crying)
DISGUST (apprehending a "bad smell")

the deliberate expression of emotion was interpreted as supporting the notion of a special role of the right hemisphere in emotional processing (see Borod, Koff, & Caron, 1983, for review of the literature).

Lateral dominance. When the data were analyzed by handedness group, there were no differences between right- and left-handers for facial asymmetry. In fact, among those subjects showing asymmetries, the same proportion, i.e., 70%, of each handedness group was left-sided. Although these findings suggested that facial asymmetry was unrelated to handedness, it occurred to us that there could be a *quantitative* relationship such that strongly lateralized right-handers might be more left-faced than strongly lateralized left-handers. Accordingly, we administered to each of the 51 subjects an extensive lateral dominance battery (Borod, Caron, & Koff, 1984; Borod, Koff, & Caron, 1984), which included *performance* measures for strength of leg, arm, and hand and for manual speed and accuracy, and *preference* measures for hand, foot, and eye (see Table 8.2). When we correlated overall facial asymmetry scores with these measures, no correlations were significant, with the exception of eye preference (rho = +.27). The association between facedness and eyedness may reflect peripheral rather than central processing, since the

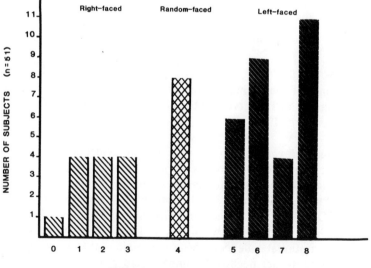

Fig. 8.1 Number of subjects with left-sided facial asymmetry for eight expressions of emotion (Borod, Koff, and Caron, 1983). SOURCE: E. Perecman (Ed.), *Cognitive processes in the right hemisphere.* New York: Academic Press, 1983

Table 8.2 Lateral Dominance Battery

Dimension	Task Description
Strength	Upper leg (pressure cuff)[†] Forearm (pressure cuff)[†] Hand dynamometer*
Speed	Signing name* Hitting targets Dotting circles* Tracing spirals
Accuracy	Target test Spiral test Simultaneous (mirror) writing*
Preference	Hand preference* Foot preference* Eye preference: Eye usage* ABC Eye Test (Miles, 1929)* Hole-in-Card Eye Test*

[†]Pressure in kg. which the subject was able to exert on a blood-pressure cuff by pressing his/her upper leg against the underside of a desk or his/her dorsal forearm against a wall.
*Tasks from the Harris Tests of Lateral Dominance (1958).
SOURCE: *Cortex,* 1981, *17,* 381–90.

neuroanatomy of the cranial nerves suggests interaction and communication between the facial nerve and the nerves that innervate the eye (Gray, 1959; Wartenberg, 1946).

Emotional valence. In view of recent evidence suggesting relatively greater right-hemisphere involvement in negative (i.e., unpleasant) emotion and relatively greater left-hemisphere involvement in positive emotion (Ahern & Schwartz, 1979; Dimond & Farrington, 1977; Reuter-Lorenz & Davidson, 1981; Sackeim, Greenberg, Weiman, Gur, Hunger-buhler, & Geschwind, 1982), we also considered our asymmetry data with respect to emotional valence. Those expressions that were significantly left-sided were in fact negatively toned; these were Disapproval, Confusion, Disgust, and Grief. Most of the expressions that were relatively less lateralized were positively toned: these were Smile of Greeting, Flirtation, and Clowning.

Conclusions

To summarize this study, facial asymmetry during posed expression of emotion was significantly left-sided, and unrelated to measures of handedness and footedness. Further, our data suggested that negatively toned expressions might be more lateralized than positively toned ones.

STUDY II: FACIAL ASYMMETRY RELATED TO HEMIFACE SIZE AND MOBILITY IN NORMALS

While it is certainly the case that this left-sided facial asymmetry could be related to central, that is, right-hemisphere mechanisms, the finding also seemed amenable to another explanation—namely, that the phenomenon was a function of more peripheral factors. For instance, were the two sides of the face or the two "hemifaces" to differ in degree of muscular activity, the side with the greater mobility might be perceived as more expressive. Further, that side might have developed greater facility over time and hence might be able to move more extensively during emotional expression. Along the same lines, were the hemifaces to differ in size, the expression mapped on the smaller side might be perceived as more extensive. To explore these possibilities, we performed two studies; in one, we examined the relationship between hemiface mobility and facial expression asymmetry, and in the other, the relationship between hemiface size and hemiface mobility.

Method and Results

Hemiface mobility. To explore the effects of mobility, 37 right-handed normal adults (19 female, 18 male) were videotaped while producing five different facial expressions of emotion, and while executing unilateral nonemotional facial movements (Borod & Koff, 1983). Mobility of the upper face was assessed by asking subjects to close one eye, and mobility of the lower face by asking subjects to make three unilateral movements: moving the mouth at 45°, 90°, and 135° with respect to a vertical midline. Judges later rated the emotional expressions for degree of facial asymmetry in the lower face and the nonemotional facial movements for hemiface facility. Although the left hemiface was rated as being more extensive during emotional expression and as being more facile during nonemotional movement than the right hemiface, these two asymmetry ratings were not significantly related to each other.

Hemiface size. To look at the effects of size, we examined hemiface size and mobility in 21 right-handed and 21 left-handed normal adults, equally divided by sex (Koff, Borod, & White, 1981). Size was measured from photographs of the full face in frontal view, and mobility was measured from videotapes of the subjects making unilateral nonemotional facial movements. The right hemiface was measured as significantly larger than the left hemiface, and the left hemiface was judged to be significantly more facile than the right hemiface (see Figure 8.2). Parenthetically, it is interesting to note that in a separate study of hemiface size in 40 neonates (3 days old) and 40 preschoolers (2–4 years old), the right hemiface also was measured as significantly larger than the left (Koff, Borod, & Strauss, 1985). Just as handedness seemed unrelated to facial asymmetry in our Study I, handedness did not seem to be related to hemiface size or to hemiface mobility. We also examined the relationship between hemiface size and mobility in light of some evidence that highly practiced unilateral limb usage may be associated with increased muscle

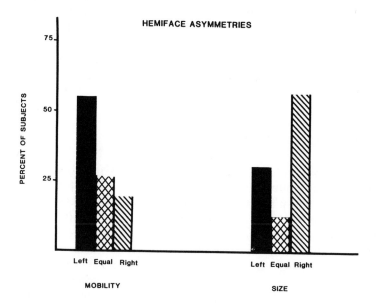

Fig. 8.2 Percent of subjects (N=42) with left, equal, or right asymmetries for hemiface mobility and size.

size and strength (Buskirk, Andersen, & Brozek, 1956). Our analysis of the data, however, revealed no systematic relationship between hemiface size and mobility.

Conclusions

These findings suggest that coincidental rather than causal factors could explain why emotional expression distributed over the generally smaller and more mobile left hemiface appears to be more extensive and/or intense than that on the right hemiface.

STUDY III: FACIAL ASYMMETRY DURING POSED AND SPONTANEOUS EXPRESSION IN NORMALS

At this point, since we had found left-sided asymmetries for both posed emotional expressions and for deliberate nonemotional movements, we wondered whether these findings might reflect a special role for the right hemisphere in the voluntary movement of the facial musculature. Therefore, we next tried to look at what could be thought of as more spontaneous expressions of emotion. Whereas we defined *posed* expressions as deliberate or volitional movements clearly intended by an individual or executed in response to a request (after Myers, 1976), we thought of *spontaneous* or involuntary movements as unintended reactions to appropriately evocative emotional situations. If the right hemisphere has a superordinate role in the expression of emotion, we felt there should be no difference between spontaneous and posed expressions; both should be left-sided. The clinical neurological literature, however, has long suggested a distinction between posed and spontaneous expression (Damasio and Maurer, 1979; Geschwind, 1975), which has been interpreted as reflecting different and possibly independent neuroanatomical pathways (Kahn, 1964; Tschiassny, 1953). Pyramidal control has been implicated in volitional facial movement, in that cortical lesions have been shown to impair the ability to produce an expression—for example, a smile—to command but not spontaneously. Nonpyramidal systems have been implicated in the opposite situation, where volitional movements are intact but spontaneous responses are impaired. Although clinical-behavioral evidence, such as that mentioned above, suggests a distinction between posed and spontaneous facial behavior, the neuroanatomical evidence in humans regarding the origins and course of the neural pathways for spontaneous emotional expression has not been clearly documented. There is, in particular, a lack of consensus about whether pathways for spontaneous expressions are crossed or uncrossed, and just how they are distributed to the upper and lower face.

The following study (Borod, Koff, & White, 1983) was specifically designed to compare facial asymmetries in posed and spontaneous expressions of emotion in the same subjects. In accordance with our earlier observations concerning emotional valence, we included positive and negative expressions.

Method

Subjects were 37 right-handed college students, 19 females and 18 males. For the spontaneous condition, subjects were videotaped while viewing slides designed by Buck (1978) to elicit expressions of positive and negative emotion. For example, a negative slide shows a surgical procedure, and a positive slide shows a little baby picking flowers. Each subject was seated alone facing a one-way mirror, behind which a videocamera recorded his/her responses. A headrest was positioned to keep the subject's head relatively immobile for later asymmetry ratings. There were two posed subconditions: verbal command and visualization. In the first, subjects were requested to pose two positive expressions (happiness, sexual arousal) and two negative expressions (sadness, disgust) to verbal command. In the second, they were instructed to deliberately produce facial expressions appropriate to the slides.

Later, three trained observers, naive with respect to the hypotheses of the study and to the elicitation condition or emotion type being viewed, rated the expressions for type of emotion, overall intensity, and asymmetry in the lower face. The results to follow are based on asymmetry ratings for only those facial expressions perceived as emotional and rated as appropriate to the particular stimulus situation; nonemotional facial movements were excluded from our analysis.

Results

Effects of Condition, Valence, and Sex. A three-way analysis of variance of the facial asymmetry ratings was conducted to examine the effects of Condition, Sex, and Emotional Valence. There were no significant differences in facial asymmetry between elicitation conditions. The percentage of left-sided relative to right-sided expressions is similar across all three conditions—posed verbal, posed visual, and spontaneous. For emotional valence, overall, there was a marginally significant difference between asymmetries for positive and negative emotions. The negative expressions were significantly left-sided, while the positive expressions were more randomly lateralized. Finally, for sex of subjects, there was a significant interaction with emotional valence. This result is presented in Figure 8.3, where the females' score for positive emotions was significantly different from their score for negative emotions and from the males' scores for both positive and negative emotions. Sex-by-valence interactions have also emerged in other studies of facial asymmetry (Borod & Caron, 1980; Schwartz, Ahern, & Brown, 1979; Strauss & Kaplan, 1980). One possible explanation for these findings is that factors intrinsic to the experimental conditions and/or to intrapersonal variables may have produced a differential pattern of responding as a function of sex.

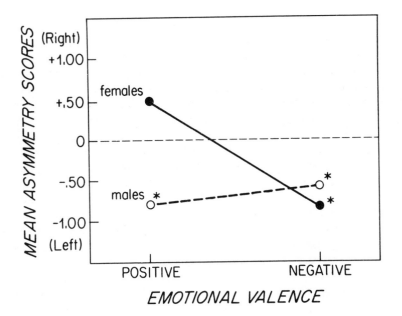

Fig. 8.3 Mean facial asymmetry scores for positive and negative expressions of emotion, by sex of subject. *Note:* An asterisk indicates a score is significantly different from zero, using a two-tailed *t*-test (Borod, Koff, and White, 1983). SOURCE: *Brain and Cognition*, 1983, *2*, 165–75.

Direction of asymmetry. To determine the direction of facial asymmetry, *t*-tests were conducted against the null hypothesis of no difference between the two sides of the face. When all the data for the 37 subjects were considered, facial expressions were significantly left-sided. Since we were measuring asymmetries only in the lower portion of the face (which is predominantly contralaterally innervated), these findings support the notion of a dominant role for the right hemisphere in the facial expression of emotion and are compatible with the existing literature on right-hemisphere specialization for emotion.

In light of the lack of significance in the analyses above, we collapsed across elicitation conditions and examined sex and valence separately. For all subjects, negative emotions were significantly left-sided while positive emotions were not systematically lateralized. When broken down by sex of subject, negative emotions were significantly left-sided for both males and females. Positive emotions were significantly left-sided for males but not for females.

Conclusions

Thus, when patterns of facial asymmetry in posed and spontaneous expressions of emotion were compared, no significant differences emerged. We believe that ours is the first study to address this issue with a substantial number of both posers and expressions. Regardless of whether the production of an expression was intended or not, the pattern of facial lateralization observed in one condition was comparable to that observed in the other condition. Further, posing to verbal command or to visual imagery did not produce differential patterns of lateralization. The use of the posed visualization subcondition afforded us experimental control by requiring the subject to attempt a deliberate re-creation of the spontaneous experience, and by using the identical visual stimulus.

A separate study (Koff, Borod, & White, 1983) may shed some light on the lack of difference among the three conditions: that is, posing to verbal command, posing to visual imagery, and spontaneously reacting to a visual stimulus. Informal observations during our facial studies suggested that subjects were using visualization to prompt themselves while posing emotional expressions. We thought it would be interesting to inquire directly about the subjective experience while posing expressions to verbal command. Accordingly, we asked 43 college-aged student subjects to pose a series of emotional facial expressions and to describe their strategies for creating the expressions. Eighty-six percent of the subjects reported prompting themselves with some sort of visualized cue. Parenthetically, among those who used visualization, the most likely place where the situation, scene, or image was pictured was to the left. Sixty-two percent of the subjects visualized something to the left, 32% saw something straight ahead, and 5% saw something to the right. Thus, all three conditions may involve similar underlying processes, although the elicitation procedures vary.

STUDY IV: FACIAL EXPRESSION IN BRAIN-DAMAGED PATIENTS

Two studies that more directly examine the neuroanatomical correlates of facial emotional expression were undertaken. Each study examined the role of the right hemisphere in emotional expression by comparing the performance of patients with right-hemisphere pathology to those with left-hemisphere pathology. In the first study (Part A), spontaneous expression was examined, and in the second (Part B), both posed and spontaneous expression were examined.

PART A: SPONTANEOUS EXPRESSION

This study (Buck & Duffy, 1980) was designed to examine spontaneous expression of emotion in patients with right- or left-hemisphere brain damage. These patients were compared to a hospitalized control group with non-neurological symptoms and to a group of patients with Parkinson's Disease.

Method

Subjects were 37 male patients hospitalized in a V.A. Medical Center (median age = 65 years) for at least 4½ months. The sample was composed of four groups. There were 8 patients with medical evidence of left-hemisphere damage (right-sided sensory/motor impairment) with a PICA (Porch, 1967) score profile consistent with the diagnosis of aphasia

(LHDs); 10 patients with medical evidence of right-hemisphere damage (RHDs); 9 patients with a medical diagnosis of Parkinson's Disease (PDs); and 10 patients with no known history or medical evidence of neurological damage (NCs). The latter included patients with heart, lung, and stomach symptoms, and amputees. Any patient whose medical diagnosis was unclear, or who had significant visual problems or evidence of bilateral cerebral damage, was excluded from the study. The groups were not significantly different in age, years of education, or (for the LHDs and RHDs) time since onset or incidence of hemiplegia.

The slide-viewing paradigm (Buck, 1978) described in Study III was used to elicit spontaneous expressions of emotion in the patients. Subjects were shown a series of emotionally laden color slides while their facial reactions were videotaped from behind a one-way mirror. Slides were of familiar people (nurses and other well-known hospital personnel), unfamiliar people, unpleasant scenes, and unusual scenes. Raters, a panel of college-students who were unaware of patient diagnosis, viewed the videotapes and attempted to guess the types of slides shown. The resulting accuracy scores indicate the "sending accuracy" (or emotional expressiveness) of the subjects, defined as the ability of the raters to guess the types of slides viewed.

Results

Results indicated that right-hemisphere-damaged patients showed significantly lower sending accuracy relative to left-hemisphere-damaged and patient controls. In fact, right-hemisphere-damaged patients did not differ significantly in sending accuracy from the sample of patients with Parkinson's Disease. The Parkinson's group had been selected because a lack of facial expression (i.e., "masked facies") is recognized as one of the most common and reliable symptoms of Parkinson's Disease (Best & Taylor, 1966), and it thus served to establish a baseline level of emotional expressiveness in a group clinically recognized to be nonexpressive. Finally, observers could determine the category of slides viewed by the left-hemisphere-damaged aphasic patients as well as they could from the facial expressions of non-brain-damaged controls (see Figure 8.4).

The pattern of sending accuracy of the different patient groups across the different slide categories proved to be of interest. The non-brain-damaged control patients exhibited a pattern of accuracy that was remarkably similar to the pattern previously obtained from 24 preschool children (Buck, 1977). Communication was best on "familiar people" slides and at a chance level on "unpleasant" slides. Right-hemisphere-damaged

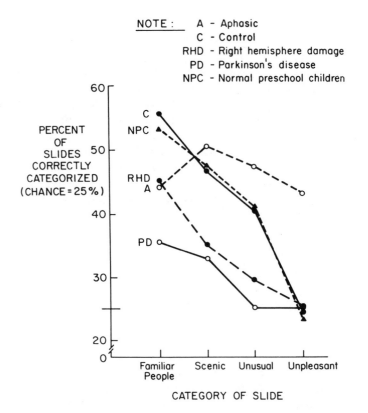

Fig. 8.4 Spontaneous sending accuracy of different patient groups across slide categories.

and Parkinson's Disease patients showed the same tendency, albeit at lower overall levels of communication accuracy. The left-hemisphere-damaged aphasic patients, in contrast, did not respond more to the familiar than the unpleasant slides.

Conclusions

In summary, results indicate that RHD and PD patients were significantly less emotionally expressive than were LHD aphasic patients or hospitalized normal controls under spontaneous elicitation conditions. These findings seem to support the notion that the right cerebral hemisphere is dominant for spontaneous nonverbal expressiveness.

The groupings by slide-type differences were not predicted, and any explanation must be highly tentative. However, it is possible that the differential expressiveness elicited by familar versus unpleasant slides, as evidenced by most of the subjects, is due not to brain mechanisms at all but to the psychological phenomenon of *display rules*. Specifically, we learn to emphasize our positive reaction to people we know (*facilitatory* display rule), and to inhibit our negative response to unpleasant stimuli (*inhibitory* display rule). All groups except the aphasic patients showed this pattern of response. Indeed, the aphasic patients responded in an equally expressive manner to all of the slides: they were less expressive than the controls on the familiar slides but more expressive on the unpleasant. Perhaps left-hemisphere damage acts to lessen the influence of display rules—either facilitatory or inhibitory—on the spontaneous expression of emotion.

PART B: POSED AND SPONTANEOUS EXPRESSION

Our Study III suggested that posed and spontaneous facial expressions have similar patterns of facial asymmetry (i.e., left-sided) in the normal subject, presumably reflecting right-hemisphere mediation. Further evidence for this hypothesis comes from the study just reviewed of patients with unilateral cerebral lesions under spontaneous elicitation conditions. Since spontaneous expression has been considered to reflect different neural pathways and origins than does posed expression, it seemed important to study the expression of emotion in brain-damaged patients under both conditions. In this study (Borod, Koff, Perlman Lorch, & Nicholas, in press) subjects were patients with unilateral right- or left-hemisphere lesions; a demographically similar normal control group was also studied. In light of the valence findings reported above, both positive and negative emotions were elicited.

Method

Subjects were 12 patients with right-hemisphere brain damage (RHD or RBD), 15 with left-hemisphere damage (LHD or LBD), and 16 normal controls (NC). Evidence of a unilateral lesion was confirmed by CT scan. Patients were examined at least one month post onset of illness, with a median of 7.5 months, and were included if their lesions resulted from cerebrovascular accident (e.g., occlusion, embolism, thrombosis). Patients were excluded if they had a history of psychiatric disorder, psychotropic drug treatment, or additional neurological disorder. A similar majority of each brain-damaged group had hemiplegia, visual-field deficits, and facial paralysis on the side contralateral to their lesion. All subjects were right-handed, and the majority were right-footed and right-eyed. The three groups did not differ significantly from each other on demographic variables, with an overall mean age of 57 years, an average of 13 years of education, and middle class as the typical socioeconomic level.

To study the expression of emotion, we videotaped subjects as they viewed positive (pleasant scenes, familiar people, unfamiliar people, and sexual material) and negative (unpleasant and unusual materials) emotionally-toned slides previously described, and as they deliberately posed a range of facial expressions to verbal command or in visual imitation of photographs of prototypical expression (Ekman & Friesen, 1975). Subjects posed positive (happiness, sexual arousal, pleasant surprise) and negative (sadness, anger, fear, disgust, confusion) expressions. All responses were videotaped for later quantitative and qualitative analysis.

Two judges viewed the videotapes of the experimental sessions and scored each expression for accuracy. Each expression was scored as accurate (1) or inaccurate (0). To be successful, an expression had to occur and had to be appropriate for the particular stimulus. Lack of success in the spontaneous condition typically reflected "no response," while in the posed condition it usually meant an inappropriate response. For data analysis, expressions were pooled according to valence. To simplify the presentation and interpretation of results, and since there were no differences between the verbally and visually elicited posed subconditions, data were combined across these subconditions.

Results

Quantitative. An ANOVA on the accuracy ratings was conducted to examine the effects of Group, Condition (posed, spontaneous), and Valence (positive, negative). Overall, RBDs were significantly less accurate in expressing facial emotion than either the LBDs or the NCs (see Figure 8.5). A significant Group-by-Valence interaction suggested that this finding was especially the case for positive emotions. There were also significant differences between the conditions; subjects were less impaired in the posed condition than in the spontaneous one. Finally, there was an interaction between valence and condition; subjects were more accurate

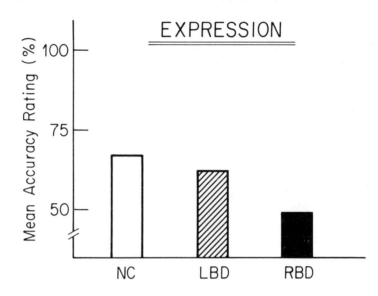

Fig. 8.5 Mean accuracy scores for the expressions of facial emotion, by subject group.

in expressing negative emotion during the spontaneous condition and positive emotion during the posed condition. Since we were concerned that we had included expressions, specifically sexual arousal and confusion, that are not considered part of the canon of basic emotions (Ekman & Friesen, 1975; Izard, 1971), these expressions were removed and the analysis repeated. Again, there were significant differences between the groups, with the RBDs the most impaired.

Qualitative analyses. In addition to quantitative differences in the performance of RBDs relative to LBDs on tasks of facial expression, the quality of responses also differed. During the expression tasks, a variety of inappropriate responses were observed. Among these were what we have termed "paramotias" (a part of the gestalt facial expression was inaccurate), unrecognizable facial expressions, facial groping (a disorganized performance of multiple facial movements without production of any one specific gestalt configuration), and vocalization (e.g., saying "happy" when requested to look happy). RBDs demonstrated significantly more paramotias, unrecognizable facial expressions, and facial groping than NCs, and tended to show more paramotias and unrecognizable expressions than LBDs. LBDs produced significantly more vocalizations than RBDs or NCs.

Conclusions

In summary, these data show that patients with right-hemisphere pathology have more difficulty producing facial expressions of emotion than do patients with left-hemisphere pathology or normal controls. This appears to be the case for both spontaneous and posed expressions of emotion. That RBDs are impaired relative to both LBDs and NCs in expressing and perceiving facial emotion is consistent with the notion that the right hemisphere has a predominant role in the processing of emotional stimuli. As long ago as 1912 (Mills), it was suggested that right-brain-damaged patients are impaired in emotional processing. Prior to the present data, however, most of the findings had been based on studies of perception and comprehension of emotion (e.g., Heilman, Scholes, & Watson, 1975; Cicone, Wapner, & Gardner, 1980), and relatively little work had focused on impairments in emotional expression.

SUMMARY AND CONCLUSIONS

The research described in this chapter focused on the neuropsychology of emotional expression, using the face as a behavioral index of emotion. We have described four studies concerning hemispheric specialization in the control of facial expression.

First, we examined facial asymmetry during volitional emotional expression and then related the asymmetries to traditional measures of lateral dominance (Borod & Caron, 1980; Borod, Caron, & Koff, 1981a). Overall, facial expression was more extensive on the left than on the right side of the face; this was especially the case for expressions of negative emotion. Asymmetries in facial expression seemed to be independent of handedness and footedness but correlated with eyedness. Second, we examined the possible confounding effects of hemiface mobility and hemiface size on observed facial asymmetries (Borod & Koff, 1983; Koff, Borod, & White, 1981). While hemiface mobility was left-sided and hemiface size larger on the right side, these peripheral factors did not appear to relate to the direction of facial asymmetries. Third, we compared facial asymmetries observed during posed expression to those during spontaneous expression and examined their relationship to the emotional valence of the expression, i.e., positive or negative (Borod, Koff, & White, 1983). Overall, the majority of expressions were judged to be asymmetric and significantly left-sided. There were no differences in patterns of facial asymmetry between posed and spontaneous expressions, but there were asymmetry differences as a function of emotional valence and sex. Again, negative expressions were more left-sided than positive ones. Finally, we examined spontaneous and posed facial expressions of emotion in brain-damaged patients (Borod, Koff, Perlman, & Nicholas, 1983; Buck & Duffy, 1980). Right-brain-damaged patients, relative to left-brain-damaged patients and normal controls, were impaired in the communication of facial emotion. Taken together, these studies of normal and brain-damaged adults support a dominant role for the right hemisphere in the expression of facial emotion.

THEORETICAL SPECULATIONS

The Role of the Right Hemisphere in Emotion

The general findings of greater left hemiface involvement in the expression of emotion in normals *and* facial expression deficits in patients with right-hemisphere pathology appear to be related to the special role of the right hemisphere in emotional processing (Borod, Koff, & Caron, 1983; Ley & Bryden, 1982; Tucker, 1981, and chapter 10 of this book). At this point we can only speculate about how and why the right hemisphere became dominant for emotion. Such speculation can be offered at the psychological, neuroanatomical, and developmental level.

At the *psychological* level, emotional processing involves strategies and functions for which the right hemisphere has been described as superior: strategies variously termed nonverbal, holistic, synthetic, and gestalt, and functions variously characterized as visuospatial organization, pattern perception, and visual imaging. Gardner and his colleagues (Gardner, Brownell, Wapner, & Michelow, 1983) have suggested that the critical demand of emotional processing that engages the right hemisphere is a spatial one, that is, a sensitivity to relationships among emotions that entails some determination of which behavior is appropriate for a particular situation. The right hemisphere appears to have a capacity for multimodal integration and organization and thus may be particularly attentive and sensitive to changes in the environment. This suggestion is supported by research observing that unilateral neglect of space accompanies with much greater frequency damage to the right parietal lobe than to the left (Hécaen & Albert, 1978; Heilman, 1982; Walsh, 1978). Heilman (1982) has suggested that the right hemisphere may be more in touch with certain subcortical systems which are important for both arousal and intention. Support for this theory comes from studies with right-lesioned patients, in whom reaction times are found to be very slow and GSRs (galvanic skin responses) difficult to obtain.

At the *neuroanatomical* level, what we know about the structure of the right hemisphere is consistent with the strategies and functions associated with emotional processing. A higher concentration of white to grey matter in the right hemisphere compared to the left suggests a greater degree of neuronal interconnectivity among regions (and possibly among functions) of the right hemisphere (Gur, Packer, Hungerbuhler, Reivich, Obrist, Amarnek, & Sackeim, 1980). This neuroanatomical finding seems to agree with Semmes' behavioral observations (1968) about the diffuse, integrative processing dimension of the right hemisphere. Although there is ample documentation that limbic system structures are intimately involved in emotion (Lamendella, 1977; Papez, 1937), there is currently no neuroanatomical evidence for greater or more direct limbic system connectivity to the right rather than to the left hemisphere (Geschwind, 1979; Pandya, 1979). This speculation may, of course, be borne out eventually.

From a *developmental* perspective, Brown and Jaffe (1975) have suggested that the right hemisphere may be dominant in infancy, when the organism is predominantly responsive to such emotionally laden environmental cues as faces, nonverbal sounds, intonational aspects of speech, and somatosensory input, and that this hemisphere may retain a sensitivity for emotional information throughout development. It has further been postulated that, in the early neonatal state, the right hemisphere is more active than the left (Carmon & Nachshon, 1973) and becomes responsible for the initial elaboration of emotional arousal (Ley, 1979; Tucker, 1981). Head-turning in infants does, in fact, show a spontaneous right bias as early as 24 hours after birth (Michel, 1981; Turkewitz, Gordon, & Birch, 1965). Thus, from very early on, it is possible that the left visual field, the left ear, and the left side of the head may receive selectively more exposure to the environment than the right side of the body, with profound implications for later behavior.

Emotional Valence and Laterality

While the studies reviewed in this chapter indicate that the right hemisphere is specialized for emotional processing in general, the normal data from Studies I and III suggest that this is especially the case for emotions that are negatively toned. In light of these findings, we reviewed the papers on facial asymmetry, attending particularly to the elicitation condition employed and the emotional valence of the expressions studied (Borod & Koff, 1984). There were 15 studies examining posed expressions and seven studies of spontaneous expression. Table 8.3 displays the number of studies in which a significant majority of posers displayed left-sided or right-sided facial asymmetry or no differences between the two sides of the face (i.e., equal).

When considering the findings for negative emotions, we see that the left hemiface (and by implication, the right cerebral hemisphere) was involved more frequently than the right hemiface in the deliberate production of negative emotion. Since so few studies have addressed the spontaneous production of negative emotion, it seems premature to attempt a generalization about these data. For positive emotion, the majority of studies have found that the left and right hemifaces were involved with relatively equal frequency; these findings obtained for both posed and spontaneous expression. These studies, then, do not appear to support the hypothesis that positive emotions are predominantly right-sided and (by implication) innervated by the left hemisphere; if any conclusion is to be drawn, it is that there is bilateral involvement in the expression of positive emotion (see Strauss, chapter 7 of this book).

How can we explain what appears to be a right-hemisphere specialization for negative emotions? It may be that the answer lies in the quality of the emotional processing upon which an emotional response is based. The quality of the decision one has to make in the case of negative emotions may be different than that for positive emotions. If negative emotions are linked with survival, e.g., removing oneself from a dangerous situation, then a system would be required that is sensitive to a variety of different multimodal inputs, only a part of which would be necessary for a decision to be made. One would not necessarily need resolution of fine detail upon which to base a response, but would need only to be able to quickly scan and evaluate the entire situation. This type of behavior seems to be

Table 8.3 Number of Studies in Which a Significant Majority of Posers Displayed Facial Asymmetry

| Emotion | Condition | Asymmetries | | |
		Left	Equal	Right
Positive	Posed	3	12	0
	Spontaneous	1	6	0
Negative	Posed	10	4	0
	Spontaneous	2	1	0

more linked to gestalt, synthetic processing than to discrete, focused analysis. Support for this comes from Denenberg's work (Sherman, Garbanati, Rosen, Yutzey, & Denenberg, 1980) with animals showing that spatial choice and conditioned fear are mediated by the same (right) hemisphere; Denenberg and his colleagues have postulated that "spatial territoriality" might, in fact, be the basis for fight and flight behaviors. An independent elaboration of this theory has been proposed by Heilman (1982), who described negative emotions as those associated with preparation for action, high arousal levels, and vigilance to further incoming stimuli. These are processes that seem more apposite to the right than to the left hemisphere.

At this point, one can only speculate about why negative emotions would be lateralized at all (and more so than positive emotions). One possibility is that negative emotions are more critical in terms of mobilizing the organism. One might argue that rapid, efficient activity is not the typical response to a positive emotion, while it may be more so for negative emotions (e.g., fight, flight). From an evolutionary perspective, this seems logical, since laterality is thought to reduce the potential for intrahemispheric conflict. It may, in fact, be more important to survival to avoid such conflict than to build redundancy. One could argue that the generation of a motoric response is generally unilateral and possibly more efficient in that respect, because it avoids the need for fine coordination between the two sides of the body.

If one considers positive emotions, on the other hand, there may be reasons why they tend to be less lateralized and/or less dominated by right-hemisphere processes. We have suggested that expressions of positive emotions, for example, the smile, are often more communicative and linguistic than reactive and emotional, thus possibly reflecting more left-hemisphere involvement in their execution (Borod, Caron, & Koff, 1981b). In general, most pleasant emotions are communicative, while most unpleasant ones tend to be reactive. There are, obviously, exceptions to this notion; for example, "joy" can be thought of as positive and reactive, and "anger" as negative and communicative. The communicative/reactive dichotomy gains support from findings (LoCastro, 1972) that expressions of love and anger are better communicated through verbal content (a left-hemisphere function) that are expressions of sadness and joy, which are better communicated through facial expression (presumably a right-hemisphere function). Further, the dimensions of pleasantness and communicativeness can be related to yet another dimension, i.e, approach/withdrawal, suggested as salient in emotional expression (Ahern & Schwartz, 1972; Izard, 1979). Kinsbourne, in fact, has made an argument for left-hemisphere involvement in approach behaviors and right-hemisphere involvement in withdrawal behaviors (1980).

Another explanation for differences between positive and negative emotions is related to their response characteristics. Smiles of happiness are generally defined by their bilateral symmetry; a unilateral smile appears bizarre and may thus be perceived as more negative—for example, a sneer, a leer, a quizzical look. Thus, in studies where raters selected those responses that looked happy or where experimenters worked carefully with their posers to produce prototypical smiles, the facial expressions were likely to be symmetrical or, if not, slightly nonsymmetrical and not consistently lateralized to one or the other hemiface. Negative expressions, on the other hand, are often more one-sided, e.g., sneering or disdain.

Sex Differences and Display Rules

In addition to finding differences in facial asymmetry as a function of emotional valence, we also found interactions between sex of poser and valence of expression, whereby patterns of facial asymmetry for females were more affected by emotional valence than were those for males. Similar sex-by-valence interactions have been reported in other studies of facial asymmetry (Schwartz, Ahern, & Brown, 1979; Strauss & Kaplan, 1980). In speculating about what accounts for the sex differences, several explanations were posited. One is that such differences reflect structural differences between male and female brains. Another is that interpersonal variables may induce different modes of responding for males and females. Clearly, subjects' tendencies to behave in a particular way in social situations could influence their performances in studies of affect.

Another explanation for these sex-by-valence findings derives from social-psychological theories about display rules. Buck (1982, 1984) and Tucker (1981, and chapter 10 of this book) have suggested that the right hemisphere is associated with general affective processes (both positive and negative) and the left hemisphere with the control (i.e., facilitation and inhibition) of these processes according to display rules.

A final explanation could be that factors intrinsic to the experimental conditions, e.g., sex of experimenter, may affect the subjects' behavior in a significant way. This possibility has to be considered in light of our first study on facial asymmetry (Borod & Caron, 1980) in which there were sex-by-valence interactions but in different directions than in the Borod, Koff, and White study (1983). In the Borod and Caron study (1980), positive emotions were left-lateralized for females but not for males, while negative emotions were left-lateralized for both females and males. Experimenter variables may have been a factor since in the Borod and

Caron study (1980), the experimenter was a man, and in the Borod, Koff, and White study (1983), in which the interaction went in the opposite direction, the experimenter was a woman. In both studies, expressions were significantly left-sided, regardless of valence, when the sex of the experimenter was opposite to the sex of the subject. It has been pointed out that left-sided, relative to right-sided, facial expressions are more frequent when subjects are embarrassed (Alford, 1982) or self-conscious (i.e., face-to-face with the examiner; Rinn, 1984); in a similar vein, left-directed lateral eye movements are more frequent when subjects are asked questions designed to elicit shame and embarrassment (Libby & Yaklevich, 1973). In studies of personality, Lynn and Lynn (1938) found that shy and insecure subjects tended to be more left-faced than confident subjects, and Libby and Yaklevich (1973) found that high self-abasing subjects typically avert their gaze to the left. (It is interesting to note that these studies just reviewed perhaps provide support for Wolff's speculation [1933] that the left side reflects the unconscious self.)

ACKNOWLEDGMENTS

This work was supported, in part, by United States Public Health Service Grant No. MH37952 to New York University School of Medicine, USPHS Grant No. NS06209 to Boston University School of Medicine, and Bio-Medical Research Support Grant 1-SO7RR07186-02 to Wellesley College. We are grateful to Mary Hyde and Errol Baker for assistance in statistical analysis, and to Jerry Martin and Karen Olsen for assistance in videotaping. We are especially grateful to the Medical Research Services of the Boston and Cleveland Veterans Administration Medical Centers, and to the Aphasia Research Center, Department of Neurology, Boston University School of Medicine.

REFERENCES

Ahern, G. L., and Schwartz, G. E. (1979). Differential lateralization for positive versus negative emotion. *Neuropsychologia, 17,* 693–98.

Alford, R. (1982). Personal communication.

Best, C., and Taylor, N. (1966). *The physiological basis of medical practice.* Baltimore: Williams and Wilkins.

Borod, J. C., and Caron, H. S. (1980). Facedness and emotion related to lateral dominance, sex, and expression type. *Neuropsychologia, 18,* 237–42.

Borod, J. C., Caron, H. S., and Koff, E. (1981a). Asymmetry of facial expression related to handedness, footedness, and eyedness: A quantitative study. *Cortex, 17,* 381–90.

Borod, J. C., Caron, H.S., and Koff, E. (1981b). Asymmetries in positive and negative facial expressions: Sex differences. *Neuropsychologia, 19,* 819–24.

Borod, J. C., Caron, H. S., and Koff, E. (1984). Left-handers and right-handers compared on performance and preference measures of lateral dominance. *The British Journal of Psychology, 75,* 177–86.

Borod, J. C., and Koff, E. (1983). Hemiface mobility and facial expression asymmetry. *Cortex, 19,* 355–61.

Borod, J. C., and Koff, E. (1984). Asymmetries in Affective Facial Expression. In N. Fox and R. Davidson (Eds.), *The psychobiology of affective development.* Hillsdale, NJ: Erlbaum and Associates.

Borod, J. C., Koff, E., and Caron, H. S. (1983). Right hemispheric specialization for the expression and appreciation of emotion: A focus on the face. In E. Perecman (Ed.), *Cognitive processes in the right hemisphere.* New York: Academic Press.

Borod, J. C., Koff, E., and Caron, H. S. (1984). The Target Test: A simplified laterality measure of speed and accuracy. *Perceptual and Motor Skills, 58,* 743–48.

Borod, J. C., Koff, E., Perlman, M., and Nicholas, M. (1983). Expression and appreciation of facial emotion in brain-damaged patients. Paper presented at the International Neuropsychology Society, Mexico City.

Borod, J. C., Koff, E., Perlman Lorch, M., and Nicholas, M. (in press). The expression and perception of facial emotion in brain-damaged patients. *Neuropsychologia.*

Borod, J. C., Koff, E., and White, B. (1983). Facial asymmetry in posed and spontaneous expressions of emotion. *Brain and Cognition, 2,* 165–75.

Brodal, A. (1957). *The cranial nerves: Anatomy and anatomical-clinical correlations.* Oxford, England: Scientific Publications.

Brown, J. W., and Jaffe, J. (1975). Hypotheses of cerebral dominance. *Neuropsychologia, 13,* 107–10.

Buck, R. W. (1977). Nonverbal communication of affect in preschool children: Relationships with personality and skin conductance. *Journal of Personality and Social Psychology, 35,* 225–36.

Buck, R. (1978). The slide-viewing technique for measuring nonverbal sending accuracy: A guide for replication. *Catalog of Selected Documents in Psychology, 8,* 63.

Buck, R. (1982). A theory of spontaneous and symbolic expression: Implications for facial lateralization. Paper presented at the International Neuropsychology Society Meeting, Pittsburgh.

Buck, R. (1984). *The communication of emotion.* New York: Guilford Press.

Buck, R., and Duffy, R. J. (1980). Nonverbal communication of affect in brain-damaged patients. *Cortex, 16,* 351–62.

Buskirk, E. R., Andersen, K. L., and Brozek, J. (1956). Unilateral activity and bone and muscle development in the forearm. *Research Quarterly, 27,* 127–31.

Carmon, A., and Nachshon, I. (1973). Ear asymmetry in perception of emotional nonverbal stimuli. *Acta Psychologia, 37,* 351–57.

Cicone, M., Wapner, W., and Gardner, H. (1980). Sensitivity to emotional expressions and situations in organic patients. *Cortex, 16,* 145–58.

Damasio, A. R., and Maurer, R. G. (1978). A neurological model for childhood autism. *Archives of Neurology, 35,* 777–86.

Darwin, C. (1872). *The expression of the emotions in man and animals.* Reprint, New York: D. Appleton and Company, 1890.

Dimond, S. J., and Farrington, L. (1977). Emotional response to films shown to the right or left hemisphere of the brain measured by heart rate. *Acta Psychologia, 41,* 255–60.

Ekman, P., and Friesen, W. (1975). *Unmasking the face.* Englewood Cliffs, NJ: Prentice-Hall.

Gainotti, G. (1972). Emotional behavior and hemispheric side of the lesion. *Cortex, 8,* 41–55.

Gardner, H. (1975). *The shattered mind: The person after brain damage.* New York: Alfred A. Knopf.

Gardner, H., Brownell, H., Wapner, W., and Michelow, D. (1983). Missing the point: The role of the right hemisphere in the processing of complex materials. In E. Perecman (Ed.), *Cognitive processes in the right hemisphere.* New York: Academic Press.

Geschwind, N. (1975). The apraxias: Neural mechanisms of disorders of learned movement. *American Scientist, 63,* 188–95.

Geschwind, N. (1979). Personal communication, June 15.

Gray, H. (1959). The cranial nerves. In C. M. Gross (Ed.), *Anatomy of the human body.* Philadelphia: Lea and Febiger.

Gur, R. C., Packer, I. K., Hungerbuhler, J. P., Reivich, M., Obrist, W. D., Amarnek, W. S., and Sackeim, H. A. (1980). Differences in the distribution of gray and white matter in human cerebral hemispheres. *Science, 207,* 1226–28.

Hécaen, H., and Albert, M. L. 1978. *Human neuropsychology.* New York: John Wiley and Sons.

Heilman, K. (1982). Discussant comments. In J. C. Borod and R. Buck (organizers), *Asymmetries in facial expression: Method and meaning.* Symposium presented at the International Neuropsychology Society Meeting, Pittsburgh.

Heilman, K. M., Scholes, R., and Watson, R. T. (1975). Auditory affective agnosia. *Journal of Neurology, Neurosurgery and Psychiatry, 38,* 69–72.

Izard, C. D. (1971). *The face of emotion.* New York: Appleton-Century-Crofts.

Izard, C. (1979). Emotions and human development. Paper presented at the Social Relations Psychology Colloquium, Harvard University.

Kahn, E. A. (1964). Facial expression. *Clinical Neurosurgery, 12,* 9–22.

Karch, G. R., and Grant, C.W. (1978). Asymmetry in perception of the sides of the human face. *Perceptual and Motor Skills, 47,* 727–34.

Kinsbourne, M. (1980). The attempt to find an organizing principle for the specialized function of each hemisphere. Paper presented at the Society for Research in Development Symposium, "The development of emotion and cerebral asymmetry." Tarrytown, New York.

Koff, E., Borod, J. C., and Strauss, E. (1985). The development of hemiface asymmetry. *Cortex, 21,* 153–56.

Koff, E., Borod, J., and White, B. (1981). Asymmetries for hemiface size and mobility. *Neuropsychologia, 19,* 825–30.

Koff, E., Borod, J. C., and White, B. (1983). A left hemispace bias for visualizing emotional situations. *Neuropsychologia, 21,* 273–76.

Kuypers, H. G. J. M. (1958). Corticobulbar connections to the pons and lower brain-stem in man. *Brain, 81,* 364–90.

Lamendella, J. T. (1977). The limbic system in human communication. In H. Whitaker and H. A. Whitaker (Eds.), *Studies in neurolinguistics.* New York: Academic Press.

Ley, R. G., and Bryden, M. P. (1982). Consciousness, emotion, and the right hemisphere. In R. Stevens and G. Underwood (Eds.), *Aspects of consciousness.* New York: Academic Press.

Libby, W. L., and Yaklevich, D. (1973). Personality determinants of eye contact and direction of gaze aversion. *Journal of Personality and Social Psychology, 27,* 197–206.

Lindzey, G., Prince, B., and Wright, H. K. (1952). A study of facial asymmetry. *Journal of Personality, 21,* 68–84.

LoCastro, J. (1972). Judgment of emotional communication in the facial-vocal-verbal channels. Unpublished Ph.D. Thesis, University of Maryland.

Lynn, J. G., and Lynn, D. R. (1938). Face-hand laterality in relation to personality. *Journal of Abnormal and Social Psychology, 33,* 291–322.

Michel, G. F. (1981). Right-handedness: A consequence of infant supine head-orientation preference? *Science, 212,* 685–87.

Mills, C. K. (1912). The cerebral mechanism of emotional expression. *Transactions of the College of Physicians of Philadelphia, 34,* 147–85.

Myers, R. E. (1976). Comparative neurology of localization and speech: Proof of a dichotomy. *Annals of the New York Academy of Science, 280,* 745–57.

Pandya, D. (1979). Personal communication, May 3.

Papez, J. W. (1937). A proposed mechanism of emotion. *Archives of Neurology and Psychiatry, 38,* 725–43.

Porch, B. E. (1967). *Porch Index of Communicative Ability.* Palo Alto: Consulting Psychologists Press.

Reuter-Lorenz, P., and Davidson, R. (1980). Differential contributions of the two cerebral hemispheres to the perception of happy and sad faces. Paper presented at the International Neuropsychological Society Meeting, San Francisco.

Rinn, W. E. (1984). The neuropsychology of facial expression: A review of the neurological and psychological mechanisms for producing facial expression. *Psychological Bulletin, 95,* 52–77.

Sackeim, H., Greenberg, M., Weiman, A., Gur, R., Hungerbuhler, J., and Geschwind, N. (1982). Hemispheric asymmetry in the expression of positive and negative emotions: Neurologic evidence. *Archives of Neurology, 39,* 210–18.

Schwartz, G. E., Ahern G. L., and Brown, S. L. (1979). Lateralized facial muscle response to positive and negative emotional stimuli. *Psychophysiology, 16,* 561–71.

Seinen, M., and Van Der Werff, J. J. (1969). The perception of asymmetry in the face. *Nederlands Tijdschrift voor de Psychologie en Haar Grensgebieden, 24,* 551–58.

Semmes, J. (1968). Hemispheric specialization: A possible clue to mechanism. *Neuropsychologia, 6,* 11–26.

Sherman, G. F., Garbanati, J. A., Rosen, G. D., Yutzey, D. A., and Denenberg, V. H. (1980). Brain and behavioral asymmetries for spatial preference in rats. *Brain Research, 192,* 61–67.

Strauss, E., and Kaplan, E. (1980). Lateralized asymmetries in self-perception. *Cortex, 6,* 283–93.

Stringer, R., and May, P. (1980). Attributional asymmetries in the perception of moving, static, chimeric and hemisected faces. Internal report, Katholieke Universiteit, Nijmegen.

Tschiassny, K. (1953). Eight syndromes of facial paralysis and their significance in locating the lesion. *Annals of Otology, Rhinology, and Laryngology, 62,* 677–91.

Tucker, D. M. (1981). Lateral brain function, emotion, and conceptualization. *Psychology Bulletin, 89,* 19–46.

Turkewitz, G., Gordon, E., and Birch, H. (1965). Head turning in the human neonate: Spontaneous patterns. *The Journal of Genetic Psychology, 107,* 143–58.

Walsh, K. S. (1978). *Neuropsychology: A clinical approach.* New York: Churchill Livingstone.

Wartenberg, R. (1946). Associated movements in the oculomotor and facial muscles. *Archives of Neurology and Psychiatry, 55,* 439–88.

Wolff, W. (1933). The experimental study of forms of expression. *Character and Personality, 2,* 168–73.

9 Sensitivity to Nonverbal Communication in Normal, Psychiatric, and Brain-Damaged Samples

Robert Rosenthal and Larry I. Benowitz

Through the centuries the study of human communication has focused primarily on verbal language, perhaps because of the rich informational content of the spoken or written word, perhaps because the stream of consciousness is accompanied by inner speech, or perhaps because language has been regarded as a central feature of what is uniquely human. The wealth of information communicated by cues such as facial expressions, body movements, or intonational qualities of the voice, on the other hand, received little systematic attention prior to Darwin's (1872) seminal investigation into the cross-cultural, ontogenetic, physiological, and evolutionary aspects of emotional expression (Sebeok & Rosenthal, 1981). The recent growth of interest in research in nonverbal communication can be traced in part to contemporary appreciation of Darwin's biological perspective (e.g., Ekman, 1982).

As the reader has seen in chapters 7 and 8, studies of psychiatrically and neurologically impaired subjects not only contribute to our appreciation of the constituent elements of nonverbal communication and of their relationship to particular brain structures, but also afford us insights into the impairments in intellect and interpersonal relationships of these individuals. Such insights are valuable to the clinician as well as to the researcher.

In the case of psychiatric patients we are well aware of their disordered thinking and affect but are less aware of their disorders of processing environmental stimuli. The most important of these stimuli for humans are the human stimuli, which are increasingly being recognized as having crucial nonverbal components (Ekman, 1982). In this chapter we shall show that psychiatric patients are particularly impaired in their ability to decode nonverbal cues. This impairment may or may not have contributed to the development of their psychiatric conditions, but is very likely to be a significant source of continuing difficulty in the understanding of their human environment. A better descriptive, etiological, and prognostic understanding of such patients may help our efforts at prevention, treatment, and rehabilitation.

In the case of brain-damaged patients, although a diminished sensitivity to nonverbal cues is not of etiological significance, it very likely will, as with psychiatric patients, cause them difficulties in responding appropriately to the human environment. Over and above this clinical problem, working with brain-damaged patients can be of special value in increasing our understanding of biological and psychological aspects of human communication. Since we can often be fairly precise in localizing brain damage, these locations can be correlated with various deficits in communication. This has been done classically in the domain of linguistic communication. With the development of standardized measures of decoding nonverbal cues, we are now also able to specify portions of the brain that appear to be essential to the decoding of specific channels of nonverbal communication. Some of the research regarding hemispheric implication in decoding nonverbal communication is reported in the last section of this chapter; all the chapters in Part II report research on various aspects of the relation between brain functions and nonverbal communication.

In this chapter, we summarize our investigations into the relationship between either psychiatric impairment or brain damage and the ability to decode facial expressions, body movement, and tone of voice. The results we report have implications (a) for a better understanding of the relationship between brain and behavior, (b) for a better understanding of the social consequences of psychiatric and neurological impairment, and (c) for the further development of instruments to help in the processes of differential diagnosis.

PROFILE OF NONVERBAL SENSITIVITY (PONS) TEST

The instrument we have employed in these investigations is the PONS test, the Profile of Nonverbal Sensitivity (Rosenthal, Hall, DiMatteo, Rogers, & Archer, 1979; Rosenthal, 1979). This test was developed as an outgrowth of earlier work suggesting the important role of nonverbal cues in the mediation of interpersonal expectation effects (Rosenthal, 1963, 1964, 1966, 1969, 1976, 1981, 1985a, 1985b). A brief description of the PONS test has been given in chapters 3, 4, and 5; a somewhat fuller discussion follows.

Description of the PONS Test

The PONS test is a 45-minute videotape or 16-mm sound film comprised of 220 two-second auditory and/or visual segments. The printed answer sheet employed by the viewer has 220 pairs of descriptions of real-life situations. From each pair of descriptions, the viewer circles the one that best fits the segment that has just been seen and/or heard. Twenty scenarios are represented in each of eleven nonverbal "channels":

1. *Face:* Only the sender's face is on screen.
2. *Body:* Only the sender's body from the lower neck to the knees is on screen.
3. *Face + Body:* Both the sender's face and body are on screen.
4. *Randomized Spliced Voice:* Only the voice can be heard, the sound track having been scrambled randomly to eliminate the content.
5. *Content-Filtered Voice:* Only the voice can be heard, the sound track having been treated electronically to filter out high frequencies so as to eliminate the content.
6. *Face + Randomized Spliced Voice:* Combined channels 1 + 4.
7. *Face + Content-Filtered Voice:* Combined channels 1 + 5.
8. *Body + Randomized Spliced Voice:* Combined channels 2 + 4.
9. *Body + Content-Filtered Voice:* Combined channels 2 + 5.
10. *Face + Body + Randomized Spliced Voice:* Combined channels 3 + 4.
11. *Face + Body + Content-Filtered Voice:* Combined channels 3 + 5.

The twenty scenarios were selected such that half were judged to communicate positive affect and half were judged to communicate negative affect. Orthogonally to the positive-negative dimension, half the scenarios were judged to reflect dominant affect and half to communicate submissive affect. Thus, there are five scenarios in each of the following four quadrants: Positive-Dominant, Positive-Submissive, Negative-Dominant, and Negative-Submissive. The scenarios in each quadrant are as follows:

Positive-Dominant: (1) expressing motherly love; (2) talking to a lost child; (3) admiring nature; (4) talking about one's wedding; and (5) leaving on a trip.

Positive-Submissive: (6) expressing deep affection; (7) trying to seduce someone; (8) helping a customer; (9) expressing gratitude; and (10) ordering food in a restaurant.

Negative-Dominant: (11) nagging a child; (12) expressing jealous anger; (13) criticizing someone for being late; (14) expressing strong dislike; and (15) threatening someone.

Negative-Submissive: (16) talking about the death of a friend; (17) asking forgiveness; (18) returning a faulty item to a store; (19) saying a prayer; and (20) talking about one's divorce.

The eleven channels and four quadrants can be conceptualized in terms of an analysis of variance model so that each person assessed provides five replications (scenarios) in each cell of a 2 × 2 × 11 design (positive-negative × dominant-submissive × channels). A more useful model is based on the assumption of a hypothetical 12th channel called "no video, no audio." The expected accuracy rate for this channel, if subjects simply guessed, is 50% but adding it to the model permits a more powerful and more compact analytic model: 2 × 2 × 2 × 2 × 3 or (a) Positive vs. Negative, (b) Dominant vs. Submissive, (c) Face Shown vs. Face not Shown, (d) Body Shown vs. Body not Shown, and (e) No Audio vs. Randomized Spliced vs. Content-Filtered.

For each person or for any homogeneous group of persons, this model permits an evaluation of accuracy in nonverbal communication as a function of these five orthogonal factors and the 2-, 3-, 4-, and 5-way interactions among them. In addition, individuals and groups can be compared with one another on the relative importance to each person or to each group of all five factors taken singly or in interaction.

For some purposes a sixth factor of order or learning is added. Thus, within each combination of channel and scene type there are five scenes which can be arranged for analysis into the order in which they are shown in the PONS test. This order or learning factor with its five levels is fully crossed with the five factors listed above. The one-*df* contrast for linear trend is an overall index of improvement over time in PONS performance. Individuals and groups can, therefore, be compared for their degree of learning as well as their level of performance. In addition, the interaction of the one-*df* learning contrast with other one-*df* contrasts provides interesting information on such questions as which channels show greater learning, which content quadrants show greater learning, and various combinations of such questions.

The Reliability of the PONS Test and Some Basic Findings

The reliability of the PONS is quite adequate, ranging from .86 to .92 for internal consistency with a median retest reliability of .69. The voice, body, and face channels of the PONS contribute to accuracy in judging the scenes in that order: voice least, then body, and face most. The factor analysis of the 11 channels of the PONS yielded four factors essentially equivalent to (1) the six channels showing the face (face present); (2) the three channels showing only the body (body only); (3) the Randomized Spliced channel taken alone (RS); and (4) the Content-filtered channel taken alone (CF).

For 133 samples comprising 2,615 subjects, sex differences consistently favored females: they were especially superior to males at judging cues of negative affect. In general, younger children were less accurate than older children and young adults at decoding nonverbal cues. However, younger samples showed a *relative* advantage at judging audio as opposed to video cues, a result suggesting that the ability to read vocal nonverbal cues may develop prior to the ability to read visual nonverbal cues.

Some 3,000 subjects from 20 nations have taken the PONS. It has been found that those subjects who performed best were from nations more similar linguistically to the United States and more similar culturally in terms of general modernity (e.g., steel consumption) and development of communicatons (e.g., television, radio, and telephone).

PONS performance was not highly correlated with intellectual ability, though it did tend to be correlated with cognitive complexity. Further, people scoring high on the PONS tended to be better adjusted, more interpersonally democratic and encouraging, less dogmatic, more extraverted, more likely to volunteer for behavioral research, more popular, and more interpersonally sensitive as judged by acquaintances, clients, spouses, or supervisors. These results, based on dozens of studies, contribute strongly to the construct validity of the PONS.

Many special groups have been tested with the PONS, and of these the best performers have been actors, students of nonverbal communication, and students of the visual arts. Clinical psychologists, psychiatrists, and other clinicians scored no higher than college students, but clinicians rated as more effective by their supervisors scored significantly higher than did those rated as less effective by their supervisors.

NONVERBAL SENSITIVITY AMONG PSYCHIATRIC AND ALCOHOLIC PATIENTS

Samples, Methods, and Results

Initially, five samples of psychiatric patients were available for testing with the PONS, all of them hospitalized at the time of testing. Two samples came from different psychiatric hospitals in the Belfast area of Northern Ireland ($n = 11$ and 15); two samples came from a single private psychiatric hospital in the Boston area of the United States ($n = 11$ and 9); and one sample came from a psychiatric hospital in the Sydney area of Australia ($n = 22$). A preliminary analysis of variance showed no significant differences among the five samples in total PONS score, in differential performance in the 11 channels, or in differential performance in the four quadrants. All five samples were, therefore, combined to form a single sample of neuropsychiatric (NP) patients ($n = 68$).

Two samples of alcoholic patients were also available for testing with the PONS, all of them enrolled in residential treatment programs of a "halfway-house" nature. One of the samples was from an urban setting in the Boston area ($n = 17$), the other from a rural setting in Kansas ($n = 44$). A preliminary analysis of variance showed no significant differences between these two samples in total PONS score, in differential performance in the 11 channels, or in differential performance in the four quadrants. The two samples were, therefore, combined to form a single sample of alcoholic patients ($n = 61$).

The PONS performance of the psychiatric patients and alcoholics was then compared with the PONS performance of a large ($n = 482$) norm group of non-psychiatric subjects, all of whom were high school students sampled from the east and west coasts and the midwestern part of the United States. Table 9.1 shows the results of this comparison. For each of the 11 channels of the PONS the mean accuracy is given in percentage form for each of the three samples. The performance of the 482 normal subjects conforms very closely to that of the smaller, more preliminary norm group ($n = 359$) which was the basis for the construction of the standard scoring sheet and which constituted a subset of the total sample of 482 normal subjects. The performance of the NP patients and the alcoholics are quite similar to each other but are consistently lower than the performance of the normal subjects. These results are consistent with those of Guthrie and Smouse (1981), Turner (1964), and Vandenberg and Mattsson (1960), all of whom found psychiatric patients to perform significantly more poorly than normal controls in the decoding of affects.

Effects of Adding Information

By means of the analysis of variance, the patient groups were compared with the normal subjects on the effects on accuracy of adding the information from tone of voice, body, and face channels of nonverbal communication. Because the alcoholic and psychiatric patients performed so similarly, they were combined into a "patient" group for these analyses. Table 9.2 shows the mean level of accuracy obtained by patients and normals with or without the presence of tone of voice cues. For this analysis, the row means of Table 9.1, listed in the right-hand column, were the basic data, with presence of tone of voice defined by the mean of the accuracy obtained in the content-filtered and random-spliced chan-

Table 9.1 Mean Accuracy (Percentage) Obtained in All Channels by Alcoholic Patients, Psychiatric Patients, and Normal Subjects

Subject Type	Audio Channels	Video Channels				Mean
		None	Body	Face	Both	
Alcoholic Patients (N = 61)	None	50.0%[a]	72.2%	75.8%	74.2%	68.0%
	Content-Filtered	57.9	65.8	74.2	78.6	69.2
	Random-Spliced	56.9	70.3	82.8	79.7	72.4
	Mean	54.9	69.4	77.6	77.5	69.9
Psychiatric Patients (N = 68)	None	50.0[a]	71.7	74.8	72.4	67.2
	Content-Filtered	58.6	64.9	75.7	75.8	68.7
	Random-Spliced	57.4	71.3	80.5	79.7	72.2
	Mean	55.3	69.3	77.0	76.0	69.4
Normal Subjects (N = 482)	None	50.0[a]	77.6	81.0	80.6	72.3
	Content-Filtered	60.9	72.0	82.5	85.4	75.2
	Random-Spliced	63.0	76.6	88.8	84.0	78.1
	Mean	57.9	75.4	84.1	83.3	75.2

[a]Theoretical accuracy.

Table 9.2   Mean Accuracy (Percentage) Obtained by Patients and Normal Subjects With and Without Tone of Voice Cues

	Tone of Voice Cues		
	Absent	Present	Weighted Mean
Patients	67.6%	70.6%	69.6%
Normals	72.3	76.6	75.2
Weighted Mean	69.2	72.6	71.5

Table of Contrasts:

Contrast	$F(1,608)$	P	Effect Size $(r)^a$	Error Term
Patients vs. Normals	58.65	.001	.30	1.06
Presence of Audio Cues	151.19	.001	.45	.15
Interaction	5.17	.025	.09	.15

[a] Computed from $r = \sqrt{\dfrac{F}{F + df \text{ error}}}$

nels. The lower half of Table 9.2 shows, for each of the three relevant contrasts, the F ratio, p level, effect size (r), and the error term for each F ratio. It should be noted that the larger error term is associated with a "between subject" effect while the smaller error terms are associated with the "within subject" effects. Normals were significantly more accurate overall than patients, and adding tone of voice cues led to improved performance overall. The significant interaction, though small in magnitude, shows that normals were able to make significantly better use of the addition of the audio channels than were the patients. When we examine the marginal means, the difference between the patients and normals is greater in percentage units than is the difference between the conditions of presence versus absence of voice cues. Yet the former difference is associated with a smaller F and hence a smaller effect size than the latter difference. This apparent anomaly is due to the smaller sampling fluctuation associated with the within-subject effects compared to the between-subject effect.

Table 9.3 shows the mean level of accuracy obtained by patients and normals with or without the presence of body cues. The lower half of Table 9.3 shows again that normals were significantly more accurate than patients and that adding body cues led to very greatly improved performance overall. The significant interaction effect, though small in magnitude, shows that normals were able to make significantly better use of the addition of the channels carrying body cues than were the patients.

Table 9.4 shows the mean level of accuracy obtained by patients and normals with or without the presence of face cues. The lower half of Table 9.4 shows again that normals were significantly more accurate than

Table 9.3   Mean Accuracy (Percentage) Obtained by Patients and Normal Subjects With and Without Body Cues

	Body Cues		Weighted Mean
	Absent	Present	
Patients	66.2%	73.0%	69.6%
Normals	71.0	79.4	75.2
Weighted Mean	67.8	75.1	71.5

Table of Contrasts:

Contrast	$F(1,608)$	P	Effect Size (r)	Error Term
Patients vs. Normals	58.67	.001	.30	.70
Presence of Body Cues	589.55	.001	.70	.15
Interaction	5.52	.02	.09	.15

patients and that adding face cues led to enormously improved performance overall. The significant interaction effect, though modest in magnitude, shows that normals were able to make significantly better use of the addition of the channels carrying face cues than were the patients.

A summary of the results presented in Tables 9.2, 9.3, and 9.4 will be useful. All three analyses show that, overall, normal subjects are more accurate than our patient groups in reading nonverbal communications. All three analyses are based on the same data in testing this effect so that the three results are really three restatements of the same result. The three analyses also tell us that the addition of tone of voice, body, and face cues, each considered independently of the others, all increase the level of accuracy obtained and to increasing degrees: $r = .45$ for audio

Table 9.4   Mean Accuracy (Percentage) Obtained by Patients and Normal Subjects With and Without Face Cues

	Face Cues		Weighted Mean
	Absent	Present	
Patients	62.2%	77.0%	69.6%
Normals	66.7	83.7	75.2
Weighted Mean	63.7	79.3	71.5

Table of Contrasts:

Contrast	$F(1,608)$	p	Effect Size (r)	Error Term
Patients vs. Normals	58.67	.001	.30	.70
Presence of Face Cues	2412.87	.001	.89	.15
Interaction	11.18	.001	.13	.15

cues, r = .70 for body cues, and r = .89 for face cues. For the PONS test, then, adding body cues adds more information than does adding tone of voice cues, and adding face cues adds more information than does adding body cues. Finally, the three analyses tell us that the addition of tone of voice cues, body cues, and face cues is differentially more advantageous to normal subjects than to our patient groups. While all of these effects are modest in magnitude, they are remarkable in their consistency. Taken together they suggest strongly that psychiatric patients and alcoholic patients are less able than normal subjects to profit from the addition of further channels of nonverbal information considered independently of one another.

The finding that patients are less able than normals to profit from the addition of channels of nonverbal communication is consistent with a number of findings reported in the literature of psychopathology. Maher (1966) has summarized the general attentional problems often found in schizophrenic patients generally, and Meiselman (1973) has noted that chronic schizophrenics may be especially impaired when required to process information from two sense modalities simultaneously. There are also specific theoretical and empirical formulations suggesting that psychiatric patients differ from normals in the efficiency with which they can deal with stimuli carried in the auditory and visual channels. McGhie (1973), for example, has suggested that schizophrenics perform relatively more effectively in the auditory than in the visual channel and, in addition, that adding visual information to auditory information may have relatively disruptive effects. Although the authors cited were writing specifically of schizophrenia, or even of restricted subtypes of schizophrenia, their formulations could be tested on our more heterogeneous group of hospitalized psychiatric patients.

Table 9.5 shows the mean accuracy obtained by the psychiatric patients (n = 68) and the normal subjects (n = 482) for the pure audio channels (content-filtered and random-spliced) and the pure video channels (face, body, face + body). Despite the diagnostically and nationally heterogene-

Table 9.5   Mean Accuracy (Percentage) Obtained by Psychiatric Patients and Normal Subjects in Pure Audio and Pure Video Channels

	Audio	Video	Difference
Psychiatric Patients	58.0%	73.0%	15.0%
Normal Subjects	62.0	79.7	17.7
Difference	4.0	6.7	2.7[a]

[a]$F(1,608)$ = 6.70, $p <$ .01, effect size (r) = .10.

ous nature of our patient sample, their performance was what McGhie would have predicted for schizophrenic patients. Their performance was relatively better on the audio than on the video channels.

The work of both McGhie and of Meiselman would suggest further that psychiatric patients should be more impaired when confronted with channels combining audio with video information than on pure channels. We examined this suggestion by obtaining for each of our patients and normals a "pure channel" accuracy score based on single mode channels (CF, RS, face, body, face + body) as well as a "mixed channel" accuracy score based on the remaining six channels having both audio and video components. Table 9.6 shows that the psychiatric patients were more impaired in their performance relative to normal subjects when confronted with mixed channel information than when confronted with pure channel information, though the effect was small in magnitude.

Alcoholic patients were also compared to normal subjects both for their relative performance in audio versus video channels and for their relative performance in pure versus mixed channels. In both comparisons, alcoholic patients' performance was in the direction of psychiatric patients' performance (i.e., better performance on audio than video, better performance on pure than on mixed channels) but not significantly so.

It seemed likely, in view of the results presented thus far, that psychiatric patients might be relatively more impaired in handling greater amounts of information regardless of the specific sense modality involved. For the 11 channels of the PONS the definition of information transmitted is the mean accuracy score obtained by a large norm group ($n = 482$). Those channels in which accuracy is greatest are assumed to be those in which the most information was transmitted. If psychiatric patients were to be most impaired in channels conveying the most information, there should be a sizeable correlation between a channel's information level and the degree to which psychiatric patients would be disadvantaged in performing in that channel relative to the normal subjects. The correlation obtained was quite substantial ($r = .65$), suggesting that the more

Table 9.6   Mean Accuracy (Percentage) Obtained by Psychiatric Patients and Normal Subjects in Pure and Mixed Channels

	Pure	Mixed	Difference
Psychiatric Patients	67.0%	74.6%	7.6%
Normal Subjects	72.6	81.6	9.0
Difference	5.6	7.0	1.4[a]

[a]$F(1,608) = 3.04$, $p < .09$, effect size (r) = .07.

information available in a channel, the less efficiently would psychiatric patients be able to utilize that information. The analogous correlation employing alcoholic rather than psychiatric patients was in the same direction, but smaller in magnitude ($r = .43$).

An alternative definition of channel information level was also employed to avoid the problem that accuracy-as-judged-by-normals entered into both the definition of information level and the degree of disadvantage of the patient groups. In the alternative analysis, a weight of 1 was given to a channel if tone occurred (RS or CF), a weight of 2 was given if body was shown, and a weight of 4 was given if face was shown. Channel weights varied, then, from 1 for RS and CF to 7 for figure RS and figure CF. These weights were based on the earlier analyses weighting patients and normals equally so that they contributed equally to the results. The correlation between channel information level defined by these weights and degree of disadvantage was .57 for psychiatric patients and .33 for alcoholic patients. By this different definition of amount of channel information, we again found that the more information that is carried in a channel, the less efficiently the patient groups, especially the psychiatric patients, utilize that information.

Effects of Affect Quadrants

The performances of the psychiatric patients and the alcoholics were also compared with the performance of the normal subjects on each of the four affect quadrants. Table 9.7 shows the results. For all three samples,

Table 9.7   Mean Accuracy (Percentage) Obtained in Four Quadrants by Alcoholic Patients, Psychiatric Patients, and Normal Subjects

	Negative	Positive	Mean
Alcoholic Patients ($N = 61$)			
Submissive	70.3%	66.4%	68.4%
Dominant	77.0	65.8	71.4
Mean	73.6	66.1	69.9
Psychiatric Patients ($N = 68$)			
Submissive	69.5	67.3	68.4
Dominant	76.7	64.2	70.4
Mean	73.1	65.8	69.4
Normal Subjects ($N = 482$)			
Submissive	74.5	71.8	73.2
Dominant	82.9	71.6	77.2
Mean	78.7	71.7	75.2

higher accuracy was obtained on negative than on positive affect scenes and on dominant than on submissive orientation scenes. The advantage of the dominant over submissive scenes was greatest for the normal subjects and smallest for the psychiatric patients: $F(1,608) = 7.69$, $p < .01$, effect size $r = .11$. Perhaps the patient groups, especially the psychiatric patients, found the dominant orientations of the female sender sufficiently unpleasant so that they reduced their attention to these scenes, with a corresponding drop in relative accuracy. Such a speculation stems more from a psychodynamic framework than from a framework of information processing.

A thorough understanding of the effects of the quadrants on the accuracy of our patient groups required that we analyze also the effects of the quadrant location of the incorrect alternatives paired with the correct alternatives of each of the four quadrants. Table 9.8 shows the results for each of the three groups under discussion. For all three samples, accuracy was lowest when the incorrect alternative was from the same quadrant as the correct alternative, highest when the incorrect alternative was from the quadrant diagonally opposite to the quadrant of the correct alternative (i.e., the quadrant that differed on both dimensions of positiveness and dominance). This result, that greater confusion occurs when both the correct and incorrect alternatives are from the same quadrant, adds to our understanding of the reliability of the quadrants of the PONS and is summarized in Table 9.9. The effects are very large in size for all three samples, attesting to the within-quadrant reliability of all three samples. The bottom half of Table 9.9 shows the residuals when the effects of quadrant similarity and of sample have been removed. These residuals show that normals obtain the greatest benefit from having dissimilar incorrect alternatives, while psychiatric patients obtain the least benefit. This appears to be yet another instance, then, when adding information to the test situation is relatively least useful to the psychiatric patient, more useful to the alcoholic patient, and most useful to the normal subject.

Effects of Practice

There is one more result suggesting that psychiatric patients are less able than normals to profit from the addition of information, in this case prior exposure to PONS scenes. Psychiatric patients showed essentially no improvement whatever in going from the first half to the last half of the PONS, while normal subjects showed very substantial gains (effect size $r = .44$) in going from the first half to the last half of the PONS. Alcoholic patients showed gains as large as those of the normal control samples.

Table 9.8 Mean Accuracy (Percentage) Obtained in Four Quadrants as a Function of Quadrant Location of Incorrect Alternative

Subject Type	Correct Alternative	Incorrect Alternative	Correct Alternative			
			Dominant		Submissive	
			Dominant	Submissive	Dominant	Submissive
Alcoholic Patients	Positive	Positive	62.8%	64.4%	70.8%	54.9%
		Negative	69.2	72.5	80.9	55.4
	Negative	Positive	74.3	83.8	78.2	72.7
		Negative	70.6	87.0	80.5	53.9
Psychiatric Patients	Positive	Positive	62.3	62.5	68.0	60.1
		Negative	64.6	68.7	75.9	57.0
	Negative	Positive	75.5	82.0	75.4	71.7
		Negative	65.0	80.1	75.5	49.9
Normal Subjects	Positive	Positive	68.5	74.1	73.5	64.2
		Negative	72.8	75.6	87.9	59.1
	Negative	Positive	81.8	90.0	84.2	77.6
		Negative	74.0	91.0	85.4	52.4

Table 9.9 Mean Accuracy (Percentage) Obtained at Three
Levels of Similarity of Incorrect to Correct Alternative

	Quadrant Similarity		
Subject Type	Most	Intermediate	Least
Alcoholic Patients	60.6	71.8	78.8
Psychiatric Patients	59.3	69.4	75.5
Normal Subjects	64.8	76.9	84.4
Table of Residuals:			
Alcoholic	−0.1	0.0	+0.1
Psychiatric	+0.9	−0.1	−0.9
Normal	−0.9	+0.1	+0.7

Analysis of Omitted Items

For most samples, only a very few persons omit any items in the administration of the PONS. However, it was observed that alcoholic patients, and especially psychiatric patients, left a fairly large number of items unanswered. Tables 9.10 and 9.11 list the percentage of items omitted for all channels and all quadrants by alcoholic and psychiatric patients. Inspection shows that psychiatric patients omitted many more items than did alcoholic patients; $F(1,138) = 20.35$, $p < .001$, effect size $r = .36$. It is interesting to note that the overall accuracy rates of alcoholic and psychiatric patients are very similar despite the very much greater rate of omissions by the psychiatric patients.

Although the alcoholic and psychiatric patients differed in several ways in their patterns of omitted items, there were a great many points of similarity. Generally, if one group omitted many items in a given channel, the other group was also likely to omit many items in that channel (Pearson correlation = .674, $p < .015$). Table 9.12 shows the percentage of items omitted in all channels by the two groups combined, as well as the resulting analysis of variance. The three significant main effects each tell a very clear story. Adding audio, body, or face cues serves to reduce significantly the rate of omission of items. Thus, as we might expect, when more information is added to make the task a bit easier, fewer items are omitted. The significant interaction between the body and face channels appears to be due primarily to the fact that giving both body and face cues does not reduce omissions much beyond the level achieved by giving either body or face cues. These results suggest that, in general, omission might be positively related to the overall difficulty of a channel; harder items might be omitted more. This formulation was checked by

Table 9.10 Percentage of Items Omitted in All Channels by Alcoholic Patients and Psychiatric Patients

Audio Channels	None	Video Channels			Mean
		Body	Face	Both	
Alcoholic (N = 61)					
None	3.0[a]	2.9	1.9	1.7	2.4
Content-Filtered	1.7	1.5	1.3	0.3	1.2
Random-Spliced	1.7	0.7	0.7	0.9	1.0
Mean	2.1	1.7	1.3	1.0	1.5
Psychiatric (N = 79)					
None	18.2[a]	13.4	11.8	11.7	13.8
Content-Filtered	15.9	10.9	7.6	8.7	10.8
Random-Spliced	14.2	9.6	9.6	8.4	10.4
Mean	16.1	11.3	9.7	9.6	11.7

[a]Estimated value, Snedecor & Cochran (1967, p. 318, or 1980, p. 275).

Table 9.11 Percentage of Items Omitted in Four Quadrants by Alcoholic Patients and Psychiatric Patients

	Negative	Positive	Mean
Alcoholic Patients ($N = 61$)			
Submissive	1.0	1.7	1.4
Dominant	1.6	1.4	1.5
Mean	1.3	1.5	1.4
Psychiatric Patients ($N = 79$)			
Submissive	10.9	12.2	11.6
Dominant	9.2	12.0	10.6
Mean	10.0	12.1	11.1

computing the correlation between the rate of item omissions of a channel and the difficulty of a channel defined by the performance of the norm group. This correlation was .771, $p < .01$.

Finally, Table 9.13 shows the percentage of items omitted in four affect quadrants by the two patient groups combined. There were significantly fewer omissions when affects were negative rather than positive, and there was a tendency for fewer omissions to occur on dominant rather

Table 9.12 Percentage of Items Omitted in All Channels by Alcoholic Patients and Psychiatric Patients Combined ($N = 140$)

	Video Channels				
Audio Channels	None	Body	Face	Both	Mean
None	10.5[a]	8.1	6.8	6.6	8.0
Content-Filtered	8.8	6.2	4.7	4.5	6.0
Random-Spliced	7.9	5.1	5.2	4.6	5.7
Mean	9.1	6.5	5.6	5.2	6.6

[a]Estimated value, Snedecor & Cochran (1967, p. 318, or 1980, p. 275).

Table of Variance:

Source	df	MS	F	P
Audio	2	6.145	21.15	.001
Body	1	6.457	22.23	.001
Face	1	16.807	57.85	.001
Audio × Body	2	0.042	—	
Audio × Face	2	0.462	1.59	
Body × Face	1	3.849	13.25	.001
Audio × Body × Face	2	0.006	—	
Error	1380	0.290		

Table 9.13   Percentage of Items Omitted in Four
Quadrants by Alcoholic Patients and Psychiatric
Patients Combined ($N = 140$)

	Negative	Positive	Mean
Submissive	5.9	6.9	6.4[b]
Dominant	5.4	6.7	6.0[b]
Mean	5.6[a]	6.8[a]	6.2

[a]Differ at $p < .001$, $F(1,414) = 18.15$, $r = .20$.
[b]Differ at $p < .20$, $F(1,414) = 1.71$, $r = .06$.

than submissive affects. Both of these results are consistent with the finding that omissions increase as the difficulty level of items increases. Omissions, then, appear to reflect uncertainty.

Schizophrenic/Neurotic Patients versus Patients with Character Disorders

For our Australian sample of psychiatric patients we had available a subsample of 10 patients diagnosed by the hospital staff as having character disorders and a subsample of 11 patients diagnosed by the hospital staff as schizophrenic or severely neurotic. All these patients had made self-ratings of the degree to which they felt they understood (a) other people, (b) social situations, (c) tone of voice, (d) body movements, and (e) facial expressions. These self-ratings, made on a nine-point scale, were correlated with PONS performance. Table 9.14 shows the correlations between total PONS performance and five self-ratings for the schizophrenics/neurotics, the patients with character disorders, and all patients combined. The combined group of patients included four that could not be diagnosed as either having character disorders or being schizophrenics/neurotics. Examination of the correlations suggests that schizophrenic/neurotics tend to be more accurate, on the whole, in their self-ratings of interpersonal sensitivity than the character disorder patients. In addition, of all the self-ratings made, ratings of how well patients felt they understood facial expressions correlated most strongly with total PONS score.

   The five self-ratings of understanding shown in Table 9.14 were highly intercorrelated, the correlations rating from .37 to .65 with a median of .48. Therefore, a new composite variable of self-rating of understanding was generated by summing over the five self-ratings. Table 9.15 shows the

Table 9.14   Correlations Between Total PONS Accuracy and Self-Ratings by Australian Psychiatric Patients

Self-Ratings of Understanding of:	Schizophrenic/ Neurotic ($N = 11$)	Character Disorder ($N = 10$)	All Patients ($N = 25$)
Other people	+.33	+.33	+.38
Social Situations	+.62*[a]	−.06[a]	+.42*
Tone of Voice	+.46	+.21	+.35
Body Movements	+.54	+.04	+.17
Facial Expressions	+.64*	+.68*	+62**
Median	+.54	+.21	+.38

*$p < .05$
**$p < .001$
[a]z *of difference* = 1.51

correlations between this composite variable and PONS channel scores for three groups of patients. As we would expect on the basis of Table 9.14, the schizophrenic/neurotic patients tended to show higher correlations between PONS scores and self-ratings of understanding than did the character disorder patients. Before leaving this section we should note that, in general, our Australian psychiatric patients were much better able to tell us, via their self-ratings, how well they would perform on the PONS than were our American samples of normal students and adults. For these American samples, subjects' self-ratings of interpersonal sensitivity showed near-zero correlations with PONS scores, although subjects' spouses' ratings of subjects' interpersonal sensitivity did correlate positively with subjects' PONS performance (Rosenthal, Hall, DiMatteo, Rogers, & Archer, 1979).

ADDITIONAL PONS TESTING OF PSYCHIATRIC PATIENTS: THE LYLE RESEARCH

Jack Lyle of the University of Sydney conducted an extensive study of psychiatric patients drawn from several psychiatric hospitals in the greater Sydney area. Complete PONS scores were available for 82 of these patients and the mean accuracy obtained in all channels is shown in Table 9.16. Compared to the earlier sample of 68 psychiatric patients (Table 9.1), the present sample performed slightly lower (68.4% versus 69.4%).

Table 9.15 Correlations Between Composite Self-Rating and PONS Channel Scores for Australian Psychiatric Patients

Patient Type	Audio	Video				Marginals
		None	Body	Face	Both	
Schizophrenic/Neurotic (N = 11)	None	—	+.45	+.42	+.36	+.47
	CF	+.58	+.40	+.38	+.66*	+.55
	RS	−.26	+.77**	+.49	+.50	+.47
	Marginals	+.15	+.58	+.44	+.59	+.61*
Character Disorder (N = 10)	None	—	+.28	+.32	+.33	+.52
	CF	+.15	+.06	+.23	+.34	+.47
	RS	−.12	+.40	+.38	+.40	+.57
	Marginals	+.43	+.54	+.54	+.53	+.33
All Patients (N = 25)	None	—	+.33	+.34	+.37	+.48*
	CF	+.38	+.31	+.32	+.53**	+.51**
	RS	−.07	+.56**	+.51**	+.50*	+.55**
	Marginals	+.36	+.55**	+.51**	+.57**	+.50*

*$p \leq .05$
**$p \leq .01$

Table 9.16   Mean Accuracy (Percentage) Obtained in All Channels by 82
Psychiatric Patients (after Lyle)

| | Video Channels | | | | |
Audio Channels	None	Body	Face	Both	Mean
None	50.0%*	68.7%	73.4%	71.9%	66.0%
Content-Filtered	56.0	63.8	75.4	74.9	67.5
Random-Spliced	58.2	70.1	80.8	78.1	71.8
Mean	54.8	67.5	76.5	75.0	68.4

*Theoretical accuracy

The profiles of the two samples of psychiatric patients were quite similar, however. For each of the 11 channels the performance of each sample of patients was subtracted from the performance of the norm groups subjects (n = 482, Table 9.1) and the resulting differences were correlated for the two of the norm group subjects (n = 482, Table 9.1) and the resulting differences were correlated for the two samples. The correlation between these difference scores for the two samples was +.830. Subtracting the performance of the patients from the performance of the normal subjects serves to reduce the effect of the very strong channel differences in difficulty which would otherwise inflate the correlation between the two psychiatric samples. When the 11 channel scores of the two samples were correlated directly, without correcting for the performance of the norm group, the correlation of +.830 increased to +.990.

Earlier, we saw that the addition of information was of significantly less benefit to the patient groups than to the normal group (Tables 9.2, 9.3, 9.4). Table 9.17 shows the results of the analogous analysis for the patients studied by Lyle. The first column of Table 9.17 shows the benefits in percentage points that accrued to Lyle's patients when tone of voice, body, and face cues were added. The last column of Table 9.17 shows the analogous benefits of added information that accrued to the normal subjects. The second column of Table 9.17 shows the extent (in r) to which Lyle's patients benefited less than did the normals from the addition of tone, body, and face cues. The third and fourth columns review the analogous results obtained from the patients discussed earlier in this chapter.

In general, the results based on Lyle's patients are quite similar to those obtained from the earlier samples of patients. For both sets of patients the addition of facial, body, or tone of voice cues was less helpful than it was to normals, though the magnitude of this effect was modest, r about .10. It should be emphasized that Lyle's psychiatric patients, although they did profit less than normals from the addition of further nonverbal cues, nevertheless did benefit substantially from the addition of

Table 9.17 Improvement in Accuracy Due to the Addition of Tone of Voice, Body, and Face Cues for Three Samples

Cue Type	Lyle's Patients		Prior Patients		Normals
	Percentage	(Effect Size)[a]	Percentage	(Effect Size)[a]	Percentage
Tone of Voice	3.7%	.04	3.0%	.09%	4.3
Body	5.6	.16	6.8	.09	8.4
Face	14.6	.14	14.8	.13	17.0
Mean	8.0	.11	8.2	.10	9.9

[a]Effect size (*r*) comparing percentage improvement of patients with percentage improvement of normals.

such cues. With these benefits expressed in terms of r, the addition of tone of voice, body, and face cues improved performance by $r = .43$, $r = .68$, and $r = .92$, respectively. The analogous benefits for the patients described earlier combined with the normals were $r = .45$, $r = .70$, and $r = .89$, respectively. The agreement between these two sets of effect sizes was excellent; an r of $.998$ reflected the great similarity in the patterns of the two sets of three scores and a t of 0.20 reflected the small degree of mean difference between the two sets of r's.

Earlier we saw that psychiatric patients were relatively more accurate in the pure audio than in the pure video channels in comparison to the normal subjects. We were able to make the analogous comparison for Lyle's patients, and the results were quite consistent with those of the earlier analysis. Whereas the magnitude of the effect had been $r = .10$ for the earlier group of patients, the magnitude of the effect for Lyle's patients was $r = .13$. The mean percentage accuracy for the latter group was 57.1% for the audio channels and 71.3% for the video channels. The analogous scores for the earlier samples were given in Table 9.5.

We also saw earlier that psychiatric patients were relatively more accurate in either the pure audio or pure video channels than in the mixed channels (having both audio and video information) in comparison to the normal subjects. This effect was small, however (effect size $r = .07$), and though the trend was in the same direction for Lyle's patients, the effect was smaller still in magnitude ($r = .04$). The mean percentage accuracy for this group was 65.6% for the pure channels and 73.8% for the mixed channels. The analogous scores for the earlier samples were given in Table 9.6.

All indications were that psychiatric patients might be most impaired in those channels conveying the most information. If that were the case, we suggested earlier, we might expect a sizeable correlation between the amount of information carried in each of the 11 channels and the degree to which psychiatric patients might be disadvantaged in performing on each of the 11 channels relative to normal subjects. The correlation obtained for our earlier group of patients was substantial ($r = .65$), suggesting that the more information carried in a channel, the less efficiently would psychiatric patients be able to utilize that information. The analogous correlation was computed for the patients tested by Lyle and the results were remarkably consistent: this time the correlation was equally substantial ($r = .64$).

Table 9.18 shows the mean accuracy obtained in each of the four affect quadrants by Lyle's patients. These results were quite consistent with those obtained by the earlier group of psychiatric patients (Table 9.7). The earlier analysis had suggested that the psychiatric patients benefited significantly less from scenes showing dominant affects than did the nor-

Table 9.18 Mean Accuracy (Percentage) Obtained in Four Quadrants by 82 Psychiatric Patients (after Lyle)

	Negative	Positive	Mean
Submissive	68.4	66.0	67.2
Dominant	75.3	64.1	69.7
Mean	71.8	65.0	68.4

mal controls. That same result was also obtained when the analogous comparison was made for the later group of patients. This time the effect size was slightly smaller than in the original analysis ($r = .08$ instead of $r = .11$).

Of the 82 patients tested by Lyle, 27 had been clearly diagnosed as neurotic, 28 had been clearly diagnosed as psychotic, and 10 had been clearly diagnosed as having personality disorders. The neurotic patients performed significantly ($p < .05$) better (73.4%) than did the psychotic or personality disorder patients (67.7%), who did not differ from each other. Table 9.19 shows the point biserial correlations between having been diagnosed as neurotic (versus psychotic or personality disordered) and performance on the various PONS channels, quadrants, and marginals. In every

Table 9.19 Correlations Between Neurotic Status and PONS Scores for 65 Psychiatric Patients (after Lyle)

Channels

Audio	None	Body	Face	Both	Marginals
		Video			
None	—	+.20	+.19	+.25*	+.26*
CF	+.24	+.26*	+.19	+.15	+.26*
RS	+.30*	+.23	+.30*	+.21	+.32**
Marginals	+.37**	+.27*	+.28*	+.23	+.31*
Face 120	+.27*				
Body 120	+.26*				

Quadrants

	Negative	Positive	Marginals
Submissive	+.34**	+.22	+.32**
Dominant	+.14	+.31*	+.25*
Marginals	+.26*	+.31*	+.31*

*$p \leq .05$
**$p \leq .01$

channel, quadrant, or marginal the neurotic patients scored higher than did their presumably more severely disturbed fellow patients.

Less severely disturbed patients often show a higher level of intellectual functioning, as was the case for the present sample. The neurotic patients showed a significantly higher score on the Simpson Vocabulary Scale (point biserial $r = .29$). In addition, scores on the IQ scale were positively correlated with scores on the PONS total score ($r = .30$), raising the question of whether the superior PONS performance of the neurotic patients might not be due to their higher IQ. The correlation of .31 between status as a neurotic and PONS total score was recalculated partialing out the effect of IQ. The results showed only some shrinkage due to the "removal" of the effects of IQ, from $r = .31$ to $r = .24$.

The greatest advantage of the neurotic patients over the remaining patients had been found in the scores on the 40 items of tone only ($r = .37$). This subtest of the PONS was also significantly correlated with IQ ($r = .27$), and once again we partialed out the effect of IQ from the relationship between neurotic status and PONS performance. Once again there was some shrinkage, but the partial correlation of .32 was still substantial. The superior performance of the neurotic patients could not simply be attributed to their superior intellectual functioning. Perhaps their superior PONS performance was related to their presumably superior social adjustment when compared to the psychotic or more characterologically involved personality disorders.

In this research Lyle had administered two scales of psychoticism to his patients: one described by Overall, Hunter, and Butcher (1973) and one described by Eysenck and Eysenck (1968, see also Claridge & Chappa, 1973). The correlation between these scales was +.45; each correlated −.20 with patients having been classified as neurotic; and the Overall et al. and Eysenck measures correlated +.16 and +.10 respectively, with patients having been psychiatrically classified as psychotic. The less psychotic or the better adjusted patients were found to be on these two scales, the better was their total PONS performance. The correlations were −.30 and −.29 respectively, both correlations reaching significance at the .01 level. Both measures of psychoticism were found to be negatively related to IQ, so partial correlations were again computed to "remove" the effects of IQ from the relationships between psychoticism scale performance and PONS performance. The resulting partial correlations did not show much shrinkage, with the original correlations of − .30 and −.29 reduced only to −.24 and −.25 respectively.

Thus, whether defined by psychiatric diagnosis or by scores on two different scales of psychoticism, more severely disturbed patients appear to perform less well on the PONS even after the effects of differences in IQ have been removed through partialing.

BRAIN-DAMAGED PATIENTS AND THE PONS

Hemispheric Involvement

Three doctoral dissertations employing the PONS had implicated the right hemisphere of normal subjects in the processing of nonverbal cues. Dwyer (1975), employing a dichotic listening task, found that, for a verbal task, most subjects showed a right-ear (left hemisphere) advantage, while for the content-filtered items of the PONS employed by Dwyer, most subjects showed a left-ear (right hemisphere) advantage. Domangue (1979) found that left-eye (right hemisphere) dominant subjects performed significantly better on the content-filtered items of the PONS than did subjects who were right-eye (left hemisphere) dominant. Domangue also found that subjects showing familial left-handedness were superior to right-handed subjects at decoding content-filtered speech. Finally, Young (1979) found that, when presented with PONS stimuli, the right hemisphere was more activated (as defined by EEG alpha variables) relative to the left hemisphere, which was more activated when presented with verbal stimuli.

A more definitive investigation of the role of each hemisphere in the processing of the nonverbal cues of the PONS test was undertaken by administering the PONS to 10 patients with radiologically lateralized damage to only one cerebral hemisphere (Benowitz, Bear, Rosenthal, Mesulam, Zaidel, & Sperry, 1983). Following the format employed in Table 9.1, Table 9.20 shows the PONS scores for these left- and right-hemisphere-damaged patients and the differences between them. Overall, patients with damaged left hemispheres performed better at the PONS than did patients with damaged right hemispheres; $t(8) = 1.96$, $p = .043$ one-tailed, effect size $r = .57$. Examination of the differences between the groups, displayed in the bottom third of Table 9.20, shows that the three largest differences all occur in the column listing the three face channels: face alone, face plus content-filtered speech, and face plus random-spliced speech. Thus the three face channels show the greatest deficit of the right-brain-damaged patients compared to the left-brain-damaged patients, $F(1,24) = 5.84, p = .03$, effect size $r = .65$.

Comparison of Table 9.20 with Table 9.1 shows that both brain-damaged groups performed more poorly than did the normal controls in every one of the 11 channels. In general, however, the left-brain-damaged patients performed better than the alcoholic and psychiatric patients while the right-brain-damaged patients performed worse, especially on the three face channels (Face alone, Face + CF, and Face + RS).

Earlier, in our discussion of psychiatric patients, we noted that even

Table 9.20 Mean Accuracy (Percentage) Obtained in All Channels by Patients with Left and Right Brain Damage

Damage	Audio Channels	Video Channels				Mean
		None	Body	Face	Both	
Left Damage (N = 4)	None	50.0[a]	77.5%	80.6%	76.2%	71.1%
	Content-Filtered	57.5	62.5	80.6	81.9	70.6
	Random-Spliced	58.8	73.1	87.5	80.0	74.8
	Mean	55.4	71.0	82.9	79.4	72.2
Right Damage (N = 6)	None	50.0[a]	71.2	67.1	71.2	64.9
	Content-Filtered	59.6	62.9	73.3	75.8	67.9
	Random-Spliced	55.4	68.8	71.7	73.8	67.4
	Mean	55.0	67.6	70.7	73.6	66.7
Left Minus Right	None	00.0	6.3	13.5	5.0	6.2
	Content-Filtered	-2.1	-0.4	7.3	6.1	2.7
	Random-Spliced	3.4	4.3	15.8	6.2	7.4
	Mean	0.4	3.4	12.2	5.8	5.5

[a]Theoretical accuracy

when patients could not profit as much as normals from the addition of channels of nonverbal cues, the addition of tone, body, and face cues was helpful in absolute terms. The same result was found for our sample of 10 brain-damaged patients. Table 9.21 shows the magnitude of benefit (in terms of the effect size index r) of adding tone of voice, body, or face cues for our norm group, for two samples of psychiatric patients, and for our brain-damaged patients. For all samples, all channels are very informative; but in all cases body cues are more informative than tone of voice cues and face cues are more informative than body cues for these PONS–based measures. The final column of Table 9.21 shows the strength of these four results and the homogeneity of these four results; the obtained r's ranged from .92 to 1.00.

Additional Patients and a New Analysis

Additional patients with damage to the right hemisphere gradually became available, although they were tested only with the four basic channels of the PONS: Face alone, Body alone, Random-Spliced, and Content-Filtered (Benowitz, Bear, Mesulam, Rosenthal, Zaidel, & Sperry, 1983; Benowitz, Finklestein, Levine, & Moya, 1986).

Including data from the patients from whom full PONS scores were available, there are now data from 18 patients on the four basic channels of the PONS. Four of the patients had damage in the left hemisphere, five had damage in the right hemisphere but with no temporal lobe involvement, and nine had damage in the right hemisphere including temporal lobe involvement. Performance was originally scored and reported in percentile ranks; for our present purpose these percentile ranks were transformed to radians by means of the standard arcsin transformation.

Table 9.21 Magnitude of Effect (r) of Adding Information from Tone of Voice, Body, or Face for Four Samples

Samples	Channel			
	Tone	Body	Face	$r(1)^a$
Normals ($N = 482$)	.51	.74	.91	.996
Psychiatric I ($N = 129$)	.38	.66	.88	.998
Psychiatric II ($N = 82$)	.43	.68	.92	1.000
Brain-Damaged ($N = 10$)	.53	.88	.93	.918

[a]Shows magnitude of linear increase in information in going from tone to body to face for the four samples.

Table 9.22 Mean Performance in Four Channels by Three Brain-Damaged Samples (Units are in Radians)

Samples	Channel				
	Face	Body	Random-Spliced	Content-Filtered	Mean
Right Damage +Temporal ($N = 9$)	.22	.81	1.28	1.24	.89
Right Damage NoTemporal ($N = 5$)	1.24	1.18	.24	1.09	.94
Left Damage ($N = 4$)	1.68	1.64	1.16	1.39	1.47
Mean	1.05	1.21	.89	1.24	1.10

One patient in the right hemisphere with temporal lobe involvement sample was actually a composite patient; one patient who had been tested only with the face and body channels and one who had been tested only with the two tone of voice channels (RS and CF). The effect of this combining is, in general, to increase the error variance and, therefore, leads to a small increase in type II errors or errors of the conservative type. & 9.23

Table 9.22 presents the mean performance in all four channels for all three groups of patients, and Table 9.23 shows the analysis of variance of these data. There were two main results. First, the overall performance of the patients with damage to the left hemisphere was superior to the performance of patients with damage to the right hemisphere, an effect

Table 9.23 Analysis of Variance of Mean Performance Scores: Unweighted Means Procedure

Source	df	MS	F	p	r
Between Patients	17				
Samples	2	.4132	2.91	.09	—
a. Left vs. Right	1	.8214	5.79	.04[a]	.53
b. (Right + T) vs. (Right *No* T)	1	.0050	—	—	.05
Patients (within samples)	15	.1418			
Within Patients	54				
Channels	3	.0772	1.08	—	—
Channels × Samples	6	.2223	3.12	.015[b]	—
Channels × Patients	45	.0712			

[a]Employing proportional model rather than unweighted means procedure also yields p of .04.

[b]Employing proportional model rather than unweighted means procedure yields $p = .004$.

that was significant statistically and large in magnitude ($r = .53$). Second, the interaction of channels × samples was significant, indicating that differences among samples varied significantly for different channels.

Interactions can be interpreted properly only when the residuals defining them are examined (Rosenthal & Rosnow, 1984). These residuals are computed by subtracting off the row and column effects of a two-way design. The residuals defining the interaction of the four channels with the three samples are shown in Table 9.24. The fact that rows and columns all show means of zero indicates that the entries of the table are proper residuals. An especially useful way to examine interaction residuals is by way of contrasts (Rosenthal & Rosnow, 1984, 1985). The contrasts computed in this case were not planned, so we should not attach too much importance to the exact significance levels obtained. However, we are protected from type I errors by virtue of the statistical significance of the overall interaction effect.

The first contrast. The top half of Table 9.25 gives the weights defining the first contrast, for which $F(1,45) = 14.90$, $p = .0005$, and effect size $r = .71$. The nature of this contrast is essentially a profile statement saying (a) for right-brain-damaged patients with temporal involvement, the face will be decoded especially poorly, while the random-spliced speech will be decoded especially well relative to (b) the right-brain-damaged patients with no temporal involvement, who will show the opposite profile (i.e., relatively "too good" on face and "too poor" on random-spliced speech).

These findings would be of great diagnostic benefit if a simple difference score could be formed (e.g., the difference between face and random-spliced speech measured in this example in the arcsin transformed percentile ranks) that would discriminate right-brain-damaged patients with and without temporal involvement. We have at least preliminary evidence that such difference scores may be useful. Of the 8 patients with temporal involvement who showed a nonzero difference, all 8 did better

Table 9.24   Residuals Defining the Interaction of Four Channels × Three Samples

	Channel				
Samples	Face	Body	RS	CF	Mean
Right, + Temporal	−.62	−.19	.60	.21	0
Right, No Temporal	.35	.13	−.49	.01	0
Left Damage	.26	.06	−.10	−.22	0
Mean	0	0	0	0	0

Table 9.25 Contrast Weights Employed in the Interpretation of a 4 × 3 Interaction

	Channel				
Samples	Face	Body	RS	CF	Mean
Contrast I					
Right, + Temporal	−1	0	+1	0	0
Right, No Temporal	+1	0	−1	0	0
Left Damage	0	0	0	0	0
Mean	0	0	0	0	0
Contrast II					
Right, + Temporal	−2	−2	+2	+2	0
Right, No Temporal	+1	+1	−1	−1	0
Left Damage	+1	+1	−1	−1	0
Mean	0	0	0	0	0

on random-spliced than on face cues. Of the 4 patients without temporal involvement who showed a nonzero difference, all four did better on face than on random-spliced cues. This degree of accuracy of categorization (100%) was significant at $p = .004$, two-tail by Fisher's exact test.

The second contrast. The bottom half of Table 9.25 gives the weights defining the second contrast, for which $F(1,45) = 13.71$, $p = .0006$, and effect size $r = .69$. The nature of this contrast is also essentially a profile statement saying (a) for right-brain-damaged patients with temporal involvement, the visual cues (face and body) will be decoded especially poorly, while the audio cues (RS and CF) will be decoded especially well relative to (b) all the other brain-damaged patients, who will show the opposite profile (i.e., relatively "too good" on video and "too poor" on tone of voice).

These findings would also be of great diagnostic benefit if a simple difference score could be formed (e.g., the difference between the mean of the video channels and the mean of the audio channels measured in this example in the arcsin-transformed percentile ranks) that would discriminate right-brain-damaged patients with temporal involvement from the other two samples of patients. We have at least preliminary evidence that such difference scores may be useful. Of the 9 patients with temporal involvement, 8 did better on audio than on video cues, while only 1 did worse. Of the 9 remaining patients showing no right-hemisphere temporal involvement, 8 did better on video than on audio cues while only 1 did worse. This degree of accuracy of categorization (89%) was significant at $p = .0034$, two-tail by Fisher's exact test.

Two findings or one? The two contrasts we have described were both very effective in helping us to explain the obtained significant interaction of channels × samples. The first contrast accounted for 79.5% of the variation among the 12 residuals of Table 9.24, while the second accounted for 73.2% of that variation. The two contrasts were, of course, not independent and the weights shown for the two contrasts were correlated with $r = .577$. The question we must then ask is whether these contrasts were really saying two different things or, because of their high intercorrelation, were essentially making the same statement.

One approach to address this question is to observe whether the percentage of the variation in the residuals of Table 9.24 accounted for by the two contrasts together is appreciably greater than the percentage of that variation accounted for by each of the contrasts individually. This approach showed that, together, the contrasts accounted for 97% of the interaction variance, while individually they had accounted for only 80% and 73%, respectively. A more conservative multiple-correlation approach is to predict not the residuals of Table 9.24 but the sum of squares of the contrasts plus the sums of squares of the error term for testing the significance of the contrast. In that situation we find that the two contrasts together predict 62% of the variance, while they predict only 50% and 48% individually.

An additional approach to address the question of "two findings or one" is to employ partialing procedures. In this approach we correlate each set of contrast weights with the residuals of Table 9.24 while controlling for the effects of the other contrast. When this procedure was employed, both correlations of contrast weights with residuals actually increased slightly: from .892 to .90 and from .855 to .86, respectively. A more conservative partialing approach is to predict not the residuals of Table 9.24 but the sum of squares of the contrasts plus the sum of squares of the error term for testing the significance of the contrast. In that situation we find that partialing reduces the first contrast's effect size (r) from .71 to .53, while reducing the second contrast's effect size (r) from .69 to .48. Each of these reduced partial correlations is still significant statistically at $p < .05$ after removing the effects of the other contrast.

The results of the preceding analyses are in good general agreement: there are two independently useful results. First, patients with right temporal lobe damage perform relatively better on random-spliced tone of voice cues than on face cues, while right-brain-damaged patients with no temporal lobe involvement perform relatively better on face cues than on random-spliced tone of voice cues. Second, patients with right temporal lobe damage perform relatively better on tone of voice cues than on video cues, while the brain-damaged patients of our other two samples perform relatively better on video cues than on tone of voice cues.

CONCLUSION

The results we have summarized here, in particular about the decoding of facial cues, fit well what we know and suspect about the role of the right hemisphere in decoding nonverbal cues (Benowitz, Bear, Mesulam, et al., 1983; Benowitz, Bear, Rosenthal, et al., 1983; Benowitz et al., 1984; DeKosky, Heilman, Bowers, & Valenstein, 1980; Galaburda, LeMay, Kemper, & Geschwind, 1978; Kolb & Taylor, 1981; Ley & Bryden, 1979; Rosenthal et al., 1979; Sperry, 1982; Zurif, 1974). The newer results involving differences in profiles of sensitivity to different sources of nonverbal cues in different types of patients are sufficiently provocative so that extended replications are very much in order.

The results of these studies show, then, that psychopathology or focal brain damage can severely compromise one's ability to appreciate the wealth of information about social relationships, emotional state, and emphasis that are communicated nonverbally. The consequences of these losses are profound, and are frequently manifest in the insensitivity and misperceptions seen in impaired subjects. As enunciated so eloquently by Darwin, nonverbal "intelligence" appears to be an integral, universal feature of normal human social interactions and, like verbal language, appears to involve specific structures of the brain. The underlying neurology may in fact be genetically specified to handle these functions, and may well determine the development of our competence. Whether any types of psychopathology reflect selective impairments in those brain structures that mediate nonverbal abilities remains to be determined.

ACKNOWLEDGMENTS

Preparation of this chapter and much of the research described was supported by the National Science Foundation. Portions of this chapter constitute an expanded version of results described in chapter 12 of Rosenthal, R., Hall, J. A., DiMatteo, M. R., Rogers, P. L., & Archer, D. (1979). *Sensitivity to nonverbal communication: The PONS test.* Baltimore: Johns Hopkins University Press.

REFERENCES

Benowitz, L. I., Bear, D. M., Mesulam, M. M., Rosenthal, R., Zaidel, E., & Sperry, R. W. (1983). Contributions of the right cerebral hemisphere in perceiving paralinguistic cues of emotion. In L. Vaina & J. Hintikka (Eds.), *Cognitive constraints on communication.* Dordrecht, Holland: D. Reidel Publishing Company.

Benowitz, L. I., Bear, D. M., Rosenthal, R., Mesulam, M. M., Zaidel, E., & Sperry, R. W. (1983). Hemispheric specialization in nonverbal communication. *Cortex, 19,* 5–12.

Benowitz, L. I., Finklestein, S., Levine, D. N., & Moya, K. (1986). The participation of the right cerebral hemisphere in evaluating configurations. In C. B. Trevarthen (Ed.), *Brain circuits and functions of the mind: Essays in honor of Roger W. Sperry.* Cambridge: Cambridge University Press, in press.

Claridge, G. S., & Chappa, H. J. (1973). Psychoticism: A study of its biological basis in normal subjects. *British Journal of Social and Clinical Psychology, 12,* 175–187.

Darwin, C. (1872). *The expression of the emotions in man and animals.* Chicago: University of Chicago Press, 1965 reprint.

DeKosky, S. T., Heilman, K. M., Bowers, D., & Valenstein, E. (1980). Recognition and discrimination of emotional faces and pictures. *Brain and Language, 9,* 206–14.

Domangue, B. B. (1979). Hemisphere dominance, cognitive complexity, and nonverbal sensitivity. Unpublished doctoral dissertation, University of Delaware.

Dwyer, J. H., 3d. (1975). Contextual inferences and the right cerebral hemisphere: Listening with the left ear. Unpublished doctoral dissertation, University of California, Santa Cruz.

Ekman, P. (Ed.) (1982). *Emotion in the human face* (2nd ed.). New York: Cambridge University Press.

Eysenck, S. B. G., & Eysenck, H. J. (1968). The measurement of psychoticism: A study of factor stability and reliability. *British Journal of Social and Clinical Psychology, 7,* 286–94.

Galaburda, A. M., LeMay, M., Kemper, T. L., & Geschwind, N. (1978). Right-left asymmetries in the brain. *Science, 199,* 852–56.

Guthrie, P. T., & Smouse, A. D. (1981). Perception of emotions and attribution of acceptance by normal and emotionally disturbed children. *Journal of Nonverbal Behavior, 5,* 253–63.

Kolb, B., & Taylor, L. (1981). Affective behavior in patients with localized cortical excisions: Role of lesion site and side. *Science, 214,* 89–91.

Ley, R. G., & Bryden, M. P. (1979). Hemispheric differences in processing emotions and faces. *Brain and Language, 7,* 127–38.

Maher, B. A. (1966). *Principles of psychopathology: An experimental approach.* New York: McGraw Hill.

McGhie, A. (1973). Psychological studies of schizophrenia. In B. Maher (Ed.), *Contemporary abnormal psychology.* Harmondsworth, England: Penguin.

Meiselman, K. C. (1973). Broadening dual modality cue utilization in chronic nonparanoid schizophrenics. *Journal of Consulting and Clinical Psychology. 41,* 447–53.

Overall, J. E., Hunter, S., & Butcher, J. N. (1973). Factor structure of the MMPI-168 in a psychiatric population. *Journal of Consulting and Clinical Psychology, 41,* 284–86.

Rosenthal, R. (1963). On the social psychology of the psychological experiment: The experimenter's hypothesis as unintended determinant of experimental results. *American Scientist, 51,* 268–83.

Rosenthal, R. (1964). Effects of the experimenter on the results of psychological research.

In B. A. Maher (Ed.), *Progress in experimental personality research* (Vol. 1). New York: Academic Press.

Rosenthal, R. (1966). *Experimenter effects in behavioral research.* New York: Appleton-Century-Crofts.

Rosenthal, R. (1969). Interpersonal expectations. In R. Rosenthal and R. L. Rosnow (Eds.), *Artifact in behavioral research.* New York: Academic Press.

Rosenthal, R. (1976). *Experimenter effects in behavioral research* (rev. ed.). New York: Irvington.

Rosenthal, R. (Ed.). (1979). *Skill in nonverbal communication.* Cambridge, MA: Oelgeschlager, Gunn & Hain.

Rosenthal, R. (1981). Pavlov's mice, Pfungst's horse, and Pygmalion's PONS: Some models for the study of interpersonal expectancy effects. In T. A. Sebeok and R. Rosenthal (Eds.), *The Clever Hans phenomenon.* Annals of the New York Academy of Sciences, No. 364.

Rosenthal, R. (1985a). From unconscious experimenter bias to teacher expectancy effects. In J. B. Dusek, V. C. Hall, & W. J. Meyer (Eds.), *Teacher expectancies.* Hillsdale NJ: Lawrence Erlbaum Associates, in press.

Rosenthal, R. (1985b). Nonverbal cues in the mediation of interpersonal expectancy effects. In A. W. Siegman & S. Feldstein (Eds.), *Nonverbal behavior in interpersonal communication.* Hillsdale, NJ: Lawrence Erlbaum Associates.

Rosenthal, R., Hall, J. A., DiMatteo, M. R., Rogers, P. L., & Archer, D. (1979). *Sensitivity to nonverbal communication: The PONS test.* Baltimore: The Johns Hopkins University Press.

Rosenthal, R., & Rosnow, R. L. (1984). *Essentials of behavioral research.* New York: McGraw-Hill.

Rosenthal, R., & Rosnow, R. L. (1985). *Contrast analysis: Focused comparisons in the analysis of variance.* New York: Cambridge University Press.

Sebeok, T. A., & Rosenthal, R. (Eds.). (1981). *The Clever Hans phenomenon.* Annals of the New York Academy of Sciences, No. 364.

Snedecor, G. W., & Cochran, W. G. (1967). *Statistical methods,* 6th ed. Ames: Iowa State University Press.

Snedecor, G. W., & Cochran, W. G. (1980). *Statistical methods,* 7th ed. Ames: Iowa State University Press.

Sperry, R. W. (1982). Some effects of disconnecting the cerebral hemispheres. *Science, 217,* 1223–26.

Turner, J. le B. (1964). Schizophrenics as judges of vocal expressions of emotional meaning. In J. R. Davitz, *The communication of emotional meaning.* New York: McGraw-Hill.

Vandenberg, S. G., & Mattsson, E. (1960). *The interpretation of facial expressions by schizophrenics, other mental patients, normal adults and children.* Proceedings of the 16th International Congress of Psychology, Bonn.

Young, L. D. (1979). Differential involvement of the cerebral hemispheres in sensitivity to nonverbal communication: A psychophysiological investigation. Unpublished doctoral dissertation, Harvard University.

Zurif, E. B. (1974). Auditory lateralizaton: Prosodic and syntactic factors. *Brain and Language, 1,* 391–404.

10 Neural Control of Emotional Communication

Don M. Tucker

Research on nonverbal communication has added an important perspective to our understanding of cognitive functioning in natural situations. By some estimates (Mehrabian, 1972), over 90% of the emotional information in interpersonal interactions is conveyed through nonverbal channels. For cognitive science to be relevant to clinical issues, or to everyday human interactions, it must consider nonverbal as well as verbal cognition.

This chapter begins with a brief review of evidence that the right hemisphere is particularly important to nonverbal communication. It is intrinsically interesting to find that verbal and nonverbal forms of communication are differentially lateralized. However, more important is what the study of lateralization can tell us about the cognitive processes underlying nonverbal communication. In the second section of this chapter I will consider nonverbal communication in light of the general literature on hemispheric specialization for cognition. This literature should help provide a positive characterization of the cognitive processes involved in "nonverbal" communication; rather than understanding this cognition only as "nonverbal," the study of the right hemisphere should help describe what this cognition is as well as what it is not. Separating verbal and nonverbal communication between the two hemispheres raises questions of how the communication process as a whole is integrated. In a third section I will discuss current models of hemispheric integration and what these might mean for understanding the control of the communication process.

Appreciating the lateral organization of the brain may yield new perspectives on understanding adaptive, real-world cognition. But lateral asymmetry is only one dimension of brain organization, as chapter 7 has reminded us, and at least two other dimensions are fundamental: the anterior/posterior dimension and what may be termed a vertical dimension, the distinction between cortical controls and the more primitive influences from subcortical systems. In a fourth section I will discuss how the balance of control between anterior and posterior regions, and that between cortical and subcortical systems, should be included in a comprehensive neuropsychological model of communication.

If a neuropsychological approach is to be meaningful, it must not only analyze the person into neural subsystems, but it should help us to understand whole brain function. In a final section I will speculate on implications of a neuropsychological model for clinical work.

RIGHT HEMISPHERE CONTRIBUTIONS TO UNDERSTANDING AND EXPRESSING EMOTION

Understanding Facial Expressions

Recognizing familiar faces is a cognitive process that occurs so automatically that it is easily taken for granted, and may not be considered an important aspect of intelligence. Yet there are complex configurational processing skills required for facial recognition, as chapter 7 has noted. The uniqueness of these skills is emphasized by the inability of certain brain-injured patients to identify faces even when other cognitive skills remain intact. Although bilateral lesions produce the most severe deficits, when matched groups of unilateral lesioned patients are contrasted, the right-hemisphere-damaged group is more severely impaired (De Renzi & Spinnler, 1966; Russo & Vignolo, 1967).

Clinical observations have suggested that right-hemisphere-damaged patients often show social inappropriateness; a contributing factor seems to be their difficulty in understanding the emotion communicated in facial expressions (Cicone, Wapner, & Gardner, 1980). An initial question in this research has been whether the right hemisphere's role in interpreting emotion in faces is due solely to its skill in facial recognition, or whether it provides a unique contribution in understanding the emotion itself. With right-hemisphere-damaged patients, Cicone et al. (1980) observed that in addition to their facial recognition deficit, these patients had difficulty interpreting the appropriate emotion in drawings of emotional situations, indicating that the right hemisphere's contribution to understanding emotion may be a general one.

Research with normal subjects has also indicated that the right hemisphere's skill in interpreting emotion in facial expressions goes beyond a strictly visuospatial process. The standard procedure in this research is tachistoscopic presentation of photographs of faces to the left and right visual half fields, lateralizing the initial reception of the stimuli to the right and left hemispheres, respectively (see chapter 7). With this technique, Suberi and McKeever (1977) found a right hemisphere (left visual field) advantage as subjects recognized faces they had memorized, and an even greater right hemisphere advantage when the faces to be memorized portrayed emotions. In other research with normals, Ley and Bryden (1979) showed that both the recognition of emotion and the identification of specific cartoon characters in line drawings of faces produced a right hemisphere advantage with tachistoscopic presentation. The right hemisphere advantage for the emotional expressions was greater for those expressions with greater emotional intensity, further indicating that understanding emotion and not just perceiving faces requires the right hemisphere. Ley and Bryden (1979) proposed that the right hemisphere's capacity in gestalt integration and its skills in imagery afford the cognitive capacity for evaluating emotional information.

In a visual half field experiment on facial recognition, Safer (1981) asked his subjects how they interpreted the emotion in the faces. Safer found that some subjects performed well on the task by empathizing with the emotion in the face to facilitate identifying the emotion. In subsequent research Safer trained some subjects to identify emotion through empathy, and found that this approach produced a substantial right hemisphere advantage. This study provides important evidence that the right hemisphere's role in emotional communication goes beyond its visuospatial skills; in this study the right hemisphere appeared important to the subject's ability to process his or her own emotional response to the facial expression.

The results of research on normal facial recognition are usually expressed in terms of group data, and may not reflect the substantial individual differences in normal hemispheric involvement in interpreting facial expressions (Galper & Costa, 1980; Safer, 1981; see Levy, Heller, Banich, & Burton, 1983). Although any generalizations from group data must be tempered by realization of the uniqueness of individual brains, the findings with normals confirm those from brain damage studies, indicating that at least for most right-handed persons the right hemisphere is specialized for interpreting emotion in facial expressions.

Asymmetry of Facial Displays

Neurologists have known for some time that hemiplegia (unilateral paralysis) may be associated with a loss of voluntary facial movement contralateral to the lesion (e.g., on the right side of the face with a left hemisphere lesion), while spontaneous emotional expressions remain symmetric (Monrad-Krohn, 1924). Monrad-Krohn described cases in which emotional expressions were exaggerated following brain damage. He concluded that in the normal brain there may be a tonic inhibition of emotional movements, an inhibition closely associated with voluntary control. Although Monrad-Krohn did not address the intrinsic lateralization of emotional processes, the issues that were important in his clinical observations, such as tonic inhibition and the distinction between voluntary and spontaneous expressions, remain important in current research on facial expression of emotion in normals.

Campbell (1978) found that when normal subjects were asked to smile to have their photographs taken, the smile was often more extensive on the left half of the face. Because the innervation of the lower face is divided (Thompson, 1982), a greater left side intensity suggests right hemisphere control of emotional expression. Examining a variety of posed emotions, Borod and Caron (1980) also found greater left-sided intensity, as reported in chapter 8. Sackeim, Gur, and Saucy (1978) took photographs of posed expressions of emotion and developed split half composites from each half-face and its mirror image; the left half composites were found to portray more intense emotion. The use of posed, voluntary emotional expressions is an important issue in these studies. Ekman, Hager, and Friesen (1981) suggested that a greater left-sided intensity occurs only for posed expressions. In their study of facial muscle movements as subjects watched pleasant or aversive slides, Ekman et al. found that spontaneous expressions are likely to be more intense, whether on the right or on the left side of the face.

A number of methodological issues in this research require further study (Dopson, Beckwith, Tucker, & Bullard-Bates, 1984; Koff, Borod & White, 1981; Thompson, 1982; see Sackeim & Gur, 1982, for a review). For example, observation of more intense emotional expressions on the left side of the face has been interpreted to indicate the right hemisphere's expressivity; in light of the neurologic evidence on inhibitory control of facial expressions (Monrad-Krohn, 1924; see Sackeim & Gur, 1982), this asymmetry could as easily reflect a tonic inhibitory influence of the left hemisphere on the right side of the face (Dopson et al., 1984).

Whereas several important issues remain to be resolved, recent evidence does address one important question raised by initial studies in this area: Spontaneous as well as posed emotions appear to be more intense on the left side of the face. Moscovitch and Olds (1982) found a greater left-sided intensity in two studies, one in which they observed facial expressions occurring during restaurant conversations, and a second study in which they surreptitiously examined facial expressions as subjects described emotional experiences. Dopson et al. (1984) compared spontaneous with posed emotions directly. Split half composites were made from photographs taken without the subject's knowledge during happy and sad mood induction procedures. Subjects were than asked to pose happy and sad expressions, and a second set of composites was made. For both happy and sad emotions, and for both spontaneous and posed expressions, greater intensity was observed for the left side of the face. This finding about the right hemisphere's functioning is consistent with the research reported in chapters 7, 8, and 9.

Emotion Conveyed by Tone of Voice

In the last century Hughlings Jackson (1879) observed that emotional aspects of speech are often spared in aphasia. Monrad-Krohn (1947) conducted clinical studies of the effects of brain dysfunction on the ability to convey meaning through tone of voice, and through the emphasis and timing of speech. Monrad-Krohn termed these melodic aspects of speech "prosody," and observed characteristic prosodic patterns of psychiatric as well as neurologic disorders (Monrad-Krohn, 1963).

The preservation of the emotional intonation of speech in aphasia would suggest that the intact right hemisphere may be responsible for handling this aspect of vocal communication. Heilman, Scholes, and Watson (1975) examined this possibility by testing the ability of right- and left-hemisphere-damaged patients to judge the emotion conveyed by the tone of voice of taped sentences. The right-lesioned group showed a significant impairment on this task. Tucker, Watson, and Heilman (1976) replicated this finding and showed that right-lesioned patients also were impaired in the ability to express emotions through vocal intonation.

Further evidence of right hemisphere involvement in prosodic comprehension was provided when Deglin (1973) observed that electroconvulsive therapy administered to the right hemisphere impaired the patients' abiltiy to recognize emotion expressed by tone of voice. Ross and Mesulam (1979) describe two patients with right hemisphere lesions whose verbal productions were grammatically correct, but lacked the appropriate emotional emphasis. The problems in daily living suffered by these patients because of their loss of prosodic ability are convincing evidence of the adaptive significance of the nonverbal information in vocal communications. Ross and Rush (1981) propose that the right hemisphere has both receptive and expressive centers for emotional communication, paralleling the receptive and expressive speech regions in the left hemisphere. Rosenthal and Benowitz, in chapter 9, find that right temporal lobe involvement is decisive in the ability to decode tone of voice cues.

Although most of the research on lateralization of auditory perception in normals has focused on verbal stimuli with the dichotic listening method, some studies with normals have presented nonverbal information, and have found it processed more efficiently by the right hemisphere (see chapter 7). Knox and Kimura (1970) found that children by age 5 showed a left-ear superiority in recognizing nonverbal sounds in the environment. In contrast to the right-ear advantage observed in most studies of speech, Haggard and Parkinson (1971) found a left-ear advantage when normal subjects were asked to identify the emotional tone of natural speech. Using a monaural rather than dichotic presentation, Safer and Leventhal (1977) asked subjects to judge whether sentences were emotionally positive, neutral, or negative, without instructing them whether to attend to the verbal content or the tone of voice of the sentence. With left ear presentation, the subjects showed a significant tendency to make judgments based on the speaker's tone of voice rather than the verbal content.

This evidence of right hemisphere specialization for sending and receiving emotional information through vocal intonation is important in showing that the right hemisphere's role in emotional communication extends beyond dealing with facial expressions. Certainly the right hemisphere's nonverbal perceptual skills are important to its specialization for emotional intonation. But the cognition most relevant to hemispheric specialization appears to be at a more complex level than simply processing the vocal intonations. When the intonation serves to delineate the phrase structure rather than emotional tone of the verbal utterance, normals show a right-ear advantage (Zurif & Mendelsohn, 1972).

Although more research is required to examine hemispheric contributions to the comprehension of complex or subtle emotional communications, there have been several indications that the right hemisphere's role extends beyond the perception of faces or vocal intonations. Gardner, Ling, Flamm, and Silverman (1975) found that both left- and right-lesioned patients had difficulty understanding the humor in cartoons. The patients with left hemisphere lesions had difficulty understanding the verbal captions. Right hemisphere lesions appeared to produce a more general deficit in affective response; these patients laughed inappropriately or not at all at the cartoons, confabulated answers to questions, and often drew impossible inferences from the cartoons. Gardner et al. suggest that right hemisphere lesions often lead to inappropriate behavior, and that at least one important factor is the patient's impaired ability to understand the affective significance of situations. In their research on emotional facial recognition, Cicone et al. (1980) also emphasize a higher-order impairment in emotional comprehension; the right-hemisphere-damaged patients showed errors suggesting they did not understand the semantic relations among various emotions.

In considering emotional communication in social interactions, or the understanding of the emotional meaning of life situations, it is certainly necessary to appreciate the importance of verbal cognition. Strauss, in chapter 7 and previously (1983), suggests that the right hemisphere's contribution to emotional communication is particularly relevant to nonverbal features, and that left hemisphere involvement is important to verbal representation of emotion. Some authors (Flor-Henry, 1983; Tucker, 1981) propose that the left hemisphere regulates the right hemisphere's emotional processing; it would seem that this regulation would draw heavily on the verbal mediation of emotion. However, even when the task involves strictly verbal material, right-hemisphere-lesioned patients show a qualitative pattern of responding that indicates a higher-order impairment of emotional understanding. Wechsler (1973) found that both right and left lesions impaired recall of the information in stories, but that right-lesioned patients were particularly unable to recall accurately the stories relevant to their own emotional situation. These patients showed personal, egocentric distortions of the emotional information.

NEUROPSYCHOLOGICAL ORGANIZATION OF NONVERBAL COMMUNICATION

All the chapters in Part II of this book make clear that the distinction between verbal and nonverbal communication appears overly imprecise, particularly with regard to hemispheric specialization (see also Buck & Duffy, 1980). Certain gestures that are important in regulating the flow and emphasis of verbalizations may be organized within the left hemisphere. However, for spontaneous as opposed to symbolic nonverbal communications, as chapter 8 points out, right hemisphere specialization seems fairly well documented. By considering the general characteristics of right hemisphere cognition, it may be possible to understand better the operational principles underlying the spontaneous expression of emotion through nonverbal messages.

Representational Form

The first psychological distinction between right and left hemisphere functions contrasted the nonverbal nature of right hemisphere skills, in auditory and visual modalities, with the left hemisphere's known verbal ability (Kimura, 1977). More recently, other distinctions, such as between analytic and holistic modes of organizing information (Levy, 1969; Nebes, 1978; Sergent & Bindra, 1981; Tucker, 1976), have been shown to be important to hemispheric specialization, and exceptions to the verbal/nonverbal dichotomy have been pointed out in chapter 9 and elsewhere (Bever & Chiarello, 1974; Russo & Vignolo, 1967). Although these exceptions show that each hemisphere has a characteristic approach to organizing information, whether verbal or nonverbal, it is important not to overlook the verbal/nonverbal distinction, especially when considering nonverbal communication. For most of its cognitive operations, each hemisphere seems specialized for a specific representational mode.

Verbal cognitive representation entails the substitution of an internal code, a word, for sensory experience. Although some students of language have argued that the phonetic characteristics of words often harbor inherent reflections of their referents (Jakobson, 1965; Werner & Kaplan, 1963), a linguistic code is essentially an arbitrary substitution for the original information. This representational format offers important advantages to an information processing system over the analog representation that occurs in the initial, iconic or echoic, representation of concrete perception. In computer terms, a digital, substitutive code is relocatable, its semantic packages portable from one area of memory, or one brain, to the next. In this form, the substitutive code can be organized and processed according to fixed and repeatable rules, such as those of algebra or grammar. The capacity for repeatable, regularized cognitive operations is essential to complex instances of human cognition, and may be intrinsic to the left hemisphere's operation (Goldberg & Costa, 1981). In his description of the development of cybernetic operations in biological systems, Bertalanffy (1968) stated that only when processes become routinized, i.e., stable and repeatable, are they amenable to feedback from their outcome, perhaps the most fundamental aspect of structured cybernetics.

Nonverbal cognitive processes involve a fundamentally different form of internal representation: They are analogical. There is no transformation of the continuous sensory data into a discrete, substitutive code; rather, the internal representation of the information is an analog of the sensation, mirroring the environment. An image retains the sensory quality of the sight or sound, and the cognitive processing of the image must occur through analogical, as opposed to logical or propositional, transformations (see Kosslyn, 1980).

The analogical nature of the right hemisphere's information processing may be important to an understanding of the nature of the information transfer in nonverbal communication. Buck (1982 and with Borod & Koff, chapter 8) suggests that nonverbal communication operates through a biologically shared signal system, rather than the socially or culturally shared signal system of language. Buck cites Darwin's (1872) speculation that emotional displays have evolved to reflect the individual's internal affective state so as to facilitate social coordination. Unlike the arbitrary symbols of language, nonverbal emotional displays have an inherent relation to their referents. The analogical form of the information representation causes the message to reflect its meaning in a continuous fashion. An extensive or fast gesture of the hand portrays a continuously greater amplitude of the sender's meaning than a smaller or slower gesture. The speaker's intonation conveys information not in an arbitrary code, but through mirroring an internal emotional state analogically. Because of its continuous nature, a subtle nonverbal cue is often of the same form but less intense than a more direct message. The child recognizes the firmness of the parent's admonition by the continuous amplitude of the message's affectively modulated intonation contour.

The analogical nature of the data transfer is particularly important on the receiving end. The perception of the message requires an internal representation of the information; because the message is a concrete and continuous reflection of the sender's affective state, the simple mental representation of this information in the process of perception tends to elicit the corresponding affective state in the receiver. With verbal representation there is an inherent distance between the semantics of the message and the perceiver's affective response that is afforded by the indirect, substitutive nature of the verbal code. With nonverbal communication the analogical format of the information allows the communication to elicit emotion concretely and directly.

In both verbal and nonverbal forms of interpersonal information transfer, the communication process synchronizes the information processing operations of the participants. At least one view of speech perception holds that effective comprehension draws on the listener's capacity to parallel covertly the speech generation process to activate the appropriate semantic pathways (Neisser, 1967). In nonverbal communication, the continuous and analogical form of the information transfer facilitates the receiver's paralleling the sender's affective state. The synchronization of the participants' neural operations is continuous, direct, and emotionally immediate.

Cognitive Structure and Process

The capacity for handling analog representation thus seems integral to the right hemisphere's involvement in communication. In addition to the verbal/nonverbal distinction between left and right hemisphere cognition, recent neuropsychological research has shown that the two hemispheres differ in terms of cognitive structure and process. Considering this research suggests that in expressing and interpreting emotion the right hemisphere's cognition is holistic, handling multiple channels of communication simultaneously.

In some of the early studies contrasting the performance skills of matched groups of left- and right-hemisphere-damaged patients, left as well as right hemisphere damage impaired the patient's ability to perform certain visuospatial tasks. Russo and Vignolo (1967), for example, found that performance of Gottschaldt's embedded figures test was even more difficult for aphasics than for right-hemisphere-lesioned patients, even though the test was nonverbal. The important difference in hemispheric function appeared to involve not just the content of the information, verbal versus nonverbal, but how it was structured. The left hemisphere appeared particularly suited to the analytic organization of even visuospatial information, breaking the perceptual configuration down into its constituent elements.

This lateral specialization for cognitive structure was apparent to Levy-Agresti and Sperry (1968) in their study of the different strategies of task performance taken by the two hemispheres of the commissurotomy patients. In these patients, the fiber tracts connecting the hemispheres were severed to prevent the spread of epileptic seizures. The left hemisphere appeared to analyze the stimulus materials and deal with specific details, whereas the right hemisphere attempted a more global or synthetic approach. Levy (1969) speculated that the lateral specialization of the human brain may have occurred in evolution to avoid the incompatibility that occurs when analytic and synthetic modes of organization occupy the same neural regions.

The relevance of structural aspects of cognition to lateralization was shown further by Nebes (1978) in his study of hemispheric performance by commissurotomy patients: the right hemisphere appeared particularly important to those visuospatial tasks requiring the perception of part-whole relations, synthesizing the parts to perceive the whole. In an electroencephalographic study of cognition in normals (Tucker, 1976) I found that, at least for males, greater right than left hemisphere alpha suppression predicted performance on a synthetic visuospatial task (the Mooney Closure Faces) but not on an analytic task (the Embedded Figures Test).

A recent review of tachistoscopic studies of face perception (Sergent & Bindra, 1981) concluded that the typical right hemisphere advantage in this research occurs particularly when the task calls for holistic processing of the face; when an analytic strategy is required, a left hemisphere advantage may be observed.

The two hemispheres' differing approaches to structuring information has been perhaps the most important characterization of cognitive lateralization beyond the verbal/nonverbal dichotomy. However, a distinction has also been drawn in terms of process, how cognitive operations are carried out over time. Cohen (1973) suggested that the left hemisphere is particularly adept at sequential processes, those which must be ordered serially, while the right hemisphere is better able to handle parallel operations. In their review of the literature on cognitive lateralization, Bradshaw and Nettleton (1981) questioned whether the current characterizations of hemispheric differences, in terms of analytic versus holistic structure and sequential versus parallel processing, may not both reflect some more fundamental dimension.

All that seems necessary to unify these dimensions is to assume that the same forms of neuropsychological organization are applied to spatial as to temporal domains: The analytic organizational skill that the left hemisphere applies to spatial information would, when applied to events occurring over time, allow the capacity to differentiate and sequentially order those events. The same holistic approach that affords the right hemisphere its competence in spatial conceptualization would seem to allow its processing resources to be allocated more efficiently across multiple operations in time.

Verbal communication is inherently a linear process; the semantic integrity of the message requires that the order of the information be interpreted correctly. The left hemisphere's speech regions must not only analyze the continuous flow of auditory information into discrete units of verbal data, but must also decode the sequential relations among the units according to the conventions of grammatical order. The left hemisphere's capacity for focal attention (Kinsbourne, 1974; Tucker & Williamson, 1984) seems requisite to maintain the appropriate order in the information processing operations required for language.

In contrast, nonverbal communication entails parallel streams of analog data—from the speaker's facial expression, gestures, posture, intonation. Effective comprehension of the communication requires a strategy for allocating cognitive resources to encompass these several input streams in parallel; this is the kind of strategy that the right hemisphere contributes in experimental research (Bradshaw & Nettleton, 1981; Cohen, 1973).

The meaning of nonverbal communication cannot be decoded in the linear and focal manner used to interpret the relatively discrete and definite meanings of words. Rather, the meaning is a latent content, emergent from a complex of often subtle cues. The communication of interpersonal attraction, for example, is essential in forming and maintaining relationships in a variety of settings. The relevant communication is seldom verbal, or even explicit. Such cues as a facial expression displaying interest, a slightly prolonged eye contact, or an encouraging tone of voice can communicate that the interaction is important and enjoyable. Because they are in continuous, analog form, the strength or amplitude of the meaning of these cues is also continuous. Unlike a discrete verbal message, the meaning in these analog cues cannot be decoded explicitly, but must be appreciated in proportion to the continuous magnitude of the cues. Because the receiver's cognitive resources are allocated over a number of parallel information channels, and because many of the cues are subtle, the receiver may not be able to access the meaning of any cue consciously. The meaning of the communication is "atmospheric" (Werner, 1957), arising from the capacity to experience the confluence of the parallel sources of information in the message together with the intrinsic affective responses they elicit.

The Developmental Context of Emotional Communication

Werner's (1957) study of development suggested to him that affective factors are inseparable from cognition in the developmental process. The child's psychological organization is syncretic, with cognitive, emotional, postural, and visceral elements fused in an undifferentiated experiential matrix. Independently of Werner, Monrad-Krohn's (1947; 1963) clinical studies of brain function and communication led him to similar conclusions. For the child, the verbal content of speech is inseparable from the prosodic features. Monrad-Krohn (1963) described how a child understands a phrase in a certain tone of voice, but may not recognize the same phrase spoken in a different tone. The communication is what Werner (1957) termed "holophrastic," its semantics undifferentiated.

The syncretic nature of the child's involvement in communication suggests that humans begin communicating with emotional features as integral to the process, and only later, with the emergence of verbal competence, develop the capacity for communication with other purposes than the exchange of emotional information. The neuropsychological research on the right hemisphere's holistic conceptual organization seems relevant to the child's experience of communication. Several lines of evidence indicate that the right hemisphere becomes functionally mature earlier than the left. Whitaker (1978) reviews this evidence: Children often show spatial skills, such as recognizing faces or environmental sounds, before they are competent to acquire language. The alpha rhythm of the EEG, which appears at a later stage of maturation than slower frequencies, is observed first over the right hemisphere. Whitaker points to Taylor's (1969) observation of more seizure foci in the left hemisphere in the first year of life; Taylor argues that since immature neural tissue is susceptible to seizures, the left hemisphere's maturation lags behind that of the right.

Other electrophysiologic evidence supports Whitaker's view. Research on infants' EEG response to photic driving shows a greater response, suggesting greater neural maturity, in the right hemsphere (Crowell, Jones, Kapuniai, & Nakagawa, 1973). In addition to the finding of earlier alpha development in the right hemisphere, extensive observations of children's EEGs have shown a higher abundance of theta activity in the left hemisphere (Walter, 1950). Since the developmental progression in EEG frequencies is toward decreased delta and theta and increased alpha, the frequency characteristics of left and right hemisphere EEGs in childhood indicate earlier maturation on the right.

The developmental psychology literature suggests that the child's experience of the communication process is initially holistic and undifferentiated. From neuropsychological research we find that the right hemisphere's conceptual skills in holistic, supramodal intergration appear integral to the expression and comprehension of emotion, in facial displays and vocal intonations. Although tentative, the evidence on brain maturation suggests that, for whatever adaptive reasons, the brain develops with the right hemisphere operational earlier than the left. Combining these perspectives, we gain the impression that communication in its primary form is nonverbal, organized in the brain with the emotional meaning of the communication fused with the message. In the process of development, as the left hemisphere becomes capable of analytic, logical encoding, the child gains the capacity to differentiate the cognitive features of communication. This increasing verbal differentiation allows the child's communication important new capacities for semantic definiteness, complexity, and flexibility, as the communication becomes more articulated from its primitive, syncretic, and inherently egocentric context (Werner, 1957).

But differentiation applies to some domains more than others; the evidence on the lateralization of nonverbal communication is instructive in showing that the primary emotional features of the communication remain embedded within their early, analogical form, organized and interpreted in neural regions separate from those of differentiated verbal semantics. This is an interesting model of communication, a differentiated and structured verbal semantic system operating within the context of a more primitive, but emotionally powerful, nonverbal cognitive system. Because communication is so essential to the child's formation of an identity, it seems reasonable to conclude that this neuropsychological substrate of communication is also relevant to the organization of personality.

LATERALIZED CONTROL PROCESSES IN COMMUNICATION

For a comprehensive view of how communication is controlled, it is insufficient just to characterize lateralized neural systems; the question becomes how their contributions are coordinated. Although neuropsychological research has only begun to consider hemispheric interaction, the existing evidence may suggest how verbal and nonverbal communications are, or are not, integrated.

Hemispheric Parallelism

In recent work in cognitive psychology, an issue has been whether an individual's cognitive resources are limited to one channel of operation at a time, or whether resources can be allocated across several tasks concurrently (Posner, 1978; Posner & Boies, 1971). At least in some experimental situations, multiple cognitive pathways can be activated simultaneously. If subjects are asked to attend to phonetic aspects of a letter presented visually, later tests show that they processed the physical, orthographic features of the letter simultaneously (Posner, 1978). Although this research has not considered lateralization, experiments presenting letters in different typefaces to the left and right visual half fields (Bryden & Allard, 1978) have shown that at least complex orthographic features require right hemisphere processing, while the linguistic decoding of the letters occurs more efficiently in the left hemisphere. The possibility that the two hemispheres carry out independent and parallel processing of a given stimulus has been considered in laterality research (Moscovitch, Scullion, & Christie, 1976); what is not well understood is how the results of separate processing can be integrated.

Friedman and Polson (1981) proposed that the two hemispheres represent independent pools of information processing resources. A cognitive load applied to one hemisphere would thus draw capacity from only that resource pool. Friedman and Polson reviewed several dual-task experiments which they found consistent with their notions. Hellige and Wong

(1983) used a dual-task method in dichotic listening studies. As with other lateralization effects (Levy, Heller, Banich, & Burton, 1983) individual differences in hemispheric usage were important in this research. When these were taken into account, Hellige and Wong observed that the interference effects of secondary tasks were hemisphere-specific, further indication that the two hemispheres represent independent resource pools.

If this is the case, the two hemispheres' specialized processing operations could proceed in parallel during interpersonal communication. Hemispheric function would then not be dichotomous, with attention directed at one time to the verbal message and at another time to the nonverbal message, but would be simultaneous, with two separate transmission channels active during the communication. At the same time as linguistic-processing regions of the brain are decoding the lexical units of speech from the continuous auditory input stream, ordering them within appropriate syntactical schemas, and activating relevant verbal semantic domains, other regions are operating on the analogical features of the sender's voice, gestures, and facial expression, combining these into a supramodal representation that allows the receiver to mirror the affective status of the sender. Strauss, in chapter 7, presents evidence of such parallel processing.

Although parallel processing of information by the two hemispheres seems likely to occur, especially in the early stages of perception (Moscovitch et al., 1976), there must be some capacity for these parallel cognitive operations to influence each other. The question of information exchange between the hemispheres has received only limited attention in lateralization research. Because each hemisphere is specialized for a particular form of representation, digital or analog, some sort of analog-to-digital conversion must occur for a successful interhemispheric transfer. Considering this process even at a simplistic level presents some interesting issues for interhemispheric integration. Is there an asymmetry in the translation? Is verbally characterizing an analogical representation more efficient than generating a nonverbal, analog reconstruction from a verbal message? Would an asymmetry in the analog-to-digital conversion have implications for the question of which hemisphere controls the exchange? Are individuals similar in the degree of interhemispheric coordination of verbal and nonverbal messages, or do some persons maintain greater independence between the two hemispheres in handling communication?

The task of coordinating hemispheric responses would become particularly difficult if the verbal message were incongruous with the nonverbal one. In a communications-theory analysis of schizophrenic interactions, Bateson and associates proposed that a child's response to a communication could become distorted if the message's ostensible content were incongruous with an implicit meaning, a metacommunication (Bateson,

Jackson, Haley, & Weakland, 1956). The resultant double bind, the incongruity between verbal and nonverbal messages, could produce a hemispheric incongruity as the child attempts to understand the emotional meaning of the communication (Galin, 1974). A child hearing her mother say, "Yes, of course I love you," while feeling the mother stiffen and withdraw from her embrace may organize the relationship with the mother in incompatible ways within the two hemispheres. To the extent that the child's sense of self emerges from these early interactions (Sullivan, 1953), distortions in communication could produce distortions in the neuropsychological organization of personality. Some current research on brain function in schizophrenia actually suggests that this disorder is associated with faulty integration of information between the hemispheres (Beaumont & Dimond, 1973). Although other studies do not find that schizophrenics have callosal information transfer deficits (see Walker & McGuire, 1982), the coordination of lateralized cognitive and emotional processes remains an important issue in research on psychopathology.

The normal child's capacity to integrate verbal and nonverbal processes has been questioned by recent findings. Galin, Johnstone, Nakell, and Herron (1979) compared the ability of 3- and 5-year-olds to integrate tactile information intra– or inter-hemispherically. The younger children showed particular difficulty in comparing the tactile stimuli between the two hands, suggesting a developmental immaturity in interhemispheric transfer. Although further research on this issue is required before drawing conclusions, an interesting possibility is that early in life integration between the hemispheres is minimal and that hemispheric parallelism is the normal state of affairs. Lateralized contributions to communication thus may develop before the child has the capacity to coordinate them.

Reciprocal Inhibition: Dominance Revisited

Although a degree of hemispheric parallelism probably occurs during normal cognition, some coordination of hemispheric contributions must occur. An elementary mode of coordination may be reciprocal inhibition. In addition, there are several indications that the left hemisphere has priority when attentional resources are scarce. Controls exerted by the left hemisphere over the right may be an important higher order feature of the neuropsychological regulation of emotion.

The demonstration that each hemisphere is capable of independent cognitive operations was probably the most striking aspect of the human commissurotomy studies. The phenomenon of parallel hemispheric processing was first examined in commissurotomy studies in monkeys

(Sperry, Gazzaniga, & Bogen, 1969); monkeys with sectioned commissures could be trained to perform certain simultaneous tasks more efficiently than intact animals. Experiments with human commissurotomy patients showed that their left and right hemispheres could also perform separate tasks at the same time, as long as the tasks were simple and the two hemispheres maintained a common mental set (Sperry et al.,1969). These constraints were important; tasks with greater attentional demands showed that the capacity for hemispheric paralleling in the commissurotomy patients was limited (Kinsbourne, 1974).

Kinsbourne (1974) reviewed evidence that a balance of control is often achieved through reciprocal inhibition between brain regions. Because the right hemisphere may fail to develop language after left hemisphere damage, whereas the right hemisphere can develop language after left hemispherectomy (when the entire left cortex is removed), Kinsbourne suggested that the left hemisphere normally inhibits the right hemisphere's capacity to develop language. Pointing to the opponent process organization of several brain systems, such as in the auditory pathways of the brainstem, Kinsbourne proposed that the two hemispheres normally interact through reciprocal inhibition, mediated across the corpus callosum to control the direction of attention to the left and right halves of perceptual space.

Reciprocal inhibition has been shown to occur between homologous regions in the two hemispheres, as when simultaneous stimulation is not perceived on the side contralateral to a lesion due to reciprocal inhibition from the intact hemisphere (Birch, Belmont, & Karp, 1967). However, the nature or extent of reciprocal inhibition between the hemispheres for higher order cognitive processes is not well understood. In interpersonal communication, reciprocal inhibition would cause an emphasis on one hemisphere's mode of communication to decrease processing of the other mode. A person with a hysteric personality, for example, shows a global and holistic cognitive style (Shapiro, 1965) that seems to entail a predominance of right hemisphere processing (Smokler & Shevrin, 1979). In an interpersonal interaction, the hysteric's impressionistic and affectively responsive approach to understanding the communication would result in a primary emphasis on nonverbal cues. If reciprocal inhibition operated to decrease left hemisphere processing, the hysteric's capacity for rational, analytic understanding of the verbal message would be expected to be impaired. Consistent with this line of reasoning, observation shows that poor analytic skills are an important feature of the cognitive deficits of the hysteric personality (Shapiro, 1965).

Although individual differences in styles of emotional self-control are clearly important, other evidence suggests that inhibitory effects across the corpus callosum usually support left hemisphere dominance. Kinsbourne (1974) described observations with commissurotomy patients indicating that the left hemisphere has priority for attentional resources. When the two hemispheres of these patients were trained to perform difficult tasks in parallel, the left hemisphere appeared attentionally competent, while the right hemisphere responded automatically and inappropriately to each stimulus presented. If the patients were required to respond with the right hand or to give a verbal answer, their inattention to the left half of space was particularly striking. While tapping simultaneously with both hands, a commissurotomy patient was asked a difficult question. As she thought of her answer, she stopped tapping with the right hand but continued with the left, suggesting that the left hemisphere was most important to actively directing her attention to the question (Kinsbourne, 1974).

The hypothesis that each hemisphere represents an independent pool of processing resources (Friedman & Polson, 1981; Hellige & Wong, 1983) does not take reciprocal inhibition into account, nor does it address the possibility of hemispheric asymmetries in attentional control, asymmetries that may exist in the degree and kind of attention controlled by a hemisphere (Heilman & Van Den Able, 1980; Kinsbourne, 1974; Tucker & Williamson, 1984). Some findings using the dual-task paradigm with lateralized presentation methods are not consistent with the notion of separate and symmetric hemispheric resources. Hayne, Antes, and Tucker (1981) found that a secondary task of a button press to a tone interfered with nonverbal primary tasks in both auditory and visual modalities among normal subjects. When the secondary task was presented during verbal primary tasks, however, no interference of the primary tasks occurred and performance on the secondary task was impaired. These findings with normals suggest an attentional priority for left hemisphere operations not unlike that observed in the commissurotomy studies (Kinsbourne, 1974).

Because the right hemisphere does appear to control cognitive operations when a task requires holistic, spatial cognition (Bradshaw & Nettleton, 1981), and because some persons seem predisposed toward right hemisphere processing (Smokler & Shevrin, 1979; Gur & Gur, 1975; Swenson & Tucker, 1983), the left hemisphere apparently assumes control or dominance only under certain conditions. Kinsbourne (1974) proposes that, although both hemispheres must collaborate to balance attention between the left and right halves of perceptual space, the left hemisphere is specialized for focal attention. Several aspects of attentional control processes in the brain, reviewed below, are congruent with Kinsbourne's notion. An active, internally directed, "intentional" control of cognitive resources appears to be associated with left hemisphere dominance. Recent studies suggest further that a person's attentional orientation and degree of left hemisphere dominance may be important determinants of emotional responsivity, both as experienced subjectively and as displayed in nonverbal communication.

Buck and Duffy (1980) examined the effects of unilateral brain damage on nonverbal displays of emotional responses to aversive or pleasant photographic slides. By having raters examine videotapes of the subject's facial expression and attempt to determine which slides the person was viewing, Buck and Duffy obtained an objective rating of the subject's intensity of emotional display. An interesting finding with this procedure was that normals tend to inhibit their responses more to unpleasant than pleasant slides. With the brain-lesioned patients, Buck and Duffy found that left-hemisphere-damaged subjects were rated as more emotionally expressive, particularly while viewing the unpleasant slides. One way of interpreting this finding is to emphasize the importance of an intact right hemisphere in organizing emotional expressions. However, the left-lesioned patients were more expressive than normals. This finding, together with the observation that it was particularly the unpleasant slides for which patients' nonverbal displays were apparent, suggests that the left-hemisphere-damaged patients were deficient in the ability to inhibit their emotional responsivity voluntarily.

With normal university students, Shearer and Tucker (1981) presented pleasant and unpleasant slides and asked the students either to facilitate or to inhibit their emotional responses to the slides. The students were then asked to describe how they tried to accomplish the inhibition or facilitation: Blind ratings of their introspective reports showed that verbal and analytic cognition was more frequently reported for inhibition, whereas imaginal and global ideation was more frequent for facilitation. Tucker and Newman (1981) used a similar procedure, but trained students to inhibit their emotional responses to the slides, using a cognitive strategy that was either verbal and analytic or imaginal and global: For both subjective ratings of emotional response and a skin temperature measure of peripheral vasoconstriction, the verbal and analytic strategy was a more effective method of emotional inhibition. In both these experiments with normals one can infer that the cognitive strategies, naturalistic or trained, involved differential hemispheric function. In the Buck and Duffy (1980) research, asymmetric hemispheric involvement in nonverbal displays was clearly present because of unilateral lesions. Taken together, these three studies suggest that emotional communication depends not only on the right hemisphere's capacity to affectively modulate nonverbal behavior, but also on the left hemisphere's inhibitory regulation of this process.

The clinical significance of left hemisphere inhibition of emotional communication may be relevant to psychopathology as well as brain damage. The most consistent finding in neuropsychological research on schizophrenia is left hemisphere overactivation, apparently associated with the characteristic verbal deficits of these patients (Flor-Henry, 1976; Gur, 1978; Walker & McGuire, 1982). High left hemisphere activation is particularly characteristic of acute or paranoid schizophrenics (Flor-Henry, 1983); may decrease as patients become familiar with the testing situation (Gruzelier & Hammond, 1976); and can be normalized with phenothiazines (Serafetinides, 1973). These results are consistent with the hypothesis that the left hemisphere overactivation observed in schizophrenics results from pathological anxiety (Tucker, 1981; Walker & McGuire, 1982). Clinical observation suggests that the cognitive deficits of schizophrenics include not only deviant verbalizations but also disordered comprehension of emotional situations. An important diagnostic feature of schizophrenia, blunted affect, is manifested through the channels of nonverbal communication that appear to be mediated by the right hemisphere. A reasonable hypothesis is that coincident with left hemisphere overactivation in schizophrenia there is a suppression of right hemisphere functioning (Alpert & Martz, 1977).

   An interesting perspective on control processes in emotion is suggested by the schizophrenic's nonverbal communication. Although a patient's characteristic state is a flat, restricted emotionality, at certain times the same patient suddenly manifests inappropriate affect. The chronic inhibition of right hemisphere processing seems to produce disorganized and poorly modulated right hemisphere functioning when it does occur. An investigation of schizophrenics' ability to interpret emotional meaning from tone of voice showed their performance to be both worse and more variable than that of normals (Turner, 1964).

   In less pathological cases of high anxiety there are also indications of exaggerated left hemisphere function, together with a corresponding decrement in the right hemisphere's contribution to affective, nonverbal displays. Several features of the cognitive style of the obsessive-compulsive personality, including an overly focused attention, detail-oriented perception, and a heavy reliance on verbal, intellectual ideation (Shapiro, 1965) suggest that the chronic anxiety of this syndrome is associated with a predominance of left hemisphere processing. Some experimental results with normal obsessive-compulsive personality styles (Smokler & Shevrin, 1979) have been consistent with this formulation. The high level of left hemisphere control in the psychological functioning of the obsessive-compulsive appears to result in a restriction of the right hemisphere's contribution to nonverbal communication; these persons appear emotionally inhibited in interpersonal interaction (Shapiro, 1965).

   In normal university students, high levels of trait anxiety have been found to be associated with a right ear attentional bias, an impairment of right visual half field performance (Tucker, Antes, Stenslie, & Barnhardt,

1978) and a detail-oriented perceptual strategy (Tyler & Tucker, 1982) that suggest high activation, and in some cases dysfunction, of the left hemisphere. In a high anxious sample including patients as well as normals, a particularly strong color-word interference effect for right hand responses on the Stroop test (Newman, 1982) is also consistent with exaggerated and inflexible left hemisphere control in these persons. The possibility of suppressed or impaired right hemisphere processing in anxiety was suggested by low levels of left lateral eye movements in high trait anxious students (Tucker et al., 1978).

In his important early studies of disorders in prosody, Monrad-Krohn (1963) observed that states of high anxiety in normals could be associated with a restriction of the emotional intonation of speech. In research on lateralized cognitive styles, we have observed that a left hemisphere style is associated with greater introversion as well as higher trait anxiety (Swenson & Tucker, 1983). The possibility that introverts rely more on left hemisphere processing, whereas extraverts show greater right hemisphere processing, has been suggested on theoretical grounds (Levy, 1982; Tucker & Williamson, 1984) and receives support from research on individual differences in visual half field performance (Charman, 1979). Although personality theorists since Jung (1921) have emphasized that cognitive and attentional differences between introverts and extraverts are at least as important as differences in sociability, this personality dimension has become popular with the general public because it characterizes observable differences in how people relate socially. Consistent with the altered nonverbal communication in psychopathology, the normal introvert's reliance on left hemisphere processes of self-regulation seems associated with a restricted affective modulation of communication, whereas the extravert's right hemisphere style causes affective displays to be strong and frequent (see Buck, Miller, Savin, & Caul, 1972; Levy, 1982; Tucker & Williamson, 1984).

CONTROL STRUCTURE OF THE BRAIN

Considering the brain only in its lateral aspect may cause other important neuropsychological perspectives to be overlooked. The brain shows a major functional differentiation between anterior and posterior regions. Furthermore, any student of the brain must appreciate its hierarchic organization. The human brain is only the latest edition of successive evolutionary transformations of vertebrate neural architecture. Because each new level of brain organization could not replace existing structures, but had to achieve its advantages through modulating primitive systems that remained operational, the brain has an inherent vertical dimension to its organization that is perhaps more fundamental than its differentiation in either the laterality or the caudality dimensions (Hughlings Jackson, in Taylor, 1958). Although the control of communication may appear to be a unified process experientially, it is carried out by multiple interlocking networks of neural systems, as observed in chapter 7.

Intrahemispheric Control and Verbal Self-Regulation

The process of reciprocal inhibition appears important to maintaining a balance not only between the two hemispheres, but between anterior and posterior regions within a hemisphere. An interesting example of problems occurring when this balance is upset is the speech dysfunction of Wernicke's aphasia, caused by lesions of the speech comprehension areas of the posterior left hemisphere. Although the regions of the anterior left hemisphere organizing the motor output of speech are intact, many patients with this dysfunction produce speech that is syntactically disorganized and often meaningless (Hecaen & Albert, 1979). Benson and Geschwind (1975) contrast the effects of anterior and posterior lesions in the left hemisphere. Whereas Broca's aphasics (with anterior left damage) may speak only a single word at a time, the word is usually meaningful; Wernicke's aphasics are fluent, but their speech is often incomprehensible, an uncritical mixture of circumlocutions, stock phrases, and neologisms. The left posterior regions seem to monitor ongoing speech as it is generated, offering a set of syntactic and semantic constraints that must be satisfied to produce meaningful communication.

The disorganization of speech control that occurs in jargon aphasia may be instructive in understanding emotional aspects of speech. The "word salad" produced by some schizophrenics appears lacking in the self-regulatory constraints provided by the self-monitoring of verbal output. Normal personality differences may be associated with different degrees of inhibitory control in verbal output: Some people choose words with parsimony and precision, while the verbal fluency of others seems unconstrained. The child's development of appropriate verbal self-monitoring skills is important to attentional control and personality (Luria, 1982; Meichenbaum, 1974). Given the evidence of high left hemisphere activation in anxiety (Tucker et al., 1978; Tyler & Tucker, 1982), it seems likely that increased verbal self-monitoring would be associated with the heightened self-consciousness of anxious persons (Sarason, 1975). Although relative hemispheric activation is important to the effects of anxiety on verbal cognition, the regulation of verbal behavior seems to depend on anterior-posterior interactions within the left hemisphere as well.

Frontal Regulation and Emotional Valence

The differentiation of the brain on the anterior-posterior axis has been a major feature of mammalian brain evolution. Pribram (1981) describes two major functions of brain systems. One, termed the epicritic function, serves to develop and maintain an internal representation of the external environment. The second, termed the protocritic function, regulates sensory and motor operations according to homeostatic needs. At the level of the cortex, the representational function is handled by the receptive areas and their parietal integration in the posterior brain, while the regulatory function is carried out largely by the frontal cortex. Given its unique pattern of interconnections with limbic and brainstem structures as well as with other cortical regions (Fuster, 1980), the frontal cortex is well suited to directing the brain's information processing operations adaptively.

The effects of lesions to the frontal lobe suggest that an important aspect of frontal regulation is inhibition of other brain regions. Patients with frontal damage often show what has been termed the disinhibition syndrome (Hecaen, 1964; Luria, 1973). The patients are inappropriately impulsive in social settings, and make crude jokes and sexual advances. On the basis of his clinical observations, Luria (1973) concluded that the left and right frontal regions are not equivalent in their regulatory functions. Although left frontal lesions produce marked deficits in planning and goal-oriented behavior, it is damage to the right frontal lobe that is most often associated with inappropriate affective responses and disinhibition of impulses.

Recent studies of the emotional effects of brain lesions are consistent with Luria's observations. Although denial of illness and inappropriate optimism have been attributed to right hemisphere lesions in general (Gainotti, 1972), Finsett (1983) has found that these are characteristic only of anterior lesions; patients with more posterior right hemisphere lesions may show depressive affect. Robinson, Kubos, Starr, Rao, and Price (1984) also found that the caudality of the lesion, its location in the anterior/posterior dimension, is important to hemispheric differences in the emotional effects of brain damage. Examining both left- and right-hemisphere-lesioned groups, Robinson et al. observed that lesions in the right hemisphere produced greater denial and inappropriate cheerfulness the closer they were to the frontal pole. For the left hemisphere the caudality of the lesion was also important, but to an opposite emotional valence: The closer the lesion to the frontal pole, the more negative the patient's affective response. This opposite caudality-valence interaction for the left hemisphere is consistent with the Benson and Geschwind (1975) observation that Broca's aphasics are often depressed, whereas Wernicke's aphasics may show a more positive affect associated with verbal disinhibition and denial of problems.

The inclusion of both laterality and caudality as determinants of the emotional effects of brain lesions may help unite the conventional clinical observations on the frontal disinhibition syndrome with the studies showing laterality effects in emotional response to brain damage (Kinsbourne & Bemporad, 1984). For some time it was observed that left hemisphere lesions may produce a depressive-catastrophic reaction (Goldstein, 1952). Gainotti's (1972) systematic clinical observations confirmed this, and showed the contrasting effects of denial of illness and occasional euphoria following right hemisphere lesions. The problem in understanding the general significance of these observations has been the difficulty of interpreting which hemisphere's normal affective tendency is released by the unilateral lesion. On the basis of an extensive review of the neurological literature, Sackeim et al. (1982) concluded that a lesion releases the emotional functioning of the contralateral hemisphere. Following the suggestions of Hall, Hall, and Lavoie (1968), I have argued that the lesion may disinhibit or exaggerate the affective characteristics of the lesioned hemisphere (Tucker, 1981); this interpretation would appear more consistent with emotional lateralization in normals and psychiatric patients.

The marked differences in emotional response to unilateral lesions suggest that some fundamental control processes in the brain have different effects on the two hemispheres. Because the traditional observations of the disinhibition syndrome suggest that frontal regions exert inhibitory controls over emotional processes (Flor-Henry, 1977; Hecaen, 1964), the recent demonstrations that the characteristic emotional responses to unilateral lesions occur only with frontal damage (Finsett, 1983; Robinson et al., in press) seem to support the notion that these emotional responses reflect an ipsilateral release, and thus an exaggeration of a hemisphere's normal affective tendency. However, alternative interpretations of the recent findings are possible: Given the substantial interconnections between right and left frontal lobes across the corpus callosum and anterior commisure, it could be argued that a frontal lesion impairs reciprocal inhibition of the contralateral hemisphere—an argument consistent with Sackeim et al. (1982).

The issue of how to interpret frontal regulation of lateralized emotional processes has also been important in research involving EEG measures of normal emotion. Davidson and associates (Davidson, 1984; Davidson,

Schwartz, Saron, Bennett, & Goleman, 1979) observed that negative emotion in normals, associated with viewing an aversive videotape, was associated with EEG activation of the right frontal region, whereas during a positive emotional condition left frontal EEG activation was observed. In line with the Sackeim et al. (1982) interpretation of the brain-lesion evidence, Davidson et al. interpret their frontal lobe findings to indicate the left hemisphere's role in positive emotion, and the right hemisphere's more negative affective tendency. My associates and I made similar observations of frontal EEG asymmetry in emotional states, but suggested an opposite interpretation (Tucker, Stenslie, Roth, & Shearer, 1981). Students in an experimentally induced depressed mood showed greater EEG activation of the right frontal lobe, not unlike the effects observed during negative emotion by Davidson et al. However, because a previous experiment had suggested that a depressed mood is associated with impaired imagery and decreased right hemisphere activation on an attentional bias measure, and because psychiatric depressives show poor right hemisphere performance (Goldstein, Filskov, Weaver, & Ives, 1977; Kronfol, Hamsher, Digre, & Waziri, 1978), we interpreted the frontal lobe activation to represent an inhibitory influence, possibly suppressing the cognitive representational functions of the posterior right hemisphere (Tucker et al., 1981).

Neural and Cognitive Control

The finding that asymmetries in frontal lobe function can be observed during normal emotional states indicates that the issues raised by clinical observation of brain lesions may now be addressed by studies combining the systematic methods of experimental psychology with the measurement sophistication of quantitative electroencephalography. Until further studies with normals are conducted, however, the most theoretically significant evidence is the emotional changes following focal lesions. The most recent findings indicate that the caudality of the lesion interacts with its laterality in determining affective valence, suggesting something of a diagonal model of emotional organization in the brain. The right anterior and left posterior regions appear to exert important inhibitory controls on emotional functioning. Patients with lesions in these areas, although suffering from cognitive and sensorimotor impairments, often show inappropriately positive affective responses (Benson & Geschwind, 1975; Finsett, 1983; Robinson et al., 1984).

A psychological consideration of the cognitive controls on emotion offered by each hemisphere may help explain the lesion effects. Lesions disrupt the balance between anterior and posterior regions within a hemisphere may impair control of that hemisphere's cognitive functioning. Because of their differing representational capacities, the two hemispheres differ in their cognitive regulation of emotion. Lesions that disinhibit the representational functioning of one hemisphere could thus have different, and in some ways opposite, effects on emotional control than similar lesions of the opposite hemisphere.

The right hemisphere's holistic and analogical representational format appears to facilitate the emotional modulation of nonverbal cues. This mode of representing emotional information seems to be more subjectively powerful than verbal representation. With verbal cognition, the information is packaged in a substitutive code, affording greater distance from a syncretic, concrete, and immediate affective response.

The anxious person shows not only a reduction of nonverbal emotional expressivity, but often a restriction of verbal productions as well, as in speech or test anxiety (Sarason, 1975). Given the increased self-consciousness of anxiety, it seems as if the verbal self-monitoring operations of the posterior left hemisphere are exaggerated, just as they are apparently deficient in jargon aphasia. When anxious children are trained in verbal self-monitoring and self-instruction methods to cope with anxiety, their performance suffers and their reports of anxiety increase (Fox & Houston, 1981). In severely obsessive-compulsive patients, neuropsychological testing indicates impaired function of the left frontal lobe (Flor-Henry, Yeudall, Koles, & Howarth, 1979); Flor-Henry et al. suggested that the ruminative verbal ideation symptomatic of this condition results from the loss of the left frontal lobe's normal inhibitory influence on posterior left hemisphere cognitive processes. The increased depression ratings with anterior left hemisphere lesions observed by Robinson et al. (1984) may also reflect augmented anxiety associated with an unmodulated posterior left hemisphere. Although features of depression and anxiety often overlap, Gainotti (1972) cautions that the emotional response to left hemisphere lesions is not true depression, but has more catastrophic features.

While many factors interact to determine the affective status of a brain-injured patient or normal person, the cognitive self-regulatory operations of the posterior left hemisphere may serve an important function in emotion and personality, perhaps not unlike that attributed to verbal cognition by Freud (see Galin, 1974). This could explain why posterior left hemisphere damage may cause disinhibited and uncritical verbalizations (Benson & Geschwind, 1975).

Emotional disinhibition can occur with right anterior lesions (Finsett, 1983; Luria, 1973; Robinson et al., 1984), and intrahemispheric controls may be important here as well. Because of its mode of cognitive and perceptual elaboration of experience, the right hemisphere seems to facilitate emotional influences on behavior, whether in specific nonverbal communications or in general life decisions. The adaptive failure of many patients showing the disinhibition syndrome (Hecaen, 1964; Lezak, 1976) suggests that normal personality functioning requires frontal inhibitory regulation of the right hemisphere's involvement in interpersonal interaction. When this regulation is disrupted, and the right hemisphere's contributions to experience and behavior are unconstrained, the patient's behavior is socially inappropriate and, although emotions may be labile, the patient's characteristic affective state is usually positive. This effect is consistent with the evidence that higher posterior right hemisphere function is associated with a more positive mood (Goldstein et al., 1977; Kronfol et al., 1978; Tucker et al., 1981).

To account for the existing evidence on how emotion is controlled in the brain requires a more differentiated model of brain systems than left versus right (Kinsbourne & Bemporad, 1984). Even adding the anterior/posterior dimension is insufficient to deal with the complexity of brain organization, and it will be necessary to develop further specificity in terms of interactions of frontal, temporal, and parietal neural networks with limbic and brainstem systems. However, particularly when the topic is communication, it is also important to consider the cognitive characteristics of the brain, and the research on hemispheric function has provided the most explicit account of the cognitive capacities of brain systems. The control of emotion, and its communication, are cognitive as well as neural operations. The individual's mental representations serve as a defining context for evaluative, emotional self-regulation. Although made of biological stuff, the brain is a cognitive organ.

Active and Receptive Controls

Stimulated by studies of cognitive lateralization, recent neurosciences research has discovered anatomical and neurophysiological asymmetries of the brain indicating that functional specialization of the hemispheres in the course of evolution has also entailed neurophysiologic specialization. The evidence of asymmetries in brain organization now includes findings of asymmetries in the distribution and function of the neurotransmitter pathways of the reticular and mesencephalic activating systems. Since some abnormality in these neurotransmitter pathways has been implicated in psychopathology by the success of pharmacologic treatments, understanding the significance of their asymmetry is clearly important to a working knowledge of emotional control in the brain. Because these neurotransmitter-specific control systems have integral roles in directing the organism's attentional capacity as a function of adaptive concerns, a theoretical model that considers their specific effects may explain important aspects of hemispheric differences in cognition. The evidence on these systems is still tentative, and substantial speculation is required to formulate how their regulatory influences may figure in lateralized emotional and cognitive processes. But if it can be properly interpreted, this evidence promises a unique and novel perspective on emotional control in the brain. In addition to lateralized cognitive processes regulating emotion, a "top-down" view, it may be possible to consider a "bottom-up" view, how asymmetric attentional control systems have intrinsic emotional characteristics, and how their qualitatively distinct effects on information processing may underlie hemispheric differences in cognition.

To understand the asymmetry of these attentional control systems, it may be helpful once again to consider the interaction of hemispheric specialization with the anterior-posterior differentiation in the brain. The regulatory importance of left posterior and right anterior regions, discussed above, seems to coincide with the functional importance of brain regions on the opposite diagonal. The left anterior and right posterior regions appear to have major functional roles, due to differential hemispheric specialization for motor and perceptual processes.

Hughlings Jackson (Taylor, 1958) developed concepts of hemispheric specialization at the end of the last century that remain consistent with current evidence. Largely because of the left hemisphere's language skills, he described it as specialized for expressive functions. Observing impairment in various forms of perception following right hemisphere damage, Jackson suggested the right hemisphere is specialized for receptive functions. More recently Pribram (1981) has made a similar distinction, describing the left hemisphere as effective and the right hemisphere as affective.

The left hemisphere's importance to the direction of higher order motor organization has been recognized since Liepmann's initial clinical studies (Kimura, 1977). Various forms of apraxia are more common with left hemisphere lesions (Heilman, 1979). Although behavioral programming involves primary contributions from anterior motor regions, complex motor cybernetics also seem to depend on ongoing feedback from receptive—somatosensory and kinesthetic—centers in the left parietal region (Kolb & Milner, 1981), perhaps not unlike the regulatory influence of the posterior speech comprehension area on verbal productions (Hecaen & Albert, 1978).

Many of the right hemisphere's special skills involve the holistic integration of perceptual data, and this requires the coordination of bilateral perceptual input from the receptive fields of the posterior brain. Consistent with Semmes's (1968) initial formulation of the right hemisphere's role in developing multimodal representation, recent anatomical evidence has been interpreted to suggest greater cross-modal integration in the right hemisphere (Goldberg & Costa, 1981); this would also require right hemisphere control of bilateral receptive fields of the posterior brain. In the specific perceptual process of depth perception, information must be coordinated from the visual half fields of both eyes, and thus from the left and right occipital cortex. The right hemisphere is specialized for this process (Carmon & Bechtolt, 1969).

A schematic representation of differential hemispheric specialization for motor and perceptual processes is shown in Figure 10.1. This functional asymmetry may be supported by asymmetries in neural circuitry. A greater proportion of white than gray matter in the right hemisphere has been observed, particularly for anterior regions (Gur et al., 1980). Gur et al. found a relatively higher proportion of white matter in the left hemisphere for some posterior detectors. Since white matter occupies more space than gray matter, computerized radiologic studies provide converging evidence, showing that the right frontal lobe and left occipital lobes are larger than their counterparts (Galaburda, LeMay, Kemper, & Geschwind, 1978; LeMay, 1979).

We have observed that the resting EEG of right-handers also shows different asymmetries for anterior and posterior regions (Tucker, Roth, & Bair, 1984). Although electrophysiologic covariance among right hemisphere regions was generally higher than among left hemisphere areas, interhemispheric EEG coherence showed the right anterior region to covary closely with the left hemisphere, while the left occipital region covaried with the right hemisphere.

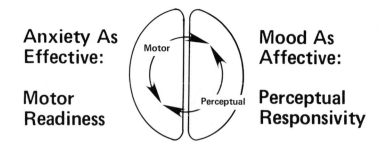

Anxiety As Effective: Motor   Perceptual   **Mood As Affective:**

Motor Readiness   **Perceptual Responsivity**

Fig. 10.1 Schematic model of how motivational and emotional processes interact with the lateral and anterior/posterior dimensions of the brain organization.

Although confident interpretation of the functional significance of these anatomical and electrophysiological findings must await further studies, asymmetries in the circuitry of neural networks seem clearly different for the front and back of the brain. The substantial interconnections between the left occipital region and the right hemisphere could exist to support the right hemisphere's integration of bilateral visual information; the interconnection of right anterior regions with the left hemisphere could support that hemisphere's bilateral motor control (Tucker et al., 1984).

Recognizing the differential involvement of the two hemispheres in input and output functions may lead to principles of lateralized information processing. In its specialization for motor organization, the left hemisphere may have developed cognitive processes that are congruent with the form of attentional control required by the motor output functions of the anterior brain. In its receptive processing, the right hemisphere may have evolved to draw on a different form of attentional control, a mode of control intrinsic to perceptual systems.

The issue of emotional control of brain operations must translate at some level to the regulation of the operational characteristics of neural networks. Although psychology has considered arousal as a diffuse phenomenon, there are multiple neurophysiological systems regulating neural activity, each with qualitatively distinct effects. Pribram and McGuinness (1975) draw on a variety of evidence to differentiate between an Activation system supporting tonic motor readiness and an Arousal system producing a phasic increment in neural activity in response to novel perceptual input.

Williamson and I (Tucker & Williamson, 1984) have attempted to develop the Activation and Arousal notions further by considering the operational characteristics of the neurotransmitter pathways that seem integral to these control systems. When the function of the dopamine pathways supporting motor readiness is augmented with drugs in animals or humans, the effect is not a diffuse increase in behavior, but a tight restriction of motor function, until the behavior becomes stereotyped and repetitive (Iversen, 1977). A qualitatively different change in neural function seems to occur with increased functioning of the locus coeruleus norepinephrine pathway, a primary aspect of the neural substrate of the Arousal system. The animal appears more active, but this activity habituates rapidly (Kempf, Greilsamer, Mack, & Mandel, 1974).

The controls on the level of activity in neural systems thus seem to offer distinct regulatory characteristics. Tucker and Williamson (1984) reviewed evidence that these systems are asymmetric in the brain; this is consistent with differential hemispheric specialization for motor and perceptual processing. The regulatory features of these attentional controls may be integral to lateralized cognitive functions. The increased redundancy in the information flow with Activation would seem to facilitate focal attention as well as constancy in motor function; this may be integral to the left hemisphere's analytic organization of cognition. In contrast, the habituation bias of Arousal seems to lead to a broader attentional coverage, as each item in the stimulus array receives only transient attention. This more expansive coverage may figure importantly in the right hemisphere's capacity for global conceptualization of multimodal sensory data.

The constructs of Activation and Arousal present some interesting theoretical possibilities. Not only do they suggest a congruence of higher conceptual processes with the cybernetic characteristics of elementary attentional controls: these are inherently adaptive controls. McGuinness and Pribram (1980) suggested that Activation is related to a more internally directed, motivational function, while Arousal has more emotional, affective features.

In other work, Pribram (1981) has described how the frontal cortex seems to facilitate internal control of behavior by increasing the redundancy of the brain's information processing. Tucker and Williamson (1984) proposed that redundancy is a direct result of dopaminergic Activation, and that internal control is important not only to motor operations but also to the active, avoidant, and vigilant attention that animal research suggests is dopaminergic (Iversen, 1977). The effects of augmented dopamine function in humans may help explain the link between left hemisphere function and anxiety. Abnormally high dopamine function in amphetamine addiction (Kokkinidis & Anisman, 1980) is associated with an overly focused, detail-oriented perceptual style (Ellinwood, 1967; Matthysse, 1977) that may reflect high left hemisphere activation. These addicts also show a hypervigilance that indicates not only chronic anxiety but an avoidant, internally directed attentional mode.

The blockade of dopamine transmission with neuroleptic antipsychotic drugs is an important treatment for schizophrenics, for whom anxiety, an autistic internal attentional focus, and paranoid hypervigilance are frequent signs. It seems relevant that neuroleptic treatment decreases left hemisphere activation in both schizophrenics (Serafetinides, 1973) and normals (Laurian, Gaillard, Le, & Schopf, 1983). Neuroleptics were first found to be clinically useful in treating motor stereotypies of severely obsessive-compulsive patients (Matthysse, 1977). This seems congruent with the animal literature on dopamine function and with the suggestion that high left hemisphere activation is important both to the anxiety and to the cognitive disorders of obsessive-compulsives.

The pathological routinization observed with excessive modulation by the Activation system may be an extreme form of a regulatory control that is integral to adaptive left hemisphere function. Goldberg and Costa

(1981) have formulated an important model of lateralized cognition from their review of the hemispheric specialization literature. Consistent with Kinsbourne's (1974) notions is their suggestion that the left hemisphere is specialized for focusing attention on a single modality, or on a single aspect of a task. This not only allows analytic organization of information, but facilitates the integration of practiced, routinized skills that can then be performed automatically and efficiently. The redundancy bias of Activation would seem a necessary regulatory influence in producing routinization. This cybernetic mode may have been essential in allowing the left hemisphere to develop verbal communication. The capacity for routinization and automatization would appear requisite to allow efficient use of an arbitrary, substitutive code according to structured syntactical schemas.

From the regulatory characteristics of the Arousal system comes a different influence on cognitive organization that may also be tied to adaptive functions. Through facilitating habituation to repetitive input, the Arousal system allows the perceptual apparatus to orient to novelty in the environment. This seems important to the right hemisphere's capacity to handle the diverse features of new problem-solving situations (Goldberg & Costa, 1981). The expansive attentional coverage produced by a habituation bias may allow the right hemisphere its capacity in holistic integration of data from several sensory modalities, such as in nonverbal communication. Through biasing the brain to orient to novel input, the Arousal system generates an external mode of control of the brain's information flow, similar to the participatory mode Pribram (1981) attributed to posterior cortex. Rather than focusing on constancy in internally directed operations, Arousal maintains a constant flow of new input from the environment, such that the available representational capacity is maximally reflective of the external surround.

The emotional characteristics of increased Arousal may be inherent to producing these regulatory effects. The facilitation of orienting to novelty and habituation to unrewarding cues produced by norepinephrine activity in the brain may be important to reward effects (Tucker & Williamson, 1984). In humans, augmented norepinephrine function is produced by a number of recreational drugs, at least in the initial euphoriant stages of their use, including amphetamine (Kokkinidis & Anisman, 1980), cocaine (Cooper, Bloom, & Roth, 1974), and alcohol (Borg, Kvande, & Sedvall, 1981). The leading biochemical hypothesis of the affective disorders has suggested increased norepinephrine function in mania, and decreases in depression (Schildkraut, 1965; Schildkraut et al., 1978). Given the evidence that norepinephrine pathways may be right-lateralized in the brain (Oke, Keller, Mefford, & Adams, 1978; Pearlson & Robinson, 1981), the changes in right hemisphere function with changes in mood (Kronfol et al., 1977; Tucker et al., 1981) seem consistent with the notion that the individual's affective status is an important determinant of Arousal, the right hemisphere's contribution to conceptual organization, and the brain's level of participation in the information flow of the immediate environment.

There are many regulatory systems determining the nature and level of neural activity. It is probably not possible to understand the effects of norepinephrine and dopamine systems without considering their interactions with serotonin, acetylcholine, GABA, the endogenous opiates, and other neurochemically specific processes in the brain. Yet even an incomplete model of how the brain self-regulates its function through Activation and Arousal shows the bottom-up continuity in the control of cognition in the brain. The most basic regulatory systems have qualitative influences on information processing that seem intrinsic to the most complex cognitive characteristics of the cerebral hemispheres. And these regulatory systems are not just neural entities, but are coincident with subjectively meaningful motivational and emotional states.

DIALECTICS OF COMMUNICATION

Cognitive Regulation

The effects of Activation and Arousal include inherent regulatory constraints. With increasing Activation the animal's motor output is not simply increased, but becomes restricted in its range, more focused and routinized. With greater Arousal, the brain becomes responsive to perceptual input, and yet habituates rapidly to a given stimulus. Each of these major regulatory processes applies an integral inhibition to its target system. Increasing the activity of the brain's input or output operations includes a form of negative feedback to modulate those operations (Tucker & Williamson, 1984).

The balance or stability built into the effects of these control systems at an elementary level may be maintained at higher levels. Drawing on the Activation system to provide constancy and sequential control to its handling of motor operations, the left hemisphere seems to have become specialized for a tightly controlled and routinized form of cognitive processing. The left hemisphere carries out its verbal expressive functions through application of regulatory constraints from the self-monitoring operations of posterior comprehension centers. If these constraints are disrupted by lesions, both verbal productions and affect may become disinhibited. The importance of the posterior left hemisphere to self-regulation suggests that to balance its role in handling higher-order motor control of the anterior brain the left hemisphere has capitalized on the regulatory features of Activation in developing inhibitory control from posterior self-monitoring regions.

The right hemisphere's cognitive skills seem specialized to draw on the regulatory characteristics of the Arousal system. Its holistic integration of novel sensory data seems facilitated by the broad attentional coverage associated with a habituation bias. Given the characteristics of Arousal, even the higher functions of the right hemisphere are inherently responsive and labile. The term *emotion* applies to affective, receptive processes, and the right hemisphere's capacity to integrate the representational functions of the posterior brain seems essential to its role in emotional experience and emotional communication. But representational skills alone are not sufficient to explain the right hemisphere's emotional functions; there must be an evaluative component to determine which representations are meaningful. Similarly, a habituation bias in its elementary form selects for any novel stimulus; there must be some direction from frontal limbic cortex to regulate the habituation bias according to the organism's current adaptive needs. Although the nature of this regulation is unclear, the disinhibitory effects of right frontal lesions suggest that in the normal brain the right hemisphere's affective responsivity must be modulated by inhibitory frontal control.

Balance through reciprocal inhibition thus seems to occur between anterior and posterior regions within each hemisphere, complementing hemispheric specialization for active and receptive attentional modes. Activation is achieved almost paradoxically through increased redundancy in the motor system; elaborating on this regulatory mode, the representational operations of the posterior regions of the left hemisphere are inherently tight and restrictive. Because responsiveness to novel input is facilitated in the perceptual apparatus by Arousal, the right hemisphere's representational operations tend to be loose and expansive. These features of lateralized cognition seem to be important to the control of emotional communication. There appears to be a continuity between each hemisphere's cognitive handling of emotion and its elementary cybernetic characteristics.

The top-down and bottom-up views thus may represent different perspectives on the same regulatory systems. At one level we can see how a hemisphere's higher cognitive skills are important in emotional control, and at a more elementary level we find the specific attentional control features of Activation and Arousal. Both aspects of these systems are functional at any given time, and they are obviously interdependent. The extent to which the bottom-up or top-down directions of control predominate seems to depend on the overall adequacy of the individual's functioning and the degree of current environmental stress.

Under favorable conditions, higher cognitive features are important: The person uses verbal structure to rationally order decisions and uses imaginal ability to conceptualize a given situation holistically. Each of these cognitive operations draws on its associated regulatory system. In its rational functioning the left hemisphere requires the analytic organization and sequential order afforded by the redundancy bias of Activation. As it provides a broad, imaginative conceptualization of a new situation, the right hemisphere draws on the more flexible data handling mode of Arousal. It is important to consider that, although required by cognitive operations, an increment in Activation or Arousal may not be free of affective implications. A certain degree of anxiety may be required for analytic rationality, whereas a sufficient mood level may be required for a global perspective.

Under less than optimal conditions, the cognitive, semantic determination of brain operations may deteriorate, and the primitive cybernetics of one of these systems becomes exaggerated. With chronic anxiety, the individual's behavior is obsessive-compulsive, showing the routinization and fragmentation from over-modulation by Activation. In addition, the inherent increment in the left hemisphere's cognitive functioning is apparent, not only in verbal ruminations, but in driven intellectualization. When mood level becomes pathologically high in mania, the person's attention cannot be focused, but flits from one object or topic to the next, over-modulated by a habituation bias. In addition, the manic's cognition reflects the structural features of an exaggerated right hemisphere contribution, with overly global and expansive conceptualization. Understanding the regulatory influences of these neural systems may suggest how thought disorders manifest specific forms of cybernetic distortion.

Communication and Self-Control

Neuropsychology has convincingly divided the brain, but has yet to find how it can be integrated. It is at least theoretically, if not phenomenologically, disconcerting to consider the mind as dualistic. How are lateralized processes coordinated? This question becomes more difficult, and perhaps even more interesting, when we consider the different effects of Activation and Arousal on internal versus external control of the brain's information flow.

Hegel proposed in his *Phenomenology of Mind* (1807) that the nature of the mind is to be found not within the self, but in the interaction of self with the world. Most of us think of the mind as something within us, something that each of us owns privately. Similarly, research on the brain may consider the brain as a thing in itself, and may fail to consider that brain systems have evolved embedded within an ecological context (Gibson, 1979). Among the regulatory effects of the Activation and Arousal systems, perhaps the most adaptively significant is the bias toward internal versus external determination of the information flow. With its redundancy bias, Activation maintains a constancy in internal representations that facilitates the use of these representations as contextual referents in directing ongoing perception and behavior. Operating under habituation, Arousal selects for novel input, and thus fills representational capacity with a continual flow of new environmental data. The novel features of the environment then gain control over the organism's information processing.

Tucker and Williamson (1984) discussed the possible adaptive effects of regulating the degree of internal versus external control that are suggested by animal research on the neurotransmitter substrates of these neural control systems. Activation seems important to establishing internal control in vigilance and avoidance behavior, whereas Arousal seems to facilitate external control when the animal is in a potentially rewarding context. Findings with humans appear congruent. The overactive left hemisphere associated with the excessive dopaminergic Activation in schizophrenia is accompanied by an autistic internality. When abnormally high dopaminergic function is produced by chronic amphetamine abuse, pathological internality is shown by hypervigilance and paranoia (Ellinwood, 1967). In contrast, disorders that seem to be associated with reliance on right hemisphere processing involve more external attentional control. With high mood level and low anxiety, manics and psychopaths are easily bored, reflecting the habituation bias of Arousal, and these persons become controlled by the need for novel stimulation. When mood level is decreased in depression, the orientation toward potentially rewarding features of the environment is decreased, and the person's externality is inappropriately restricted.

Because of their inherent regulatory biases, the most elementary neural control systems simultaneously determine the brain's activity level and the nature of its relation with the environment. For human brains, the most significant environment is social, and the development of emotional self-regulation occurs within the context of social communication. Human juveniles are behaviorally incompetent, and acquire self-control skills only with substantial parental direction. As a result, the child's ways of handling communication become integral to developing strategies of self-control. The emotional controls on communication are no more important than the communication controls on emotion.

A developmental view of self-regulation in the context of social communication may be informative. The child seems to begin in an external control mode. The brain develops with posterior, receptive regions maturing before anterior, motor ones (Hughlings Jackson, in Taylor, 1958). This seems congruent with the earlier maturation of the norepinephrine substrate of Arousal prior to the dopaminergic substrate of Activation (Kokkinidis & Anisman, 1980), and with the evidence that the right hemisphere matures before the left (Taylor, 1969; Whitaker, 1978). Because regulation by Arousal is not balanced by Activation, and cannot be appropriately modulated by the immature frontal cortex, external input exerts a powerful control. The infant shows "obligatory attention" when presented with a stimulus: the stimulus captures the infant's attention, and after several seconds of uninterrupted viewing the infant shows distress but cannot redirect its attention (Posner & Rothbart, 1981).

Those who have considered early emotional development have been impressed with the child's emotional dependency in the first months of life. Mahler (1968) suggests that the child must move from an initial functional autism toward a stage of symbiotic fusion with the mother. Recent observational research with infants is congruent with Mahler's formulations, suggesting that establishing an appropriate interpersonal attachment is perhaps the first psychological task of life (Ainsworth, 1973). This task can only be accomplished through nonverbal communication. The child is receptive to the parents' nonverbal displays, and is capable of paralleling them, reciprocating the parents' attention and establishing an emotional bond that is the prototype for later relations.

From this syncretic embeddedness, the child soon moves toward greater autonomy and individuation. This is not necessarily a smooth transition, since autonomy is achieved at least in part through negativism and rebellion to counter the initial dependency (Harvey, Hunt, & Schroder, 1961). Mahler (1968) describes this transition as the separation-individuation stage. It seems neuropsychologically significant that the competence to begin to establish internal control occurs at the same time as rapid developments in motor control and language acquisition. The maturation of left hemisphere cognition seems coincident with the development of motoric Activation, and the internal control afforded by the redundancy bias may be significant for personality development.

Verbal communication is an important mode of data transfer between parent and child, and much of the child's developing self-control seems to occur through internalizing parental verbal directives (Luria, 1982; Meichenbaum, 1974). Thus the child's emotional dependency can be supported by verbal as well as nonverbal communication. But the young child's early struggles with individuation may be instructive in showing that the internal control of attention supported by Activation is essential for developing autonomy.

It may be that these early experiences with active attention will be formative for developing and maintaining identity in the context of interpersonal relationships. Field-independent children are more conceptually as well as interpersonally differentiated, and they approach problem-solving situations with analytic cognitive skills (Witkin, Dyk, Faterson, Goodenough, & Karp, 1962). The most widely used measure of field independence, the embedded figures test, is unique among spatial tasks in requiring the left hemisphere's analytic processing (DeRenzi & Spinnler, 1966; Tucker, 1976). Witkin et al. propose that the capacity to analyze figure from the ground is a general cognitive skill, applying to social as well as perceptual fields. Although verbal cognition does not guarantee independence, the same analytic cognitive capacities that the left hemisphere uses in inhibitory self-regulation seem important to the child's capacity to differentiate a sense of identity from the embedding interpersonal context.

Whole Brain Function

An account of how the two hemispheres' psychological functions are integrated must consider not only regulatory interactions within the brain but also inherent alterations in the brain's participation in the information of its external context (Pribram, 1981; Kinsbourne & Bemporad, 1984). And the integrity of the psychological function of the brain must arise in spite of these two cybernetic modes that are not only different but opposite. Whereas the left hemisphere is analytic, the right is holistic; the left handles sequential processing and the right operates in parallel; the left is digital and the right is analogical; the left is routinized and the right is novel; the left supports autonomous processing and the right is contextually embedded.

A psychological theory that accounts for these neuropsychological subsystems should have a sufficient range of convenience to include not only their cognitive features but also the emotional and interpersonal features that are adaptively important. Psychoanalytic theory has this broad range, and there are a number of interesting parallels between hemispheric specialization and Freud's notions of primary and secondary process functions (Galin, 1974). However, a Freudian account seems to remain dichotomous: if we attribute ego, and perhaps superego, functions to the left hemisphere, and id or primary process functions to the right hemisphere, the resulting model fails to explain interhemispheric integration. It is possible to consider overall control achieved by one side dominating the other at any given time, but there is no account of superordinate functioning: levels of cognitive organization that include left and right hemisphere contributions.

The stability and integrity of the brain's control structure may arise not in spite of but because of the intrinsic opposition between its subsystems. In psychological theory the idea of hierarchic or synergic levels of organization emerging from the opposition of basic processes is found in the application of Hegel's dialectical philosophy to developmental psychology (Riegel, 1975). TenHouten (1978) has applied dialectical thinking to hemispheric relations, suggesting that human intellectual function does not have to be divided into left or right hemispheric modes, but can on occasion include a third mode integrating lateralized processes. In his description of the fundamentals of dialectical thought, Riegel emphasized three points: (1) psychological issues are viewed developmentally, understood as processes evolving in time; (2) the individual cannot be understood except as considered in the context of interaction with the environment; and (3) developmental progression is often achieved through the integration of opponent processes.

Each of these points seems congruent with the operational characteristics of brain systems. Hegel described the development of ideas as proceeding from an initial proposition, a thesis, through a critical and negative evaluation of that proposition, an antithesis, toward a new level of organization, the synthesis. The synthesis is not a simple modification of the thesis, nor a compromise, but a new construction necessitated because both the thesis and antithesis are true, and their apparent opposition can be resolved only when they are reformulated at a higher level of abstraction.

This sort of dialectical model is an interesting way to consider a unified neuropsychology. The important lateralized cognitive operations may not be the pure forms characterized by research, but rather the ones supporting interhemispheric integration: verbal and analytic processing of imaginative constructions; global representations supporting verbal metaphors. Abstract cognitive functioning may require both analytic and global, differentiated and integrated, forms of conceptual organization (Harvey, Hunt, & Schroder, 1961; Werner, 1957). Similarly, the individual's relation with others is dichotomized into internal versus external modes of control only in pathological states; the optimal mode finds a harmonic balance of these regulatory influences that allows abstractness in relation as well as cognition. The synergic level of functioning may thus represent the optimal state that is approximated in various forms by normal brains. But it is important to consider that whatever organizational stability is achieved exists with the inherent tension of opponent processes. And the developmental process of dialectical organization may not just occur with ideas, as expressed in Hegel's epistemology, but may characterize a modal progression of how conceptual development is orchestrated by neural systems in everyday living.

In orienting to a variety of new situations, the primary attentional mode seems to be Arousal. Representational capacity is opened up to handle a broad range of potentially relevant information. As Goldberg and Costa (1981) suggested, the right hemisphere seems especially suited to dealing with novel input. The external control intrinsic to Arousal is an important aspect of this stage, the thesis: the new idea, person, or situation captures attentional capacity. This is a primitive but fundamental regulatory mode, where first impressions are made, often through nonverbal features of communication.

For Hegel, moving beyond the initial thesis required an antithetical stage, and in many situations this may involve critical verbal analysis. In the child's development the appearance of autonomy coincides with maturing left hemisphere cognition, and the child's success in individuation may require analytic cognitive skills. It may be that, in a variety of situations, an initial orienting through right hemisphere processing is followed by a more critical and deliberate appraisal mediated by rational, verbal representations. The internal control provided by Activation allows the individual's cognitive processes to develop an autonomous approach to the new situation.

If the appropriate dialectical tension is maintained between these cognitive, and affective, modes, the result is a more complex and abstract organization of the concepts through which the individual relates. From this perspective, it may not be possible to separate conceptual development from interpersonal development (Harvey et al., 1961). The child's handling of interpersonal communication, balancing the dialectical modes of relation, is a major determinant of how the brain's information processing resources will be allocated to the tasks of cognitive development.

Dialectics of Clinical Work

An example of what may be dialectical processes in interpersonal orientation is found in the transference phenomenon in psychotherapy. In group or individual therapy, a client may show an unexpectedly positive evaluation of the therapist, attributing great virtue and power to the therapist (Whitaker & Malone, 1955). Although clinicians are understandably reluctant to deny these characteristics, some clients are sufficiently childlike in their orientations to appear as if they are recapitulating earlier parental relations. The extreme form of this is a psychotic transference, in which a severely disturbed person experiences an identity fusion with the therapist. In later stages of therapy, a negative transference may occur, in which the client becomes critical of the therapist (Whitaker & Malone, 1955; Tucker, 1973).

Although, given the therapist's perspective, a negative transference may be interpreted as more pathological than a positive one of equal intensity, both of these may be important modes of relation. Through the initial holistic and positive mode the client orients to the novel situation, calling on earlier experiences with dependency. The development of a mature relation with the therapist may require the dialectical opposition of this orientation through a period of negative independence, and the therapist who subverts the client's autonomy strivings may preclude the client's developmental work in therapy.

A dialectical analysis of emotional controls and modes of relationship in clinical work need not focus only on the client. The clinician's ability to develop an understanding of, and relation with, the client is also an issue of real life epistemology, and it is important to consider the neuropsychological processes in the clinician's communication skills.

Perhaps the most straightforward implication of neuropsychological research on emotional communication is that right hemisphere skills are required to understand nonverbal cues. The psychologist, physician, or other professional will have had substantial academic education, but may not have had any real training in understanding the emotional meaning of gestures, tone of voice, or facial displays. These comprehension skills are considered part of "clinical judgment," and not only is there little training in these skills, there are seldom formal attempts to assess them (Davitz, 1964). Clarification of the cognitive skills required to send or receive nonverbal messages (Rosenthal, 1979) could suggest specific procedures for assessment and training.

Some of the initial research on individual differences in ability to understand nonverbal communication found that cognitive factors may be more important than personality (Davitz, 1964). A recent study by Hayne (1983) found that personality characteristics were predictive of skill in sending and receiving emotional communications only for the more intelligent subjects, for whom cognitive skills appeared not to be a limiting factor. By characterizing the specific aspects of cognition that are important in handling emotional communications, neuropsychological research could contribute to developing skills training for clinical judgment.

The emotional aspects of hemispheric function may help clarify the emotional and attentional controls directing the clinician's approach to the clinical interaction. For example, to appreciate the multiple channels of analogical information in the client's vocal intonation, facial expression, and posture, a holistic and receptive attentional mode may be required. Furthermore, to understand the more subtle nuances of emotional meaning in the client's communication, it may be necessary for the clinician's own emotional responses to be free to be elicited empathically (cf. Safer, 1981). Optimal function of the clinician's right hemisphere seems important to dealing with analogical information, and a variety of emotional and attentional constraints may be detrimental. If the clinician is depressed, right hemisphere skills may suffer (Goldstein et al., 1977; Kronfol et al., 1977; Tucker et al., 1981). Factors that augment the clinician's anxiety, such as a critical therapy supervisor or difficult material brought up in the session, could produce an overly analytic and restricted attention (Tyler & Tucker, 1982) that impairs the reception of nonverbal cues. Also important are characterological issues; students who survive professional training must be task-oriented and focused, and may not be experienced in the receptive, externally directed attentional mode that seems important to the right hemisphere's comprehension of emotional communication.

The importance of empathy and a receptive attitude are well known in psychotherapy (see chapter 3); what a neuropsychological analysis may offer is a new perspective on the cybernetic characteristics of these psychological processes. There also may be adverse effects of the clinician's relying on right hemisphere processing in relating to the client. Operating under Arousal, the clinician's attention will be drawn to issues that are novel and stimulating, and these may not be relevant to therapy objectives. Sensitive to the clinician's cues, the client may be directed to produce material that arouses the clinician. Adopting a right hemispheric mode of functioning, the clinician's experience is syncretic, with internal emotional responses and external perceptions closely fused. Although there are important advantages of this experiential mode (Werner, 1957) that can facilitate therapy, there is an unavoidable loss of objectivity. Because they are fused in this attentional orientation, the client's messages and the therapist's own idiosyncratic responses may be difficult to sort out.

When the clinician is maximally receptive to the client's nonverbal cues, these cues elicit parallel, analogical responses in the clinician. The nonverbal communication thus operates directly on the clinician's emotional matrix, with minimal intellectual mediation. One effect of this direct, externally controlled cybernetic mode is to put the clinician's own psychological state at risk. Clients often experience tragic life events, and particularly if these are interpreted through a disorganized personality, the emotional response is powerful. Paralleling this response without intellectual mediation requires substantial psychological investment. To cope with his or her personal response, the clinician may adopt strategies that are counterproductive for therapy.

The form of empathy mediated by the right hemisphere's analogical processing is in its elementary form primitive and undifferentiated. It is a direct affective response to the perception of nonverbal cues, and as such represents emotional contagion rather than any real understanding of the client's perspective. Children show a strong sensitivity to nonverbal emotional cues well before they have the cognitive capacity to take the perspective of the other person. The personality type most affected by emotional contagion, the extraverted or hysteric personality, is also the least able to understand the subjective perspective of others. This paradox may be found in recent research on personality and nonverbal communication. Given the indications that extraverts rely on right hemisphere cognitive and affective processing (Charman, 1979; Levy, 1980), it is not surprising that they are nonverbally expressive of emotion (Buck, Savin, Miller, & Caul, 1972; DePaulo & Rosenthal, 1979). But, although the findings are mixed, some studies find them to be less able to understand nonverbal cues than more anxious, introverted subjects (DePaulo & Rosenthal, 1979; Boice, 1983).

It may be that right hemisphere processing is a necessary but not sufficient condition for effective empathy. In the course of development, a major challenge for the child is to appreciate that others have a different perspective on the world. This understanding requires conceptual differentiation. The child must be sufficiently individuated to recognize that he or she has a unique view of events, and thus others could have equally unique views. The field independence supported by the left hemisphere's analytic cognition allows the child to become separate at least temporarily from egocentric fusion with the world and to adopt the abstract, "as if" position of another's point of view.

The dialectical struggle for the clinician is to be maximally receptive to the primary, syncretic experience of the client's nonverbal communication, and then to differentiate this perception so as to consider not just what it elicits in the receiver, but what it might mean from the sender's perspective. This requires distance from the client and the interaction, a distance afforded by the more active, internally directed attentional mode associated with analytic cognition. The experienced clinician will have skilled, routinized ways of analyzing the client's messages that can balance syncretic perception. The development of an optimal understanding of the client requires integrating the opposite perspectives of active and receptive attentional modes. Because of their intrinsic emotional substrates, these modes may be determined by the clinician's ongoing affective status. The clinician with high anxiety and low mood may be overly focused and task-oriented, insensitive to the emotional meaning of subtle nonverbal cues, and perhaps restricted in the emotional resonance conveyed to the client. The clinician with low anxiety and high mood, on the other hand, may easily synchronize with the client nonverbally, but may not be sufficiently tenacious in the work of therapy.

Most probably the effective clinician moves between these alternative attentional modes, drawing from each as the situation demands. But a dichotomous alternation of these modes cannot produce concepts that are both differentiated and integrated. An abstract understanding of the client's communication can come only from a superordinate integration of these modes, an integration requiring the struggle of holding both analytic and syncretic perspectives simultaneously. Since most books on therapeutic practice emphasize the analytic perspective, this book concentrates on the syncretic side—specifically, sensitivity to nonverbal communication in the clinical context.

REFERENCES

Ainsworth, M. D. S. (1973). The development of infant-mother attachment. In B. M. Caldwell & H. N. Riccinti (Eds.), *Review of child development research* (Vol. 3). Chicago: University of Chicago Press.

Allen, M. (1983). Models of hemispheric specialization. *Psychological Bulletin, 93*, 73–104.

Alpert, M., & Martz, M. J., Jr. (1977). Cognitive views of schizophrenia in light of recent studies of brain asymmetry. In C. Shagass, S. Gershon, & A. J. Friedhoff (Eds.), *Psychopathology and brain dysfunction*. New York: Raven Press.

Bateson, G., Jackson, D. D., Haley, J., & Weakland, J. H. (1956). Toward a theory of schizophrenia. *Behavioral Science, 1*, 251–264.

Beaumont, J. G., & Dimond, S. J. (1973). Brain disconnection and schizophrenia. *British Journal of Psychiatry, 123*, 661–62.

Benson, D. F., & Geschwind, N. (1975). The aphasias and related disturbances. In A. B. Baker & L. D. Baker (Eds.), *Clinical neurology*. New York: Harper & Row.

Bertalanffy, L. von. (1968). *General systems theory: Foundations, development, applications*. New York: Braziller.

Bever, T. G., & Chiarello, R. J. (1974). Cerebral dominance in musicians and nonmusicians. *Science, 185* 137–39.

Birch, H. G., Belmont, I., & Karp, E. (1967). Delayed information processing and extinction following cerebral damage. *Brain, 90*, 113–30.

Boice, R. (1983). Observational skills. *Psychological Bulletin, 93*, 3–29.

Borg, S., Kvande, H., & Sedvall, G. (1981). Central norepinephrine metabolism during alcohol intoxication in addicts and healthy volunteers. *Science, 312*, 1135–37.

Borod, J. C., & Caron, H. S. (1980). Facedness and emotion related to lateral dominance, sex and expression type. *Neuropsychologia, 18*, 237–41.

Bradshaw, J. L., & Nettleton, N. C. (1981). The nature of hemispheric specialization in man. *The Behavioral and Brain Sciences, 4*, 51–91.

Bryden, M. P., & Allard, F. (1978). Dichotic listening and the development of linguistic processes. In M. Kinsbourne (Ed.), *Hemispheric asymmetry of function*. London: Cambridge University Press.

Buck, R. (1982). A theory of spontaneous and symbolic expression: Implications for facial lateralization. Paper presented to the meeting of the International Neuropsychological Society, Pittsburgh.

Buck, R., & Duffy, J. (1980). Nonverbal communication of affect in brain-damaged patients. *Cortex, 16*, 351–62.

Buck, R., Savin, U. J., Miller, R. E., & Caul, N. F. (1972). Communication of affect through facial expressions in humans. *Journal of Personality and Social Psychology, 23*, 362–71.

Campbell, R. (1978). Asymmetries in interpreting and expressing a posed facial expression. *Cortex, 14*, 327–42.

Carmon, A., & Bechtolt, H. P. (1969). Right hemisphere dominance for stereopsis. *Neuropsychologia, 7*, 29–34.

Charman, D. K. (1979). Do different personalities have different hemispheric asymmetries? A brief communique of an initial experiment. *Cortex, 15*, 655–57.

Cicone, M., Wapner, W., & Gardner, H. (1980). Sensitivity to emotional expressions and situations in organic patients. *Cortex, 16*, 145–58.

Cohen, G. (1973). Hemispheric differences in serial versus parallel processing. *Journal of Experimental Psychology, 97*, 349–56.

Cooper, J. R., Bloom, F. E., & Roth, R. H. (1974). *The biochemical basis of neuropharmacology*. New York: Oxford University Press.

Crowell, D. H., Jones, R. H., Kapuniai, L. E., & Nakagawa, J. K. (1973). Unilateral cortical activity in newborn humans: An early index of cerebral dominance: *Science, 180*, 205–8.

Darwin, C. (1872). *Expressions of the emotions in man and animals*. London: John Murray.

Davidson, R. J. (1984). Affect, cognition and hemispheric specialization. In C. E. Izard, J. Kagan, & R. Zajonc (Eds.), *Emotion, cognition, and behavior*. New York: Cambridge University Press.

Davidson, R. J., Schwartz, G. E., Saron, C., Bennett, J., & Goleman, D. J. (1979). Frontal versus parietal EEG asymmetry during positive and negative affect. *Psychophysiology, 16*, 202–3 (Abstract).

Davitz, J. R. (1964). *The communication of emotional meaning*. New York: McGraw-Hill.

De Renzi, E., & Spinnler, H. (1966). Visual recognition in patients with unilateral cerebral disease. *Journal of Nervous & Mental Disease, 142*, 515–25.

DePaulo, B. M., & Rosenthal, R. (1979). Ambivalence, discrepancy, and deception in nonverbal communication. In R. Rosenthal (Ed.), *Skill in nonverbal communication: Individual differences*. Cambridge, MA: Oelgeschlager, Gunn & Hain.

Deglin, V. L. (1973). Clinical-experimental studies of unilateral electroconvulsive shock. *Journal of Neuropathology and Psychiatry, 11*, 1609–21.

Dopson, W. G., Beckwith, B. E., Tucker, D. M., & Bullard-Bates, P. C. (1984). Asymmetry of facial expression in spontaneous emotion. *Cortex, 20*, 243–51.

Ekman, P., Hager, J. C., & Friesen, W. V. (1981). The asymmetry of emotional and deliberate facial actions. *Psychophysiology, 18*, 101–6.

Ellinwood, E. H. (1967). Amphetamine psychosis: I. Description of the individuals and process. *Journal of Nervous and Mental Disease, 144*, 273–83.

Finsett, A. (1983). Depressive behavior, outburst of crying and emotional indifference in left hemiplegics. Paper presented at the Second Annual Symposium of Models and Techniques of Cognitive Rehabilitation, Indianapolis.

Flor-Henry, P. (1983). Hemispheric laterality and disorders of affect. In R. M. Post & J. C. Ballenger, (Eds.), *Neurobiology of mood disorders*. Baltimore: Williams and Wilkins.

Flor-Henry, P., Yeudall, L. T., Koles, Z., & Howarth, B. (1979). Neuropsychological and power spectral EEG investigations of the obsessive-compulsive syndrome. *Biological Psychiatry, 14,* 119–30.

Fox, J. E., & Houston, B. K. (1981). Efficacy of self-instructional training for reducing children's anxiety in an evaluative situation. *Behavior Research & Therapy, 19,* 509–15.

Friedman, A., & Polson, M. C. (1981). Hemispheres as independent resource systems: Limited-capacity processing and cerebral specialization. *Journal of Experimental Psychology: Human Perception & Performance, 7,* 1031–58.

Fuster, J. M. (1980). *The prefrontal cortex: Anatomy, neurophysiology and neuropsychology of the frontal lobe.* New York: Raven Press.

Gainotti, G. (1972). Emotional behavior and hemispheric side of the lesion. *Cortex, 8,* 41–55.

Galaburda, A. M., LeMay, M., Kemper, T. L., & Geschwind, N. (1978). Right-left asymmetries in the brain. *Science, 199,* 852–56.

Galin, D. (1974). Implications for psychiatry of left and right cerebral specialization: A neurophysiological context for unconscious processes. *Archives of General Psychiatry, 31,* 572–83.

Galin, D., Johnstone, J., Nakell, L., & Herron, J. (1979). Development of the capacity for tactile information transfer between hemispheres in normal children. *Science, 204,* 1330–33.

Galper, R. E., & Costa, L. (1980). Hemispheric superiority for recognizing faces depends upon how they are learned. *Cortex, 16,* 21–38.

Gardner, H., Ling, P. K., Flamm, L., & Silverman, J. (1975). Comprehension and appreciation of humorous material following brain damage. *Brain, 98,* 399–412.

Gibson, J. J. (1979). *The ecological approach to visual perception.* Boston: Houghton Mifflin.

Goldberg, E., & Costa, L. D. (1981). Hemispheric differences in the acquisition and use of descriptive systems. *Brain and Language, 14,* 144–73.

Goldstein, K. (1952). The effect of brain damage on the personality. *Psychiatry, 15,* 245–60.

Goldstein, S. G., Filskov, S. B., Weaver, L. A., & Ives, J. (1977). Neuropsychological effects of electroconvulsive therapy. *Journal of Clinical Psychology, 33,* 798–806.

Gruzelier, J. H., & Hammond, N. (1976). Schizophrenia: A dominant temporal-limbic disorder? *Research Communications in Psychology, Psychiatry, and Behavior, 1,* 33–72.

Gur, R. C., Packer, I. K., Hungerbuhler, J. P., Reivich, M., Obrist, W. D., Amarnek, W. S., & Sackeim, H. A. (1980). Difference in the distribution of gray and white matter in human cerebral hemispheres. *Science, 207,* 1226–28.

Gur, R. E., & Gur, R. C. (1975). Defense mechanisms, psychosomatic symptomatology, and conjugate lateral eye movements. *Journal of Consulting & Clinical Psychology, 43,* 416–20.

Gur, R. E. (1978). Left hemisphere dysfunction and left hemisphere overactivation in schizophrenics. *Journal of Abnormal Psychology, 87,* 226–38.

Haggard, M. P., & Parkinson, A. M. (1971). Stimulus and task factors as determinants of ear advantages. *Quarterly Journal of Experimental Psychology, 23,* 168–77.

Harvey, O. J., Hunt, D. E., & Schroder, H. M. (1961). *Conceptual systems and personality organization.* New York: Wiley.

Hayne, C. H. (1983). Cognitive ability and cognitive style in the comprehension and expression of emotion. Doctoral dissertation, University of North Dakota.

Hecaen, H. (1964). Mental symptoms associated with tumors of the frontal lobe. In J. M. Warren & K. Akert (Eds.), *The frontal granular cortex and behavior.* New York: McGraw-Hill.

Hecaen, H., & Albert, M. L. (1978). *Human neuropsychology.* New York: John Wiley & Sons.

Hegel, G. W. F. (1807). *The phenomenology of mind.* Translated by J. B. Baillie. New York: Humanities Press, 1966.

Heilman, K. M., Scholes, R., & Watson, R. T. (1975). Auditory affective agnosia: Disturbed comprehension of affective speech. *Journal of Neurology, Neurosurgery, and Psychiatry, 38,* 69–72.

Heilman, K. M. (1979). Apraxia. In K. M. Helman & E. Valenstein, *Clinical Neuropsychology.* New York: Oxford University Press.

Hellige, J. B., & Wong, T. M. (1983). Hemisphere-specific interference in dichotic listening: Task variables and individual differences. *Journal of Experimental Psychology: General, 112,* 218–39.

Iversen, S. D. (1977). Brain dopamine systems and behavior. In L. L. Iversen, S. D. Iversen, & S. H. Snyder (Eds.), *Handbook of Psychopharmacology,* Vol. 8, *Drugs, neurotransmitters and behavior.* New York: Plenum Press, 333–84.

Jackson, J. Hughlings. (1879). On affections of speech from diseases of the brain. *Brain, 2,* 203–22.

Jakobson, R. (1965). Quest for the essence of language. *Diogenes, 51,* 21–37.

Jung, C. G. (1971). *Psychological Types.* In Collected Works, Vol. 6. Princeton: Princeton University Press (first German edition, 1921).

Kempf, E., Greilsamer, J., Mack, G., & Mandel, P. (1974). Correlation of behavioral differences in three strains of mice with differences in brain amines. *Nature, 247,* 483–85.

Kimura, D. (1977). Acquisition of a motor skill after left-hemisphere damage. *Brain, 100,* 527–42.

Kinsbourne, M. (1974) Mechanisms of hemispheric interaction in man. In M. Kinsbourne & W. L. Smith (Eds.), *Hemispheric disconnection and cerebral function.* Springfield, IL: Charles C. Thomas.

Kinsbourne, M., & Bemporad, B. (1984). Lateralization of emotion: A model and the evidence. In N. Fox & R. J. Davidson (Eds.), *The Psychobiology of affective development.* Hillsdale, NJ: Erlbaum.

Knox, C., & Kimura, D. (1970). Cerebral processing of non-verbal sounds in boys and girls. *Neuropsychologia, 8,* 227–37.

Koff, E., Borod, J. C., & White, B. (1981). Asymmetries for hemiface size and mobility. *Neuropsychologia, 21,* 273–76.

Kokkinidis, L., & Anisman, H. (1980). Amphetamine models of paranoid schizophrenia: An overview and elaboration of animal experimentation. *Psychological Bulletin, 88,* 551–78.

Kolb, B, & Milner, B. (1981). Performance of complex arm and facial movements after focal brain lesions. *Neuropsychologia, 19,* 491–503.

Kosslyn, S. M. (1980). *Image and Mind,* Cambridge, Massachusetts: Harvard University Press.

Kronfol, Z., Hamsher, K., Digre, K., & Waziri, R. (1977). Depression and hemisphere functions: Changes associated with unilateral ECT. *British Journal of Psychiatry, 132,* 560–67.

Laurian, S., Gaillard, J. M., Le, P. K., & Schopf, J. (1983). Topographic aspects of EEG profile of some psychotropic drugs. In D. Kemali & C. Perris (Eds.), *Advances in biological psychiatry.* Oxford: Pergamon Press.

Levy, J. (1969). Possible basis for the evolution of lateral specialization of the human brain. *Nature, 224,* 614–15.

Levy, J., Heller, W., Banich, N. T., & Burton, L. A. (1983). Are variations among right-handed individuals and perceptual asymmetries caused by characteristic arousal differences between the hemispheres? *Journal of Experimental Psychology: Human Perception and Performance, 9,* 29–359.

Levy-Agresti, J., & Sperry, R. W. (1968). Differential perceptual capacities in major and minor hemispheres. *Proceedings of the United States National Academy of Sciences, 61,* 1151.

Ley, R. G., & Bryden, M. P. (1979). Hemispheric differences in processing emotions and faces. *Brain and Language, 7,* 127–38.

Lezak, M. D. (1976). *Neuropsychological assessment.* New York: Oxford University Press.

Luria, A. R. (1973). *The working brain: An introduction to neuropsychology.* New York: Basic Books.

Luria, A. R. (1982). *Language and cognition.* New York: John Wiley & Sons.

Mahler, M. S. (1968). *On human symbiosis and the vicissitudes of individuation.* New York: International University Press.

Matthysse, S. (1977). Dopamine and selective attention. *Advances in Biochemical Psychopharmacology, 16,* 667–69.

McGuinness, D., & Pribram, K. (1980). The neuropsychology of attention: Emotional and motivational controls. In M. C. Wittrock (Ed.), *The brain and psychology.* New York: Academic Press.

Mehrabian, A. (1972). *Nonverbal Communication.* Chicago: Aldine Atherton.

Meichenbaum, D. (1974). Self-instructional methods. In F. H. Kanfer & A. P. Goldstein (Eds.), *Helping people change.* New York: Pergamon.

Monrad-Krohn, G. H. (1924). On the dissociation of voluntary and emotional innervation in facial paresis of central origin. *Brain, 47,* 22–35.

Monrad-Krohn, G. H. (1947). Dysprosody or altered melody of language. *Brain, 70,* 405–15.

Monrad-Krohn, G. H. (1963). The third element of speech: Prosody and its disorders. In L. Halpern (Ed.), *Problems of dynamic neurology.* New York: Grune & Stratton.

Moscovitch, M., Scullion, D., & Christie, D. (1976). Early versus late stages of processing and their relation to functional hemispheric asymmetries in face recognition. *Journal of Experimental Psychology: Human Perception & Performance, 2,* 401–16.

Moscovitch, M. & Olds, J. (1982). Asymmetries in spontaneous facial expressions and their possible relation to hemispheric specialization. *Neuropsychologia, 20,* 71–81.

Nebes, R. D. (1978). Direct examination of cognitive function in the left and right hemispheres. In M. Kinsbourne (Ed.), *Asymmetrical function of the brain.* London: Cambridge University Press.

Neisser, U. (1976). *Cognition and reality: Principles and applications of cognitive psychology.* San Francisco: W. H. Freeman & Company.

Newman, J. P. (1982). Hemispheric specialization and the processing of Stroop color-word stimuli. Doctoral dissertation, University of North Dakota.

Oke, A., Keller, R., Mefford, I., & Adams, R. (1978). Lateralization of norepinephrine in human thalamus. *Science, 200,* 1411–13.

Pearlson, G. D., & Robinson, R. G. (1981). Suction lesions of the frontal cerebral cortex in the rat induce asymmetrical behavioral and catecholaminergic responses. *Brain Research, 218,* 233–421.

Posner, M. I. (1978). *Chronometric explorations of mind.* Hillsdale, NJ: Erlbaum.

Posner, M. I., & Boies, S. J. (1971). Components of attention. *Psychological Review, 78,* 391–408.

Posner, M. I., & Rothbart, M. K. (1981). The development of attentional mechanisms. In J. H. Flowers (Ed.), *Nebraska symposium on motivation.* Lincoln: University of Nebraska Press.

Pribram, K. H., & McGuinness, D. (1975). Arousal, activation and effort in the control of attention. *Psychological Review, 82,* 116–49.

Pribram, K. H. (1981). Emotions. In S. K. Filskov & T. J. Boll (Eds.), *Handbook of clinical neuropsychology.* New York: Wiley–Interscience.

Riegel, K. F. (1975). The development of dialectical operations. *Human Development, 18,* 1–128.

Robinson, R. G., Kubos, K. L., Starr, L. B., Rao, K., & Price, T. R. (1984). Mood disorders in stroke patients: Importance of location of lesion. *Brain, 107,* 81–93.

Rosenthal, R. (Ed.) (1979). *Skill in nonverbal communication: Individual differences.* Cambridge, MA: Oelgeschlager, Gunn, and Hain.

Ross, E., & Mesulam, M. M. (1979). Dominant language functions of the right hemisphere? Prosody and emotional gesturing. *Archives of Neurology, 36,* 144–48.

Ross, E. D., & Rush, A. J. (1981). Diagnosis and neuroanatomical correlates of depression in brain-damaged patients. *Archives of General Psychiatry, 38,* 1344–54.

Russo, M., & Vignolo, L. A. (1967). Visual figure-ground discrimination in patients with unilateral cerebral disease. *Cortex, 3,* 113–27.

Sackeim, H. A., & Gur, R. C. (1982). Facial asymmetry, perceiver biases and the communication of emotion. In J. T. Cacioppo & R. E. Pety (Eds.), *Social Psychophysiology.* New York: Guilford Press.

Sackeim, H. A., Gur, R. C., & Saucy, M. C. (1978). Emotions are expressed more intensely on the left side of the face. *Science, 202,* 434–36.

Safer, M. A. (1981). Sex and hemisphere differences in access to codes for processing emotional expressions and faces. *Journal of Experimental Psychology: General, 110,* 86–100.

Safer, M. A., and Leventhal, H. (1977). Ear differences in evaluating emotional tone of voice and verbal content. *Journal of Experimental Psychology: Human Perception and Performance, 3,* 75–82.

Sarason, I. G. (1975). Anxiety and self-preoccupation. In I. G. Sarason & C. D. Spielberger (Eds.), *Stress and Anxiety,* Vol. 2. New York: Wiley.

Schildkraut, J. (1965). The catecholamine hypothesis of affective disorders: A review of supporting evidence. *American Journal of Psychiatry, 122,* 509–22.

Schildkraut, J. J., et al. (1978). Toward a biochemical classification of depressive disorders. *Archives of General Psychiatry, 35,* 1427.

Serafetinides, E. A. (1973). Voltage laterality in the EEG of psychiatric patients. *Diseases of the Nervous System, 34,* 190–91.

Sergent, J., & Bindra, D. (1981). Differential hemispheric processing of faces: Methodological considerations and reinterpretation. *Psychological Bulletin, 89,* 541–54.

Shapiro, D. (1965). *Neurotic styles.* New York: Basic Books.

Smokler, I. A., & Shevrin, I. (1979). Cerebral lateralizations and personality style. *Archives of General Psychiatry, 36,* 949–54.

Sperry, R. W., Gazzaniga, M. S., & Bogen, J. E. (1969). Interhemispheric relationships: The neocortical commissures; syndromes of hemisphere disconnections. In P. Vinken & C. Bruyn (Eds.), *Handbook of clinical neurology,* Amsterdam: North Holland.

Strauss, E. (1983). Perception of emotional words. *Neuropsychologia, 21,* 99–103.

Suberi, M., & McKeever, W. F. (1977). Differential right hemispheric memory storage of emotional and non-emotional faces. *Neuropsychologia, 15,* 757–68.

Sullivan, H. S. (1953). *The interpersonal theory of psychiatry.* New York: Norton.

Swenson, R. A., & Tucker, D. M. (1983). Lateralized cognitive style and self-description. *International Journal of Neuroscience, 21,* 91–100.

Taylor, D. C. (1969). Differential rates of cerebral maturation between sexes and between hemispheres. *Lancet, July,* 140–42.

Taylor, J. (Ed.) (1958). *Selected writings of John Hughlings Jackson.* New York: Basic Books.

TenHouten, W. D. (1978). Hemispheric interaction in the brain and the propositional, compositional, and dialectical modes of thought. *Journal of Altered States of Consciousness, 4,* 129–40.

Thompson, J. K. (1982). Neuroanatomy, hemisphericity, and facial asymmetry. *Neuropsychologica, 20,* 699–702.

Tucker, Daniel M., Watson, R. G., & Heilman, K. M. (1976). Affective discrimination and evocation in patients with right parietal disease. *Neurology, 26,* 354.

Tucker, Don M. (1973). Some relationships between individual and group development. *Human Development, 16,* 249–72.

Tucker, D. M. (1976). Sex differences in hemispheric specialization for synthetic visiospatial functions. *Neuropsychologia, 14,* 447–54.

Tucker, D. M. (1981). Lateral brain function, emotion, and conceptualization. *Psychological Bulletin, 89,* 19–46.

Tucker, D. M., Antes, J. R., Stenslie, C. E., & Barnhardt, T. N. (1978). Anxiety and lateral cerebral function. *Journal of Abnormal Psychology, 87,* 380–83.

Tucker, D. M., & Newman, J. P., (1981). Verbal versus imaginal cognitive strategies in the inhibition of emotional arousal. *Cognitive Therapy and Research, 5,* 197–202.

Tucker, D. M., Roth, D. L., & Bair, T. B. (1984). Functional connections among cortical regions: Topographic patterning of EEG coherence. Manuscript in preparation.

Tucker, D. M., Stenslie, C. E., Roth, R. S., & Sherrer, S. L. (1981). Right frontal lobe activation and right hemisphere performance during a depressed mood. *Archives of General Psychiatry, 38,* 169–74.

Tucker, D. M., & Williamson, P. A. (1984). Asymmetric neural control systems in human self-regulation. *Psychological Review, 91,* 185–215.

Turner, J. le B. (1964). Schizophrenics as judges of vocal expressions of emotional meaning. In J. R. Davitz (Ed.), *The communication of emotional meaning.* New York: McGraw-Hill.

Tyler, S. K., & Tucker, D. M., (1982). Anxiety and perceptual structure: Individual differences in neuropsychological function. *Journal of Abnormal Psychology, 91,* 210–20.

Walker, E., & McGuire, M. (1982). Intra-and inter-hemispheric information processing in schizophrenia. *Psychological Bulletin, 29,* 701–25.

Walter, W. G. (1950). Normal rhythms—Their development, distribution and significance. In D. Hill and G. Parr (Eds.), *Electroencephalography.* London: McDonald.

Werner, H. (1957). *The comparative psychology of mental development.* New York: Harper.

Werner, H., & Kaplan, B. (1963). *Symbol formation: An organismic-developmental approach to language and the expression of thought.* New York: John Wiley & Sons.

Whitaker, C. A., & Malone, J. P. (1955). *Roots of psychotherapy.* New York: Blakiston.

Whitaker, H. A. (1978). Is the right leftover? Commentary on Corballis & Morgan, "On the biological basis of human laterality." *Behaviorial and Brain Sciences, 1.*

Witkin, H. A., Dyk, R. B., Faterson, H. F., Goodenough, D. R., & Karp, S. A. (1962). *Psychological differentiation: Studies of development.* New York: Wiley.

Zurif, E. B. & Mendelsohn, M. (1972). Hemispheric specialization for the perception of speech sounds: The influence of intonation and structure. *Perception and Pscyhophysics, 11,* 329–32.

Indexes

AUTHORS

Page numbers in bold type refer to chapters in this book.

SUBJECTS